To Marik

Let es nort or
To vertroy !

MW00974053

Post-Liberalism

Post-Liberalism

The Death of a Dream

Melvyn L. Fein

Transaction Publishers
New Brunswick (U.S.A.) and London (U.K.)

Library of Congress Catalog Number: 2011049669
ISBN: 978-1-4128-4608-0
Printed in the United States of America

Library of Congress Cataloging-in-Publication Data

Fein, Melvyn L.
    Post-liberalism : the death of a dream / Melvyn L. Fein.
        p. cm.
    ISBN 978-1-4128-4608-0
  1. Liberalism. 2. Liberalism—Philosophy.   I. Title.
    JC585.F3945 2012
    320.51—dc23

                                                    2011049669

It is true that you may fool all of the people some of the time;
you can even fool some of the people all of the time;
but you can't fool all of the people all the time.

—Abraham Lincoln

Contents

1

When Prophesy Fails

A Premature Burial

Several years ago H. W. Brands wrote a small book entitled *The Strange Death of American Liberalism*. In it he argued that liberalism was on its way out. As a historian, he believed that America was reverting to its national heritage. Cognizant of the anti-governmental sentiments that motivated the Founding Fathers, Brands suggested that conservative attitudes were deeply ensconced in the national psyche. Thomas Jefferson, he reminded his readers, regarded a robust federal authority as anathema. The nation's third president envisioned a country of independent yeoman farmers each of whom was sturdy enough to meet his (or her) own needs without submitting to the equivalent of a George III. Monarchy might be acceptable to fainthearted Europeans, but Americans who grew to maturity by taming a wild frontier possessed the courage to regulate their own fortunes. They did not require a central administration to tell them what to do.

According to Brands, liberalism is about governmental control. It seeks to concentrate social services in a central authority that is theoretically under the control of the people. As a result, liberals promise programs and regulations intended to promote personal welfare. They also dream of expanding *social justice*. Under their tutelage, representatives of the people will legislate projects to defend the weak from the strong. For liberals, the government is all-wise, all-knowing, and eternally beneficent. It is a friend that can be relied upon to thwart the greedy assaults of the wealthy because it is founded on the proposition that defending the natural rights of the individual is the central mission of a democratic government.

Yet, Brands argued, this attitude is of recent vintage. According to him, Americans have always been wary of aristocratic pretensions. They understood that a government strong enough to provide extensive benefits was strong enough to threaten their freedoms. Only practical necessity modified this attitude. The dangers presented first by the Civil

1

War, then industrialization, the two World Wars, the Great Depression and finally the Cold War prompted them to turn to national authorities for services once jealously guarded by individuals. Despite their misgivings, they asked the federal government to provide security in an increasingly insecure world.

Nor were they disappointed in their hopes. After all, wasn't it the federal government that rescued them from the Depression and then defeated the Axis powers? Wasn't it also the federal government that gave them the War on Poverty, Civil Rights, and Social Security? Brands believed that the apogee of liberal success occurred during the Cold War. This was when the Soviet Union seemed most threatening. Only later, once government tendrils began to extend too deeply into the daily lives of ordinary citizens, did they rebel and embrace the Reagan counterrevolution. Ultimately, even Bill Clinton declared that the era of Big Government was over.

Nevertheless, like the reported death of Mark Twain, the demise of liberalism was greatly exaggerated. Liberalism is not dead. It is merely dying. As the election of Barack Obama demonstrated, liberal fervor can occasionally be as great as ever. The movement has merely entered a period of decline.

Death Throes

It was midmorning, and the sun was shining brightly into my suburban living room. All seemed right with the world as I sat reading a book. Consequently, I was unprepared for the strange crashing sound that assaulted my ears. It appeared to come from the large trapezoidal window that overlooked my front driveway; hence I got up to investigate. At first I saw nothing. But then in the middle of the pane, I noticed a mysterious smudge. Not quite certain of its origin, I leaned across the window seat to scrutinize it more closely. There, in the center of the smear, was a tiny feather. Almost too small to be seen, it impelled me to look down to determine if a bird had collided with the window. Sure enough, one had. It was lying on the concrete directly beneath my gaze. Unfortunately, I could not make out whether the creature remained alive. Only a firsthand inspection would reveal its condition.

Upon descending the front staircase, I quickly became aware that the diminutive creature was still living. But it was in a perilous state. Its small chest was heaving great sighs, while its head was contorted into an angular position. As best I could tell, it had broken its neck. Taken aback by this development, I wondered what to do. Should I bring the injured bird upstairs and nurse it back to health? Or should I move it to the side of the driveway and allow it to expire in peace? Unsure of which course to follow, I wandered toward the street to ponder my options. Within minutes, however, my attention was diverted by a commotion behind me. Surprisingly, it was the little bird thrashing about. Its wings were flapping so energetically it seemed poised to fly off. At this, I concluded I had been mistaken. The creature was less seriously injured than I imagined.

When I turned to walk toward it, however, I was met by another surprise. As suddenly as the thrashing began, it ended. By the time I reached the creature there was no movement at all. The little animal had died. Despite an astonishing burst of vigor, it was past saving. What I witnessed were its death throes. While fighting desperately to live, it expended its last ounce of energy. This brief show of vitality had been deceptive. What seemed to betoken a return to normality was the opposite. The creature's struggle against death was actually evidence of its imminent passing.

This fatality was, in the great scheme of things, a minor tragedy. A piece of me mourned the death, but birds have short lives. Of far more consequence are the current death throes of liberalism. This enormously influential political movement, this fundamental source of contemporary Western ideals, is in the process of passing from the scene. Nevertheless, most people, including liberals, remain unaware of its impending collapse. From their viewpoint, liberalism is very much alive. Thus, when Senator Ted Kennedy passed from the scene, he was praised as the Last Lion of Liberalism. Television screens from coast to coast showed him defending the cause. There he was in the flush of youth declaring as stridently as ever that "[t]he dream will never die!" He believed it, as did many millions of his fellow liberals. For them, *the dream* is the touchstone of their existence. It is an eternal verity that will always be with us.

Yet appearances can be mistaken. At this instant, liberalism is undeniably vigorous. Indeed, not long ago it recaptured both the American Congress and the presidency. Moreover, it did so in dramatic fashion. Furthermore, it subsequently spent trillions of dollars to advance its aspirations. Nevertheless, it is thrashing about. Decidedly not in an unchallenged ascendancy, within months of its greatest successes, it inspired a dynamic Tea Party Movement and then endured a terrible defeat in the midterm elections. As a result, just as with that tiny bird, liberals are currently flapping wildly about in an attempt to ward off their inevitable death. Spitting invectives at their adversaries, fanning the flames of class warfare, and promising to come back stronger than ever, left-leaning activists may seem in robust health, yet their very forcefulness is evidence of an underlying weakness. Liberalism is, in fact, succumbing to a fatal malady. It is dying of "inconsistency poisoning." Contrary to the declarations of its partisans, liberalism is not on the side of history. It is not the wave of the future. Far from being "progressive," it is marching rapidly toward the rear.

Ironically, in seeking to defend the indefensible, liberal partisans are hastening this demise. For almost two centuries, they have accused capitalism of being riven by contradictions. As a result, they have awaited the self-immolation of a system regarded as terminally unjust. Yet it is liberalism that is about to meet this fate. Despite claims of representing the 99 percent, its defenders are unprepared to halt this suicidal plunge precisely because they are looking elsewhere. They are not seeking to repair what is broken because they do not perceive themselves as in trouble.

Liberals, for all their bravado, are about to pay the price for self-delusional inconsistencies. Far from heralding a brave new world, they seek to resurrect a very old one. Just as was the case with the Soviet Union, their collectivist political philosophy has grown sclerotic. Because it is grounded in decrepit totalitarian traditions, it too must founder on the shoals of uncongenial truths. Far from being inevitable, liberalism is about to perish thanks to its unstable internal architecture. Having broken its neck after crashing into what appeared to be a window of opportunity, the very expectations that fueled liberalism's upward flight will ultimately destroy it. Needless to say, its advocates are fighting against this fate. They are determined to make their own predictions come true. Yet despite their efforts, they cannot ward off destiny. That which the facts of human existence will not permit, cannot become reality. Dreams grounded in a misunderstanding of the human condition are analogous to a broken neck. They too cut off vital life juices.

A Failed Prophesy

Liberals are idealists. They predict a glowing future once their aspirations are realized. According to them, after the petty rivalries of capitalism are laid to rest, the underlying goodness of humanity will come to the fore. In the words of Obama's acceptance speech at the

Democratic nominating convention, "we must . . . rise or fall as one nation; [our] fundamental belief [must be] that I am my brother's keeper; I am my sister's keeper." As for his critics, they foolishly dismissed this philosophy as so much "happy talk." Yet their attitude merely fed "into the cynicism that we all have about government." But we must not be fooled. We must instead "fix our eye not on what is seen, but what is unseen, that better place around the bend." More recently, he has invoked the hallowed dream of total "fairness." For him this must inspire a "New Nationalism" under which we rededicate ourselves to our mutual welfare.

Regrettably, liberals are not just idealists—they are utopians. They do not merely expect a better world, they long for a perfect one. As a result, they forecast a time when people will join hands to form a single family of humankind. And when this occurs, the conflicts and insecurities that have haunted our species will disappear as we realize our destinies are tied to a common global village. Much as Saint Thomas More once envisaged an island from which selfishness was banished, they expect government mediation to produce complete equality and endless prosperity. People will then cease vying to outdo one another and instead work for the common good. The difference between then and now is that Thomas More knew his island was a fantasy, whereas contemporary liberals genuinely believe their dreams will come true.

As troublesome as this utopianism is the fact that most liberals refuse to acknowledge counterevidence. Completely certain of their visions, they will not allow them to be disconfirmed. Those of More's readers who believed his island paradise actually existed were soon disabused by the discoveries of the intrepid mariners then crossing the Atlantic. None came back with confirmation of an actual place called Utopia. Amazingly, today's liberals, despite their intellectual pretensions, refuse to countenance similar journeys. They balk when asked to venture into uncongenial ideological territory. True believers of the most adamant sort, they are the secular equivalent of fundamentalist Christians. Theirs is a faith. It may be secular, but it is as independent of empirical verification as any religious belief system.

Why then do liberals refuse to see what is happening? Why, if liberalism is in its death throes, are those closest to its focal point unaware of this development? Could it be that liberalism is not really dying? Could it be that they know something less committed observers do not? Or is it that their faith induces a kind of moral blindness? Many liberals are unquestionably intelligent. Many are even intellectuals. How then can they be oblivious to something so profound? The answer is that they are human. Just as their political aspirations are undermined by the human condition, so is their ability to see what they do not wish to see.

What is nowadays occurring politically was explored more than half a century ago by social psychologists. Back in 1956, Leon Festinger, Henry Reicken, and Stanley Schacter published a book entitled *When Prophecy Fails.* Based on research conducted two years earlier, the investigators scrutinized, not a political party, but a religious cult. They wondered what would happen when a worldwide catastrophe predicted by this group did not materialize. Would its adherents become disillusioned? Would the scales fall from their eyes? Or would they continue to believe in a misguided faith? The answer turned out to be the latter. Most of its members strengthened their commitment. Their convictions, far from being shaken, were reinforced.

Dorothy Martin (in the book called Mrs. Marian Keech) and her collaborators Charles and Lillian Laughead (alias Thomas and Daisy Armstrong) believed they channeled messages from extraterrestrials. These cosmic communiqués first predicted landings by flying saucers and later prophesized a great flood that would engulf everyone on December 21. So convinced were they and their followers that on three separate occasions they trekked to the predicted landing sites. In the end, they assembled at Martin's home to await salvation by the saucers delegated to pick them up before the deluge. Some even quit their jobs and gave away their earthly possessions in anticipation of being whisked skyward.

Festinger (who is well known for his theories of cognitive dissonance) suspected that rather than admit to error these true believers would find a way to rationalize these disconfirmations. Discomfort with inconsistent perceptions would induce them to reconceptualize what occurred so as to produce the appearance of consistency. This, of course, is what transpired. When the original saucer landings did not take place, the leaders and their adherents interpreted these as tests of faith. They were being asked to demonstrate their steadfastness in the face of disappointment. Something similar occurred when the deluge failed to materialize. At this point, Martin announced the reception of a message explaining that the Earth had been spared. Thanks to the group's dedication, the cataclysm had been cancelled.

Indeed, subsequent to this, Martin and the Armstrongs increased their proselytizing. Far from being discouraged, they continued to believe. More certain than ever, they even sought publicity for their ideas. Unabashed at having been proven wrong, they saw no reason to apologize. So far as they were concerned, they were not mistaken. To the contrary, they were responsible for saving humanity. Moreover, the continued security of the planet depended upon others joining their mission. It was the scoffing unbelievers who were being imprudent.

Half a century later, Diana Tumminia engaged in a more extensive study of a saucer cult. Her account in *When Prophecy Never Fails* demonstrates that the earlier tendencies remain with us. Humanity has not become more sensible during the intervening years. Tumminia found that so-called Unarians were similarly unperturbed by the failure of predicted saucer landings. They too found reasons to explain why these had not occurred. Other uncomfortable events, such as the deaths of their leaders, were similarly incorporated into an elaborate mythology that entailed previous lives on distant planets. Fervent in their conviction that souls are reborn, they construed current events as indicators of previous happenings in earlier incarnations. This allowed them to characterize their analyses as "scientific." Others might sneer, but this was because they were unenlightened. Members of the group knew better. Commending one another on their own perceptiveness, they were convinced of their insights.

Contemporary liberals are not unlike these Unarians or the Martin circle. They too hold fast to disconfirmed beliefs. They also remain unperturbed when events contradict their predictions. Thus, when a massive stimulus failed to revive a dismal economy, they claimed it had rescued the nation. Or when a massive reform of the medical system did not reduce costs, they pretended it would. Few liberals admit their errors, but neither did the Unarians. True believers do not perceive themselves as mistaken. Nor do they believe themselves irrational. To the contrary, they are convinced they are correct. For them, their commitments are never disconfirmed. Instead, the facts are reinterpreted to corroborate their assertions. It is thus their critics who are mistaken. It is they, for example, the conservatives, who are irrational. Such mean-spirited reactionaries are obviously out of touch with reality.

But what if the liberals are the real Unarians? What if they are blinded by a need for consistency? Few would disagree that religious cults hunger for salvation. Their members generally hope to be saved from a world perceived as iniquitous—or at minimum disappointing. But don't liberals seek a similar salvation? Aren't they too transfixed by the injustices of a world they did not shape? Liberals may not anticipate extraterrestrial saviors, but they do expect to lift the downtrodden out of their misery. They likewise intend to bring peace on earth and fulfillment to the masses. In other words, they too cling to extravagant hopes.

Liberals are also like the Unarians in that they wish to decode a complex and mystifying world. Why, they wonder, do unexpected events so frequently disturb our fondest expectations? Liberals may not share a mythology involving thirty-three planets arranged in the shape of a vortex. Nor do they urge earthlings to build a power tower to unite the spiritual energy of the universe. Nevertheless, they have their own explanatory myths. They, for instance, believe in the ultimate equality of all human beings. For them, our natural parity has been undermined by an unjust economic system. They further believe in a redistribution of wealth to correct these disparities. This is why Obama has frequently recommended taxing the rich. Liberals, of course, do not consider these myths. But what if they are? What if they are simply intellectualized efforts to make sense of unpleasant realities? Wouldn't liberals be as guilty of simplistic thinking as the Unarians? Some progressives get around this hurdle by claiming there are no truths, only opinions. Nevertheless, they insist their own views are valid.

Another quality shared by liberals and Unarians is that they live their faith. Both put their money where their mouths are. Festinger argued that irrevocable actions often bind people to their beliefs. Once publicly committed to a position, it is difficult to back away without a loss of face. Indeed, reflect on how hard it is to admit a mistake. The words "I was wrong" choke in most of our throats. Many of us prefer to protect an error rather than seem foolish. If we can convince others we are right, their agreement is taken as proof that we were not wrong. This was clearly the case with the Unarians who wrote books to defend their predictions. It was especially true of those who went to the predicted landing sites. There they happily posed for pictures carrying welcome signs. Nor were they embarrassed by newspaper stories of their exploits. If anything, those who publicly identified as Unarian became more devout.

But isn't this also true of liberals? Those most adamant in their public demonstrations of faith are likewise the least apt to abandon them. Moreover, liberals too vocally proclaim their devotion. Their political attitudes are not hidden under a bushel basket. Instead they are flaunted at Occupy Wall Street demonstrations; announced on bumper stickers; and made known in a myriad of private conversations. Nor are liberals above proselytizing. If they could, they would convert everyone to their viewpoint. Nonetheless, these efforts begin with public declarations of faith. Liberals are not shy about telling others what to believe. They are ardent witnesses for their version of social justice. They similarly donate to the cause, vote for its candidates, and send letters to legislators pleading for the orthodox programs. Moreover, few change their minds. If we need an example, which of those who marched against the Vietnam War have since decided the conflict was justified? And who among those who supported Obama's stimulus program have subsequently admitted it did not work?

Finally, liberals, like Unarians, revel in public encouragement. In fact, they receive more of it than mere cultists. Liberalism is one of the two major political outlooks of contemporary Western society. For more than a century it has been in the vanguard setting our social agenda. Even people who do not subscribe to its tenets must respond to its initiatives. In universities, newspaper offices, and welfare institutions it is so dominant that nary a dissenting voice is heard. Indeed, in many such places, it is possible to imagine that liberalism is the only viable perspective. So rarely is opposition expressed that it may be thought nonexistent. On the other hand, affirming the party line draws smiles of approbation. Not only do heads nod in agreement, but voices chime in with reinforcing comments. Liberals tend to create the reverse of Thomas Nast's responsibility circles. Nast famously depicted members of New York City's infamous Tweed ring as standing in a circle pointing the finger of blame at an adjacent partner. With liberals, it is pats on the back and nominations for Pulitzer Prizes that make the rounds.

I can personally testify to liberal solidarity. As a sociologist, I am exposed to an incredible thirty-to-one ratio of liberals to conservatives among my colleagues. Sociologists therefore expect unfamiliar sociologists to be comparably liberal. Add to this that I was raised a New York Jew and it is generally assumed that I too must be liberal. As a result, I am regularly treated to candid expressions of liberal opinion. Time and again, I hear jokes about conservative stupidity. Thus, during Ronald Reagan's presidency, the fact that he majored in sociology was a source of embarrassment. How could one of our own be so dense? Steadfast liberals, in contrast, are regarded as intellectual paragons. Their views, whatever their accomplishments, are celebrated. At one point I witnessed a respected colleague propose either Oprah Winfrey or Tom Hanks for president. What is more, this suggestion was greeted with warm applause. No one suggested that these might be inappropriate choices. In stark contrast, dismissive comments about Karl Marx draw hostile gazes.

Liberal solidarity is further reinforced by shared reactions to its opponents. Commentators such as Fox News' Bill O'Reilly help both to define and buttress liberal cohesion. Such evil outsiders provide targets to be attacked and opinions to be contradicted. Thus, when O'Reilly harangues against "secular humanists," liberals cheerfully accept this mantle. Or when he takes up the cudgels against those in favor of saying "Happy Holidays" at Christmas, they insist on using the phrase. They are not like O'Reilly. He is the "other," whereas they are enlightened insiders. It does not even bother them that O'Reilly is more of a populist than conservative. That he obviously disagrees with liberal opinions is sufficient to draw their ire.

Nor are liberals averse to attacking nonliberals. They trust that their friends can be mobilized by provoking fights with common enemies. If one's cause is seen as endangered, the faithful will rally to its defense. This is why O'Reilly is so hated. Were he less popular, he could be ignored, whereas his success is perceived as a red flag. Clearly, O'Reilly must be stopped before he corrupts the inadequately committed. The Mormons suffered a similar fate when they backed a California proposition asserting that marriage must be between a man and a woman. Since their money was seen as tipping the balance against gay marriage, they became anathema. Almost immediately the pickets went up against their institutions and those who made donations to the church lost their jobs. In fact, attacking these bad guys became a recruiting tool. Making them more visible helped energize those sitting on the fence. It crystallized their faith so as to make it more difficult to renounce.

Putting the pieces together, liberal orthodoxy fits the Festinger criteria for heightening commitment. Just as with the Unarians, observable declarations of faith result in irrevocable actions that reinforce the faith. Consequently, when events discredited their beliefs, they continued to champion failed prophesies. This was especially evident after Obama's minions were repudiated in a midterm election. Instead of admitting that they had not ended an inherited economic recession, they boasted of having created or saved millions of jobs. And rather than acknowledge that ObamaCare would cost trillions of dollars, they insisted it saved trillions. They even refused to cut the budget deficit on the grounds that Republicans were mean-spirited alarmists. So far as they were concerned, their own policies were correct no matter what the evidence showed. Thus, while a Greece might go bankrupt, the United States never would no matter how much the government spent.

Enthusiasms and Simplifications

Liberals often argue that they must be correct because their opponents are so wrong. Moreover, their own view of history has to prevail because conservatives cannot be allowed to win. This latter alternative would be unthinkable. Partisans of social justice must therefore rally to its defense rather than allow the forces of reaction to succeed. Too much progress has been made to permit a new dark age to descend upon humanity. Liberalism is *not* a false prophesy! Nor are its adherents wild-eyed crazies awaiting the arrival of flying saucers.

So what is the truth? Is liberalism dying? Is it fatally flawed? Or are those who doubt its tenets afflicted by their own delusions? One thing is certain: liberalism remains vigorous. Its adherents are louder and more aggressive than ever. Merely going on the Internet to read contributions to Moveon.org or the fulminations on the Daily Kos confirms this. These blogs, and hundreds of others, are dedicated to promoting the cause. Widely read, and boasting legions of contributors, they bespeak a sizeable community of activists. Indicative of the same phenomenon were the huge number of donors to the Obama campaign. So is the zeal of the enthusiastic crowds that show up for his rallies. The gleam in their eyes demonstrates a profound commitment. These people care. Indeed, many are convinced a new millennium is about to arrive.

Sadly for the liberal cause, this vigor itself suggests trouble. When people become wild in their adoration, there is a good chance they are feeding on their own hopes. Emotional frenzies often camouflage underlying reservations. As has often been said, that which seems too good to be true generally is. Successful con men understand that the most vulnerable marks are subverted by their own desires. People who too passionately want to get rich are likely to believe promises of effortless wealth. Similarly, those desirous of political salvation are more likely to be taken in by promises of government-based salvation. Assuming this is so, the very enthusiasm of the Obama crowds is evidence of inflated aspirations. Who but the overly enthusiastic would believe that the government could spend additional trillions of dollars, lower taxes for 95 percent of Americans, and still reduce the national debt? Who could believe that a Democratic administration would eliminate wasteful government spending when none has previously? Such naiveté is not a sign of political health, but desperation.

Nor is the vitriol of contemporary liberals an indicator of confidence. Partisans addicted to calling their opponents fascists have gone over the top. By the same token, when they make movies depicting the assassination of a president they despise or paint pictures of postage stamps with a gun pointed toward his head, they have abandoned the pretense of civility. Correspondingly, when they steal college newspapers that disagree with their positions on affirmative action or shout down opposing speakers, they emulate the fanaticism of movements they presumably loath. In these cases, they have morphed into an American version of the Storm Troopers. Though they deny this, if they knew more about German history, the parallels would be undeniable. Much as George Santayana once warned, those who do not remember the past are condemned to repeat it.

There is, of course, a huge difference between liberals and Nazis. Contemporary liberals are not as violent as Hitler's supporters. Nor do they sponsor final solutions. Their violence is largely rhetorical, although many of their protests are physically destructive. While they revel in intimidating their foes, their promises of bloodshed are primarily for effect. Still, they are anything but gracious. For the most part, they refuse to sit down to reason with their opponents. They prefer "non-negotiable demands" instead. Also different is that the Nazi marchers prevailed. They not only got their man appointed chancellor, they imposed the Third Reich. Their totalitarianism was thus actual. Although liberals are not nearly as despotic, they are as ambitious. They too intend to remake society. The difference is that they are unlikely to succeed. The United States is not Germany and the current economic downturn is not the Great Depression. American voters are therefore less likely to tolerate cosmic changes. They desire improvements, not radical remedies. The extremism of contemporary liberals has therefore provoked opposition. It has unleashed passions that are apt to be its undoing.

Here then is another paradox. If the underlying insecurities of today's liberalism precipitated vociferous demands for change, while the implementation of these has generated a backlash, why have their programs been so widely embraced? Why have so many good people—people who genuinely want to improve the human condition—flocked to its banner? And why have so many moderates—people not blinded by liberal enthusiasms—opted for a president who promised dramatic change? The answer has to do with the nature of political persuasion. Politicians are prey to simplifications. Those who wish to be elected understand that they cannot afford to be subtle. If they hope to assemble large coalitions of supporters, they cannot be byzantine. Complexities are confusing and uninspiring. Crowds do not—and will not—gather to hear academic disquisitions on economic theory. They prefer red meat. They want to be aroused by glowing promises of a better life.

Consider Obama's primary appeal. He told the American people he represented "[c]hange—you can believe in." His administration would profoundly alter the status quo. He did not, however, say what form this change would take. Nor did he reveal how he would produce it. He did not even explain why this transformation would be for the better. Nevertheless, none of this mattered. The Republicans countered with the claim that change was not necessarily an improvement, that it could make things worse. Yet this ignited no fires. The voters instead yawned. They wanted change, not verbal niceties. And so the cheers persisted because Obama's audiences could read into his pledge whatever they chose. The poor could imagine their bills being paid by the government, while the wealthy anticipated the return of prosperity. Homosexuals could foresee the legalization of gay marriage, while straights envisaged an end to the Iraq War. Unspecified change is, in essence, a Santa Claus sack full of unopened presents. It is a blank slate upon which people project their fondest desires. This allows those with different expectations to subscribe to what seems the same agenda.

As much as anything, voters were swayed by Obama's preternatural self-confidence. His tone of voice and imperturbable style suggested that he could be trusted. Moreover, his obvious intelligence indicated that he would deliver workable solutions. There was no need to quibble about the specifics. The man's character spoke for itself. In addition, his mixed race allowed voters to congratulate themselves on their tolerance. Alongside this, questions regarding whether particular programs were feasible paled to insignificance. Discussions of technical qualifications seemed trivial in comparison. They made those who offered them sound uncertain. Better to leave the details to someone you trusted rather than get mired in the weeds.

13

Putting liberal enthusiasms and campaign simplifications together, we come up with a reason to doubt the validity of liberal assertions. Liberals, and suggestible moderates, might have been impressed with vociferous claims and ambiguous promises, but these did not add up to much. They certainly did not prove that liberalism is free of fallacious prophecies. Then again, they did not establish it is riven with them either. Demonstrating the latter requires evidence. So far, all we have deduced is a set of questions. Nor have we suggested a viable alternative. Even if liberalism is dying, this does not demonstrate that conservatism is poised to inherit its mantle. It too may be rent by contradictions.

Why Liberalism Cannot Work—An Overview

Liberalism is about dreams. It pretends to be about the future, but actually peddles fantasies of salvation. Liberals claim to be hardheaded realists who have harnessed science to improving the human condition, whereas they are more like small children listening for the hooves of Santa's reindeer on the roof. There is an old adage that has been attributed to everyone from Benjamin Disraeli to Winston Churchill which goes as follows: "If you are not a socialist when you are twenty, you do not have a heart. But if you are still a socialist at forty, you do not have a head." This observation is severe, but it contains more than a grain of truth. So does the claim that people tend to become more conservative as they grow older. It is therefore the very young who are most moved by liberal sentiments. It is they who find its promises most attractive. This is why Obama's campaign pinned its hopes on mobilizing their enthusiasm. It is also why advertisers aim to persuade the young rather than the affluent elderly.

To be blunt, liberalism is not merely about dreams, but immature dreams. Its greatest attraction is for those who do not understand how the world works and/or who do not possess the strength to control their own destinies. In appealing to their sense of social concern, the young are persuaded that compassion is sufficient to reform the world. If they care enough about the poor and downtrodden, this will, of itself, generate the power to change history. The old and the wealthy cannot, and will not, do the job because they are bitter and selfish. As the hippies once warned, we should not (with a few exceptions such as Obama) trust those over thirty. They failed to build a new world because they were inadequately educated and corrupted by power. Hence, as Obama asserted, old folks such as John McCain just "don't get it." They are out of touch. It takes fresh eyes and pure hearts to clean out the Augean stables of a society in shambles.

So what is the Liberal Dream? By now its outlines should be familiar. At least as widely disseminated as Christian ideals, its tenets are deeply ensconced in our political platitudes, educational objectives, and public entertainments. Liberalism begins by extolling *universal love*. Instead of competing with one another, people are urged to be collaborative. They are asked to be mutually supportive on the assumption that widespread cooperation is in everyone's interest. If people care enough about one another, they will be mutually helpful. This is what socialism is about. Its central goal is putting the good of the community above personal desires. As social creatures, we human beings must understand that our individual destinies are tied to our joint welfare. Furthermore, the well-being of the whole can only be ensured by what used to be called "brotherhood." As Obama clearly affirmed, we must ultimately be each other's keepers. One might even assert that it is in our interest to become one large and loving village.

Next liberalism asserts that the *government* must mediate this collective love. As the sole agent of all the people, its power must be dedicated to furthering the interests of all. It has to set up, and enforce, rules that guarantee mutual respect. In the process, it needs to develop massive programs that do for individuals what they are unable to do for themselves. In the final analysis, it is up to the government to protect people from themselves and their neighbors. In the modern context, this translates into establishing a welfare state. The government needs to create a safety net that does not allow people to be injured. Their bodily wants, health, and even emotional well-being must all be safeguarded. To do less is callous. It would demonstrate a lack of compassion.

But we need not fear a mammoth government becoming oppressive. Liberals perceive themselves as social democrats. The government they sponsor will protect people because it is made up of the people; in other words, it will be "a government of the people, by the people and for the people." Moreover, those running it will be among the *best and brightest* because, themselves liberals, their compassion and competence will dictate that they pursue shared objectives. And because the government will employ the best minds and the most effective organizers, they will do a better job of helping people than they could do for themselves. A veritable "brain trust" will certify that only rational policies are implemented in a compassionate manner. What amounts to a kindhearted collection of village elders will see to this. They might even be described as philosopher kings, albeit without crowns or a divine mandate.

The result of all this intelligent concern is that there will be *no wars, no discrimination, no pollution, no disease, no ignorance, and no poverty.* All of these are irrational and will therefore be banished. Since capitalism breeds these horrors, it must be consigned to the ash heap of history. Instead an elemental Marxism will become the order of the day. Each person must be asked to contribute to society according to his or her abilities, while receiving according to his or her needs. Selfishness, being illogical, must be dispensed with. Since no one will be in want; no one will be in fear. Everyone will be cared for and thus will feel secure.

As an additional consequence of this effective, egalitarian concern, everyone will be *equal*. No one will lord it above anyone else because everyone will recognize that no one is better than anyone else. With social resources intelligently distributed, no one will possess an excess of goods; hence no one will use these to gain superiority. But with no superiority, there can be no inferiority. Relationships based on a disparity of power will thus disappear. Indeed, the whole notion of power becomes obsolete. As a result, no one will ever again have to worry about being forced to serve the whims of others. As their own masters, they will be on a par with every other individual.

In order to achieve this, special attention will be paid to the weak. These *underdogs* need to be lifted out of inferiority. They will thus not be allowed to suffer in silence as they do in capitalism. Social leaders must recognize their special responsibility to the oppressed and make them the focus of their efforts to achieve equality. Thanks to liberalism bullying will not be permitted. No longer will it be allowable to blame the victims for their misery.

Furthermore, with complete equality will come universal *liberty*. As potential oppressors are cut down to size, individuals will be able to realize their potentials. They will be able to engage in *self-actualization* so as to achieve their best selves. No longer obliged to defend themselves against the demands of selfish elites, their energies will be freed to undertake personal growth. Whether their private bent leads them to the arts, the sciences, or athletics, they can become as good as is possible without fear over-shadowing others. In this way, the whole of humanity will be elevated to a level never previously achieved.

Finally, liberalism promotes *niceness*. One of its central tenets is that goodness begets goodness. In a society in which people care for one another, their concern must elicit concern from others. Goodness is, as it were, contagious. Genuine morality, of its very nature, is communicable. People who are not attacked, but rather befriended, are not destructively defensive. They allow their naturally helpful inclinations to emerge. In the end, an absence of coercion is self-sustaining. Gentleness and courtesy become the norm, with people, if not joining hands to sing Cumbaya, at least joining hearts in a global family based on universal amiability. The bad old day of jealousy and greed will thereby be banished.

How could anyone object to this? Is there any part of this agenda a decent human being would find unworthy? To suggest there is seems peevish. It contradicts a multitude of universal human aspirations. Many decent people are, in fact, drawn to the Liberal Dream. The young and dispossessed, in particular, find it congenial. So do secular moralists. In emphasizing compassion and universal equality, it makes them feel morally superior. Conversely, to bridle at the Liberal Dream is to label oneself a curmudgeon. Being against niceness and equality sounds absurd. Likewise, rejecting personal growth or interpersonal concern appears malevolent. Worse still, defending oppression is insane. As a consequence, few do. Certainly not most enlightened Americans. They know better.

So why object to liberalism? And why claim that it is dying? Isn't this equivalent to predicting a bleak future for humanity?

Well, no it is not. It is, in fact, to do the opposite. The primary reason for rejecting liberalism is that it is dishonest and unrealistic. As described above, it has never existed and never will. Fundamentally inconsistent with human nature, it cannot be actualized. Total liberalism has never been implemented, not because a clique of selfish elitists has stood in the way, but because the facts of human existence make it impossible. It is, and forever will remain, a dream that exists solely in the imagination. Fraught with hypocrisies, it is dead on arrival. People may find comfort in its promises, but they will never experience its benefits. Sadly, liberalism specializes in hope, not its realization.

This becomes clear when we examine how liberalism has been operationalized. The specific programs and regulations it has inspired have hardly ever lived up to their billing. Most are typically launched with wildly exaggerated claims, struggle through a period of disappointing accomplishment, and then limp off-stage, only to be replaced by equally exaggerated promises. Like the War on Poverty, they are introduced with a flourish of trumpets only to disappear from the public agenda several years later without so much as an admission of failure. Sadly, this has not happened only once. Rather, it is standard operating procedure for liberal causes. In the abstract they seem optimistic, whereas in the flesh they fail to deliver.

One of the central areas in which liberalism has sought reform is *economic justice*. The goal has been to create a prosperity so dynamic that everyone partakes of it. Franklin Delano Roosevelt (FDR) expressed this aspiration by promising "freedom from want." He would end the Great Depression by confiscating the ill-gotten gains of the rich and channeling them to the less well-off. The trouble is that his policies did not end the depression, nor lift the poor out of it. Lyndon Baines Johnson (LBJ) later expressed this same aspiration by promising to eliminate poverty. He asserted that a nation as affluent as the United States should be ashamed to tolerate destitution in its midst. The poor must immediately be empowered to enter the middle class. Only they weren't. An alphabet soup of government agencies could not put the Humpty Dumpty of individual privation together. Millions of people remained stubbornly below the poverty line. Then Jimmy Carter told us that welfare was "a disgrace to the human race" and he would end it. But he did not. The dependency fostered by government handouts was not reduced until a Republican Congress forced reform on a reluctant Democratic president.

Related to economic justice is the distribution of such fundamental goods as education and health. Liberals believe these should be universally accessible. They want the government to provide them from cradle to grave. Described as *rights*, it is assumed that the quality of these services will thereby be improved. No longer will the underprivileged have to line up at hospital emergency rooms. No longer will the children of the poor have to accept menial jobs from want of a college education. Whether a government-supplied education can be superior is, of course, another matter. The same can be said of health care. Can government-organized clinics supply the quality of care available in the marketplace? Considering the experience of other nations, the answer is uncertain.

Another aspect of liberal reform is social justice. Not only must economic disparities be evened out, so must social inequalities. Basic to this objective has been family reform. Back in the 1920s the goal was "free love." The paternalistic family was to be dismantled so as to liberate men and women from its oppressive obligations. Bertrand Russell actually suggested that the government support children so that husbands and wives need not be enslaved. More recently the call has been for the multicultural family. This is essentially a recommendation that families be constructed anyway people desire, whether this entails gay couples or single-parent households. There has also been a loosening of marriage vows to make divorce more acceptable. Even swinging marriages are held to be unobjectionable. Everyone must be allowed to handle relationships as they choose. Yet have these innovations improved the life circumstances of those affected? This is doubtful. The family is an ancient institution not likely to be disassembled so lightly.

Social justice has also focused on eliminating disparities between social categories. No group is supposed to exercise more power than any other. Gender, race, religion, ethnicity, and sexual orientation are all supposed to make no difference in determining social status. With respect to gender, the goal is androgyny. Any discrepancies between men and women are held to result from disparities in socialization. Thus many liberals assert that if the manner in which boys and girls are raised is comparable, divisive differences will evaporate and the traditional male hegemony will be consigned to the history books. With respect to race, the goal was once integration. Now it is equal representation in every aspect of society. With respect to sexual orientation, the aim was formerly toleration. Currently it is equal rights in areas such as marriage and adoption. With respect to religion, the target was also once toleration. Nowadays a separation of state and religion is interpreted as ejecting religion from the public scene. Fundamentalist beliefs are condemned as inherently oppressive.

Nor has it been considered sufficient to encourage the elimination of social differences. These are to be radically expunged through legal and programmatic means. Political correctness is no longer a matter of informal social sanctions. It has been transformed into laws about such things as hate crimes. Even more widespread has been the use of affirmative action to redistribute people according to their proportion in the population. In school, on the job, and in government, representation is dictated not by ability or desire, but social category. Education too has been mobilized to teach the proper attitudes. Even the very young are instructed that it is perfectly fine that Sally has two mothers. And as for recalcitrant adults, sensitivity training is the

19

order of the day. If they do not learn to express the correct opinions, they may find their positions in jeopardy.

Then too there is the issue of defending the downtrodden. Criminals are asserted to have unalienable rights, as do the mentally ill and drug abusers. Parents who use corporal punishment to discipline their children are now condemned as abusive, whereas murders are scrupulously protected from overzealous law enforcement agents. Even living out on the street is protected. Where once the homeless were described as vagrants and jailed, they are now objects of compassion. All of these outcasts, save for wayward parents, are understood to be victims. If they have offended the rules, either the rules are barbaric or social pressures to honor them are extreme. In the first case, the rules need to be loosened, and in the second, ordinary people must be more tolerant. In other words, niceness must be applied to rule breakers, not just rule keepers. The root causes of their deviance have to be understood so that these can be eliminated. Punishment is therefore the problem, not those punished.

As with economic justice, however, there is a question about whether these measures have the intended effect. Has feminism actually improved the situation of women? Or has it protected the interests of young children? And what about rehabilitating criminals? Has treating them with kindness reduced levels of criminality? As for affirmative action, has it elevated the status of blacks and women? There is reason to believe not. Education too may have achieved less than what was promised. All in all, these various social justice projects have had mixed results. Just how mixed must await further examination. In the meantime, it should be noted that passionate proclamations of liberal success ought to arouse skepticism.

As if this were not enough, liberalism promises *environmental justice*. It blames capitalism for polluting our environment and assures us that a more equitable society will be less contaminated. Once market-oriented greed is tamed, the cleanup will begin in earnest. Global warming will come under control, as both air and water are returned to a pristine condition. Ours will also become a less energy prolific world as people learn to reign in their appetites and respect the ecology. No longer will urban sprawl be allowed to desecrate the forests or oil wells defile the landscape. Automobile traffic too will be reduced as people congregate in central cities and rely on mass transportation. Eventually the skies will clear and people will once again see the stars.

There is no doubt that the environment has improved in recent years. Nor is there any doubt that pure air and water can foster an increased life span. What is not as certain is whether liberal measures will have the advertised effects. Ironically, efforts to reduce global warming may have little effect either because the problem is not of human origin or because draconian actions cannot succeed. And what about the possibility that reduced energy production will result in impoverishment? Many liberal activists say they do not care, that what matters is saving the planet. Some even urge that the earth's population be reduced by a factor of seven. They tell us that the carrying capacity of the planet is about a billion people. But then they do not say who should volunteer for elimination.

Lastly liberals seek *moral justice*. They want a world characterized by civility and mutual respect. People are asked be one another's keepers, but not each other's police officers. In fact, morality is said to be relative. Because what is right for one person may not be for another, everyone must decide for him or herself what is correct. As a consequence, moral tolerance needs to be universal, with guilt trips held to a minimum. People must not be told that they are at fault for the persons they are. Religious authorities must understand, for example, that they are not authorities for everyone. Their fire and brimstone nonsense must accordingly be identified for what it is. A civilized society cannot permit inquisitions or witch hunts. The trouble is that in practice tolerance tends to be confined to liberals' ranks. Dissenters are not so fortunate. Whereas free speech is said to apply to everyone, nonliberal voices, such as the Tea Party members, are shouted down. They are accused of undermining the coming millennium and are thus exempt from protection. Nor is relativism quite as relative as liberals pretend. It does not apply to attitudes with which they disagree. Female circumcision, for instance, is condemned as "genital mutilation." It is not accorded respect on the grounds that other cultures approve of it.

In general, liberals believe their programs can come to fruition only if several conditions are achieved. They begin by denouncing property rights. The Bible tells us that the love of money is the root of evil, whereas liberals believe property ownership is more insidious. They argue that if everything is owned in common, interpersonal envy can be eliminated. Moreover, with everyone allowed equal access to goods and services, no one will be in want. People can take what they require, as required. Likewise no one will be able to manipulate others by rewarding them with a paycheck, nor buy their way out of trouble with a bribe. Lobbying legislators with goodies will be a thing of the past and even marrying for money will lose its significance. Instead, generosity will be of the spirit, not the wallet.

Liberals also believe it necessary to eliminate hierarchical distinctions. They remind us that people are people, with no one inherently better than anyone else. Most would approve of Thomas Jefferson's observation that no human being is born with a saddle on his back or spurs on her heels. These accoutrements are acquired later on. If people learn to look to each other's humanity, not their status, status will prove an artificial anachronism. People will then treat each other according to their desserts, not their symbolic accomplishments. When this occurs, tyranny will become impossible. Nor, with genuine equality the norm, will anyone be ashamed of his/her origins.

Many liberals would also like to eliminate risk. They believe that as long as things can go wrong, some people will be unhappy. They do not merely want to furnish a social safety net; they intend to wrap everyone in cotton batting. Thus, universal health care is supposed to keep everyone healthy, while job security keeps people employed. Furthermore, multicultural families will afford everyone love on their own terms. Most liberals, however, are not enamored of entrepreneurs. They distrust innovations that upset comfortable apple carts. They do not want changes to eject anyone onto the proverbial street. Life is supposed to be predictable and its dangers held to a minimum. In short, everyone is supposed to wear a bicycle helmet and every ladder must carry a warning that it is unsafe to perch on the top step.

Once more most of this sounds reasonable—until one examines the details. It turns out that a majority of the liberal programs have not worked very well. Nonetheless, there is a more serious objection. The problem is that most can *never* work. They depend upon conditions that cannot be achieved. For starters, property rights will never be eliminated. Human beings are property-owning creatures. We all wish to exercise control over some physical goods. Whether these are toothbrushes or forty acres of land, we are prepared to defend them. Moreover, we are prepared to defend the property rights of others. Even parents scold a child who takes a cookie from a weaker sibling. To imagine a world in which this is not so is to imagine a world in chaos. But not to worry. Such a state has never existed. Nor will it ever exist—not even if everyone becomes liberal. Even liberals like to accumulate pretty toys. They are not about to give up their Gucci loafers or morning cups of Starbucks coffee.

Nor will hierarchical distinctions disappear. We human beings are given to ranking one another according to relative power. No one wants to be at the bottom of the greasy pole. None of us wants to be less important than others. Some years ago a Broadway song asked If I ruled the world. In so doing, it appealed to a widespread fantasy of being so powerful as to be able to do anything one desires. By the same token, no wants to be a slave. None of us wishes to be so powerless as to always defer to others. Liberals suggest this is why people need to be equal, but this ignores our persistent desire to gain an advantage over others. Such a craving for superiority amounts to nothing less than a yearning to be special. And who does not want to be special? Yet in a world where everyone is special, no one is. It is one where none stand out. In such a world not only would no one be rich, but no one would be a rock star. Such a universe would embrace mediocrity. As a consequence, it is a place where few would want to live. In the real world, we compete for priority. We always have and always will. To imagine otherwise is to believe in fairytales.

Nor are we liable to eliminate all risks. People will continue to die no matter how advanced medicine becomes. People will also stumble in achieving their fondest hopes. Disappointment is a part of human existence. Not only is this so, but we make certain that it is. Thus, we ski down mountains for the thrill of it. We also set goals too ambitious to be reached. Moreover, the moment we get what we desire, we aim higher, thereby ensuring that at some point we fall short. Nor can we eliminate the accidents of living. Since no one can foresee, or control, all contingencies, bad things are sure to occur. We may trip over a child's skate in our driveway or invest in a new product that is overtaken by a better one. Who knows, perhaps some day an asteroid will do to us what one did to the dinosaurs.

The Liberal Dream in Its Impossible Particulars

If these observations are not sufficient to undercut the liberal agenda, then it is time to be more specific about the inconsistencies of the Liberal Dream. Liberals seek justice, but in many cases they pursue what Thomas Sowell has labeled *cosmic justice*. He argues that liberals want things to be so perfect that they guarantee they never will be as good as they predict. Liberals essentially convert the perfect into the enemy of the good. To illustrate, in desiring everyone to be rich, they ensure that people will not be as affluent as is possible. Thus, by advocating a radical redistribution of wealth, they weaken the motives that create wealth. As we have already seen, attempts to eliminate poverty have not succeeded. But the difficulty lies deeper than this. Governments do not create wealth. They are not engines of production. Indeed, they are often elaborate Ponzi schemes. They take from some people to give to others, that is, until they have exhausted the resources of those from whom they take. Nor can governments ensure that everyone works up to his or her ability. Some people inevitably drop out. Some rebel. Some are lazy. What then? Under such conditions can they be brought up to the level of the more ambitious?

Similarly, can there be complete justice with respect to education or health? It has been argued that educational fairness exists only if there is a total equality of academic results. Only if no child is left behind can it be said that every child has been provided with equivalent opportunities. The trouble with this requirement is that not every child is equally talented. Hence, if all are to obtain good grades, these must be watered down. Some people, of course, find this perfectly acceptable. They regard grades as invidious distinctions that impose unnecessary disparities. They prefer accepting children for whom they are, in which case ignorance will become the norm. Likewise, health care is said to be fair only if everyone is afforded the best of every appropriate intervention. No matter that the cost would be greater than the gross national product. No matter that some patients do not take prescribed medicines. Somehow everybody must be saved from every potential malady.

Then there are the promises of social justice. When these too become cosmic, they are likewise impossible to achieve. Thus, when status differences are totally eliminated, the injustices begin to pile up. Sadly, it is because of the presumptions of social justice that the family has been condemned. It is accused of depriving men and women of the freedom to be themselves. It is also said to be inimical to true love. In reality, however, destroying the underpinnings of interpersonal commitment annihilates the opportunity for love. Human beings who flit from flower to flower, as advised by the king in *The King and I*, do not accumulate much honey. They are more apt to die lonely and disillusioned. Similarly, children deprived of dependable parental care suffer the fate of many foster children. They do not grow into a confident, satisfied maturity, but anxious, self-sabotaging adults. Deprived of two committed parents, they remain emotionally deprived.

By the same token, eliminating the distinctions between men and women is not a prescription for universal happiness. Men and women are different. This verity is no longer politically correct, but it remains a fact. The former president of Harvard University may have lost his job for affirming this truth, but it is still the truth. It is also true that honoring these differences makes successful intimate relationships more likely. It is equally true that people are more prone to enjoying their work if it is in line with their preferences and abilities. Artificial quotas are exactly that—artificial.

Race and sexual orientation are, however, another matter. Liberals are absolutely correct in insisting that these categories should have nothing to do with a person's opportunities. The error here is in assuming that color and sexual fairness can be legally mandated. Reforming social rules can rectify some wrongs, as witness the 1960s Civil Rights legislation, but these changes can only go so far. They are able to influence our cultural evolution, but not impose it. Correcting subtle attitudes depends on the evolution of larger social trends.

As for crime and drug abuse, social justice is not a matter of crippling the legal system. No doubt there have been abuses in applying the law, but once more liberalism has gone too far. Cavalier pronouncements about how it is better to allow a hundred guilty men go free than to imprison one innocent person are incredibly shortsighted. A hundred guilty men circulating through the community are apt to inflict substantial damage. So great would their depredations be that a society exposed to them might as well not have a legal system. As a result, by converting *excuse abuse* into a cottage industry, liberals have done ordinary citizens no favor. Making it more difficult to convict criminals simply creates more criminals. As per the Broken Window Theory, it sends the message that society does not care about enforcing its rules. Unfortunately, those most injured are the innocent bystanders.

When it comes to environmental justice, the problem is a little different. Here the issue is how much is too much. If cosmic justice entails demolishing the economy, this is over the line. Almost no one is against protecting the environment. After all it was Republicans under Teddy Roosevelt who initiated the conservation movement. This being so, our current disagreements are essentially over how radically to alter our consumption and production habits. Recycling plastic bottles is not too much to ask. Nor is encouraging efficient internal combustion engines. But strangling domestic oil production or making the construction of nuclear reactors impossible is another matter. In this case, there are no absolutes. How best to balance prosperity and environmental concerns is thus an open question.

Next, with respect to moral justice, liberalism is in a bind. Liberals tend to be extreme moralists, but moralists who simultaneously deny the validity of morality. They emphatically believe that some things are wrong; nevertheless, they insist that right and wrong are in the eye of the beholder. Were this so, however, were ethical relativism correct, disinterested observers must wonder why they should subscribe to liberal values. Postmodernists tell us that morality is a matter of persuasion, but if this is the case, why should liberals rather than conservatives be persuasive? The absolutism of traditionalists may be in error, but denying the authority of moral rules, qua moral rules, is no improvement. Nor is attacking religion with mindless abandon. While it is true religious authorities have been responsible for some of the worst atrocities in human history, so have the zealous advocates of atheism. The Soviets under Stalin did a more than adequate job of ignoring human dignity. No, what liberalism is lacking is an accurate understanding of how morality operates. In its haste to do what is right, it has forgotten to scrutinize how we arrive at decisions regarding what is right.

Which brings us back to our initial depiction of the Liberal Dream. We opened up by observing that liberalism believes in universal love. The problem with this is that love cannot be universal. Love has to do with attachments to particular human beings. To pretend that these can be with everyone is absurd. While people can abstractly care for the welfare of strangers, they concretely care for the welfare of only a relative few. People play favorites. They always have and always will. Those who claim otherwise have usually been exposed as frauds. They may say they love everyone, but in reality love no one. Much as was the case with the leaders of the French Revolution, they readily commit murder in the name of protecting humanity.

Liberalism then moves on to ask the government to deliver the impossible. The state is supposed to be the guardian of comprehensive public welfare. Its programs and regulations are expected to institute cosmic justice of every sort. Yet there are limitations. Over the past century governments have indeed produced wonders. Thus, they have given us social security, public education, and a splendid infrastructure of roads and bridges. But they have not given us everything they promised. Time and again cranky bureaucracies have mismanaged its programs. Their administrators tell us they care, and then get bogged down in red tape. They may even be unfair, with those having the right political connections (such as unions or banks) obtaining the best service—including subsidies. Nor have government regulations proved adequate. Hate crime legislation, for instance, has not eliminated hate. What liberals forget is that governments are human institutions. They are run by people, some of whom are invariably imperfect.

Liberals hope to get around this by sponsoring democratic institutions administered by "the best and brightest." Confident in their own abilities and intentions, they project these onto government agencies. At the very least, they expect to institute policies that guarantee the best results. Unfortunately, they have a difficult time admitting when their calculations are off base. Examples of this tendency are manifold. Accordingly, once upon a time, liberals said that Medicare would be cheap; it wasn't. They also assured us that rent control would make housing affordable; it didn't. Nor are liberals willing to acknowledge that they too can be corrupted. As per Lord Acton's warning, no government anywhere has escaped corruption when given a monopoly of power. Liberals understand that commercial monopolies often fail to operate in the public interest; nonetheless they refuse to recognize that public monopolies can be as obtuse. Witness the Fannie Mae and Freddie Mac debacles. Their managers, public appointees all, placed their personal interests above the welfare of the nation thereby triggering a financial crisis of epic proportions. Arrogance is not confined to business people; it also afflicts the nonprofit sectors.

A comparable arrogance has prompted liberals to promise an end to wars, discrimination, pollution, disease, ignorance, and poverty. These are large orders, none of which have come close to fruition. While there have been advances, these have always been outrun by escalating aspirations. Robert Browning told us "a man's reach should exceed his grasp, or what's a heaven for?" but liberals want heaven here on earth—which is quite a reach. In particular, getting rid of capitalism, because it entails selfishness, is problematic. What sense does it make to dismantle a system that has given us unprecedented wealth and democracy in favor of an untested form of social organization? This is especially so when efforts to establish collectivist societies, as in the Soviet Union and China, have so uniformly disappointed.

Perhaps the most nonsensical element in the Liberal Dream is its call for total equality. Even Thomas Jefferson recognized this is impossible. He realized that there are always differences in ability, effort, opportunity, results, and just plain luck. In the Declaration of Independence he wrote that all men are created equal, but only with respect to their rights. According to him, everyone is entitled to life, liberty, and the pursuit of happiness. In his original draft Jefferson also included property. He believed in a market economy that defended individual ownership from government expropriation. He likewise believed in an aristocracy of merit. People were to be allowed to rise as high as they were able. To forbid this would enshrine an empire of mediocrity. It would, as many liberals have advocated, prohibit keeping score in little league baseball games on the grounds that this harms the self-esteem of the players. Nevertheless, if human beings are hierarchical animals, we will always keep score, if only in our heads. Children, in fact, do. What is more, some of us will always aspire to be better than the next guy. Happily, in doing so they will produce results that are beneficial to the entire community.

Also nonsensical is the belief that liberalism will free people to be their optimum selves. Aside from the fact that unfettered liberalism is unlikely to prevent oppression, total equality is not the best seedbed for personal growth. People need an incentive to do better. Ironically, competition, in an environment of freedom, is such a spur. People who are given whatever they want grow lethargic. Utterly dependent on others, they are bereft of ambition. Some liberals go on to advocate self-actualization. They believe that everyone possesses an inner self pressing for expression. As a result, they believe personal growth is automatic. What they do not realize is that who we become is a combination of inborn attributes and outside forces. Nature and nurture both make us what we are; hence the nurture part too needs to urge us forward. Market-based rivalries provide this encouragement.

Finally, niceness does not always beget niceness. Years ago, when I worked at a methadone clinic, I witnessed one of our clients cut open the cheek of another with a razor blade because the latter had said a kind word to a third person. Some people are evil. They may not have been born that way, but it is what they have become. To treat them with unalloyed kindness is therefore to invite attack. These people must be stopped. They need to be controlled with a force adequate to do the job. In a world where ravening wolves are allowed to wander as they please, the sheep enjoy short life spans. Nice people, who want to live in a nice world, must possess a harder edge. Daniel might have survived in the lion's den, but in our world it is wiser to follow Teddy Roosevelt's advice to carry a big stick.

All of this adds up to the conclusion that liberalism cannot work. Its ambitions rarely get beyond the dream stage. Amazingly, many liberals already know this. Given their sincerity and intelligence, they cannot help but notice the failures of their beliefs. As successful men and women, most conduct their personal lives in a manner at odds with their political convictions. They, for instance, demand achievement, not mediocrity, of their children. As a result, they are troubled by a cognitive dissonance of the sort Festinger predicted. Just as with the flying saucer cult, the pieces of their lives clash with the effect of increasing their discomfort. This is why so many liberals have become agitated. It is why their denials of collapse have become so emphatic and their promises of improvement so extreme. Contemporary liberals are in a state of panic. They are flapping their wings as fast as they can in the hopes of warding off a mental implosion. With their dreams dying before their eyes, they dread a future they do not understand.

Perhaps the biggest problem liberals face is that they cannot perceive an alternative to their vision. Nor will they go over to the enemy side. They refuse to accept what they interpret as the superstitiousness of conservatism. They also reject the notion that things cannot get better. As good people, they are committed to improvements. Fortunately, they do not have to succumb to impotent pessimism. Even as we speak, events are providing an answer to their conundrum. There is an alternative to the Liberal Dream. The problem is that it is not yet on their radar screens.

Post-Liberalism—The Professionalized Alternative

So what comes after liberalism? What will work, if liberalism cannot? This is a complex question. Indeed, it is one that requires a multipart answer. It turns out that what is possible within an intricate, techno-commercial society is contingent upon how societies are held together. As it happens, not all binding-mechanisms are equally suited to every sort of society. The measures upon which liberals pin their hopes are, in fact, more appropriate to smaller, simpler communities. Despite all their talk about being progressive, their dreams are geared to a world that disappeared millennia ago. Their aspirations are more suitable for the small hunter-gatherer bands of our remote ancestors than the massive, middle-class society we inhabit.

The central issue determining what works to maintain social cohesion is a concept with which sociologists have long been familiar, namely "social solidarity." As Thomas Hobbes asked centuries ago, how can individuals who are both selfish and dangerous live together in relative harmony? How, in their quest to obtain the best for themselves and their kin, can they keep from killing, or at least injuring, competing outsiders? Furthermore, how can creatures that evolved to live in tiny groups of no more than a hundred and fifty reside in nation-states with populations in the hundreds of millions? Why aren't they overwhelmed by torrents of undifferentiated humanity? Why don't they, at least, become confused when dealing with hordes of strangers?

Hobbes thought he had the answer. It was monarchy. He believed that people literally got together to agree to submit to an absolute ruler. In so doing, they entered into a compact that subsequently became binding on their progeny. According to him, only a special individual, one backed by everyone in the community, possessed the strength to keep potential lawbreakers at bay. Only this could control the selfishness of the strong. Today we recognize that this was not the only possible answer. Hobbes lived in a society where monarchies were the rule, but we have found that representative democracies are also workable. They too possess the requisite interpersonal restraints to keep bloodshed within bounds.

Two centuries after Hobbes, Emile Durkheim came up with a different idea. He suggested that there were two kinds of social solidarity; one he called mechanical, the other he labeled organic. The former applied to small societies. Their members presumably worked in harmony because they were alike. Given that their tasks were relatively simple, each could understand and sympathize with the others. Organic solidarity, on the other hand, was more appropriate to larger communities where people might not even know those upon whom they were dependent. These folks were able to get along because they recognized their mutual interdependence. With the tasks required for survival having grown in complexity, no one could meet all of his or her own needs. This put people at the mercy of strangers whom they had to tolerate on peril of failing to thrive. As a result, they found ways to integrate their assignments. Butchers got along with bakers and candlestick makers did business with plumbers. They may not have liked one another, but they cooperated nevertheless.

Today there is another way to understand what holds societies together. It is called Social Domain Theory. This viewpoint tells us that many forces are involved in holding societies together. Some are cultural and some structural. Among the former are normative, cognitive, symbolic, emotional, aesthetic, ritual, and material orders. Among the latter are personal relationship, social hierarchy, social exchange, social role, reconciliation, spatial, and environmental orders. For the moment we need not worry about what these entail. Their implications will be explored in greater detail later on. For now, what is important to note is that the factors holding societies together are enormously complex. What is also significant is that these transform in nature as societies move from the very small to the very large. This means that what worked for hunter-gatherers will not work for members of techno-commercial societies. That which enables the latter to cooperate is decidedly different from that which did for the former.

The simplest way to describe what has today become necessary to ensure social solidarity is *professionalization*. Much as is true of doctors and lawyers, ordinary people need to be competent at complicated tasks that are integrated with the tasks of multiple role partners. They have to be self-motivated experts in what they do so that they can do it well. Such persons cannot afford to be passively dependent upon others, but must actively strive to contribute to a multifaceted social tapestry. Were they to opt out of this interlocking community, the whole would suffer from their lack of participation, while they would be consigned to impotent isolation. Complex social roles turn out to be the key to making technological, market-oriented societies function. They are the glue holding millions of strangers together.

Knowledge and technology are also crucial in enabling such communities to function. Modern middle-class societies could not operate without the advancements in science that underlie contemporary forms of transportation, communication, and production. It is not for nothing that we today talk of an information age. Neither the prosperity in which we share, nor the democratic institutions we admire, could exist without these advances. They, as it were, help us to understand and tolerate each other despite our lack of intimate knowledge. This makes it imperative for individuals to be knowledgeable in a way their forebears were not.

Liberalism, in contrast, stresses mechanisms more appropriate for hunter-gatherers. It urges people to participate in the sort of family that flourished within hunting bands. People who depended upon cooperation with others to whom they were related were of necessity close to one another. Not only were they in physical proximity, but in emotional propinquity. Theirs was a personalized world in a way our modern one is not. The reason liberals find the family metaphor congenial—and it is only a metaphor—is that this is the kind of association for which our species evolved. Once, not long ago, all of our ancestors lived in tight-knit communities. These were the sorts of groups for which their instinctive reactions and mental abilities prepared them. This was, therefore, the sort of world they found comfortable. It is also the type we find agreeable. We resort to it in our imaginations because our genetic endowment is virtually the same as theirs. The Liberal Dream has merely hitchhiked on this legacy.

Another part of our hunter-gatherer heritage entails face-to-face hierarchies. Sometimes it is asserted that hunting bands were completely egalitarian. People who lived side-by-side under the same material conditions presumably treated each other as exactly the same. No one would have been considered better than anyone else. Certainly no one lived in a mansion or drove a Mercedes Benz. Even so, there were profound inequalities. People depended upon the leadership of community elders, shamans, and superior hunters. They understood that people differed. They also knew that unless they respected the authority of those in charge all might perish. Their equality, such as it was, was in terms of a shared humanity, not one of authority or respect. These latter were earned in face-to-face interactions and treated gingerly because it was understood that no one liked to be forced into submission.

Liberals, in misunderstanding our past, have assumed that complete equality is our natural condition. At the same time, they have assumed the mantle of hunting band elders. In arrogating to themselves the title of "the best and brightest," they imply that they deserve the right to run the community. Nevertheless, they leave out the factors that govern hierarchical arrangements in massive societies. Hundreds of millions of people cannot treat each other as if they belonged to the same village. They must, for instance, depend upon symbolic indicators of comparative rank. Moreover, what can go wrong among them is not the same as what goes wrong in tiny clearings in the forest. Thus, they have to worry about tyranny in a way their ancestors did not.

The answer to the liberal dilemma is, therefore, not a retreat into conservatism. The solution to what ails modern societies is something different. It is a vision that does not derive from long dead philosophers. Rather *professionalization* is an idea whose time has come. The difficulty is that it is so new people are not fully cognizant they are living professionalized lives. Nonetheless the possibility of such an awareness exists. Americans have experienced a reorganization of their political landscape before. It took the Civil War to establish a polarity between Democrats and Republicans, but a similar realignment may be in the works—hopefully without a comparable trauma.

If this shift is to come to fruition, more people need to become conscious of what it means to be professionalized. They have to adopt the goal of becoming self-motivated experts and accept of the implications of doing so. Still, if this occurs, the accompanying improvements will not achieve utopian proportions. Professionalization is not a cure-all. To be human is to cope with limitations. Nor will everyone benefit to the same degree. Professionalization is about ameliorization. It is about making small, albeit bona fide, improvements. A professionalized world is one that builds upon multiple successes. In contrast, political movements grounded in fantasy seldom ration their promises. Their appeal depends upon projecting colossal, although fictional, enhancements. A society based on self-motivated expertise can do better. But to the extent that it asks people to be grown-ups, it also asks them to be realistic.

Liberalism, irrespective of its intellectual pretensions, tends not to worry about facts. It does not so much prove its contentions as seduce people with tempting promises. Nor are liberals above bending the truth to make a point. A professionalized perspective ought to be different. It should at least begin by making a solid case for its projections. So far all that has been presented in this first chapter is an assemblage of unsupported assertions. Yet conviction is no substitute for evidence. It would be a grievous mistake to fall into the same trap as liberalism. The attractiveness of an idea does demonstrate its legitimacy. An effort must, therefore, be made to substantiate what has been alleged.

As a consequence, it remains necessary to document the origins of the Liberal Dream. Is that which has been described above what liberals actually believe? And if so, why do they believe it? What were the steps that brought them to this conclusion? It is also necessary to prove that liberalism has failed. The details of how its promises have gone awry must be further dissected. Particular programs and regulations have to be placed on the table and taken apart to see how they tick. Not even this will be enough however. The nature of liberal contradictions needs to be examined. Does liberalism, in fact, sponsor diametrically opposite contentions? If so, why have these inconsistencies remained obscure?

Once this is established, it will be necessary to go into greater detail regarding how societies are held together. In particular, how does Social Domain Theory explain what occurs? At this point, we will be better able to explicate why various political ideologies have exercised a broad appeal. Not just liberalism, but libertarianism, conservatism, bohemianism, anarchism, and religion will all be fair game for analysis. This is required before the superiority of a professionalized perspective can be demonstrated. Next how these alternatives square with our human and social natures must be dealt with. The result should be an exposition of why we human beings are regularly led astray by false hopes.

After this, it will be necessary to clarify the nature of a professionalized society. This must be done, lest we make the liberal error of failing to establish the manner in which a projected way of life can become reality. But this too is not enough. The details of how professionalization can be executed have to be explored. This in turn must include an explanation of how actual human beings might function in such a society. Communists once counted upon the evolution of "the new communist man," but this was wishful thinking. Professionalization has to do better. It must demonstrate that actual human beings can be sufficiently self-directed to fill the roles expected of them.

We must likewise demonstrate how people—not all people—but actual people, can save themselves from the losses that beset the human condition. If people are to become what they are capable of being, they must understand how to extricate themselves from defeats that can make life unbearable. What good would it do to prove that professionalization is possible, if individual human beings are incapable of overcoming the obstacles to professionalization? This, to be sure, is a tall order, but one that can be fulfilled.

2

The Origins of the Dream

Christianity

Traditionalists, such as Bill O'Reilly, castigate liberals for being secular progressives—and liberals return the favor. They accuse him and his allies of being fundamentalist know-nothings. The two sides of the Culture Wars are like scorpions in a bottle. They continuously spit vituperation in each other's direction. A disinterested observer might, therefore, be excused for assuming that their beliefs are completely different. Since they seem to disagree about everything, it is hard to imagine that they share a common heritage. But oddly they do. As is so often the case, a mutual loathing is exacerbated by multiple similarities. Of course, neither side will admit to this resemblance because it would dilute their respective identities. They would seem less distinctive and therefore less worthy of allegiance.

Nevertheless contemporary liberalism owes several of its more salient aspects to Christianity. Liberals share the same cultural lineage as their religious rivals. Neither would be what they are, except for concepts derived from millennia old sources. Once religion was a localized phenomenon. Hunting bands had their own Gods and early nation-states boasted of national divinities. Zeus was the chief God of the Greeks, whereas the Egyptians worshiped Isis and Ra. None of these deities were thought to be universal. The ancient Israelites took a step forward when they imagined that their God, Yahweh, was the one true God. All the same, he was their God in the sense that they conceived of themselves as his chosen people. They were the ones who received his revelations and the ones required to honor his wishes.

Christianity was an outgrowth of Judaism, but with a crucial difference. Early on, it was conceived as a universal religion. It did not belong to any particular people or nation, but to anyone willing to embrace it. As long as you believed what the church believed and honored its sacraments, you were a Christian. The faith was not the first

35

of the great international religions—that distinction probably goes to Buddhism—but it was one of the most successful. It was able to function as the glue holding the declining Roman Empire together because any Roman, no matter what his or her ethnicity, could join the Church. Saint Paul made this possible by loosening Jewish dietary restrictions and jettisoning the requirement for circumcision. Subsequently, the early Frankish rulers and the princes of Kiev were able to use the religion for the same purpose. They too found its universalism convenient for enlarging the national tent.

From the beginning, Christianity thought of its communicants as belonging to an extended family. Their God was considered a father figure and those who believed in Him were His children. Here on earth the faithful constituted an egalitarian community of brothers and sisters, while later on in heaven they would be related by even stronger bonds of adulation for their creator. Members of this quasi-kinship group were expected to be mutually supportive. They were to help each other in moments of need as if they were biologically related. In this, they were to be each other's keepers. As a consequence, charity was one of the foremost duties of a good Christian, although it was directed primarily toward fellow Christians.

God, the father, was regarded of as both omnipotent and omniscient. He was not only powerful enough to have created the world, but powerful enough to grant any wish He desired. Because God knew everything, He understood what everyone required and, because He was immensely strong, He could do anything, including suspending the laws of nature. He could even make the Sun stand still in the sky. According to Sigmund Freud, this sort of Godhead is essentially a communal projection of the "good father." Given how uncertain life can be, and how limited our biological parents are, we supposedly crave a dependable protector. God fills this bill because He is conceived of as the perfect protector. He never makes a mistake and never fails to do what is needed. We human beings may not understand His ways, but that does not make them less perfect.

Christianity is also a religion of love. Its deity so cherishes His creatures that He sent His only son to atone for their sins. Christ having come down to earth and been sacrificed on the cross, ordinary men and women were afforded the possibility of salvation. Instead of going to Hell, if they lived pious lives, they might be rewarded with eternal happiness. No longer would they be burdened by the legacy of original sin or the enduring conflicts of the mortal coil. One day they would

36

enjoy the perpetual company of their loved ones and the joy of daily praising the Lord. To benefit from this unending ardor, all they had to do was remain obedient to His wishes. Their duty was to honor God's commandments and see that His will was done—here on earth, not just heaven.

Christianity likewise believed in equality, but with some crucial provisos. God reigned supreme over all of creation, as did Christ who was a manifestation of His tripartite essence. Then came the angels who were themselves hierarchically organized. Below them came the earthly elites. In the Middle Ages, this placed the priesthood on top, followed by the various layers of the aristocracy. Equality thus had its limits, except in the sense that all of humans were the children of God. They all had eternal souls and, as long as they were baptized, were eligible for His eternal reward. No one was better than anyone else except in terms of this Great Chain of Being and the fact that some would be granted God's grace, whereas others would not.

Not all contemporary liberals believe in God, but they too subscribe to many of the same principles. They may bridle at the idea of a supernatural being, but they too think of their beliefs as universal. Anyone is allowed to be a liberal, irrespective of his or her race, religion, ethnicity, or creed. In fact, in many ways, liberalism is more universal than Christianity. It does not require anyone to join a Church or follow a particular set of sacraments. Nor does liberalism have a precise set of rituals. Its central requirement is a belief in what liberals believe. As long as a person is prepared to voice the correct sentiments and vote for the approved candidates, he or she can consider him or herself a liberal in good standing. This means that liberalism can ultimately encompass every human being on earth. Absolutely everyone is allowed to participate in making its promises come true. All that is necessary is a commitment to doing so.

Liberalism likewise advocates a family of humankind. Whether or not one is a liberal, one is theoretically eligible to be treated as a virtual sibling. Merely being human qualifies a person to be part of the same loving international village. In this case, all that is required is to join hands in our common human venture. Universal devotion is then expected to flow from acknowledging this fundamental relationship. Everyone will subsequently care about the welfare of everyone else because all are bound by a kinship of spirit. Every face will similarly smile upon every other face, with all prepared to help any other in trouble. So profound is this love that it does not even require the mediation of a Christ figure.

Liberalism, to be sure, does not boast a Godhead. It instead vests omniscience and omnipotence in the government and its minions. State run agencies are treated as if they understand everything that needs to be done to defend people from the hazards of life. These bureaucracies are likewise regarded having the power to be totally protective. They are, in addition, strongly motivated to do the right thing. Moreover, all that is required to obtain their favor is to honor their mandates. If citizens obey the injunctions of the functionaries appointed to supervise them, everyone will be better off. Peace and prosperity will descend like manna from heaven, with no one left out of this eternal bounty.

Liberalism also offers a more comprehensive version of equality than Christianity. It does not propose a Great Chain of Being in which some rank higher than others. Nor does it invest absolute authority in a superior being and his heavenly acolytes. According to liberals, everyone is on the same plane. No one deserves more, nor should any obtain more. Everyone must therefore have the exact same opportunities and enjoy the same results. Disparities of any kind are considered an anomaly. Of course, there is one small caveat. The "best and the brightest" are to be allowed to exercise greater authority than the average mortal. Because they know what is best, they must be granted the power to protect those who cannot protect themselves. But this is not considered an exception to the equality rule. It is merely a means of ensuring that it is maintained.

The bottom line is that liberalism represents an intensification of Christian ideals. It is more universal, more egalitarian, and broader in its family-like attachments. The main difference is that liberalism secularizes these principles. It invests superior protective powers in the government, rather than a spiritual being. Liberalism essentially promises heaven on earth, rather than in a mythical paradise. Indeed, it undertakes to deliver perfection in the here and now. All that is required is to defend the appropriate faith. This is necessary, for liberalism too offers a version of the devil. In standard religious terms, the devil is the Lord's eternal antagonist. He is forever attempting to lead mortals astray. If they listen to his siren song, they will disobey their Creator with the consequence that they will fall into a pit of never-ending fire. For liberals, it is conservatives who take the place of the devil. They continuously interfere with the implementation of liberal programs so as to seduce weaker souls into resisting what is best. Without the presence of these reactionary figures, progress would be inevitable. Without such selfish obtuseness, the path toward a better future would be as traffic free as a ten-lane highway.

Liberals may resist this suggestion, but the attractiveness of their ideas owes a great deal to the prior success of Christianity. Were fewer Westerners exposed to Christian ideals, these would not be available to serve as a template for the liberal variations upon them. It is the fact that these have been so deeply ingrained that makes the Liberal Dream sound reasonable. It is they that form the backdrop against which liberal promises are measured, they that make aspirations toward perfection seem sensible.

Commerce and Nationhood

This said, the Liberal Dream did not come into its own until the emergence of our modern secular world. It was the triumph of secularism that liberated human thinking from a more uniformly spiritual frame of mind. It was not until the medieval period came to an end that people began to focus on more mundane matters. Before that life was conceived of as a preparation for the after-life. Whatever happened on earth paled in comparison with what would one day happen in heaven. The high Middle Ages were a time of prosperity, but it was not until the arrival of the Renaissance and then the Enlightenment that generalized affluence came to Europe. It was only then that people began to investigate their earthly circumstances.

After the turn of the first millennium, European commerce be-gan to accelerate. It accelerated even further once the ravages of the Black Death subsided. People began to sell all sorts of goods from one end of the continent to the other. The goal became to grow rich. But richest of all were the monarchs. Because they were able to tax the merchants, and in some cases expropriate their wealth, they pos-sessed greater resources than anyone else. This had a reciprocal effect on commerce. The wealth of the kings allowed them to suppress the brigands and robber barons that preyed upon the merchants, with the effect of making it safer to engage in long-distance trade. This, in turn, redounded to the benefit of monarchial coffers. With even more money to spend, they could now buy cannons and hire mercenaries. As a result, they expanded their domains to create the beginnings of modern nation-states such as France, England, and Spain. Within these, the kings could then build lavish palaces so as to live in greater luxury than their predecessors.

These were the beginnings of the *ancien regime*. Commercial expansion was the foundation of absolute monarchies such as that of Louis XIV of France. So dominant did Louis become that he was able to build the largest palace in the Western world. So huge was this structure that he could require his nobles to spend part of the year living under his roof—so that he could keep an eye on them. Within these walls, he and they dined off gold and silver plates. They likewise wore ermine and were fawned over by legions of liveried servants. Outside the walls of Versailles, the peasants might be scratching out a living, but this was of little concern to pampered aristocrats. As long as the revenues kept coming in from the tax farmers, the living conditions of the poor were irrelevant. Out of sight, they were out of mind. Marie Antoinette actually built, and pretended to operate, a farm on the palace grounds. There she played at being a milkmaid, albeit one who could return to her luxurious apartments at a moment's notice.

Fortunately, life in places like Paris was not completely grim. Commercial success had a trickle down effect. Merchants, and those who served them, benefited from the general prosperity. Still, they were on a lower rung and knew it. They might look with envy upon the luxuries of aristocrats, but understood that this status was inherited. These members of the Third Estate, while they could improve their condition, could never break through the iron-ribbed, glass ceiling holding them down. One of those who chafed at this enforced inferiority was an immigrant from Geneva. Jean Jacques Rousseau came to the French capital in hopes of making his fortune and, in fact, did very well. After winning a major essay contest, he became a minor celebrity who was admitted into the salons of the Great Ladies. There he entertained his betters with his superior wit. But he could not become one of them. Despite his eye for women, and theirs for him, he could not hope to enter a marital alliance with a noble woman. He was, at best, the equivalent of a pampered lap dog—which irked him no end.

Rousseau got his revenge by becoming one of the philosophical gurus of the impending French Revolution. He became a font of ideas later used to legitimize tearing down the whole rotten edifice. His ideas were so profound—or at least so attractive—that they continue to be employed as a justification for contemporary liberal promises. Many liberals have no idea that they are parroting Rousseau and are even less concerned with whether he was correct. The mere fact that his theories are centuries old gives them a patina of authority that obscures their origin. They appear beyond question because, as traditional answers to important questions, they seem to have always existed. That they were concocted to suit a way of life different from our own is deemed irrelevant. For their devotees, they are self-evident.

So what did Rousseau believe? To begin with, he hated the *ancien regime*. He wished to tear it down and substitute something entirely new. Rousseau did not believe in government, as he knew it. Unlike Hobbes, he did not think a monarch necessary. Although Rousseau also posited a social compact that would be binding on subsequent generations, it would not produce a traditional sovereign. Instead, it required rulers to operate in accord with the General Will. They were mandated to be in touch with what people wanted and then to provide it. This was intended to ensure that the needs of ordinary folks were met. As a consequence, their welfare would not be an afterthought, but the loadstone around which the system revolved.

Sad to say, exactly what the General Will was, or is, remains a mystery. Somehow, there supposedly exists an underlying consensus upon which public policy is to be based. Given its presence, there can be no conflict in what is desired because, in their essential "goodness," people basically want the same things. The trouble with this expectation is that no human community has ever exhibited a complete unanimity of interests. There have always been disagreements about goals. More than this, there have continually been clashes regarding policy. Since not everyone benefits equally from every course of action, different factions support competing proposals. Nor do leaders have a convenient way of tapping into Rousseau's fictional consensus. Nowadays they use public opinion polls to establish what is desired, but these are notoriously flawed. As every pollster knows, the answers depend upon the questions asked. Moreover, the responses vary with the time and place. Lest people forget, there was a period when George W. Bush was a public favorite.

Yet Rousseau had a solution to this problem. He believed that divisions of opinion were created by disparities in wealth. Of course the rich wanted different things than the poor. What people possessed altered their desires and therefore set them at odds. The way out of this dilemma was to abolish property. If people no longer competed to obtain goods, they would be generous toward each other. The good news was that property ownership was artificial. It was an invention of our ancestors; hence it could be reversed. Pierre Proudhon would later describe property as nothing less than theft. It could therefore be outlawed. According to Rousseau, long ago someone fenced in a piece of land, thereby removing it from the public domain. Others then made the mistake of respecting this misappropriation. Had they resisted this confiscation, differences in rank would have been impossible. No one could flaunt a surfeit of resources that did not exist. But it was not too late. The damage could be undone. All that people had to do was withhold their respect from claims of ownership. This would automatically turn these pretensions into empty assertions. Saying "this is mine" would be tantamount to expelling hot air on a cold night.

Rousseau went even further. He argued that human beings were essentially good. Hobbes might have contended that people are fundamentally selfish and aggressive, but this was wrong. Human beings were by nature kind and openhanded. If they seemed otherwise, it was because they had been corrupted by disparities in property ownership. Once these were eliminated, their true character would emerge. In other words, people were, in fact, "nice." It was the system in which they were embedded that created conflicts. It was thus this system that needed to change. The way to do this was through education. If children were no longer oppressed by lessons that encouraged them to be competitive, their spontaneously high spirits would bubble to the surface. They would explore their environment with unadulterated glee and appreciate its many wonders. All that was needed was to allow them to decide for themselves what to study. In his quasi-novel *Emile*, Rousseau demonstrated how this could be done. Rather than rote recitations of materials derived from the past, the young should be allowed to explore nature on their own. They must be set free to wander through meadows and climb hillsides in accord with projects of their own design. Were this to become the norm, the young would learn what is worth knowing and consequently no longer be trapped by the iniquities of the past.

According to Rousseau, dismantling the aristocratic superstructure would liberate people to be the best they can be. In modern parlance, they would be free to self-actualize. No longer oppressed by their betters, their full potential would be realized. In the end, everyone would be completely equal, with universal love characterizing the human condition. Rousseau did not survive to see the French Revolution, never mind our modern techno-commercial society, but his projections continue to live on in the public imagination. Frenchmen who went to the barricades shouting "liberty, equality and fraternity" were his intellectual progeny. So too are contemporary liberals who believe that everyone is fundamentally nice. They are also committed to the belief that getting rid of the system, even though it is now a very different system, will liberate the human spirit. They are likewise devotees of complete equality and universal love. Just as did their intellectual forefather, they hate the government as presently constituted and would replace it with a utopian system of their own devising.

The final irony is that Rousseau was not a nice man. He was arrogant, suspicious, and craved public adulation. He also took refuge with a working-class mistress he kept in a back alley and married only late in life. Rousseau thought of himself as better than most people. He even believed himself superior to the aristocrats who snubbed him. Moreover, despite his limitations, he thought he knew best. Thus, although by his own admission, he had been incompetent as a tutor to the children of a noble family, he did not hesitate to expound upon how tutoring should be managed by others. That today many educators take his recommendations as appropriate for classes crowded with poor children should be a source of wonder. That he, a man who sent his five children to a foundling hospital so as to preserve the funds needed for fancy clothes, should be thought of as a humanitarian is beyond belief. One might think that liberals, for whom he is a paragon of virtue, might be taken aback by the failures exhibited in his personal life—but apparently not. Indeed, most are unaware of that 85 percent of orphans then died in foundling hospitals. Rousseau may have celebrated love, but he did not live by it. Instead, he self-importantly allowed his own flesh and blood to perish in quiet agony.

Industrialization

While Rousseau was preaching revolution, across the English Channel an even more momentous series of events was taking place. The Industrial Revolution had just gotten underway and was about to alter how people lived more dramatically than did purely political occurrences. James Watt's improvements upon the steam engine made it possible to liberate industrial production from water wheels and muscle power. These soon multiplied how much goods were produced and how effectively they were transported to market. No longer would ordinary people be dressed in homespuns. Increased wealth enabled them to go to stores to purchase machine made shirts and trousers. Eventually they ate steaks brought to them from hundreds of miles away by the new-fangled railroads. Soon too the population grew to previously unimagined proportions. Thus, England expanded from four million souls in the time of Elizabeth I to over sixty million under Queen Victoria.

More importantly, the way people conducted their lives was transformed. Millions moved out of their ancestral villages to take up residence in industrial cities. Instead of working agricultural fields or tending looms in their own homes, they tramped off to work in huge factories. Now required to submit to industrial discipline in smoky urban places, many were obliged to move away from their families and friends. Home life was likewise torn apart as laborers toiled twelve hours a day, six days a week. No wonder that many hated their condition. No wonder that they romanticized the villages of their youth. The fact that rural poverty was often as grinding as urban destitution was lost to their consciousness in the discomfort of their present distress.

One group of workers took matters in their own hands. These so-called Luddites set out to destroy the machines they blamed for their misery. Once these were gone, they hoped their old, less oppressive jobs would be revived. They could then go back home without having to fear unemployment or harsh working conditions. Industrialization thus created a backlash. The new ways of doing things were never acclaimed. Eventually a prejudice against industry was bequeathed to today's liberals. The latter might not work with their own hands, but they trembled at the prospect that anyone did. This also translated into an antipathy toward capitalism. Since it was blamed for introducing industrialization, it was held responsible for the blight industrialization produced.

One of the first answers to these unwelcome developments was later labeled "utopian socialism." A variety of reformers, principally in France, England, and the United States, sought to undo the havoc wrought by industrialization. They attempted to turn the clock back to a time when people lived in harmony within their traditional villages. Agriculture, and to a lesser extent small-scale industry, were extolled as creating the conditions for human happiness. It was assumed that in small communities people could function as the equivalent of an extended family. Charles Fourier theorized that 1,620 people was the optimum number for the phalanxes needed to support the appropriate intimacy. Fourier was not able to convert this prognosis into a concrete reality, but others attempted to do so. One was Claude Henri de Rouvroy, Comte de Saint-Simon. For a while, he was even able to bring a group of admirers together for the express purpose of demonstrating that brotherhood was feasible in an industrialized society.

Across the channel, Robert Owen had better luck. A successful cotton manufacturer, he was determined to prove that industry could be organized along humanitarian lines. Most notably in New Lanark in Scotland, he established the sort of ideal community he preached. It offered good sanitation, nonprofit stores, and free education. So successful did this innovation seem, that it was imported into the United States. Most impressively emulated in New Harmony, Indiana, other family style communes arose in Oneida, New York, and Amana, Iowa. Unhappily, none of these lasted in the form conceived. Most depended upon a charismatic leader to inspire dedication to their ideal. Once he left the scene or became dictatorial in his management style, the blush was off the rose. Jealousies, often sexual in nature, frequently undermined their harmony and led to their dissolution. Even religious based communes, such as those of the Shakers, and intellectual ones such as Brook Farm, succumbed to a scarcity of love. Compact villages they might temporarily have become, but experience exposed their family-oriented pretensions as extremely fragile.

Karl Marx would have none of this. He dismissed the utopian socialists as a throng of softheaded romantics. He instead sought scientifically grounded accommodations. Similarly scornful of capitalist industrialization, he believed he understood where it went wrong. Currently, most Americans are uncomfortable with being labeled Marxists, or God forbid communists; nevertheless, many have swallowed Marx's central tenets hook, line, and sinker. He is undoubtedly the central figure in the emergence of contemporary liberalism. Beating out Rousseau, who comes in a close second, his worldview is the single most influential framework upon which the Liberal Dream perches. Part of his mystique is that he outlined strategies through which his vision could be implemented. Intent on becoming the mainstay of revolutionary aspirations, he emerged as precisely this.

A successor to the idealist philosopher Georg Hegel, Marx endeavored to be more realistic. Accordingly, he developed a method of interpreting history that he called "dialectical materialism." Marx believed that the pivotal factor in human existence was economics. It was in producing goods and services, but more importantly in controlling their production, that people gained superiority over others. In looking back upon how societies evolved, Marx concluded that the engine of advancement was competition over control of the means of production. During the medieval period the fundamental clash had been between the aristocracy and bourgeoisie, while in his time it was between the capitalists and proletarians. The capitalists, who owned the factories, were now in charge, whereas the laborers chained to the factory benches were subservient. They might be the producers of wealth, but it was the owners who skimmed the gravy for themselves.

For Marx the most horrendous aspect of this arrangement was *exploitation*. The capitalists took advantage of their workers to enrich themselves, whereas the workers received only the pittance needed to keep body and soul together. Although it was their labor that produced the wealth, the bosses hoarded the excess value thereby created. These plutocrats were essentially parasites living off the sweat of their underlings. In contrast, the lot of the working person was subsistence and the threat of being fired for insubordination. Even so, the factory owners managed to keep their employees in line by convincing them that they, the bosses, had their interests at heart. As prudent employers, they were obviously concerned with the welfare of their work force. But if this ploy did not succeed, ill-educated laborers could be seduced into passivity by convincing them to subscribe to religion. Once they believed their eventual reward would come in heaven, they would cease agitating for a greater slice of the secular pie. They would instead content themselves with the realization that it was less difficult for a camel to pass through the eye of a needle than for a rich man to enter paradise.

The way out of this predicament, in Marx's view, was for the proletarians to realize their plight. Once they pierced the false consciousness that kept them in submission, they would unite to overthrow their oppressors. As the bosses concentrated more wealth in fewer hands, growing numbers of impoverished workers would understand that they had been cheated. Along the way, a cadre of professional revolutionaries would assist them in recognizing their inherent power. Because these intellectuals were the first to recognize the dynamics of exploitation, their duty was to enlighten its casualties through incessant agitation. Mired in poverty, the workers were understandably more concerned with feeding themselves and their families. Victimized, as well, by alienation and commodification, their unsatisfying working conditions had turned them into the equivalent of merchandise. Indeed, they were wage slaves.

Once *the revolution* finally arrived, ownership would be vested in ordinary people. They would become the masters of their own fate. First socialism, where the government administered the means of production in the interests of the workers, and then communism, during which the state withered away, would come into being. Once this occurred, greedy capitalists would no longer be able to order workers around. Instead, people would control their own lives. If they wanted to go fishing in the morning and amble over to the factory in the afternoon, this would be their prerogative. In any event, they would be far better off under a system that allowed individuals to contribute to the collective welfare according to their abilities, while receiving what they needed as they needed it. Thus, large families would receive a larger share of goods than would single workers, yet all would obtain enough to live in relative affluence thanks to the productivity of unleashed industrialization.

Implicit in this scenario is a belief in equality, universal love, and the essential niceness of human beings. Freed from the exploitation of the capitalists, the best selves of ordinary people would emerge so that everyone was treated with generosity. Humankind would, in essence, merge into one large village; or better yet into one super-sized extended family. None of this was particularly new. Rousseau and the utopian socialists had a similar vision. What was innovative were the strategies Marx proposed. He believed that it was essential for good people to line up on the side of the victims. They were therefore urged to sympathize with the victims, which is to say, the proletarians. It was then necessary for these compassionate onlookers to mobilize the underdogs to take advantage of their overwhelming numbers. Were these little guys to band together in the interests of economic and social justice, their power would be ineluctable. They would be transformed into an inexorable tide that would sweep all before it. In short, they would launch a revolution that remade the conditions of human existence. Old, outmoded institutions would be washed away, replaced by more rational, egalitarian ones. A dictatorship of the proletariat would then arise such that the dynamics of history were forever changed.

Many contemporary liberals cheerfully conceive of themselves as intellectuals precisely because they pride themselves on being versed in the Marxist lexicon. They accept Marx's assertions that he was a scientific socialist at face value and, therefore, was correct. They too believe their shared dream is on the side of history; and must inevitably triumph because the facts of human existence dictate that it will. Another thing they have in common with Marx is that they have failed to think through how their utopian visions will operate. As "social movement" people, they are more concerned with actualizing the revolution than administering it. Just how an industrial society can function with people fishing in the morning and voluntarily turning up at the factory in the afternoon, does not trouble them. Nor are they bothered by evidence that people do not put in peak performances simply because they are capable of them. They imagine that the opportunity to be helpful to others is sufficient to motivate an optimum effort. Workplace discipline is consequently shunned. It is regarded as the handmaiden of exploitation and thus unnecessary.

Nor are contemporary liberals discombobulated by evidence that Marx's predictions have failed. Ordinary people were supposed to become progressively impoverished with the consequence that they banded together to carry out a revolution. They instead accumulated ever-greater wealth. Today most own their own houses, drive their own automobiles, and call each other on cell phones. Furthermore, the capitalists were supposed to concentrate their assets in fewer hands, whereas the proportion of people in the upper and middle classes dramatically increased. The revolution, when it came, was theoretically to occur in an advanced industrial country, but took place instead in backward nations such as Russia and China. In addition, after the triumph of the workers, a dictatorship of the proletariat was to march majestically toward communism. People, freed of their oppressors, would evolve into the "new communist man." They were to become public-spirited as no previous generation. In fact, oppression took a new form, with totalitarian governments exploiting their peoples in ever more creative ways. Industrialization did not so much expand the wealth of its creators, as bureaucratization enhance the tyrannical methods for keeping them in subjugation. The countries that embraced communism did not transform into idyllic, extended villages. Not the Soviet Union, not Red China, not Cuba; not a single one of them made the predicted journey to one big, happy family.

Liberals who admire Marx are likewise loath to admit that his world was different from their own. The *ancien regime* that so troubled Rousseau is long gone, but so is the bourgeois universe that grieved Marx. Owner-managers dominated the industrial society in which he lived. Entrepreneurs, who built small companies into large ones, personally ran the conglomerations they put together. They could be identified as benefiting from these efforts, because they did. Modern corporations, where professional managers control daily operations, were still over the horizon. So too were large numbers of middle-class professionals performing technical chores. In Marx's day, there existed only a small cadre of office workers assisting the entrepreneur in managing his affairs. Technology was more impressive than it had previously been, but it was primitive compared with its contemporary counterpart. Automation had not yet appeared, nor was the computer more than an academic concept. Even governmental structures, as we know them, were embryonic. They were miniature compared with modern centralized governments.

Marx's anti-capitalist mentality, it must be noted, was shared by another group of revolutionaries. These were the bohemians. They too hated the effects of industrialization. Their revolution, however, was an artistic one. In painting, the impressionists; in letters, the novelists; and in music, the romantics sought new directions. They celebrated emotionality rather than scientific or industrial rationality. So devoted were they to their muses that many were prepared to live in garrets on the left bank of Paris rather than be drafted into the factory system. From their perspective, art rather than wealth was what mattered. It infused meaning into human existence, whereas material goods bespoke a shallowness of spirit. Ironically, the bohemians were financially dependent upon the bourgeoisie they despised. Without this audience prepared to purchase their output, they could not have thumbed their noses at the establishment. They would, in fact, have starved in those garrets.

The Progressive Era

As the nineteenth century came to a conclusion, the Liberal Dream acquired another dimension. While revolutionary bomb-throwers diligently labored to mobilize the proletarians, other events occurred without their assistance. Millions of people were forced to cope with the problems thrown up by the growth of capitalist production. Many of the most influential of these innovators styled themselves "progressives." They, like Marx, conceived of history as marching forward, but not quite in the same direction. Previous generations looked enviously rearward toward the glory that was Rome and Greece, whereas they were more optimistic about the future. They believed that life was getting better. As a result, they did not want to undo what had been accomplished so much as accelerate the positive achievements.

Progress was a new idea. The notion that change was inevitably for the better was a novel one. For centuries, educated people were sure that the Golden Age was behind them, that the best they could do was to slow the degeneration of civilization. But now the improvements were so obvious, they could not be denied. The railroad made it possible to cross the continent in days, rather than months. The telegraph enabled people to send messages in minutes, rather than weeks. And the electric light bulb permitted cities to illuminate the night. No longer did the successors of Abraham Lincoln have to struggle to learn their lessons by the flickering light of a fireplace. No longer did ordinary workers have to settle for a crust of stale bread or a pot of week-old peas porridge. Soon automobiles would be available to working stiffs and heavier-than-air machines would take off into the sky. Even life expectancy improved. Children did not die at the rate they once did, and public hygiene tamed the worst ravages of epidemic diseases such as cholera.

The time had consequently come to fix what was still broken. With scientific knowledge more secure than ever, answers to even the knottiest questions were, at last, available. Now that humans had mastered the power of dynamite to move mountains and the strength of steel to erect skyscrapers, what else might they accomplish? The sky was the limit. For starters, the grossly unequal distribution of wealth had to be addressed. With industrial moguls building palatial cottages in Newport, Rhode Island, at the same time that miners were dying from black lung disease in the coalfields of Eastern Pennsylvania, something had to be done. The sad truth was that power and wealth were being concentrated in fewer hands. Innovators such as John D. Rockefeller, Andrew Carnegie, and J.P. Morgan were inventing new forms of organization that enabled them to manage ever-larger empires. There was no doubt that their trusts permitted them to assemble huge monopolies from whence they could dictate prices to the nation, if not the world. At the same time, the railroads were being knit together in vast networks of monolithic routes such that they could decree the rates charged. If users did not play by their rules, they did not play at all. With nowhere else to turn for relief, they swallowed hard and did as they were told.

But not everyone was prepared to sacrifice their pride. There was thus an unintended side effect to industrial concentration. The number of workers laboring together at the same locations increased. This enabled them to compare their situations and pool their grievances.

Marx expected the workers to rise en masse against the system, but something different occurred. The workers joined together, albeit in smaller assemblages directed at their own employers. The union movement emerged. Small, and then larger, unions organized strikes against low wages and harsh working conditions. Because they too could see that wealth was proliferating, these workers wanted a share of the bounty. It wasn't equitable that the bosses lived in grand mansions, while they struggled to get by in unheated tenements. Something had to be done—and, by golly, they would do it. Even when their employers brought in goons to intimidate them, they fought back—often violently.

What was essentially evolving was a counterweight to corporate dominance. Power tends to beget counterpower, and with government agencies still of microscopic proportions, workers sought an independent power base. Social Darwinists might argue that the weak should accept their fate and allow themselves to be submerged by the strong, but there was no reason why workers should not increase their potency by joining forces. In any event, this is what they did. And in the process, they compelled the heavyweights to take notice. Change did not occur immediately. For some time the bosses were able to employ government resources, in the form of the police and military, to keep dissidents in line. The judicious use of bribery and campaign contributions also greased the wheels of collusion. Nevertheless, in the long run, democratic institutions made themselves felt. In the face of these, rather than provoke unsustainable bloodshed, the bosses made concessions. As a result, the unions were transformed into a potent counterbalance. They successfully resisted unbridled exploitation.

But the progressive era also witnessed the emergence of another potent center of power. The government became a major player. This was not because the robber barons were an unalloyed evil. John D. Rockefeller gave the public high-quality kerosene at extremely low prices, while Andrew Carnegie always adopted the most modern technology so as to produce tons of the best steel available. Even J. P. Morgan did a great deal of good by rationalizing the banking system. Nevertheless, these men were widely hated. Their enormous wealth and ruthless business practices made them feared. To stand up to them was to invite ruin. It was to risk bankruptcy for the sin of interfering with progress—as they defined it.

At the same time, another momentous phenomenon was occurring. The invention of the rotary press, coupled with widespread literacy, created cheap newspapers and sensationalistic magazines. The era of yellow journalism and muckraking reportage dawned. (Indeed, Karl Marx himself functioned as a journalist.) Where once the rich were merely envied, now they were taken to task for their misdeeds. Many were portrayed as worse than parasites. Scandalmongers, such as Ida Tarbell, made them out to be rogues and misanthropes. More than this, the consequences of their commercial practices were dissected in public. Rockefeller was pilloried for driving competitors out of business, while Morgan's bulbous nose became a symbol of degenerate greed. These insatiable "moneybags" needed to be curbed. Presently, the man to do the job arrived on the scene.

Teddy Roosevelt was genuinely offended that coalmine operators could act in unison to stiff-arm the demands of their workers. He believed this put the entire nation in jeopardy for the sake of private gains. In response, he activated dormant antitrust legislation. He intended to break up the trusts and make them less dominant. Even the success Morgan achieved in rescuing the financial system from collapse became an irritant. That the health of the nation's fiscal institutions depended upon the skill and goodwill of one avaricious old man rankled. Roosevelt intended to appropriate these responsibilities for the government. This way the public interest would take primacy. Soon he even began the process of dividing Standard Oil into a host of independent companies.

Another of Roosevelt's innovations was the Pure Food and Drug Act. Prior to this, the meatpacking industry did as it wished, while patent medicine purveyors (including Rockefeller's father) made grandiose claims they could not back up. Books, such as Upton Sinclair's *The Jungle*, frightened ordinary people about the safety of the food supply and medical supplies. The thought of rat droppings being incorporated into their sausages made readers queasy. Where once they either produced their own provisions or obtained them from merchants they knew personally, now they were at the mercy of impersonal firms that did not care about their welfare. Someone had to protect them from these industrial giants—entities they neither comprehended, nor had the power to control. Roosevelt saw to it that the government assumed this duty. Here too it would serve as a counterweight to the growing concentration of private power.

There was also another area in which the government made its presence felt. In former times, individuals were sheltered from the normal hazards of life by their families or churches. Industrialization, however, weakened these institutions. As people moved around the country to take jobs far from their ancestral homesteads, they could count less on extended families attached to inherited farms. By the same token, with immigrants flooding into the nation, religious denominations splintered. There was no single church comparable to the Roman Catholic edifice of the high Middle Ages. No single faith had the resources to underwrite the hospitals and welfare programs needed to make urban life bearable. Here too the government stepped in. It established a worker's compensation program designed to safeguard those injured on the job. It also distributed free milk to poor families to make sure their children would thrive. It even sought to outlaw alcohol on the assumption that drunkenness destroyed the family lives of the indigent.

In time, the government also sought to shield the public from the adverse implications of what Milton Friedman called "community effects." One of the consequences of an impersonal, mass society was that individuals could not independently deal with matters that required a collective solution. Railroad timetables made no sense unless everyone set their clocks to a single standard. The government achieved this by instituting common time zones. Nor could business be transacted with anything approaching rationality if every bank printed its own money. Creating a Federal Reserve System empowered to issue standardized Reserve Notes solved this problem. A national monetary system also served as a repository to which banks could repair when in need of additional funds. Then too there was the matter of protecting virgin lands from the encroachment of industrial exploitation. Water polluted by factory run-off and forests clear-cut for their timber cried out for some form of regulation. Roosevelt, who had a love affair with wild places, made a down payment on what was required by establishing the national parks and national forests. These preserved natural wonders, such as the Grand Canyon, while beginning the process of developing renewable environmental resources.

Also evolving was a more comprehensive system of public education. States such as Massachusetts had long sponsored public schools. With the advent of the twentieth century, however, these became more inclusive. Mandatory grammar school attendance became the norm, while high school attendance became common. Even the children of laborers were expected to obtain a solid grounding in literacy and civic responsibilities. College attendance was still confined to a privileged few, but it too was being reformed. In place of the old medieval emphasis on Latin and Greek, students were expected to acquire more relevant lessons. Science, of the empirical sort, flourished. So did technical education. Meanwhile, the hoary apprenticeship system was falling into disrepair. No longer able to keep up with the more complex demands of industrialization, it was replaced by government-funded schooling.

All in all, the progressive era saw a reorganization of social institutions. The nation did not see the sudden arrival of total equality, but people did witness the evolution of innovative power centers. Today we think of massive corporations as normal, but back then they were only beginning to take shape. Moreover, their very size required the introduction of bureaucratic practices. Marx had been oblivious to this development, whereas the German sociologist Max Weber brought it to public awareness. A precisely defined division of labor, under the control of a precisely defined hierarchy of authority, and governed by standardized rules and procedures became customary. This enabled large numbers of people to work in a coordinated manner, but it also increased the impersonality of their relationships. According to Weber, bureaucracies were like an "iron cage." They were less physically coercive than older forms of hegemony, but more pervasive in organizing the lives of their affiliates.

Paradoxically, as this transpired and effectively converted workers into industrial cogs, democratization was thriving. The franchise had first been extended to all adult males, with property qualifications essentially eliminated. Soon women were allowed suffrage. Like men, they were permitted to vote for their leaders. This made it important for politicians to cultivate dependable constituencies. Urban conglomerations thus saw the development of political machines such as Tammany Hall, while rural areas fell under the sway of mesmerizing orators such as William Jennings Bryant. Even so, the voice of the people was making itself felt. This meant that ordinary citizens had to be pandered too as never before. As a result, the brake was put on corporate power in the sense that large organizations also had to seek public approval. Even Rockefeller was forced to employ public relations firms. He needed to develop a positive public image lest the voters call for more extreme curbs on his interests.

In a sense, what evolved was a new balance of power. The framers of the American Constitution intended to balance the influence of the congress, the president, and the Supreme Court. They did not want any of these to become so dominant that it became tyrannical. They even balanced the congress against itself by establishing bicameral chambers. An aristocratic Senate would supposedly steady a more democratic House of Representatives. Much to the chagrin of the founders, however, these devises were soon supplemented by a two-party system. They hated the idea of what were dismissed as factions, but these, in the form of Democratic and Republican parties, kept a wary eye on each other and offered an alternative should the one in power become too monarchical. Now big government was introduced to balance big business, with both counterbalanced by an activist public. Not generalized love, not complete equality, but institutionalized competition kept the players relatively honest. They would not be corrupted by absolute power by the simple expedient of preventing power from becoming absolute. In this regard, the progressive era added big government and professionalized management to the liberal mix. They too became a part of the Dream to a degree they had not been in the Marxist universe.

Catastrophe

But just as it seemed that progress was becoming institutionalized, a catastrophe intervened. The historian Barbara Tuchman described fin-de-siècle and early twentieth-century Europe as a Proud Tower. To those involved, it finally seemed that humanity had mastered its fate. People took pride in the symbols of their success. Paris pivoted around an immense Eiffel Tower, while the United States celebrated the Columbian Exhibition with a neoclassical city of light in Chicago. Some said that everything that could be invented had been, but most people believed the innovations would keep coming. Few dreamed that bloodshed and poverty lurked around the corner. The times were too good. Revolutionaries might blow up bombs in public places, but ordinary people were grateful for the free time to journey to amusement parks such as Coney Island. They were eating better, dressing better, and being housed better than before. Why complain when the medical profession had even developed the tools to lengthen their life spans.

Then it happened. Hubris got the best of them. Competition between the European powers over their colonial empires and conflicting commercial interests boiled over. A Serbian patriot shot the heir to the Austro-Hungarian Empire and hell broke loose. The Austrians could not tolerate the insolence of the Serbians, who then applied to their Russian cousins for protection. Next, the Germans jumped into the fray on the side of their Austrian allies, which prompted the French and the English to honor their assurances to the Russians. Almost before anyone knew it, what later became known as the First World War, began. But this was no ordinary war. It was to be a bloodbath of unprecedented proportions. The Thirty Years War has seen the population of Germany reduced by a third, but that was just Germany; the Napoleonic Wars had witnessed a Grand Army of over six hundred thousand; and the American Civil War counted over six hundred thousand dead, with many tens of thousands horribly maimed. Now a slaughterhouse no one expected dwarfed all of these. It brought armies in the tens of millions into the field and led to many millions of deaths, including of civilians.

The very success of industrialization produced this calamity. A number of factors combined to generate unmatched carnage. First, all of the participants were seduced by their affluence. The optimism engendered by the Proud Tower convinced them that this war would be short and victorious. In perhaps a few weeks, it would be over and the winners could celebrate. No one imagined that four years of combat would ensue. Next, there were a plethora of technological advances. Machine guns could kill thousands of combatants in minutes. Held in place by barbwire, enemy soldiers were cut in half before they could bring old-fashioned weapons such as the bayonet to bear. Meanwhile, breach loading artillery pieces blasted infantrymen to bits, even as they hid in trenches. Overhead, airplanes spotted the best places to bombard and then added to the horror by delivering ordinance themselves. There was also poison gas wafting in the air, tanks clambering over the trenches, and dreadnoughts terrorizing the seas. Even railroads helped to increase the death toll by bringing soldiers to where they were needed. Added to this, bureaucratic techniques organized millions of soldiers and provided the supplies to keep the butchery coming. Unhappily, democratic institutions played a part as well. Ordinary men and women, who thought of their nations as belonging to them, identified with the need to win. Consequently, they did not resist being drafted into multimillion man armies. To the contrary, patriotism propelled them to heroic deeds.

All of these factors coalesced nearly to wipe out a generation of citizen-warriors. Where before optimism reigned supreme, now a resigned fatalism took its place. Perhaps things were not getting better. Perhaps everyone would wind up dead before it was possible to enjoy the fruits of economic prosperity. Maybe the best thing to do was to party hard and burn one's candles at both ends just as Edna St. Vincent Millay advised. Woodrow Wilson promised a war to end all war. He vowed to make the world safe for democracy, but events disproved his confidence. Not even he could forestall the selfishness on display at the Versailles peace conference. It dismantled ancient empires such as the Austro-Hungarian and clipped the wings of Germany, but did not introduce fairness. Progress might not be automatic after all. The collapse of so many familiar verities was too apparent for observers to imagine that everything was for the best.

The Russian Empire provided the most obvious example of collapse. This gigantic nation, one that crushed Napoleon's ambitions, found itself torn to pieces. The Czar was ripped from his throne as upstart Bolsheviks came from nowhere to take over. They now promised to bring Marx's vision to life. Styling themselves communists, they argued that they must first establish socialism in the homeland, but once this was complete, they would encourage the spread of communist ideals elsewhere. Initially, this project seemed propitious. Westerners trooped to Lenin's utopia and, in one way or another, declared that they had witnessed the future and that it worked. It wasn't until nearly a century later that economists demonstrated that Russia's economy grew more quickly under the czars than the commissars. Nor did the true believers acknowledge that the Soviet Union would not bury the West until after it collapsed. In the meantime, the collectivists, and their liberal allies, touted Russia as an example of how their dream could come true. It was indeed possible to organize a society along other than capitalist lines. It could be done, for the Soviets had done it.

Back in the United States, there had been a recession following the termination of hostilities, but this was immediately followed by a roaring upturn. The nation had never been more prosperous. Hoover was soon campaigning for the presidency by promising "a chicken in every pot and two cars in every garage." Voters, experiencing the giddy feeling of unexpected wealth, believed him. Even shoeshine boys were investing in the stock market. Meanwhile, in their better-furnished homes ordinary workers were being entertained by the radio, while out on Main Street they were amused by the movies, and in the back allies of downtown they enjoyed bathtub gin. Still hung over from the losses of the war, the old rules were discarded. This was the era of the flappers, the short skirt, and brazen sexuality. The close-knit family of yore was for suckers. It was inherently unfair. The new watchword was "free love." Why should anyone be held down by old-fashioned commitments? The intelligentsia would lead the way to a new world where people protected one another—because they genuinely cared. It had not yet occurred to these partygoers that free love was neither free, nor about love. They were to find that sexual promiscuity did not lend itself to caring about one's bed partners, never mind for the children their couplings produced. In many ways the rowdiness of the 1920s was a collective form of denial. People convinced themselves they were happy, despite the lingering insecurities introduced by the Great War.

Across the pond in Europe, things were going less well. England was wrenched apart by a general strike. Members of the Labor Party fully expected to force the government to install Marxist-style reforms by refusing to do any work. They did not succeed, except for frightening the establishment into providing additional welfare benefits. In Italy, the disorganized incompetence of the monarchial government was replaced by fascist enthusiasm. Benito Mussolini marched on Rome and soon installed a dictatorial regime. Nowadays, fascism is thought of as conservative, but in its heyday it was regarded as progressive. Cole Porter, in the song *You're the Top*, actually celebrated Mussolini as one of the best. Hadn't he made the trains run on time? Hadn't he drained the Pontine marshes around Rome? Mussolini proclaimed that he was a champion of the people. He also thought of himself as a socialist. To his admirers, his determination to elevate the little guy proved that he cared, whereas industrialists and aristocrats did not. And since he vowed to return Italy to its former glory, the people cheered.

North of the Alps events were also taking a leftward turn. During the 1920s, Germany experimented with democracy. On paper the Weimar Republic was one of the most democratic on earth. In practice, however, it was a disaster. Politicians unaccustomed to democratic institutions were negligent in their duties. Soon the nation was gripped with a monstrous inflation. The government printed money so profligately that it took a barrelful of bank notes to buy a loaf of bread. Postage stamps were literally denominated in the trillions of marks. Into this whirlwind road the Nazis. Led by an inspirational fuehrer, a journeyman painter named Adolf Hitler, they would save the nation. Hitler guaranteed to rescue the Reich from the chaos into which it had descended. Once more social discipline would prevail.

Today, as with the fascists, the Nazis are thought of as conservative. It is usually forgotten that Nazi stands for National Socialist. As Jonah Goldberg explained in *Liberal Fascism*, the Nazis were collectivists.

They believed in organizing a nation's economy from the top down. The Fuehrer might eventually become more absolutist than the Kaiser, but this was not because he believed in a market economy. An ardent advocate of elevating the German people, he considered them a single biological family. Genetically superior to other human beings, they deserved to rule over non-Germans, but only if they honored their own sense of community. Hitler would see to it that they did. He would tap into their General Will and then utilize government resources to enforce its dictates. If he seemed like a reincarnation of the Kaiser, the reality was that he utilized inherited bureaucratic institutions to impose collectivist aspirations. He was, in his own eyes, a man of the people. He believed in love and family, albeit for solely Aryans. They were the only ones worthy of the benefits of socialist unity.

Returning to the other side of the Atlantic, the Roaring Twenties came to an inglorious end. The stock market crashed and the bubble of prosperity burst. Herbert Hoover has been accused of doing nothing to relieve the suffering of the American people, but this is nonsense. Because he was a Republican, it has been assumed he was a defender of free market mechanisms. This is only partly true. It is equally accurate to describe him as an advocate of government activism. Two of the interventions of his administration, in fact, had dire consequences. One was the Smoot-Hawley Tariff. This dramatically raised the cost of international trade in the belief that it would preserve American jobs. In actuality, it discouraged trade by impelling other nations to adopt competing tariffs. This further reduced the demand for industrial products and increased unemployment. Under Hoover, taxes were also raised. He believed in pay-as-you-go policies, and since government revenues were down, he felt compelled to balance the budget with new monies. The effect was to reduce the funds available for new investments, which meant that production was reduced and unemployment elevated.

Unlike in Germany, however, the response to this calamity was not fascism. All the same, it came close. Franklin Roosevelt campaigned on the basis of conservative fiscal reforms, but upon taking office revealed himself to be a zealous advocate of collectivist solutions. Roosevelt told the nation that all it had to fear "was fear itself" and then he sought to reduce anxieties through government activism. He would shortly make the governmental expansion presided over by his cousin seem puny. Roosevelt was an ambitious man who intended to outdo Teddy. Because of his patrician, and indeed his eloquent speaking style, most of those who heard him on the radio believed him an intellectual. But FDR was nothing of the sort. He may have referred to his advisors as a "brain trust," but they were flying by the seat of their pants. Despite their apparent confidence, they did not know what would get the country out of the Depression. Most of what they did was therefore experimental. They hoped to find out in the doing what actually worked. Amazingly, much of their agenda was merely an extension of Hoover's.

In any event, the New Deal did not succeed. It did not restore the nation to prosperity. Only the advent of the Second World War managed that. What FDR achieved was to install an antibusiness mentality. Although, in hindsight, it was government interventions that prolonged the Great Depression, the president and his cronies won kudos for "doing something." Their use of public works, bank holidays, pro-union legislation, confiscatory taxes on the wealthy, and price controls for nearly everything seemed headed in the right direction. Keynesian economists explained that these interventions would "prime the pump," even though the water never really began flowing. In retrospect, they argued that they had done "too little too late," but at the time their efforts were more muscular than any previous attempts.

What Roosevelt accomplished was to give the American people hope. He was loved because his words were inspirational and his deeds provocative. The president did not sit on his hands. He tried to make things better. That's what counted. Roosevelt also gave the people someone to hate. He taught them to blame greedy business people for their plight. That is how he managed to give government intervention a good name. It was superior to a discredited adversary. Before him, people believed in rugged individualism. They cleaved to the proposition that a person's success depended upon personal effort. Afterwards most believed it was the duty of the government to save people from their disappointments. Capitalism was thought to have proven itself a failure. Its contradictions were exposed in dramatic fashion. Just as the Marxists alleged, it harbored the seeds of its own demise. Now it was the government's turn to take the lead. It represented the interests of ordinary people and hence would protect them from profligate elites. Nowadays Social Security is considered the supreme achievement of this mentality, whereas at the time no one was eligible to collect benefits. It was atmospherics, not accomplishments, which accounted for FDR's popularity.

FDR also had the good fortune to have his revolution certified by a glorious victory in WWII. Nazism instituted unexampled brutality in its homeland, but when it became the master of the European continent, its viciousness grew to rival that of Genghis Khan. If WWI was a shock to the world's body politic, its successor made this first act look paltry. Not millions, but tens of millions perished. In all, probably over a hundred million died, many in the most brutal manner. Jews and Gypsies were reduced to soap and lampshades in concentration camps, while the Japanese bayoneted babies like so many shish kabobs and starved prisoners of war into skeletons. Thousands of innocent human beings were sacrificed in experiments that treated them like laboratory animals, while millions of unlucky soldiers were offered up as canon fodder. Even civilians found no sanctuary. As the arsenal supplying the combatants, they were bombed into submission, even if firestorms killed a hundred thousand at a time. Ultimately, the atom bomb trumped every previous technological advance. It incinerated tens of thousands in the blink of an eye.

All of this butchery was terrifying. No one knew who would die next or which city would be reduced to rubble. At stake were not just life and death, but slavery versus freedom. People needed protection more than ever and Roosevelt was expert in promising it. Now he delivered the goods. He mobilized American industry to out-produce the Nazis, while overseeing a military that defeated the enemy on the field. Americans were understandably grateful. As a result, an aura of success surrounded their hero's deeds. Especially after he died, he could do no wrong. At this point, to criticize the New Deal was, in effect, to speak ill of the dead. Thus, this program benefited from the halo encircling its creator. In hindsight, it too was regarded as a great success, despite its many failures.

All of this redounded to the credit of the Liberal Dream. Idealistic youngsters who grew to maturity on a flood of liberal rhetoric internalized its assurances. They cried when Roosevelt passed from the scene, then named their children after him. This new generation blamed their parents for the stock market crash. Greed had gotten the better of their mothers and fathers. They, however, would not tolerate a comparable disaster. They would remake the world. Having imbibed the lessons of the past, from this moment forward they intended to employ the government to promote liberal causes. From now on, equality, love, and family would be the national ideals. Those who challenged these were obviously reactionary. Because they had given Roosevelt misery, henceforth their pernicious influence must be stamped out. This backward-looking old guard would not be allowed to derail the future.

The Liberal Ascendancy—Hippies and Bobos

But first there was an interregnum. The nation needed time to catch its breath. The rise of a corporate-based economy had to be consolidated and the Russian menace neutralized. Harry Truman, and then Dwight Eisenhower, served this function. They were not as exciting as Roosevelt, but they achieved crucial tasks. In the meantime, ordinary citizens enjoyed a return to prosperity. This was a time of middle-class supremacy. Almost everyone wanted to join its ranks. They expected to live in neat suburban dwellings and raise families devoted to togetherness. While not always sure how to achieve this, they took *Father Knows Best* and *Ozzie and Harriet* as role models. New fangled television sets replaced the family hearth as the point around which everyone gathered in the evening. Then, on weekends, they took the family car for pleasure drives on the new Interstates, maybe to stop for a burger at McDonald's or fried chicken at the Colonel's.

The critics, of course, were not impressed. They regarded this period as insufferably conformist. Everyone seemed to be wearing the same gray flannel suit. Suddenly, mom and pop were more concerned with accumulating material goods than fostering the emotional health of their offspring. Idealism was out of fashion, replaced by a self-satisfied conventionality. The Beatniks were among the first to object to this vapid lifestyle. In their poems, they sought to reintroduce liberal themes. They urged people to drop out of the rat race and embrace the pursuit of art instead. The way they saw it, art tapped into a deeper reality. It allowed people to be more human, which is to say, more equal and loving.

The culmination of this trend emerged just as a vibrant young president came on the scene. Much to the relief of his supporters, John F. Kennedy declared that a new generation was taking the helm. It was youthful and energetic and would not settle for having climbed out of the Great Depression. No, it would renew the effort to make the world a better place. In the vanguard of this effort were the hippies. As the pampered children of middle-class orthodoxies, they longed for something better. They would pick up where the New Deal left off and breathe new life into the Liberal Dream. First, however, they would renounce crass commercialism. Making money, for the sake of making money, was for uncouth traditionalists. What was the point of driving a big car replete with huge tailfins if what you did to obtain it robbed you of your soul? How was wealth alone going to make you happy? The answer was—it wasn't.

The hippies, who by and large did not have to worry about money because they were financed by their well-heeled parents, decided to celebrate love, equality, art, peace, and youth. They would live in crash pads in the central city, dress in frayed jeans and smoke pot. Unlike their parents, they understood that love was all you needed. Although they frequently confused love with sex, they were committed to "flower power." Intent on renouncing violence, they would be nice to everyone. Much of the time they would sing songs dedicated to peace or allow themselves to be transported to another dimension by psychedelic paintings. They agreed with Timothy Leary that the best thing to do was "tune in, turn on, and drop out." The system was fatally corrupt. The only way to save society was to abandon it. Material things did not matter. What counted was an altered state of consciousness, often obtained through chemical means.

Tragically, this outpouring of idealism came to a screeching halt. Disillusionment set in almost before chats of "never trust anyone over thirty" subsided. Events conspired to demonstrate that the world was not always as sheltered a place as the parental homes that the hippies despised. First, Kennedy was assassinated. It was almost beyond belief that a civilized nation would see a young, virile president cut down as he sought to launch much needed reforms. But there it was. He was dead and a madman did it. Or did he? Perhaps it was not Oswald, but the CIA or the Italian mob? In any event, the world had gone crazy. Soon, however, it would go crazier.

Meanwhile, the hippies themselves were under assault in havens such as Haight-Ashbury. Determined to follow the example of Mohandas Gandhi, they were defenseless when confronted by street thugs. Shortly thereafter, the Vietnam War, urban race riots, and additional assassinations further soured their vision. Nevertheless, their immediate successors did not give up. Their reaction was to become intensely politicized. Initially led by groups such as the Students for a Democratic Society (SDS), they focused on encouraging universal peace. The solution was so simple. All the politicians had to do was lay down their weapons. They were implored to declare victory in Vietnam, followed by an abrupt return home, so that no one ever again felt threatened by American belligerence. Resources must then be reassigned to the War on Poverty, not physical combat. The result would be a neo-Marxist society. It wouldn't be called Marxism—that was unduly provocative—but it would incorporate Marxist ideals. Every person and nation would eventually work together in perfect harmony. In the process, they would discover that love truly was enough. This then was the genesis of contemporary liberalism. It was a synthesis of Hippie artistic idealism and Marxist political idealism. More revolutionary and economically oriented than its predecessor, its devotees were soon marching in the streets, making non-negotiable demands. Some, such as the Weathermen, set bombs in government buildings. As the self-appointed vanguard of the revolution, they intended to shake the establishment to its senses. This would make the egotistical elite pay attention.

Now was the point at which the modern version of the Liberal Dream surfaced. The hippies were more explicit about their dedication to universal love than the New Dealers or old-style Marxists. Sometimes they got so carried away with this ideal that they literally joined hands to sing Cumbaya. Nevertheless, they had been jolted into the realization that merely spreading flower petals would not bring the new millennium. They would have to mobilize politically to bring federal resources to bear. Only the government had the money and manpower to force compliance. Since their parents were not persuaded by passionate words, equitable laws and compassionate federal programs must supplement these. In a sense, love would be given concrete form in the shape of enlightened political interventions intended to promote universal welfare.

All this would come to fruition because they, the youth of America, were the smartest and best-educated generation ever. FDR's advisors had been called the Brain Trust, while Kennedy's were labeled "the best and the brightest." Liberals knew they were more intelligent than Republican fuddy-duddies. After all, they had Kennedy and Adlai Stevenson on their side, while the opposition had Dwight Eisenhower and that scoundrel Richard Nixon. Would you actually buy a used car from the fellow? Wasn't it more sensible to place one's trust in a college-educated elite? They knew what was best, given that their professors had taught them so well. Besides, they were deeply concerned. True idealists, they were willing to sacrifice their own comfort to eradicate urban poverty.

As it happened, these nascent liberals soon adopted the causes they inherited from the old-line progressives. They began by promoting peace. Ever since they were small they had been tutored in the horrors of the atomic bomb. Having for years been asked to "duck and cover" in school, they now sought an end to the Cold War. Only if the Russians and Americans became friends would the prospect of mutual assured destruction recede. Then every one—East and West—would learn to be brothers and sisters. Soon this impulse morphed into anti-Vietnam War activism. Students paraded down the streets chanting peace slogans or cheered themselves hoarse at teach-ins. Lyndon Johnson caught the mood when he approved a television advertisement showing a little girl picking flower petals against the backdrop of a nuclear explosion. It dramatized what every good liberal knew, namely that the conservative Barry Goldwater favored war. He would risk nuclear destruction, whereas LBJ would not. Moreover, Goldwater was crazy. Like most people on the right, he was hopelessly neurotic.

Soon liberals were in the trenches fighting against poverty and discrimination. These causes meshed perfectly with their desire for total equality. Young people knew that everyone was basically the same. Whether rich or poor, black or white, male of female, their humanity was identical. It was time—past time—for the artificial barriers separating people to be torn down. Starting with civil rights legislation, but eventually spreading to affirmative action and sensitivity training, efforts were made to force people to be egalitarian. The reactionaries might not understand that this was in their interest, but a multicultural world was being born. In time, it would even include homosexuals. Ultimately, everyone would contribute to, and benefit from, a shared commitment to the public welfare.

As for liberals themselves, starting with the hippies, they were becoming the best possible human beings. By getting in touch with their inner selves, sometimes with a chemical assist, they were self-actualizing. Their art and compassion made them aware of dimensions of reality closed to their materialistic parents. They, the young, had not been commodified. They had not sold their souls for a patch of suburban grass. Left to the own devices, they genuinely enjoyed good literature and music. This internal awakening had the added benefit of opening them up to the humanity of others who might at first seem different. Themselves totally human, this intensified their empathy.

And this perhaps was the heart of the matter. Liberals were nice people. Their compassion was not a pretense. Having been educated in the humanities, they applied its lessons to their daily lives. Determined not to be corrupted by selfishness, they weren't. As a consequence, they did not look down on the homeless when they passed them on the streets. Nor did they shun the mentally ill as less than human. They could even appreciate the artistic qualities of the graffiti with which the poor festooned their neighborhoods. Nice people cared about others. Their hearts broke when they saw people in pain. As a result, they reached out to help. They did not want anyone left behind. Poverty was unthinkable in a nation as affluent as the United States. So was sending lawbreakers to jail because they could not afford legal counsel. Something had to be done, and nice people would do it.

The best part was that niceness begat niceness. As good liberals knew—for the books told them so—the root cause of crime was poverty. Eliminate the latter and the former would take care of itself. The Soviets too would appreciate compassion. Underneath their braggadocio, they favored détente. Since no one really wanted to hurt anyone else, the idea was not to put others on the defensive. Threats and insults only served to arouse hostility. This was why competition was destructive. Business types, trying to beat out their rivals, only generated antagonism. It made more sense to be cooperative. People who worked willingly with others elicited collaboration. And in the end, everyone did better as a result.

These attitudes culminated in the rise of the bobos. David Brooks insightfully coined this term. The bobos are bourgeois bohemians. They are middle-class folks who still conceive of themselves as impoverished students. The direct descendents of the hippies, many are literally grown-up versions of their former selves. Having decided that remaining poor was an undue burden, they dropped back into society and climbed the ladder of success. Still steeped in the ideals of their youth, however, their perspective remained consistent with what it had been. They continued to think of themselves as nice, egalitarian people. In their own minds, they remained underdogs fighting for the relief of other underdogs.

But it was not just the original hippies who formed the nucleus of the bobos. Society had changed in a fundamental way. As our techno-commercial civilization became more prosperous, the need for well-educated personnel swelled. Despite themselves, the hippies were the offspring of the first generation that expected its children to go to college. These youngsters thought of themselves as the best and the brightest, in part, because their parents did. Nevertheless, they were not the last cohort to be college educated. The proportion of the population obtaining a higher education, including master's degrees and doctorates, continued to rise. More than ever, good jobs required professionalization. Thus, not just doctors and lawyers, but police officers, nurses, social workers, business mangers, engineers, and even sales persons became self-motivated experts. And since the best place to acquire the appropriate skills was college, even mediocre students aspired to enter its precincts.

This had an unintended side effect. The values implicit in higher education were disseminated more broadly than previously. Liberal educators obtained an outlet to indoctrinate students in liberal verities. Their personal aspirations were consequently presented as eternal truths. Projections of a better world were not depicted as a dream, but as scientific analysis. In addition to this, academic objectives were presented as universal standards. Thus the arts faculty put forward art for its own sake as the highest ideal to which a person could aspire. Meanwhile, the social scientists lauded scientific research as the apotheosis of human existence. Needless to say, the historians and hard scientists proposed self-interested versions of the most important human goals. Impressionable students internalized these beliefs and ultimately attempted to live by them. Even after they graduated, their ambition was to write the great American novel or discover a cure for cancer. It was these objectives, not those attached to their more mundane jobs, which seemed worthy.

Bobos are bourgeois bohemians because even though they are successful members of the middle class, they conceive of themselves as academic dropouts. They do not allow themselves to recognize that they are making important social contributions, lest they abandon their youthful dreams. Some day, they will surely move to a cabin in Vermont. Who knows, the poems they have been writing on the side may become publicly acclaimed. In the meantime, since they have bosses, they feel put upon. Enmeshed in the everyday dilemmas of normal life, they do not feel special. Even their prosperity seems tainted. Although they make more money than their parents, they do not feel rich. Their houses may be larger, but they are not as nice as they would like; and their vacations may be exotic, but are not as long as they wish.

In *Bobos in Paradise*, Brooks gives a compelling account of the bobo lifestyle. Although part of the establishment, these modern success stories struggle to deny their status. If they can, they reside in latte towns, places like Burlington, Vermont and Boulder, Colorado. Eager to be close to nature, they are fond of little luxuries, that is, as long as they can pretend they are not luxuries. They spend exorbitant amounts of money on down sleeping bags, but would never purchase a fur coat. Taking an upscale cruise to observe Antarctic whales is okay, although vacationing in Newport, Rhode Island, is not. Similarly, legions of servants would be gauche, whereas spending tens of thousands of dollars to modernize their kitchen is acceptable. Much of this is pretentious, but it does not seem so to the bobos. They feel righteous in their politically correct cocoons.

Today, the bobos and their hypocritical shibboleths dominate the landscape. They control the universities, the media, and the government. They have even become the deciding factor in many boardrooms. So pervasive are their opinions that in many quarters they do not have to be defended. The Liberal Dream they propagate seems normal; it appears to be the only intellectually respectable position. Blue-collar ethnics and red neck fundamentalists may vote for blockheaded conservatives, but they never do. They are too sophisticated, too compassionate. In the end, they want their leaders to be equally sensitive and equally devoted to helping the less fortunate.

Which brings us to the present. The Liberal Dream seems secure. Safely ensconced in the imaginations of a dominant segment of society and widely perceived as progressive, it appears to be the wave of the future. Nevertheless, appearances are deceptive. The values many contemporary professionals hold are at odds with reality and even the goals they favor. That which people think will make for a better world is not necessarily what does. Fortunately, the fact that the bobos are well educated makes it likely they will, in due course, stumble over the truth. Much of what they currently defend is hypocritical, whereas they are not hypocritical by nature. Presented with the failures and contradictions of their ideals, they possess the intelligence and goodwill to recognize their errors. Nowadays many people are impatient with the pyrotechnics of the culture wars. They hate polarized fights for their own sake. The trouble is that they cannot see a way out. Paradoxically, the exit is within reach. It lies just beyond the realization that the Liberal Dream is dying. Once people mourn the passing of their juvenile hopes, they may come to terms with the world as it is.

3

Broken Promises

The Failure of the Dream

Liberals specialize in big promises. As a result, they have incurred big failures. So, of course, have others. Once, the early Christians guaranteed an immediate Second Coming. They were certain that Christ would shortly return to earth to redeem His promises of salvation. There would then be a Final Judgment, after which the faithful would receive their just deserts. The praiseworthy would be ushered into Heaven, whereas unbelievers would go to hell. Cosmic justice would be established, with God's will reigning everywhere—on earth as in heaven. The expectation of this was at times palpable. Reasonable people awaited it with as much enthusiasm as the Unarians anticipated the arrival of the Space Brothers. And they did so with joy, because the prospect was glorious. After Christ's reappearance, no one would ever have to die or be unhappy. It was this act the liberals were required to follow. It was these promises with which they had to compete for disciples.

Christ, of course, has not yet returned. But this has not dimmed the hopes of the true believers. They still expect Him to come. Nor has the Liberal Dream been fulfilled, but its devotees similarly keep the faith. That which has been promised is so magnificent its prospect is not easily relinquished. To do so would impose a duty to accept an imperfect reality. It would force people to recognize that they have not been as successful as they hoped. For many, this is unendurable. They would have to admit they were "losers." No longer could they pretend to be better than others. No longer could they insinuate they are more insightful or more moral.

Consider the Marxist component of the liberal vision. It has been an abject failure, and yet it continues to attract the allegiance of millions. They refuse to recognize that Marx's predictions fell short. Many instead persist in expecting the communist millennium to arrive. They love the vision so much they refuse to recognize it was too good to come true. Marx himself, of course, knew how to make big promises. First, he guaranteed the capitalist system would self-destruct. Its internal contradictions would catch up with it as the rich became richer and the poor became poorer. Eventually the concentration of wealth would be so extreme the misery of the poor would become universal. At this point, the social stresses would be unsustainable. Something would have to relieve the pressures.

This is where the second Marxist promise kicked in. At some juncture, fairly soon, there would be a revolution. The proletarians would rise *en masse* to take their rightful place in the scheme of things. Led, perhaps by a Christ-like figure such as Marx or Lenin, they would recognize that they had been exploited and put an end to the capitalist hegemony. Now they would take charge and begin to fashion a better and more just society. They would institute what Marx called a "dictatorship of the proletariat."

The third promise was the biggest of all. After the proletarian revolution succeeded, socialism would arrive on the scene. During this era the government would administer jointly owned resources in the interests of the community. The unexampled fairness of its operations would subsequently enable ordinary men and women to evolve onto a higher plane. They would shed the selfish defenses necessary to survive in a capitalist universe, thereby allowing their inner goodness to surface. At this point, communism would burst forth. The government would wither away and complete freedom would become the norm. Everyone would thenceforth live in unrivaled prosperity, with no one poaching on anyone else's perquisites.

Any person who is remotely honest must recognize that these promises have not been redeemed. Marx fancied himself a scientist and so he portrayed his as scientific predictions. They were presumably in harmony with the direction history was moving; hence events would soon bear him out. Only they didn't. What he said would happen, did not happen. In one respect, however, Marx was correct. Science makes predictions. It generates hypotheses with foreseeable consequences. These predictions must therefore be falsifiable. They have to be concrete and capable of being tested through actual observations. If what is predicted does not transpire, it is essential to admit the prophecy was in error.

But if verification is impossible, a forecast is not empirical. That which is deemed true no matter what the facts is essentially meaningless.

Because it has no tangible referent, it is empty. It is like declaring there is an invisible man in the room, except he can never be detected by any concrete means. Such a being would have as little substance as Paul Bunyan or his blue ox, Babe. This being so, if Marx is to be regarded as a scientist, his predictions must be subject to disconfirmation. If they do not pass this test, they must be discarded as completely as the hypothesis that mice spontaneously generate in dirty rags. That which can never be demonstrated, must be jettisoned as inherently unprovable.

Unfortunately for liberals, Marx's predictions have not fared very well. At almost every point, they have stumbled badly. First, the capitalist system did not self-destruct. It has obviously grown stronger. In fact, never, in all of history, have as many people been as well off. Wealth has not concentrated in only a few hands and workers did not slide into dismal poverty. For one thing, Marx failed to anticipate the emergence of the middle class. He did not realize that a huge cadre of self-motivated professionals would be necessary to administer massive techno-commercial enterprises. Today people eat better, are better sheltered, and have more time off than ever before—save perhaps during hunter-gatherer times. As a consequence, the stresses Marx thought inevitable never surfaced.

Second, there was no revolution—at least not the one that was predicted. Workers in advanced capitalist societies did not join together to dismantle the system. This, however, was not for want of trying. Collectivist agitators did their best to arouse the sleeping giant. But whether working through the unions or political parties, they could not generate a viable insurgency. Their general strikes either fizzled or produced disappointing outcomes. Only the Bolsheviks, and those influenced by them, caused the downfall of actual governments. Yet these insurgencies were in marginal economies such as Russia, China, and Cuba. They were not spontaneous risings of industrial workers, because, there were not enough such workers in these places. The ideology of their leaders may have been inspired by industrial developments, but their foot soldiers tended to be disillusioned members of the middle class or semi-starved peasants.

Third, socialism did not turn out as advertised, while communism remained a distant fantasy. Government control of industry and agriculture did not produce an equitable era of plenty. Worse than this, the ruling parties repeatedly degenerated into tyrannical elites. Collectivist regimes billed themselves as social democrats, but in practice

71

they ruled with a heavy hand. The apparatchiks at their apex hoarded the best products for themselves, while they suppressed dissent with undisguised violence. In Russia, Stalin killed millions of kulaks by systematically starving them to death. He simultaneously condemned millions of others to slave labor in the Gulag Archipelago. In China, the Great Leap Forward, and then the Cultural Revolution, condemned millions more to ridicule and malnourishment. In Cambodia, Pol Pot produced killing fields that reduced two million people to walls of skulls. Even in Cuba, where the regime has been applauded for promoting literacy, ordinary citizens are denied reading materials that portray the revolution as anything less than magnificent.

But despite this political repression, socialism did not produce prosperity. Thus Cuba went from being the second most affluent economy in Latin America to the second least affluent. Its leaders found that sugar production fell on collectivized farms, while vintage automobiles could be made to last for decades. Over in Russia, the commissars were able to produce first-class military equipment, but not manufacture a decent ballpoint pen. Ordinary Russians occupied tiny apartments and stood in endless lines to obtain scarce consumer goods. Meanwhile in China, the Communist party could not keep its promise to furnish an "iron rice bowl." Instead it presided over massive famines produced by ill-advised policies such as the war on sparrows. Perhaps the best example of the failure of socialist economics was found in central Europe. There, sitting cheek by jowl, were two Germanys. The one, in the West, roared ahead to become an economic powerhouse, while the other, in the East, stagnated. Germans on both sides of the wall were equally disciplined, but the latter were stripped of ambition. Forced to fulfill government plans, they became as lackadaisical as their Russian counterparts.

Still, it was in terms of their forecast of a communist utopia that the Marxists did worst. In no place, not Russia, China, or Cuba, did ideal conditions materialize. Neither their leaders nor their citizens ceased being selfish. In none of these countries did complete equality become customary. If anything, repression produced cynicism and apathy. Violence became so deeply ingrained that people survived by keeping their opinions to themselves. They did not become spontaneously loving, but collectively suspicious. Nor did they gain control over their personal lives. Far from it. The Russians took to vodka for solace, the Chinese endured wearing uniformly blue Mao suits, while the Cubans crowded into fragile boats to escape across the Florida Straits.

True believers, looking at these debacles from the security of the West, produced ready explanations. One of these accounts insisted that the leaders of the Marxist experiments were at fault. They were corrupt tyrants, not altruistic democrats. Moreover, if they were shortsighted bullies, it was because they had not been raised under suitable circumstances. Many, like Stalin and Mao, were brutal because the regimes they toppled were brutal. They had to be hard in order to prevail against harsh oppressors. Had they instead grown to maturity in places like the United States, they would have instituted a more democratic version of Marxism. Another favorite explanation was that tyranny arose as a reaction to Western hostility. If America and Western Europe had not attempted to suppress these revolutions, they would not have resorted to draconian responses. Niceness would have begotten niceness, with large-scale armies and harsh industrial discipline superfluous.

Much of this chatter, however, smacks of rationalization. It is grounded in unverifiable accounts of events that never transpired and probably never will. Of course, the true believers would do things differently—except none have. They fancy themselves as too virtuous to be corrupted; yet these are empty projections. They are no more substantial than fundamentalist predictions of the Second Coming, no more plausible than Unarian assurances the Space Brothers are about to land.

Nor have Rousseau's predictions proved more substantial. He assured his readers that the General Will would one day guide their leaders to promote universal love. Likewise, with property ownership banished from human affairs, jealousy and foolish rivalries would disappear. The problem is that these promises have not been kept. For starters, property ownership has not faded away. People still own things. In fact, more people own more than ever. Now that most people do not worry about starvation, they take pleasure in accumulating houses full of "stuff." Cautioning them that this is shallow, or a form of "theft," has little impact. Rousseau would have disapproved, but it must be remembered that he too liked to dress in fancy clothes. So, Mao notwithstanding, do the Chinese people.

As for the General Will, it has long gone aglimmering. Rousseau might have known what it represents, but no lasting consensus has emerged among his disciples. Reasonable people continue to pursue inconsistent interests. The only ostensible exceptions have occurred under totalitarian regimes. These assure us that their leaders are infallible guides to what their people desire. They style themselves

73

democratic on the assumption that they embody the spirit of their people. Some of us, however, remain skeptical. Declarations of homogeneity smack of self-serving rationalizations. They sound like verbal justifications for an unworkable idea.

Then there is the absence of the underlying niceness of which Rousseau boasted. It has not flourished in democratic societies any more luxuriantly than the universal concern alleged to characterize communism. It is not that people aren't sometimes nice. Some are. Yet when and where have human beings been completely nice? According to Rousseau, a progressive education would remedy this situation. Indeed, many educators have attempted to realize Rousseau's program. They banished rote exercises from the classroom and introduced the project method, albeit to little effect. Despite their best efforts, students still squabble with one another and malice wafts through the progressive schoolyard. Moreover, there has been no eruption of collective niceness among their graduates. A significant proportion continues to be as obstreperous.

All in all, these developments are not inspiring. They do not present an unbroken record of accomplishment. A disinterested evaluation must therefore conclude that the central promises of the forebears of liberalism have not been fulfilled. In point of fact, they have failed spectacularly. Although liberals deny this, they too are aware that events have not unfolded as predicted. Clearly, this presents a dilemma. How can their ideological aspirations continue to be advanced when the track record has been so disappointing? Their solution is similar to that of other failed prophets. They have radically reinterpreted events. History is still supposedly headed in the predicted direction. It has merely taken a few detours along the way.

The Grievance Machine

Liberals continue to believe in a collectivist revolution; only, it cannot be for the same reasons as originally propounded. People who are secure in their economic well-being are not eager to experiment with novel programs. When the trumpets sound the call to battle, they hurry home to stand guard over their possessions. They do not hate, or even envy, the more affluent. To the contrary, they hope to join them. Occasionally stirred by pangs of resentment, they are more often motivated to protect property rights. They realize that if their betters are torn from their perches, they may be next in line. It therefore makes more sense to cheer hypothetical revolutions from afar. Not so much apathetic as prudent, ordinary people are afraid of changes they may be unable to control.

But if the mass of humankind cannot be motivated by a poverty they do not experience, nor induced to tear down a capitalist infrastructure they do not regard as failed, how can they be mobilized to fight for the Liberal Dream? More particularly, which issues are serious enough to convince them that they are in immediate jeopardy? Finding such grievances has not been easy. Nevertheless, liberals have risen to the challenge. They have become well-practiced *grievance mongers*. Much of their political rhetoric is devoted to bemoaning this evil or that. One way or another, they advise the public that something must be done to fix what is broken—or the sky will fall. There is no time to wait! The crisis is upon us! In almost every election cycle, the electorate is warned that we are at a crucial crossroads. If we do not take the correct turn, horrors await. It is consequently essential to set out on the Yellow Brick Road that leads to the Liberal Oz.

Grievance mongers are specialists in hyperbole. They exaggerate the dangers of which they warn, lest the hoped for mobilization not materialize. People must be sufficiently frightened—or angered—in order to act. Their emotional juices must be set flowing or they might become too reflective. If they have time to evaluate the dimensions of the threat, they might back off. What is needed is a bandwagon effect. The anxiety or fury aroused must spread so widely as to ignite fires everywhere. Once a critical mass is formed, the inferno will then be self-sustaining. Added to this must be a large dollop of hope. People must believe the prescription offered by these change-agents will work. Here too the masses must not be encouraged to be thoughtful. Revolutionaries are determined to marshal people—not educate them. They want their followers to wage war for goals they set—not to participate in seminars on public policy.

As to the goals—these vary. The Liberal Dream is elastic. What it emphasizes at any given moment depends upon what is likely to motivate people. The grievances advanced are, therefore, targets of opportunity. Whatever is bothering potential recruits is ginned up to seem catastrophic. Small embers are fanned into a roaring blaze. But it is the heat generated, not the light produced, which matters. Should the flames abate, a new log can always be thrown on the fire. Yet if this is not enough, an entirely different conflagration can be started. An alternative grievance can be trotted out to take center stage. Normally, liberals have a lengthy, revolving list of complaints at their disposal.

Old issues are regularly revived, and new ones invented, should the existing ones falter. By now, the old standards have become second nature. What these are is easily ascertained by observing the promises made by Democratic aspirants to the presidency.

So what are these grievances? What sorts of problems make the Liberal Dream attractive enough to draw wide support? The "Social Problems" courses taught by sociologists provide object lessons. Their texts are uniformly written to appeal to liberal audiences. Hence, most begin with a plea for peace. *Peace* has been a staple of the liberal agenda for decades. Long ago, the Democratic presidential candidate George B. McClellan argued that the Civil War should be terminated. Later Woodrow Wilson said he abhorred WWI and would not get the nation embroiled in a foreign adventure. Afterwards, once re-elected, he promised to deliver peace for all time. FDR subsequently vowed he would not send American boys to fight in a European conflict, which, of course, he later did. Adlai Stevenson, in his turn, favored unilateral nuclear disarmament. He implied that Eisenhower was too militaristic and an inveterate devotee of brinkmanship. Lyndon Johnson, to be sure, escalated the Vietnam War, but this quickly drew the wrath of his left-leaning constituents. No slackers, his immediate successors learned from his example and shied away from major conflicts. Thus, Jimmy Carter was restrained in his response to Iranian hostage taking, while Bill Clinton refused to interfere when Rwanda slid into genocide. It is true that he got involved in Bosnia, but only tepidly. He even declined to capture Osama Bin Laden when presented with the opportunity.

But it was in their reaction to the Bushes that liberals revealed the depth of their adherence to peace. The first Bush had difficulty in enlisting Democrat support for the Gulf War. Even blatant Iraqi aggression against a major oil producer aroused misgivings about getting into a "quagmire" reminiscent of Vietnam. Later on, following 9/11, liberals initially supported a punitive expedition against Saddam Hussein. But when weapons of mass destruction (WMD) were not immediately uncovered, their doubts escalated into a chorus of dissent. George W. Bush was speedily transformed from a courageous defender of American interests into a trigger-happy liar. His failure to squelch sectarian violence became incontrovertible evidence that the entire adventure was ill advised. John Kerry then ran for president on the promise that he would withdraw from the war. He would apply his military experience to seek a lasting peace. Later on Obama also rushed to play the peace card. Indeed, all of his Democratic rivals did so. They vowed to end the war immediately. To have done otherwise would have courted defeat in the primaries. Obama even found it impossible to admit that the Surge worked, that changes in military tactics had gone a long way to producing victory. He knew doing so would offend the donors upon which his campaign depended.

The reason peace is a viable liberal grievance is that capitalists are alleged to be warmongers. They are accused of favoring hostilities in order to make a profit. Either they are imperialists intent on exploiting less powerful countries or they expect to make a killing by supplying weapons to the combatants. Overlooked in this analysis is the inconvenient matter that wars were fought long before capitalism arrived on the scene. Furthermore, they have since been initiated by socialist regimes. Neither the Soviet Union nor Communist China were pacifist. Nor have liberals been uniformly antiwar. FDR got the nation into WWII and won that struggle, while Harry Truman launched the Cold War and the Korean Conflict. Even John Kennedy promised to fight any foe in defense of liberty. Contemporary liberals assume he would have withdrawn from Vietnam had he lived, but his actions indicated otherwise. He was, after all, the commander-in-chief who first committed military advisors to the fray.

The difficulty with using the threat of war as a reason for pursing the Liberal Dream is that armed conflicts are not always on the horizon. It is difficult to frighten people when they feel secure. A much more reliable justification is a desire to protect the economically defenseless. Rousseau and Marx began this tradition by promising to shield the poor against the rich. They would prevent the aristocrats and/or industrialists from abusing their power. In the end, collectivist policies would extirpate oppressors root and branch. The little guys would then shelter under the liberal cloak. Once they recognized their true friends, they would unite against potential exploiters.

With respect to eliminating destitution, this undertaking reached its zenith during the War on Poverty. Liberals decided that tolerating privation was a disgrace; that an affluent nation should never allow anyone to live in squalor. Accordingly, everyone would be provided with relative comfort. What's more, the time to do so was now. They, the liberals, would see to it that every person escaped poverty. They would use governmental power to redistribute resources such that penury was eradicated. This would be a war, not in the sense that it was violent, but in being unreserved. Every effort would be made to defeat the foe. Should the capitalists balk at this undertaking, should they hoard their riches, so much the worse for them. They would be forced to comply with demands for unconditional justice. The poor deserved nothing less.

Among the tools used to eliminate poverty would be welfare programs. These were to be expanded and their benefits increased. In the process, the poor would finally be provided with a living wage. No longer would they have to skimp on necessities. No longer would they feel inferior to those who were better off. More importantly, they would not be made to feel shame. Henceforth, poverty would not be used as an excuse to belittle them. Everyone must understand that welfare was a "right." It was part of the American legacy. Old attitudes about the disgracefulness of dependency had to be eliminated. Because these benefits were part of a common patrimony, everyone, especially the poor, was eligible them. Welfare was an "entitlement." Only in this way could the underclass be abolished and equality established.

This attitude quickly metastasized to include other deserving groups. They too required social protections because they too were the victims of social oppression. First on the list were African-Americans. Having for generations been exploited by slavery and then discrimination, they needed to be offered a hand up. The constitution promised equality, hence liberals would deliver it to those previously excluded from the American Dream. To this end, the analogy between poverty and racism was invoked. Just as capitalists had taken advantage of the poor, they had misused blacks. For the sake of accumulating wealth, they erected American prosperity on the backs of their former bondsmen. The time had thus come to end this injustice. First, laws had to be rewritten to ensure equality. Then, these had to be enforced. One of the first orders of business was to protect the Civil Rights of blacks. National legislation would ensure that they exercised the franchise and utilized public facilities. No longer would demeaning practices such as separate drinking fountains be tolerated. If necessary, federal troops would make equal access a fact, not a theory.

Very quickly these assurances expanded to include other forms of inequality. Not only would *de jure* segregation of public schools be outlawed, so would *de facto* segregation. All schools would be integrated, by busing if necessary. This way black children would no longer be forced to attend inferior facilities. They too would be encouraged to excel so as to qualify for good paying jobs. Indeed, liberals demanded an equality of results. They argued that unless black achievement climbed to white levels, opportunities were not equal. Furthermore, education would not be the only front upon which the battle against discrimination was waged. Affirmative action shortly joined the armamentum of the reformers. Blacks must be hired for jobs in proportion to their percentage in the population. If they were not, this was evidence of bigotry. From now on, it would not be sufficient to refrain from excluding the racially oppressed. An active effort had to be made to correct previous wrongs.

Henceforth, black contractors were to be awarded government contracts, black students admitted to elite colleges, and black performers to appear on national television. If people objected that those so favored were unprepared, they were manifestly biased. As such, they were required to attend sensitivity training. Merely using the wrong language could now get a person in trouble. The "N-word," in particular, became taboo. Its use even played a part in allowing O.J. Simpson get away with murder. From now on blacks belonged to a protected category. Special efforts had to be made to put them on the same level as everyone else. Some even demanded reparations for slavery. They argued that compensation was due for previous eras of exploitation. This, however, was generally regarded as a bridge too far.

Meanwhile others looked on enviously at the benefits directed toward blacks. Ethnics, such as Hispanics, complained that they too had been mistreated; ergo, they should be allowed comparable advantages. Eventually, this mutated into a call for a multicultural society. Every subgroup must experience pride in its heritage. Their customs and ways of talking deserved the same respect as those of the larger community. Gone was the desire for a melting pot. Liberals discovered that this was imaginary. In its place came calls for a "tossed salad." Pluralism, not assimilation, was the goal. If people wanted to be separate, that was their choice. As long as they voluntarily decided to live among their "own kind" this should not only be allowed, but encouraged. As a result, ethnic street fairs became the rage. So did efforts to teach the young their ancestral languages. Even blacks were asked to learn Ebonics. This dialect was not inferior to Standard English, only different. Similarly Hispanic children were encouraged to attend bilingual classes. This would help them retain their Spanish at the same time that it instilled academic skills. Eventually, "diversity" came to be valued for its own sake. Everyone was said to benefit from being exposed to customs different from their own. At minimum, liberals discovered that people, who at first seemed strange, were equally human.

Next came the real discovery. Women were also an oppressed group. Just as with the poor and blacks, their weaknesses had been exploited by the dominant class. They too had been stripped of their dignity and self-determination. A male hegemony reduced them to virtual slaves. This converted half the human race into household drudges, requiring them to remain "barefoot, pregnant, and in the kitchen." Here then was a constituency of enormous proportions. With women constituting a greater percentage of the population than men, if their allegiance to the Liberal Dream could be won, victory was ensured. A combination of minorities and women would see to it that white males were outvoted. Henceforward, men would not be able to establish the standards for others. From now on, they too had to settle for equality.

Among the policies employed to ensure equity for women was affirmative action. They too would be allotted half of all sorts of jobs. The glass ceiling keeping them down would thus be shattered. Gone too would be paying women less for equal work. If necessary, the government would enforce "comparable worth." Training programs were also instituted to prepare women for nontraditional jobs, such as in construction. They would even be recruited into the military. If men balked, they were sent for sensitivity training. They would not be allowed to harass women. Thus, sexist language and catcalls were out. So was inappropriate touching. Indeed, these were grounds for dismissal. Liberals would no longer permit women to be forced into subservience. Men must learn they were not in charge. Fairness was to become the norm. From now on everything would be fifty-fifty, and androgyny the standard. Gender differences had to be consigned to the dustbin of history. Especially, given the fact that physical strength lost its advantage thanks to modern technology, women could do whatever men could. As long as boys and girls were raised the same way, they had exactly the same abilities.

Total gender equality applied at home as well. Men must learn that women were not household slaves. Nor were they to be held totally responsible for raising children. In addition, they were not going to do all of the cooking and cleaning. If necessary, women must eschew the notion of marriage. They did not need men. As Gloria Steinem put it, "A woman needs a man as much as a fish needs a bicycle." Even with respect to sexuality, women were to be liberated. The double standard was passé. If women wanted to fool around, if they wanted to ask men out, why should they be denied this prerogative? Besides, the family was an outmoded institution. The relic of a bygone era, it should no longer be allowed to furnish an excuse for female passivity. Women were not weak. It was time for them to flex their muscles, time to use their brains.

If this definition of the oppressed was not sufficiently broad, a further extension soon emerged. The grievances of another exploited group were amplified through the liberal megaphone. Amazingly, this was the criminal class. On the assumption that people became lawbreakers because they were poor, their rights became a matter of concern. The police and the courts evidently deprived these unfortunates of an opportunity to defend themselves. Thousands of accused individuals were clearly bullied into undeserved chastisements. Suspects must thus be informed of their right to counsel and allowed to refrain from self-incrimination. Illegal searches and seizures had to cease. In the future, arbitrary shakedowns at the hands of law enforcement agents were forbidden. Moreover, if necessary, illegally obtained evidence would be excluded from the courtroom. Juries must not hear coercively extracted confessions or see capriciously obtained weapons. Rather than allow innocents to be railroaded, the real bad guys, the police and judges, had to be put on a short leash.

Justice would also be guaranteed to another oppressed group. Less surly, and therefore more sympathetic, were the disabled. But they too had been excluded from normal social activities. Whether they were blind, deaf, or physically disabled, they had been treated as subhuman. Prevented from taking jobs available to the able-bodied and denied an opportunity to travel as they wished, they were being herded into handicapped ghettos. Like the poor, blacks, and women, their biological condition was used as an excuse for keeping them in subjugation. Hereafter, this would not be tolerated. The disabled too would receive government funds to compensate for their relative poverty, government training to prepare them for regular employment, and government transportation (such as kneeling buses) to take them where they wanted to go. Casual discrimination, based in a lack of respect for their humanity, was to become a thing of the past. This applied to the mentally ill as well. They too would be provided with the services they required. Furthermore, this would be done with dignity. The snake pits known as asylums were to be closed and their patients discharged.

Even the homeless would be afforded social protection. Having been thrust out of their residences by the callous greed of capitalists, they would now be given affordable places to live. The government must either subsidize their rent or construct adequate public housing. Millions of people would no longer be allowed to live in cardboard boxes, shivering themselves to sleep on cold nights. An affluent society had to provide for its citizens, even the scruffy and antisocial ones.

A still broader cause was found in the deprivation of children. They too were discovered to be an oppressed category. In fact, from the perspective of the grievance mongers, they were particularly sympathetic. Weaker even than the homeless or the disabled, they required protection on multiple levels. First, many were abused. Capitalism had converted their parents into veritable monsters who engaged in sexual, physical, or emotional abuse. These adults, having been deprived of dignity by the elite, displaced their misery onto their progeny. Sadly, this too required government intervention. Either these parents had to be reeducated or the young had to be removed to more suitable homes. In the final analysis, the community had to serve in *loco parentis*. Only it had the resources to function as the parent of last resort.

Second, the government had a responsibility to provide a quality education to every child. No youngster was to be left behind due to a lack of funding or parental apathy. Enforced ignorance was tantamount to oppression. Whatever its cause, it prevented children from taking advantage of economic and social opportunities. They were, therefore, condemned to social inferiority. Something, therefore, had to be done. What is more, it had to be done fairly. Every child deserved the same advantages. Accidents of birth ought not be allowed to result in unequal results. If this required the federal government to dip into its treasury to level school systems, so be it. If it demanded a centralized and homogeneous curriculum, this too was acceptable.

A comparably extensive cause was found in health care. Everyone, not just children, women, or the disabled, deserved first-class attention. Health was precious. Even more than education, it ought not depend on the accidents of birth. Those who were too poor, or ill-educated, to obtain the best care, possessed a valid complaint. They had every right to demand good doctors and well-equipped hospitals. If they could not afford these, the government had to make up the deficit. In the best of all possible worlds, it must furnish universal health care. Civilized people understood that no one ought to pay for so fundamental a right. In the meanwhile, Medicare would provide for the elderly, while Medicaid protected the disadvantaged. Sometime in the future, the government would be authorized to provide free medications and catastrophic care for all. As with social security, these were to be expanded to cover those who could not care for themselves. Alcoholics, drug abusers, and the mentally defective would all qualify for financial support.

Less compelling, but not for that reason to be completely abandoned, were demands for lifestyle improvements. Capitalism and industrialization produced alienation, commodification, and consumerism. People were not being treated as human. On the job, they were regarded as little more than machines, while at home they comforted themselves with things rather than relationships. Shunted into suburban seclusion, they were bamboozled into believing their unhappiness could be relieved by more of the same. Now the government had to stop building highways. It must instead concentrate on mass urban transportation. This would revive a sense of community and an awareness of our shared humanity.

Liberals also complained about a purported assault on individual rights. Freedom of speech was said to be in jeopardy from government censorship, while personal privacy was threatened by efforts to make abortion illegal. Conservative governments also illegitimately engaged in wiretapping. They claimed that this was necessary for national security, but the truth was that this was a naked power grab. Conservatives even had the temerity to deny homosexuals the right to get married. In this, they were allegedly defending traditional marriage, but they actually discriminated against gays. This too had to be stopped. A private matter, such as sexual orientation, could not be a pretext to subjugate yet another innocent group.

Finally, there were environmental concerns. Capitalism not only attacked the happiness of individuals, it raped the planet. In service to their greed, industrialists polluted the air and water, cut down the rain forests, and drove thousands of species into extinction. They did not understand that the earth had a limited carrying capacity. As a result, they encouraged soaring populations and a depletion of natural resources. Worst of all, they produced global warming. Burning coal for electricity and gasoline in internal combustion engines spewed carbon dioxide into the atmosphere where it created a greenhouse effect. Heat became trapped at ground level where it melted the ice caps and raised the sea level. Crops would soon fail, disease become rampant, and as Ted Turner opined, people be reduced to cannibalism. Our species was literally in danger of destruction. Still, the forces of greed did not care. Intent on increasing their wealth, they were prepared to see others suffer. Liberals could not allow this. It was their duty to mobilize the opposition. Marxist-style impoverishment had not occurred, but its equivalent soon would. Something had to be done. And that something was a reorganization of the market system. Only under a socialist-style system, in which everyone cared for everyone else, would people invest in drastic environmental reforms. Only then would they care enough about their shared fortunes.

To say that these liberal grievances are alarmist would be an understatement. But that was the point. Likewise, to argue that their proponents are unconcerned with economic consequences would also be accurate. Liberals only tend to promise prosperity when the economy takes a downturn. It is used as a wedge issue when conditions permit. Otherwise they agree with John Kenneth Galbraith that an affluent society ought to invest its excess production in elevating the conditions of the less fortunate. Rarely do liberals object to raising taxes. To the contrary, this is perceived as an altruistic obligation—especially when these monies come from the rich. What matters is justice. And justice comes in the shape of total equality.

Left out of these pleas are explanations of how liberal programs will achieve their objectives. The specifics of what is to be done are usually glossed over in favor of evocative attempts to elicit sympathy. Liberals tend to peddle good intentions rather than proofs of competence. The mechanics of how particular goals will be met receive less attention than the goals themselves. It is assumed that good intentions invariably produce beneficial results, that good people will see that they do. Many liberals are, to be sure, policy wonks, but even so, they are surprisingly unconcerned with the details of their proposals. No wonder that so many of their promises generate unfortunate side effects.

The Great Disruption

Francis Fukuyama has done something few social scientists before him had the perspicacity to do. He compiled, within the pages of a single book, a compendium of the consequences of the liberal hegemony. Since the time of the Great Depression, government programs have been piled upon programs and government regulations upon regulations. Republicans, not just Democrats, routinely contributed to the expansion of government services. In a sense, federal intervention became the default position of American politics. Whenever something went wrong—or was said to go wrong—the failure to add a new program was depicted as a failure to care. It was portrayed as callous indifference. Unfortunately, the overall effect has not been consistently positive. Much evil has been done in the name of doing good—and this is what Fukuyama documented.

From the 1960s through the 1990s a series of things went awry, many of which, in retrospect, derive from an excess of niceness. Time and again interventions intended to correct problems exacerbated them. One of these failures was in the area of crime. Liberalism, it must be remembered, promised to reduce crime. It was going to eliminate its "root cause," that is, poverty, and treat criminals fairly and compassionately. Violators would not be arbitrarily incarcerated or labeled criminal. Nor would they be subjected to a barbarous death penalty. Instead, they would be provided with rehabilitation programs in prison and early release for good behavior as an incentive for self-development. Some would even be offered probation, rather than imprisonment. As a result, the motivation to engage in crime would be removed. People provided with an outlet for their ambitions obviously became good citizens. They did not hurt others because there was no reason to do so.

Only a funny thing happened on the way to a crimeless society. Contrary to liberal assurances, crime escalated. Not only did it grow, but it doubled and then redoubled. Eventually, the murder rate rose to many times what it had been in the Wild West or during the heyday of Al Capone. Other crimes also became more common. Robbery rates soared, as did those for burglary and assault. So did the number of rapes. In some central cities, gangs took over the streets, while drug lords ignored international borders to engage in wholesale smuggling. For decade after decade, the dismal statistics spiraled upward. So unexceptional did this become, it seemed normal. Many observers looked at the dirty, crime-ridden streets of places like New York City and pronounced them ungovernable. Crime was as natural in these environments as trees in a forest.

Drug use also soared. Back in the 1930s the government depicted marijuana as driving people crazy. Now many regarded it as a harmless social outlet. Pot made people feel good. It expanded their senses and provided a sense of well-being. LSD also opened new vistas. Those under its influence entered a world of dazzling colors and cosmological insights. The young—but not just the young—concluded that previous generations lied about the bleak effects of various drugs. The stated objective of the authorities had been to protect people, but the real goal was to deny them pleasure. Now, a better-educated generation would experiment with a pharmacological cornucopia. Its members would determine for themselves what worked. For many thousands, heroin was no longer taboo. Shooting it up mellowed them out and made life tolerable. For others, amphetamines, then called speed, was just the ticket. It accelerated the senses and allowed its devotees to experience more than they could unaided. For millions of others, cocaine was the drug of choice. Its expense initially restricted it to the affluent—who referred to it as "nose candy." But eventually the price came down. Still, it was when it mutated into smokable crack that it migrated onto the streets. A veritable epidemic then followed. Energized by coke, many users believed they had become superhuman.

So extensive did drug use become, that those who refrained were deemed socially backward. Why not try Quaaludes or angel dust? Why not sample methampetamines or ecstasy? The utilization of these and other designer substances became a cultural trend. Parties were considered incomplete without them. Dance clubs and "raves" also depended upon them to keep the excitement flowing. Billions of dollars were made in peddling these chemicals to the young and vulnerable. Unfortunately, millions of lives were also ruined by their addictive qualities. Users usually denied that they had been hooked, but they rarely lifted themselves out of the gutters into which they had fallen.

The family, in contrast, was dismissed as obsolete. By almost any measure, its integrity was under assault. In the early 1950s, the divorce rate had been under 5 percent. Leaving one's spouse was not only unusual, in many quarters it was considered a disgrace. Togetherness was the ideal. This, however, would pass. Mom and dad with their two kids living in intimate suburban comfort would soon seem quaint. For many, this sort of closeness was regarded as stifling. Determined to escape domestic incarceration, they eschewed marriage. Why be bound by an archaic convention? It made more sense either to live with someone or, if badly married, to divorce. Relationships that did not work had to be severed so as to establish better ones. As a consequence, divorce rates soared. By the 1990s more than half of all marriages ended in the courts. Meanwhile, "shacking up" became acceptable. Among the cognoscenti, playing house was regarded as a sensible way to test out a marriage before committing. Thought of as "trial marriages," this was supposed to decrease the chances of splitting up. The opposite occurred, but it was not recognized at the time.

More adventurous souls disdained the idea of commitment. They did not intend to get married. Others tied the knot, but did not consider it binding. They preferred swinging marriages in which both parties were free to engage in sex with other partners. For many, sex became the objective. Sex felt good; hence the greatest number of orgasms with the largest cast of characters was best. Sex was love, and vice versa. As a result, the age at which teens first had sex declined—especially for girls. Where once females took pride in their virginity, this transmuted into a stigma. Hooking up and hanging out, not courtship, became the goal. Chastity was considered evidence of ignorance or timidity—or perhaps a lack of popularity. The outcome was an explosion in teenage pregnancy. Young women who possessed neither the desire, nor the aptitude, to raise a child found they had little choice. With teenage fathers unlikely to rush to their support, they were stuck with the job themselves.

Rampant sexuality thus had an abysmal effect—namely out-of-wedlock pregnancy. What had once been depicted as "illegitimacy" lost its sense of shame. Shotgun weddings went out of style, while serial monogamy came into fashion. Millions of children were now raised by single mothers, or mothers who lived with a succession of paramours. In the black community, more than two-thirds of babies would eventually be born out of wedlock. In the nation at large, more than two-fifths of babies would come into the world without a legal father. To make matters worse, these infants were generally born into impoverished households. They could not count on economic advantages and, in many cases, consigned their mothers to remain in poverty.

None of this seemed to matter the media moguls who regarded sex as a marketing tool. In films and on television, they depicted promiscuous sex as glamorous. The bygone notion that married couples should not be seen occupying the same bed was replaced with full frontal nudity. Modesty was equated with censorship, hence ridiculed. At the same time, vulgar language surged. Everyone, including the most demure young women, demonstrated their sophistication by publicly talking as coarsely as possible. In many quarters, this was seen as "cute." In others, it was deemed "authentic." Words, after all, were just words. To be ashamed of them was hypocritical. That this resulted in a lack of civility was irrelevant. Censoring oneself because others were offended was dishonest. It was better to "tell it like it is."

Also rocketing skyward were welfare rates. The country was getting richer, but the numbers on the dole increased. In many cases, a subclass of multigenerational welfare clients emerged. Unwed grand-mothers presided over households in which unwed mothers raised unwed grandchildren. None worked or intended to. All depended upon the government to take care of their needs. This was, as they were repeatedly told, a right. So pervasive was this attitude that entire neighborhoods fell into disrepair thanks to residents who did not feel responsible for their own well-being. It was not up to them to clean their homes or fix what was broken. Other people were obliged to remedy these matters. As social casualties, they were dependent upon public-spirited caretakers.

According to the media, homelessness had similarly increased. Huge numbers of people now lived on the streets. Although this was attrib-uted to a lack of residences, it was more closely correlated with two other phenomena. Roughly one third of the homeless were chemically dependent, while another third were mentally ill. Alcoholics had long wandered as derelicts in central city neighborhoods—now heroin and cocaine addicts joined them. As for the mentally ill, most had previously resided in mental hospitals. Now deinstitutionalization turned them out onto the streets. Community mental health centers and psychotro-pic medications were supposed to fill the gap, but many of these had not been built, while the laws were changed such that people could not be forced to take medications against their will. If they wanted to live in cardboard boxes, this was another right. Even if they defecated on the streets, they could not be incarcerated for vagrancy.

As for education, while it was supposed to improve, it did not. As measured by achievement tests, students were learning less, albeit going to school more. This was not for want of trying. A broad panoply of scholastic innovations had little positive effect. Thus, whole-word learning did not improve reading scores, while the new math had not elevated arithmetic abilities. Similarly, history, watered down to make it inoffensive, became boring and irrelevant. Besides, no one seemed to be counting. Students were still being tested, but their grades did not matter. They were promoted irrespective of what they knew In any event, grade inflation gave almost everyone better-looking report cards. They could then go on to college where they received comparable grades as a birthright. Actually, the reading of books was becoming optional. As modern educators knew, some students learned better visually than verbally. They were therefore provided with multimedia sources of information. As a consequence, classroom films and computer graphics replaced linear forms of learning. Even the learning disabled were accommodated. They were now allowed more time to take tests or permitted to submit personal portfolios. The experts ostensibly discovered that there were other forms of intelligence than the traditional academic ones; hence these too needed to be acknowledged and rewarded.

Replacing long-established modes of social discipline with tolerance and flexibility was also supposed to improve social attitudes. People who loved and respected themselves would love and respect others. Once more, however, the outcome was other than expected. Levels of interpersonal trust declined. People began to expect the worst of strangers. To leave one's front door open or to forget one's keys in the car ignition were now accounted foolish. Children were taught not to talk to strangers and women were asked to carry pepper spray in their purses. After President Clinton's Lewinsky debacle, many people began to say, "everyone lies and everyone cheats." They refused to condemn him for normal human behavior. Nor would they be so naïve as to expect honesty from strangers. Everyone had an angle. It was the job of enlightened people to figure these out.

This is quite a list of setbacks. A recognition that they occurred at the same time gives credence to Fukuyama's use of the appellation The Great Disruption. Something had gone unexpectedly wrong. What this was, however, was subject to interpretation. Few liberals were open to the proposition that it might be liberalism. Deeply enamored of the Liberal Dream, they looked elsewhere for an explanation. But what if liberalism was to blame? What if implementing it had caused these unanticipated problems?

Failed Prophecies

Most liberals did not intend to, but they lowered social standards across the board. In telling people they were essentially nice and that the government would protect them from a variety of threats, they implied that ordinary people were no longer responsible for their own fate. At the same time, in making promises they could not fulfill, they produced widespread cynicism. Paradoxically, people who constantly expected to be better off were led to believe they could not defend themselves, whereas those who could do so were unreliable. In the long run, this disjunction produced mental indigestion. Suspicion mixed with hope in an unholy blend of futility. The only way to survive this confusion was a willing suspension of disbelief. Intelligent people had to turn their brains off lest they short-circuit.

One of the ways in which people assuaged their consciences was by accepting assurances that what went wrong was not their fault. Indeed, nothing was anyone's fault. All human beings were the product of environmental pressures they could not control. It was therefore a mistake to blame them for their failures. It was especially wrong to blame the victims of these debacles. What misfired was imposed upon them. They were oppressed and exploited. If anyone was to blame, it was the elite. It was they who imposed the capitalistic system on others. Moreover, they did so for their own selfish purposes. If the family was in trouble, if crime was rampant, if students were doing poorly, the injured parties were not to blame. They were innocents. The authorities who dictated these events were responsible. Consequently, they should pay the price by being overthrown.

What many liberals had not counted on was the fact that people freed of a sense of personal responsibility were also freed of guilt. They would not make efforts to help themselves, or refrain from hurting others, because they believed themselves blameless. These objects of "cosmic permissiveness" had repeatedly been asked to do whatever felt right, not what was right. They were to be spontaneous and youthful. This would ensure perpetual innocence. In fact, some observers concluded that guilt was itself to blame for their problems. People burdened by a misplaced sense of culpability were frozen into impotence. Because they berated themselves for the faults of others, they lived in a perpetual state of self-subjugation. Unwilling to make things worse, they did nothing.

The answer to this quandary was to stop blaming them and allow their better selves to emerge. That this might encourage them to engage in ill-considered conduct was disregarded. More specifically, that people who did not feel responsible for their actions might not decide to get educated or would prefer to stay on welfare did not register. That married people who blamed the institution of marriage for their troubles did not work at their unions or that those engaged in promiscuous sex did not make good parents was also not allowed to intrude into consciousness. It was those other guys, the ones behind the tree, the ones living in the big houses, who were responsible. They had done it—whatever it was they did.

The Great Disruption essentially revealed a compendium of failed prophecies. Yet liberals refused to blame themselves for mistakes in judgment. In their eyes, they were not at fault. Their recommendations might not have unfolded as predicted, but that was not because they were in error. Like most failed prophets, they reinterpreted events. According to them, others caused the problems. These evildoers—mostly conservatives—gummed up the works. With a few more amply funded programs, the original predictions would still come true. Just as the Marxist Revolution had been postponed, theirs would take a little longer than originally thought. But not to worry. It would still arrive.

Unfortunately, there were a great many failed prophecies to rationalize. With so much gone wrong, there had to be a proximate cause. But what was it? Could it be that those who had been most influential in addressing social problems had no role in perpetuating them? Or was it that backward thinking people—people who were presumably not very bright—caused this disruption? Yet there is another alternative. Perhaps the Liberal Dream was flawed. With so much smoke, there might be a fire. This option is surely worth considering. Perchance the nature of what went wrong provided clues as to why things misfired so badly? A careful examination of what occurred, but also what did not, might suggest reasons most liberal predictions proved abortive.

One of the things not discussed in detail by Fukuyama is peace. Yet peace is a signature liberal concern. We begin our investigation with it because it too failed to develop as forecast. Liberals expected diplomatic niceness to deliver international harmony. Thus, they recommended unilateral disarmament as a means of terminating the Cold War. Since the Soviets were intransient, it was up to the United States to set the ball rolling. If our government renounced atomic weapons, the Russians were sure to follow. Yes, they were paranoid, but that was because history had been unkind to them. Continuously threatened by military aggression from both the East and West, they expected the worst. It was therefore up to us to demonstrate our honorable intentions. If we reduced our stockpiles of missiles, submarines, and bombers, they would be caught off guard. Perplexed by this move, they would rethink their position. Eventually, however, because they were fundamentally human, they would come around. They would realize we were sincere and join in preserving international harmony.

In fact, this is not how events turned out. The Soviets were not convinced to disarm by our prior disarmament. They joined this program, but in response to a long-term series of negotiations. First nuclear testing was abandoned and only later were warheads and missiles retargeted or decommissioned. This occurred, not because of one-sided niceness, but from balanced concessions. Ronald Reagan famously proclaimed that he would "trust, but verify." Nothing would be taken on faith. This was something the Russians could understand. It was realistic. Other "pie in the sky" proposals left them wary. They assumed these entailed trickery. Realpolitik, in which both sides protected their interests, made more sense.

Nevertheless, it was not mutual disarmament, but unbalanced rearmament that brought the Cold War to a close. Reagan was frequently reviled as a cowboy. His references to an "evil empire" were said to inflame the Soviets. When he invested billions of dollars to purchase modernized weaponry, this was taken as proof of unrestrained belligerence. Worse still was his advocacy of a missile shield against Russian projectiles. Ridiculed as unworkable "star wars," this harebrained scheme confirmed his status as a simpleminded actor. Except that this is not what the Russians thought. Other actions, such as Reagan's handling of the air traffic controller strike, convinced them he meant business. Besides, they could not afford to keep pace with the requisite spending. With their own economy in shambles, additional expenditures might push them over the edge. As a consequence, they decided to make a deal. They acceded to demands regarding Eastern Europe, and the rest was history. Ultimately, it was strength, not highminded weakness that produced results.

The Liberal Dream clearly did not bring peace between the superpowers. Nor had variants of it done so in the past. Hitler was not removed from power when Neville Chamberlain ceded the Sudetenland to him. Stalin was not prevented from gobbling up all of Europe because the United States decided not to supply Berlin by air when he imposed a blockade. In the first case an aggressor had his appetite whetted by appeasement; in the second, a show of force deterred further expansion. Nevertheless, it was the Vietnam experience that most influenced recent American thinking. Conventional wisdom now has it that this war was a mistake. Perhaps it was. But can anyone be sure that the domino effect would not have occurred without American intervention? And what would have happened years earlier had Truman accepted North Korean aggression? Would a democratic Japan have survived? Even the Iraq War is not a clear-cut example of what is best. Critics repeatedly warned that this clash was unwinnable, that even the Surge was a fool's errand. The majority leader in the Senate went so far as to proclaim that the United States was caught in a sectarian conflict from which there was no exit. But what if the United States had withdrawn? Would Iran have stood idly by? And what impact would this have had on Saudi Arabia, or oil prices. It is fashionable to dismiss oil as a symbol of capitalist greed, but what if supplies had been drastically curtailed? Wouldn't this have caused economic devastation on an international scale?

Peace is not a liberal monopoly. Others too want peace. The difference is in tactics, not the ultimate objective. Moreover, history demonstrates that those who believe in peace through strength usually prevail. Once the Chinese lived in the shadow of the Mongol hordes. Their territory was periodically devastated by nomadic invasions. As a consequence, they sought ways to diminish their peril. Some methods like the Great Wall of China were relatively passive. These depended upon turning back an incursion once it occurred. Other methods were more active. They depended upon sending armies into enemy territory to disrupt an impending attack. Events have shown that the latter strategy was far more effective. Preemptory attacks saved many Chinese lives. So it is with peace nowadays. The hawks believe in a forward strategy. They want to discourage aggression before it occurs. The doves, on the other hand, are more defense-minded. They do not want to be antagonistic. If words can deter a potential enemy, they want to try these first. Because they believe people are fundamentally nice, they do not want to resort to violence until after an enemy proves it unavoidable. Thus, they await a Pearl Harbor before swinging into action.

The trouble with passivity is that many people are not nice. Joseph Stalin, for one, believed in taking advantage of soft spots. His goal was absolute power. If he thought he could get away with something, he tried. Nor did he worry about the body count. The same, of course, was true for Adolf Hitler. What is troubling is that many on the far left do not believe this. They are convinced everyone can be saved. Not just passive, they are pacifists. Essentially anti-military, they would reduce the armed forces to an empty shell. This is not mere rhetoric. Groups such as Code Pink actively disrupt military recruiting, while less extreme liberals shut down Army Reserve training on college campuses. Meanwhile, within Congress, Democrats seem permanently in favor of trimming the military budget. Needless to say, they also hate the Central Intelligence Agency and have frequently reorganized it in order to curtail its rogue tendencies. No doubt some oversight is necessary. No doubt military appetites at times need to be curbed. Yet it is likewise true that liberals generally err on the side of military weakness. Their Pollyanna streak, left unchecked, would surely produce a dangerous vulnerability.

This obliviousness to danger has also been demonstrated with respect to crime. Liberal predictions about controlling crime were plainly contradicted by the facts. Treating the constabulary as the enemy, and seeking to disarm the police, is, in fact, a formula for chaos. Yet liberals do not see it this way. As with the military, they regard law enforcement agencies as the wellspring of violence. Often berated as "pigs," the police are regularly accused of brutality. If street thugs go too far, it is because they are defending themselves against aggression. Besides, the root cause of crime is poverty. As long as the capitalist system keeps some people in misery, they will seek to redress their grievances by breaking the rules. They are essentially "innovators" seeking a way to forestall the injustices of a failed system. Meanwhile, law enforcement agents are the acolytes of the oppressors. It is their job to thwart revolutionary attacks on the establishment. If they use excessive violence, this is because their handlers authorize whatever atrocities are necessary to keep them in power. In other words, crime, and its brutal suppression, will continue to exist as long as market-based economies remain. There is no way out except a radical reorganization of society.

Nevertheless this is not what occurred. Liberal predictions about what is necessary to control crime proved erroneous. To begin with, efforts to reduce poverty did not reduce crime. If anything, the correlation was exactly opposite. The more resources the poor were provided via welfare, social security, or Medicaid, the higher the levels of lawbreaking. Nor did curtailing police activities work. Instructing the police to refrain from enforcing rules against graffiti or turnstile jumping on the subways did not appease potential criminals. Just as with Chamberlain, pulling back only encouraged further aggression. Street thugs did not interpret police passivity as kindness. To the contrary, they perceived it as weakness. A police officer standing around doing nothing suggested they could get away with what they desired. In any event, crime went up, not down.

Amazingly, liberals looked triumphantly at this failure and insisted it demonstrated they were correct. Since capitalism remained intact, what else could one expect? Crime would remain high as long as an unjust system persisted. Only it didn't. Here too a liberal prophecy proved defective. Crime did go down, but in response to interventions said to be futile. Once police forces started enforcing the law, respect for it increased. Conservative criminologists hypothesized that enforcing all of the laws, including the petty ones, would reduce crime at every level. This turned out to be so. Implementing the "Broken Window" theory produced results. Taking the squeegee men off the street and cleaning the graffiti off the subway cars helped reduce the murder rate by more than two-thirds. So did forward policing. Being proactive and going where crime was predicted, nipped violations in the bud. These policies told potential lawbreakers there was a price to pay for their transgressions. Incarceration rates, as opposed to crime rates, soared. Now ordinary people could go back onto the street with less fear for their personal safety.

The liberal faith in rehabilitation was also punctured. Punishment was supposed to beget a resistance to punishment, whereas teaching prisoners to be upstanding citizens and providing them with the skills needed to earn a respectable living would remove the incentive to engage in crime. Only it did not. Recidivism rates were almost exactly the same whether or not prisoners were enrolled in rehabilitation programs. Nor did parole or probation make much of a difference. In time, with policies such as time off for good behavior, the average amount of time served for murder dropped to seven years. This was hardly a deterrent.

Liberal theories about crime were thus dramatically disconfirmed, but so were their speculations about the family. The family was said to be handmaiden of capitalist oppression. It tied people together in a manner that prevented them from maximizing their potential. Forced by outmoded rules to desist from self-actualization, they were less happy than if allowed to follow their instincts. If they did what felt right, which included not marrying, or if married, divorcing, everyone would benefit. Except that once more they did not. Unrestrained promiscuity was not the key to personal contentment. Divorce rates rose and trial marriages became common, whereas personal satisfaction did not go up. Sexual relationships were not the same as love relationships. The basketball player Wilt Chamberlain boasted of having had over twenty thousand liaisons, but his life was not the epitome of joy. Many Lotharios, in fact, were lonely. Perhaps freewheeling sexuality was not the philosopher's stone.

Love is important; hence the failures of liberal predictions about it were significant. Even more important, however, were the effects on children. Freeing adults from the stifling indenture of bad marriages was supposed to liberate their offspring. Released from the oppressive bickering of their parents, they too would be freed to realize their potentials. Yet this prophesy also failed. The children of divorce did

95

not flower into a generation of fulfilled adults. Sadly, the opposite occurred. On almost every measure, they did worse than the children of intact marriages. On average, they were less well educated, less productively employed, and less happily married. They also tended to have more serious health problems, including mental health difficulties. Often troubled by the failure of their parents' marriage, they frequently blamed themselves.

Even more seriously affected were children born out of wedlock. Reducing the stigma of illegitimacy was supposed to protect both the mothers and their young from opprobrium. No longer subject to social rejection, they would be released to satisfy their hopes. Only once again the prophecy went wrong. Mothers who had children as unattached teenagers had difficulty finishing high school, never mind college. Unable to get good paying jobs, they tended to be trapped in unrelieved poverty. This, of course, redounded to the detriment of their children. Poor mothers generally raise poor children. Left to their own devices, they also have difficulty imposing discipline. Teenage boys, in particular, tend to run wild. As a result, despite the best efforts of their mothers, many are ill educated, underemployed, and unmarried. Even more likely to have mental health problems than the children of divorce, they are frequently condemned to life in the underclass. Sexuality, for its own sake, has thus proven a mirage. Minutes of pleasure too often result in years of misery. Marital discipline is sometimes onerous, but its elimination is far more destructive.

Underlying much of the anarchy surrounding free love were feminist aspirations. Feminism was supposed to liberate women. Millennia of subjugation by the male hegemony were to be cast off in a burst of freedom. Women would then be able to take any jobs they desired and be paid well for doing so. No longer tied down by housework or childcare, total equality between the genders would triumph, with artificial distinctions eliminated. To this end, of course, men had to be reeducated. They needed to learn that women could do as much as they. Stripped of their privileges, they might at first resist, but in the end would benefit from genuine fairness. With everyone able to maximize their potentials, they too would profit from female contributions to the general welfare.

Only here too liberal predictions did not unfold as expected. While it is true many men resisted feminism, phenomena such as the glass ceiling largely turned out to be myths. When women entered the workforce, they did so as most people do, namely at entry-level positions. It therefore took decades to work their way up to the executive suites. But many eventually did. More than this, despite repeated allegations that women earned seventy cents on the dollar compared to men for the same work, this too turned out to be untrue. Once jobs were equated in terms of achievement, training, and difficulty of performance, the earning gap disappeared.

What had not been anticipated is that women tend to choose different jobs than men. Fewer are comfortable working on construction projects or as machinists. They prefer to supervise children in daycare centers or to function as social workers. The feminists assured everyone that the differences between men and women were due to differences in socialization, but this too was mistaken. Comparable socialization could not be provided because children resisted. They, for instance, enjoyed playing with different toys—the boys with guns, the girls with dolls. There are, it seems, biological differences between the genders that express themselves in divergent occupational choices. Women, for example, are more personal relationship oriented than men, whereas men are better at dealing with spatial relationships. Women are also more child-oriented. Given the choice between going home to care for a sick child or visiting a client several hundred miles away, they choose the former.

The feminists claimed to be seeking justice, but they overplayed their hands. In their zeal, they refused to allow women to be women or men to be men. Forecasts of gender interchangeability having proved a delusion, they insisted on forcing people into preselected molds. Equality was going to be equality, irrespective of biological differences. In time, albeit not to the satisfaction of the feminists, it became evident that men and women made different vocational choices. Even affirmative action could not produce a fifty-fifty workplace. Nor could rules about sexual harassment force men and women to interact in exactly the same ways. To ignore these discrepancies was not a reflection of justice, but of ideological commitment. It refused to allow people to decide what worked best for them.

One consequence of this intransigence was male bashing. Men were blamed for social arrangements over which they had little control. Frequently whipsawed between demands that they open doors for women or allow them to open these for themselves, they did not know which behavior was acceptable. Furthermore, whether they or their mates liked it, they were asked to perform more household tasks. In some cases, they were badgered to be Mr. Mom. This, however, proved a mixed blessing. Given that both partners were now likely to be employed, millions of husbands and wives made adjustments in accord with their work schedules. Nowadays, even though women still do most of the housework, it is often the men who do the cooking and their wives who mow the lawn. Nevertheless, most women prefer close ties with young children, while most men take the breadwinner role seriously.

Much more troubling is the friction feminist ideals introduced into intimate relationships. If men and women are to live together and cooperate in raising their children, they have to understand, and be tolerant, of each other. They cannot afford to turn their differences into grievances. Intimacy has always been difficult. Making compromises with a partner usually entails relinquishing some of one's fondest hopes. That feminists depicted women as oppressed innocents and men as unreconstructed oppressors did not help matters. It instead created suspicions and reinforced obstinacies. This made divorce more likely, with all of the negative consequences thereby implied. If this portrayal is correct, then to the degree feminists are accurate about male and female frictions, to that same degree they create a self-fulfilling prophecy. They incite the very fights of which they complain.

Turning to social class issues, liberals were also wrong in their approach to poverty. The War on Poverty did not work. It did not eliminate all vestiges of destitution. Despite Herculean efforts and imaginative interventions, the poor were not empowered to take control of their lives. Nor did the homeless disappear from our streets. Social mobility occurred, yet it had for a long time previous to this. The ranks of the middle class continued to swell, but not because community workers transformed the outlook of the poor. The poor continued to defile their neighborhoods and to look to others to defend their interests. Liberals might assert there was no culture of poverty, but just as Oscar Lewis observed, the poor continued to live disorganized, present-oriented, local-oriented, and fatalistic lives. More oppositional than ambitious, although they wanted better, few did what was necessary to obtain it.

More specifically, liberals predicted that generous welfare allowances would encourage people to lift themselves out of despair. Once freed of worry regarding their temporal needs, they would turn their attention to moving up the social ladder. Unfortunately, this was completely mistaken. Larger welfare checks simply made welfare more comfortable. People, who, if they applied themselves, could do better, were converted into clients for life. They became dependent upon a monthly check. Making them feel less guilty merely left them resigned to their helplessness. It even enabled them to be irresponsible with respect to bearing children, since they knew the government would cover the additional expenses. With respect to work, the common attitude was "why jeopardize free money for the uncertainty of the job market." Indeed, many welfare clients came to feel incapable of doing better. They literally perceived themselves as unqualified for competitive work. Having come to believe they were oppressed by the "system," they believed it deprived them of marketable skills.

Even sending welfare clients for job training did not help. This came to be regarded as an alternate form of welfare. People went for training, let us say in air conditioning and refrigeration repair, during which they received a larger check than standard. Then, once graduated, they found it impossible to find employment in the area for which they had been prepared. A few months later they entered a different training program, with similar results. In time, the welfare authorities found that the best course was to force clients into a job hunt. Once excuses about not having sufficient carfare were disallowed, many found they could secure work.

But the greatest affront to the liberal welfare reformers came from a less permissive welfare system. Once people on the dole were informed that their welfare checks would not last forever, their motivation to obtain work miraculously improved. Not long thereafter more than half of those on welfare found employment. Liberals continued to insist that disaster was around the corner, but this turned out to be a fairly long corner. The welfare rolls went down and stayed down. Suddenly people who had been dependent acquired new dignity. Contrary to liberal assertions, they found that they could care for themselves. Currently, of course, some liberals are taking credit for these reforms. Because these occurred under Clinton's administration, they conveniently forget these were thrust on him by a Republican congress.

With respect to health, billions have been expended to improve physical and mental well-being. So extensive have these efforts been that costs escalated to such an extent that the medical industry today accounts for more than one seventh of the nation's goods and services. Liberals, however, were unsatisfied. They hoped to nationalize health care. In the name of the uninsured, they insisted on overhauling the entire system. They looked to other countries for inspiration, without noting that government sponsored programs often made patients wait months for services. No one has yet figured out the best way to deliver the optimum treatment for the largest number, but this did not prevent those on the left from insisting they know the answer. Medicare and Medicaid cost far more than predicted, but this only encouraged them to impose Obamacare. Nor do the trillions this is expected to add to the budget deficit distress them. They continue to forecast only positive outcomes for their projects.

As for educational reforms, liberal policies have been no more successful. Here too a great deal of effort produced meager results. Progressive education was presumably designed to meet the needs of an industrial society. Irrelevant subjects such as ancient languages were eliminated, as was rote learning. Individualism, creativity, and critical thinking were instead to take pride of place. In other words, self-actualization was the goal. The trouble is that learning stagnated. All sorts of innovations were implemented to little avail. Classroom populations were reduced so that teachers would have more time for each student. Teacher aides were likewise introduced to provide individuated instruction. Technology also came to the classroom in the form of computers and visual aides. With respect to race, busing was touted as producing integration. Magnet schools were similarly created. These were to provide advantages for well-motivated students and parents. Even open classrooms were attempted. As per the central tenets of progressive education, these adhered to the "project method." Students would design their programs by choosing their subject matter. They would then move around as they saw fit, with teachers aiding them in these self-motivated endeavors.

Most of all, new monies were invested in equalizing classroom opportunities. State governments, and eventually the federal government, channeled tax receipts into schools at every level on the theory that this would overcome social class advantages. No longer would affluent suburbs be able to provide better facilities than inner city neighborhoods. Good teachers, computers, and up-to-date textbooks were to be available to every pupil. Ultimately, no child would be left behind. And yet, that is not what happened. School achievement remained stubbornly low. More students graduated from high school and went to college, but their achievements did not match those of former generations. Even reinstituting achievement tests made marginal differences. Study habits never seemed to rise very much.

Counter-intuitively, as early as the 1960s, James Coleman demonstrated there was virtually no correlation between the money spent and the amount of learning that occurred. His groundbreaking research showed that parental attitudes toward education mattered far more. No matter what the expenditures, the children of parents who valued education tended to do better than the children of parents who did not. Yet nobody believed this. Liberals were certain money was the key and so they insisted on throwing more of it at schools. They did not attempt to change parental attitudes because this was difficult. As a result, differences in social class attainments remained unchanged. If anything an insistence on "equal results" handicapped the better students. More money was now spent on mainstreaming mentally challenged students than supporting gifted ones. Once more, a lack of achievement was rewarded. Reformers more interested in promoting justice than learning ignored the truism that "you get what you pay for."

Nor did efforts to encourage diversity pay off. Sanitizing textbooks so that they would not offend minority groups merely produced texts that said almost nothing. Bereft of controversy, many of these were soporific. Nor did recruiting minority members into elite colleges for which they were unprepared equalize educational accomplishments. The actual consequence was that many students dropped out. Instead of learning they were as good as anyone else, they first discovered that they did not have to work as hard to obtain entrance. Then, when they were unable to keep up, they were shown the door.

As to eliminating racism from the larger society, a great deal has indeed been achieved. The election of Barack Obama as president convinced even diehards that some change occurred. Liberals therefore take pride in policies such as affirmative action. These are alleged to have made the difference. Yet here too there is reason to doubt their boasts. Paradoxically, the data shows that African-Americans made greater strides before affirmative action than after. Worse still, people promoted because they belong to a particular category are liable to be disrespected by their colleagues. If they cannot perform their jobs, they are ignored. Yes, they make more money than otherwise, but they do not obtain what they value most, namely respect for their achievements. No wonder many blacks are convinced little progress had been made.

With respect to the mentally ill, deinstitutionalization was a disaster. It has been a spur to homelessness. People for whom no appropriate facilities were available took care of their needs as best they could. For many, this meant sleeping under bridges rather than living with abusive relatives. Nor has medicalizing personal unhappiness elevated individual contentment. Drugs such as Prozac were to make people feel "better than well"—only they didn't. Once more removing individual responsibility produced unsatisfactory results. People told they did not have to put in personal effort to improve their situations did not do what they could. With the complicity of the drug companies, the United States became a nation of pill poppers.

Lastly, liberal efforts to improve the environment have had mixed results. Air and water quality have improved. Toxins of all sorts were removed from the environment. Unfortunately, the goals set were unachievable. For example, liberals hoped to spend billions of dollars to remove tiny amounts of arsenic from drinking water. Even though no more than one or two deaths per annum were attributed to this cause, they insisted on perfection. They also said that cutting down forests would result in massive extinctions. But if their figures were accurate, no living creatures should have been left on the planet by the turn of the millennium. Only most were. What is more, the percentage of forested area in the United States increased. Yet the worst liberal failure has been with respect to issues such as acid rain and global warming. Acid rain was supposed to deforest the Eastern States, but did not. Contrary to the alarmists, the largest cause of acidified lakes turned out to be other than coal-fired utilities. This, however, was small potatoes compared with global warming. According to many environmentalists, the oceans would soon rise to flood low-lying states such as Florida, while the wheat fields of the Midwest would be converted into deserts. Starvation and disease would be everywhere. Hence, only by deindustrializing society could we avert disaster.

The trouble is that Chicken Littles such as Al Gore get their science wrong. They miscalculated the speed with which the oceans were rising and the degree to which temperatures increased. They were also wrong with respect to the costs of eliminating carbon dioxide from the atmosphere or the impact doing so would have on the economy. The environmental alarmists claimed that everyone agreed with them, but this was blatantly untrue, as purloined e-mails eventually proved. Even before this, however, climatologists disputed their computer projections, while economists disputed the cost-benefits of their correctives. As of now, all that can honestly be said is that we do not yet know whether global warming will continue or even whether it is created primarily by human agencies.

Advocates of the Liberal Dream undoubtedly question many of the above assertions; nevertheless, this is a disquieting inventory of failed prophecies. It should give people pause, but, of course, those on the extreme left discount them entirely. They insist their explanations are not rationalizations. Convinced they are morally and intellectually superior, they brush negative observations aside. According to them, they are not trying to deny the undeniable, but merely attempting to promote progress. After all, they want the best for us.

4

Liberal Contradictions

Conservative Contradictions

For two centuries, its critics have predicted the demise of industrial capitalism. The system was said to be riddled with contradictions that would inevitably demolish it from within. Liberals would not have to do the dirty work of tearing down the whole rotten edifice. It would fall of its own weight. All they had to do was pick up the pieces after the collapse. Everyone from Karl Marx through Daniel Bell assured us that this was so. Even Adam Smith acknowledged difficulties with a completely free market. While he had faith in an *invisible hand*, he understood that it required assistance from time to time.

Anarchists and communists have speculated that government itself would one day become obsolete, although few conservatives have joined this prediction. Indeed, since at least Thomas Hobbes, those who have defended the existing order recognized that government interventions were frequently necessary to keep society running smoothly. If they did not believe in a "war of all against all," they were aware that humankind does not constitute a company of saints. People cheat, lie, and sometimes murder. As a result, they must occasionally be restrained. If there is going to be peace on earth, large-scale civilizations require centralized authorities. Whether in the form of armies, aristocracies, or police forces, some individuals must be designated as peacekeepers.

Conservatives have also understood that government is necessary to preserve property rights. Those who believe in a market-based system realize that trading goods and services cannot occur if the participants are insecure in the ownership of their possessions. Jean Jacques Rousseau believed property was established when someone fenced off a piece of land and said "this is mine." In his view, it was when others subsequently respected this assertion that property rights were born. Actual property owners, however, have generally understood that this scenario does not add up. They know in their bones that there have always been some people who were unwilling to respect what others possessed. These rogues happily stole whatever was not nailed down. Such folks must, as a result, be discouraged from their predations by a power greater than their own. Hobbes thought this had to be a monarch. Most contemporary conservatives recognize that democratic governments can function just as well in this capacity.

Traditionalists also understand that property rights are not absolute. Just because a person owns something does not mean he or she has a right to do whatever he pleases with it. The mere possession of a gun does not furnish a person with the right to shoot bystanders. Nor does control over an automobile bestow the right to drive it on the left side of the road (in the US). Zoning laws are a perfect illustration of this principle. A person who owns a parcel of land is not entitled to build whatever he or she desires. Because the community has an interest in where amenities are located, some areas are designated for commercial use whereas others are reserved for low-density residences. Almost no one believes that a private person should be able to build a prison in the midst of single-family dwellings.

The economist Milton Friedman argued that government is essential to regulate what he called "community effects." He realized that what a person does on his or her land may have consequences farther afield. Ownership of a factory that produces toxic chemicals does not carry with it the right to dump these poisons into a nearby stream. Given that such materials might kill innocent people hundreds of miles away—people with no knowledge of how these got into their drinking water—it is up to a larger entity—the government—to protect their interests. The same goes for less dangerous hazards—such as noise pollution. A disinterested authority must create, and enforce, rules against these communal threats. Because they are social, not individual problems, they require social solutions.

Even the marketplace requires government interventions in order to function effectively. Merely guaranteeing property rights is not enough. People lie and cheat. They tell naïve customers a product cures warts when it does not. They promise an elderly couple to repair their roof, then abscond with their money. Not only do sellers engage in false advertising, but their products can be shoddy and/or timely deliveries can be withheld. Moreover, as Adam Smith recognized, whenever competitors get together, they conspire to set prices—if they can. Because business people hate risks, they seek monopolies. Prices are set higher than costs so as to ensure stable profits. Unregulated producers also grow lax in supplying high quality goods. This is why advanced industrial nations have enacted anti-trust legislation. They learned from bitter experience that large companies are especially likely to evade the competitive features of the market.

Nowadays, even libertarians concede the above limitations. They may wish to dismantle government, but they too realize there are restrictions on what is possible. This being so, few of those who believe that capitalism is doomed do so on the grounds that regulatory safeguards are completely absent. To the contrary, they assume that the contaminants devouring capitalism go deeper. They believe that the conditions upon which a market system is dependent inevitably create consequences that obviate these very conditions. Furthermore, because the foundations of the system are supposedly rotten, the higher the structure rises, the more prone it is to collapse. This is what its critics mean by asserting that capitalism is riddled with contradictions. This is why they believe no one can prevent its imminent downfall.

Daniel Bell, for instance, argued that the factors, which once allowed capitalism to accumulate wealth, are self-defeating. He began by agreeing with Max Weber that the Protestant Revolution launched capitalism. Because the Calvinist faith claimed that only a relative handful of people were destined to go to heaven, the faithful sought the means to determine which among them were the elect. If God favored you here on earth by showering you with wealth, this was presumably an indicator of future good fortune. As a consequence, people were motivated to pursue riches. The truly religious also believed that what happened in heaven was more important than what took place on earth. As a result, they were certain God did not want them to be wastrels. Singing, dancing, gambling, wearing fancy clothes, and living in opulent homes were therefore ruled out of bounds. They might grow rich, but they would also remain ascetic. Ironically, this produced further wealth. Because they did not waste their money on frivolities, it was available to be invested in increased production.

But, said Bell, herein lies the contradiction. Asceticism allowed the early capitalists to generate investment funds, but it also created scandalously vast hoards of riches. These, however, eventually corrupted the descendents of the founding generation. They were spoiled by the luxuries they could afford, which sapped them of the ambition to create additional wealth. Instead of investing what they earned, they bought huge mansions, plush yachts, and gas-guzzling jets. No longer innovators or even good stewards of their patrimony, they saw their fortunes decline. The whole creaky structure then stagnated as people became absorbed with having fun. A preference for partying, rather than perfecting their businesses, had foreseeable results.

The trouble is that, as with other liberal predictions, this one was not born out on the ground. The market system has not stagnated. Wealth continues to accumulate. Well-heeled people continue to invest in new products and improved techniques. In fact, new modes of investment are continuously being devised. One of the most prolific, if unexpected, has been the retirement funds of ordinary workers. These have been plowed into the stocks and bonds that keep large corporations solvent. Nor have workers or executives grown lazy. They may have more leisure to take Caribbean holidays, but they also bring their laptop computers along so they can keep up with what is going on at the office. A desire to get ahead, not merely to have a nice home, keeps them in the game. While they are no longer working to get to heaven, they energetically toil for promotions, respect, and the possibility of running their own companies. In other words, they are as competitive as ever.

But this is not the end of indictments against capitalism. Karl Marx was not as impressed as Bell or Weber by the religious underpinnings of the bourgeoisie. Instead, he was obsessed with the thought that business owners are greedy and power hungry. Not content with owning the factories they possess, they aim at amassing every scrap of profit they can. Their specialty, according to Marx, is exploitation. Basically parasites, they squeeze every crumb of effort they can from their workers, then hoard the excess earnings for themselves. For Marx, the old saw that the rich grow richer, while the poor grow poorer, is the essence of capitalist logic. Capitalists use whatever mechanism they can to keep their employees in chains. As a result, these wage slaves labor six days a week for subsistence incomes, while their bosses wallow shamelessly in luxury.

For Marx, the central contradiction of capitalism is its inequitable concentration of wealth. A desire for riches motivates bosses to produce more, but greed prevents them from sharing the benefits. This inevitably produces resentments. Sooner or later the workers realize they have been exploited and band together to overthrow their masters. What the bosses do not realize is that the more affluent they become, the more visible the disparities in possessions become as well. They, in this sense, lay the foundation for their own defeat. Moreover, the larger their corporations, the better-situated workers become to

108

develop cooperative enterprises. More aware of their shared suffering, they can better communicate their dissatisfactions and coordinate their insurrections. In this scenario is found the doom of the capitalist hegemony.

Only, as we have seen, it didn't. The bosses grew richer, but so did their employees. As Gerhard Lenski observed, once profits grew there was more than enough to share with the workers. Big houses and fancy yachts were all well and good, but there comes a point when luxury is redundant. Corporate leaders found that it made more sense to buy peace with good wages than hoard resources that made only marginal improvements in their own living conditions. Even so, the wealthy had enough of a surplus to invest in their businesses. This enabled them to make even more money, while creating employment for additional workers. On top of this, countless jobs became more technical. Strong backs were no longer enough to produce productive labor. A larger proportion of workers were engaged in using their heads. But to do so, they had to become better educated. This, however, required them to be motivated—and they were. Their salaries went up, as did the discretion they exercised. As a result, the concentration of wealth that Marx expected did not materialize. The contradiction at the heart of the capitalist system turned out not to be as grim as was assumed.

By the time of the Great Depression, a different contradiction was detected at the core of capitalism. This was the business cycle. For generations, the velocity of commercial activity had fluctuated. Sometimes business was up; sometimes it was down. The problem was that these gyrations became more severe with time. The Roaring Twenties were giddy in the expectation that everyone could grow rich, while the Dire Thirties burst this bubble. One quarter of the work force was laid off and feared that their jobs would never return. The only way things were going to get better was if the government intervened. Only it had the resources to prime the economic pump.

Critics of capitalism pointed to the paradox of entrepreneurial motivation. When times were good, business owners sought to make more money by expanding their enterprises. They turned out more goods and services in the hopes of selling them at a greater profit. This allowed them to hire more workers who then purchased more of their products. Unfortunately, the bosses always became too exuberant. In their greed, they flooded the market with more goods than it could absorb. This prompted them to lay off workers, who, deprived of a paycheck, could purchase less than previously. At this point, business contracted and kept going down until the excess goods were consumed, whereupon the capitalists began producing again—only to repeat the cycle of up, then down, then up again. The problem was that with productivity grown to unprecedented proportions, the ups and downs were larger than ever. This time the down was so low millions of people were in danger of starving. Something had to be done. The system had to be modified lest it veer off the tracks completely.

Many New Deal reformers were convinced that capitalism had expired of its own selfish impulses. A more socially conscious system would therefore need to be erected to replace it. What they did not appreciate was that their own policies were a major contributor to the disaster. They argued that government had to save society, whereas government, in fact, deepened and extended the economic decline. By raising taxes on investors and overregulating the marketplace, it prevented the business cycle from taking its usual upward turn. Only WWII got the engine started again. Then, likewise contrary to predictions, it kept going for more than half a century. There was no second Great Depression. Economists having learned more about monetary policy, the Federal Reserve was able to participate in keeping business on an even keel. It turned out that capitalism was not dead; it had merely experienced a severe hiccup. By the turn of the new millennium, Western nations, and Japan, Korea, and China, were enjoying a prosperity never before realized. More people than ever were living well and surviving longer.

In the meantime, one of the lessons learned was that a huge techno-commercial society couldn't rely on exclusively private means to protect the public well-being. The Progressive era, but also the New Deal, demonstrated that there were services the government was better situated to provide than more traditional sources. Ideological purists might object, but welfare programs turned out to be a necessity, as did Social Security, Medicare, and Medicaid. The government would soon be creating interstate highways, contributing to local school districts, and sending men to the moon. Public health programs, national parks, and environmental regulations all redounded to the common good. Yes, the government could be amazingly inefficient, but it also played a critical role in balancing competing interests. Social Darwinists were prepared to let the poor and disabled suffer, but a better-informed and more prosperous electorate was not. Capitalism might not be dead, or even terminally ill, but it needed to be supplemented by a compassionate federal government.

This did not mean, however, that liberals softened their attitude toward conservatives or business people. Those who resisted additional enhancements to government programs were castigated as relics of a more primitive era. They were not nice people. They did not believe in equality. They even resisted progress. The contradictions formerly thought to destabilize capitalism might not have arrived, but those who supported unfettered capitalism undermined the effectiveness of social engineering. They were dreadful people, with three primary faults. They were stupid. They lacked compassion. And they were greedy. So consumed were they by selfish desires, that they could not see what was in our common interest. They opposed the Liberal Dream, and therefore human happiness, because they were more concerned with their personal pleasures. They might not be able to concentrate as much wealth in their hands as their predecessors, but they were as shortsighted.

As liberals saw it, those to the right of them on the political spectrum did not believe in change. Basically insecure in their approach to life, they sought to keep things the same. An obsession with tradition enabled them to conserve predictability. It prevented surprises and protected them against the unknown. Liberals, on the other hand, celebrated change. They wanted measured progress to continue into the indefinite future. More confident in their abilities, they were prepared to adjust to novel developments. Less afraid of losing what they had, they were prepared to share it with others. This meant that liberals favored improvements, whereas conservatives favored the status quo. Liberals wanted to make things better, whereas conservatives wanted them to remain the same. This might not be a contradiction, but it did impede social advancements.

The difficulty with this interpretation is that it is untrue. Conservatives may be called "conservative," but that does not mean they oppose change. Those who respect tradition do not necessarily resist modifying it. Likewise, not all liberals favor change. Many obstinately defend ineffective government programs. The notion that conservatives hate change reveals a liberal myopia regarding their adversaries. Actually, this is too benign a judgment. Many liberals misperceive conservative beliefs, whereas others knowingly disseminate false impressions. The notion that conservatives loathe change is largely liberal propaganda. It is an effort to paint their enemies as hide-bound obstructionists who cannot be trusted to promote improvements.

The odd thing is that many conservatives support change more ardently than do liberals. After all, most business people are reckoned to be conservative. Actively opposed to government interference and attracted to making money, they are deemed staunch defenders of the status quo. Yet they are also entrepreneurs. They may believe in fiscal conservatism, but they love technological innovations. These advances are, in the end, moneymakers. They give those who adopt them an edge over the competition. But this should not be surprising. Don't businesses regularly boast of new and improved products? And aren't business people expected to be self-starters who adjust to changing conditions? The idea that executives, engineers, and entrepreneurs live in a static world is nonsense. They are usually thinking ahead trying to puzzle out the next opportunity.

Liberals, in contrast, frequently resist change. For the past several decades, unions have been declining in membership, but their defenders do not welcome this development. They want to reverse the trend. By the same token, some industries are laying off workers. As they embrace automation, they require fewer human hands to keep the wheels turning. This too is unwelcome. In this case, liberals want to force employers to retain as many employees as possible. Nor did liberals want to modify the welfare system, social security, or progressive education. Thus, when conservatives suggested privatizing some aspects of social security or offering parents vouchers to choose their own schools, they went ballistic. They especially hate encroachments on the environment. The ecology is supposed to remain pristine. Environmental purity may be a good thing, but paradoxically it is also a conservative idea.

In truth, much of the impulse to condemn "conservatism" has moralistic roots. Liberals consider themselves good people and therefore their opponents must be bad ones. Moreover, since bad people do bad things, the consequences of what they want must also be bad. If conservatives propose changes in social security, this can only be because they want to reverse history. In their hatred of workers, they hope to deprive them of the safeguards generations of progressives labored to create. Such misanthropy cannot be tolerated. They, and all they stand for, must be defeated. If this requires negative portrayals, they deserve no better. Bad people must be stopped. They need to be stripped of every vestige of reactionary power.

Liberal Contradictions

Few people, however, talk of liberal contradictions. These aren't supposed to exist. Capitalism is expected to implode because of its inherent defects, but not liberalism. To the contrary, it is theoretically the wave of the future. It is about progress and continual improvements. Yet liberalism is rife with inconsistencies. Much of what its supporters say about themselves is false. In their self-congratulatory moralism, they see themselves through rose-colored glasses. They are the good guys, ergo they are good people who believe doing good. Everyone knows liberals fight for a better world. If they make mistakes, these are honest mistakes. They are certainly not such as would undermine the Liberal Dream. This vision is beyond question and exempt from error.

Nevertheless, liberals are not the sorts of people they portray themselves to be. They are nowhere near as nice. Many, especially moderate liberals, are warm-hearted and well intentioned, but in their humanity, they too are flawed. Conservatives are condemned as stupid, insensitive, and greedy, whereas liberals are presumably the opposite. Yet they are not. They have feet of clay that undermine the foundations of their most cherished beliefs. Nevertheless, a majority of liberals are not bad people. They simply do not possess a monopoly on goodness.

Superior Intelligence. Liberals routinely tell us that they are among the best and brightest. They ask us to follow their lead because they understand what is needed. Themselves among the most painstakingly educated people ever, they have analyzed our situation and discovered how to improve it. The rest of us must either join them or step aside to let them get on with their work. This attitude has been prevalent for scores of decades. During the nineteenth century, it was common for revolutionaries to refer to themselves as the intelligentsia. They had brains, whereas members of the establishment were block-headed traditionalists. As they told it, conservative defenders of the status quo mindlessly persisted in doing what they had always done. It was their critics who devised novel social solutions. It was these innovators who had their clear-thinking heads in the game.

The bobos currently take enormous pride in their superior intellects. Having always done well in school, they consider themselves the rightful heirs of FDR's Brain Trust. From their perspective, conservatives are Bible-thumping yahoos who have never consulted another book—or intend to. These ignorant louts are the kissing cousins of the antievolutionary crowd depicted in *Inherit the Wind*. They sing about the "old time religion" being good enough for them, because they hate science and learning. Too thickheaded to contemplate things they do not know, they refuse to allow others to investigate the unforeseen. If they could, they would go back to living in caves, albeit caves with stained glass windows under which to zealously praise the Lord.

But bobos are different; they are filled with curiosity. Sophisticated and subtle, they read all sorts of books. More secular in their orientation, they are interested in the here and now. Thanks to this perspective, they expect to improve this world by understanding how it functions. As a result, while they were attending university, they paid attention. They listened to their professors and understood what they were saying. Moreover, once their intellects had been cultivated, they continued to apply them. They subscribed to news magazines and talked to friends about political developments. Added to this was the fact that they cared. Knowledge mattered to them, but so did doing the right thing. These factors combined to ensure that they ascertained the truth, whereas their adversaries never discovered anything new.

No doubt many liberals are smart. A large number of them are quick learners and broadly educated. But they are also the victims of hubris. Self-satisfied in their beliefs, they are not prepared to grant that others know things they may not. Several years ago a philosophy professor at Duke University opined that the reason there were very few conservative faculty members at elite institutions was that they are not smart enough. It did not occur to him that liberal professors exhibited a bias in their hiring practices. At about the same time, the economist Larry Summers made a parallel discovery. After serving in the Clinton administration, he was appointed president of Harvard University. Not long thereafter he delivered a speech during which he wondered if the reason women were less successful in some areas was because there were biological differences between the genders. Almost immediately a firestorm erupted amidst his faculty. Didn't he understand this was heresy? Didn't he realize there were no valid distinctions between men and women and that anyone who entertained this idea was a troglodyte? So outraged were the feminist professors that they insisted Summers be fired. This was not mere rhetoric. The agitation for his dismissal was so vociferous he was forced to resign.

But Summers was not an idiot. Nor were his observations irrational. Less ideologically hidebound scientists have found numerous biological differences between the genders. There are even differences

114

in how male and female brains are constructed. For instance, women tend to have a larger corpus callosum tying the two halves of the brain together as well as a larger number of neurons in the verbal area of the cerebrum. This, however, did not matter to academics who perceived themselves as at the top of their profession. They would be the arbiters of what was correct. They knew what they knew and it was up to others to tow the line. Summers had violated this obligation. As a result, he had to go. He, of course, landed on his feet, ultimately becoming Barack Obama's chief economic advisor. The point is that many of our nation's most celebrated academics are ideologues, not disinterested scholars. Moral commitments, not genuine understandings, underlie their pronouncements.

Liberals claim to be better read than nonliberals, but this too is misleading. They read, but are very selective in their readings. Their tendency is to consult books by people with whom they agree. Liberals do not study tomes by conservatives or neoconservatives. These are dismissed out of hand without being perused. Many liberals are fond of saying they subscribe to a marketplace of ideas. They declare that the best way to discover the truth is for advocates of differing beliefs to compete openly and freely. This is what they say. It is not what they do. Liberal professors do not invite nonliberals to speak on their campuses. Nor do they assign books by nonliberals to their classes. Academic journals are supposed to be juried by accomplished academics so as to publish the best submissions. But these juries, because they tend to be liberal, filter out articles with which they disagree. Even publishing houses, because their editors are generally liberal, decline to issue conservative works. They claim these are not up to their standards, or will not be moneymakers, but this is their biases talking. As a result, conservative faculty members keep their mouths shut. They hide their opinions lest these be used to deny them tenure or promotion.

This being the reality, it is no wonder that liberals make numerous mistakes. Having silenced dissenting voices, they smugly assume their interpretations are correct. Since the colleagues they respect tell them they are right, who are they to disagree? With respect to crime, it must be admitted, this is not completely the case. Because a fairly large proportion of criminal justice faculties are conservative, they have been receptive to ideas such as The Broken Window theory. It is outside of their departments that they experience rejection of their views. The conventional wisdom among journalists, for example, is still that poverty is the root cause of crime. Most continue to believe that raising the incomes of the lower classes will solve the problem. Even the success of conservative-inspired policing practices, such as those adopted by New York City under Rudy Giuliani, did not convince them otherwise. Liberals claim to be fair-minded empiricists, but when the facts contradict their hopes, they prefer to ignore them. Their humanity overrides their intellectual convictions, and they perceive what they wish to perceive. Just as Leon Festinger predicted, they avoid cognitive dissonance by closing their eyes to unwelcome evidence.

With respect to our understandings of how families operate, the contradiction between what liberals claim and how they operate is profound. One of the favorite courses taught by sociologists is Marriage and the Family. This subject fascinates college students because so many are in the process of contemplating their matrimonial futures. One might, therefore, suppose the assigned books would be pragmatic. They are usually not. As Norvel Glenn demonstrated, the majority of these works exhibit an antimarriage bias. They tend to favor what is now called "diversity." This amounts to promoting gay marriage and single parenthood. In the name of tolerance, nonstandard arrangements are celebrated, while traditional two-parent households are described as in decline. Furthermore, readers are encouraged to do what feels right, as long as it accords with feminist sentiments.

Most of the research about the value of solid two-parent families in producing sane and successful children is consequently underplayed. So is evidence that divorce and illegitimacy have a dreadful impact on the young. In contrast, the negative aspects of marriage, such as their potential for violence, are overstated. Marriage is often portrayed as inimical to the interests of women even though research shows they too benefit from being wed. Nor is evidence that women nowadays initiate violence more frequently than men or that the level of violence among homosexual couples is as great as among heterosexual ones mentioned. Because these figures go against the intended message, they remain unattended. The point of these books is said to be knowledge, but it is actually propaganda. The goal is to encourage the sorts of relationships to which liberals are committed. That this might increase both divorce and illegitimacy is irrelevant.

As to the effects of welfare programs on poverty, there is a similar lack of intellectual candor. Welfare is routinely asserted to be a "right." Exactly what this means is unclear, except that liberals want to expand welfare benefits. Utterly immaterial is the question of whether these programs help the poor. Thus, evidence of multigenerational families on the dole leaves them unmoved. Nor do they worry about whether welfare makes people dependent. When mental hospitals were at their height, evidence accumulated that long-term patients became institutionalized. They stopped thinking for themselves and depended upon others to tell them what to do. Something similar happens to welfare clients. They too lose their initiative. They become lethargic and disorganized. How this is supposed to improve their prospects is a mystery. Nevertheless, many liberals remain convinced that money *per se* will do the trick.

One of the embarrassing facts uncovered by investigators such as Christopher Jencks is that the poor are less poor than is usually thought. Most researchers calculate their wealth in terms of their official income. They do not bother to compute how much the poor actually spend. It turns out they expend almost twice as much as they presumably make. This is because they have other sources of income. Some engage in illegal activity; others, although officially unemployed, work under the table; still others receive money from their families and boyfriends. They then spend these funds imprudently. Instead of buying fresh vegetables, they purchase frozen pizzas. Instead of acquiring sensible shoes, they purchase fancy sneakers. How increasing the public dole will correct these defects is not clear. Yet asking this question is disallowed on the grounds that it "blames the victim." The poor are treated as defective children with no control over their lives or responsibility for their own well-being.

Nor does liberal accounting make a great deal of sense. When liberals calculate how much the poor earn, they do not include transfer payments. Incorporated into their estimates are only dollars acquired in the marketplace. That which comes from welfare, Medicare, Medicaid, or Food Stamps does not count. In other words, if welfare allowances were increased tenfold, the official income of the poor would remain unchanged. Nor do liberals consider these subsidies. Because they think in terms of rights, they do not ask where the dollars come from. That these are taken from others in the form of taxes and are therefore unavailable for spending elsewhere is deemed unimportant. That the purchases others might make would increase demand and generate additional employment is ignored. Liberals do not seem to realize that governments do not create wealth; they merely move it around.

Sad to say, liberals, despite their vaunted intellectual prowess, are often economic illiterates. They may read, but few seem to study

117

economics. As the province of their enemies, this subject is disregarded. Thus, they do not talk about subsidies, but about "investments." Genuine economic investments, however, are made with an eye to producing profits, while subsidies are not. Nor are liberals concerned with the profitability of large corporations. These are thought of as bloated monoliths that can afford anything they are required to pay. Some years ago, social work students in Rochester, New York, classroom were discussing how Kodak could best provide for its disabled workers. One of them suggested the company cover all of their expenses, as well as double their retirement benefits. When another student argued that this would bankrupt the company, the first responded this did not matter. The company should do what was right whether or not it remained solvent. It did not even matter if the company failed and was unable to fulfill its obligations to retired workers. What was fair was fair. Retired workers at General Motors seem to have harbored a similar attitude.

As for the homeless, their plight is also misunderstood. The liberal media tend to portray them as intact families forced to live in tents because unemployment has removed them from their homes. That most of the homeless are either chemically dependent or mentally ill does not make it into their stories. Facts about inadequate community mental health centers or the limited effectiveness of psychotropic medications are likewise felt less newsworthy than pictures of scruffy old ladies sprawled on heating grates. Meanwhile, statistics about three million homeless wandering around city streets are bandied about as if carved in stone. The census bureau found only three hundred thousand, then cautiously estimated that there were six hundred thousand, but the media preferred the inflated figures provided by advocates for the homeless. These made the problem sound more serious, whereas the lower numbers did not.

Nor have liberal intellectuals been scrupulous in reviewing problems in education. They have, it is true, recorded the fact that American achievement tests fall below those of other nations, including less developed ones. Nevertheless, they resist documenting the failure of progressive education. That middle-class children make better use of unfettered initiative than poor ones is rarely noted. As significantly, there is almost never a suggestion that more money has not improved educational outcomes. The usual analysis concludes that not enough has been spent. Classroom sizes have declined, but where is the observation that this has not raised reading or arithmetic scores?

Nor do liberals fret over the fact that the language police have eviscerated textbooks. Quite the reverse. They applaud history standards that downplay the role of George Washington, while celebrating that of Harriet Tubman. Tubman deserves mention, but the balance has gone seriously out of whack when she becomes the star. Thanks to political correctness, a desire to demonstrate that the United States is racist and sexist has overwhelmed old-fashioned efforts to explain the evolution of our democratic institutions. Educators, more concerned with mobilizing support for liberal causes, emphasize the viciousness of Joseph McCarthy, while leaving out the accomplishments of Thomas Alva Edison. Meanwhile, in literature, they prefer the fictitious sermonizing of Rigoberto Menchu about Guatemala's economic plight to the historical novels of James Fennimore Cooper or the period romances of Jane Austin. Similarly, Paul Ehrlich's failed environmental predictions are treated kindly, Alfred Kinsey's inaccurate sexual statistics are respectfully repeated, and Margaret Mead's South Seas fantasies are related as if they were gospel. Somehow the truth gets lost in the rush to promote social justice.

Turning now to peace, its ebbs and flows have been thoroughly distorted. Peace movements are extolled, while military achievements are disregarded. Teachers tell their students that war never has made a difference, but leave out the part where Mohammad's followers bought Islam to hundreds of millions at the point of a sword. They praise the United Nations, but disregard its failures or those of its predecessor—The League of Nations. Never mentioned is the Kellogg-Briand treaty of the 1920s and scarcely discussed is the Munich agreement of the 1930s. Nowadays liberal bumper stickers proclaim that while guns kill terrorists, only love can conquer terrorism. One wonders, if the drivers of these vehicles believe this would have been enough to deter Hitler. Do they really suppose that Hamas will stop launching rockets into Israel if only the Israelis convert their tanks into tractors? Niceness and love have their limitations. Is it, therefore, smart to pretend they do not?

Despite their intellectual pretensions, liberals have a nagging habit of disregarding embarrassing evidence. They say they love facts, then refuse to examine these dispassionately. Indeed, their proclivity for simplifying issues and ignoring dissenting voices is disconcerting. Like most people they focus on specifics that strengthen their case. This is not unusual. Nor is their self-congratulatory tone uncommon. Most people, especially when in power, exaggerate their own attributes.

Less acceptable is the extent to which the fiction of superior liberal intelligence is taken at face value. Liberal control of academe and the media has allowed this fabrication to stomp across the landscape in ten-league boots. That it is nonsense should have been revealed by the adulation accorded Barack Obama during his presidential campaign. Presumably levelheaded democrats fell all over themselves in praising his saint-like qualities. They did not merely listen to his speeches— they swooned over them. Few asked how he was going to lower the sea level by a foot. Fewer still thought it improbable he could furnish 95 percent of the population with a tax cut when only slightly more than half paid taxes. In spite of boasting of their critical thinking abilities, these were nowhere in evidence. In there place were a shallow populism and a fawning obsequiousness.

Greater Compassion. Liberals tell us that they care about others more than do their rivals. They are not only nice, they are completely loving individuals. Their goal is to make everyone happy. When they perceive someone in distress, their hearts go out and they are motivated to fight for justice. After all, don't liberal chests swell with kindness whenever they observe people in despair? And don't their eyes tear up when they encounter derelicts living on the street? This is why they can be trusted. This is why their prescriptions for human progress must be honored. Conservatives, in contrast, are hard-hearted. They don't care about justice. They are not concerned about the welfare of others.

But let me offer one small quibble. Research has shown that conservatives donate far more money to charity than do liberals. Liberals describe themselves as generous, but this tends to be with other people's incomes. They may believe in helping their fellow human beings, but they devote less time to volunteering their services on their behalf. In many ways, liberal compassion is more theoretical than actual. Liberals want to help everybody, but have difficulty in helping particular individuals. Liberal compassion is thus from a distance. It is mediated via government programs. Worse still, as often as not, liberals are unconcerned about whether their policies are effective. Their efforts are largely devoted to promoting political causes. It is these they hope will succeed. Once the revolution arrives, they are sure everything will work out just fine.

Liberals never seem to have heard that "the road to hell is paved with good intentions." Far from it; their hearts overflow with noble sentiments. The problem is that they are usually unconcerned with consequences. For them, it is good enough that they want to do good. Whether they achieve it is a matter of indifference. But wait! Does this make sense? If you want to help people, but in fact hurt them, are you really being nice? If your heart goes out when you see others in pain, but you inflict further pain, are you a genuinely loving person? Aren't genuinely nice people concerned with the outcome of their efforts? This would seem common sense, but is not part of the liberal lexicon.

When welfare roles rise, when families are torn asunder, when educational systems falter, liberals shrug. Instead of reevaluating their principles, they call for more of the same. Let us consider a small example of misplaced liberal kindness. Once, about a half a century ago, young girls who got pregnant before they married were treated as pariahs. They were shipped off to relatives in another state so their reputations would not be besmirched. Liberals shuddered at the meanness of this practice. Why, they asked, damage the life of a teenager just because she made a mistake? Worse still, why harm the future of her child by labeling it illegitimate? This was cruel and irrational. Wasn't it more sensible, and compassionate, to refrain from blame? Allow her to have the child. Indeed, help her support it. In the end, this will be better for everyone.

Only it wasn't. Liberals focused on the immediate situation. They did not look to the long-term consequences. They did not perceive that this change in attitude eventually caused more grief, for many more persons. The young girls relieved of guilt were temporarily better off. But were they happier if forced to drop out of school? Meanwhile, children relieved of the stigma of illegitimacy were momentarily better off. But were they going to have superbly successful lives if raised in poverty by a single mother? Worse still—far worse—was the explosion of illegitimacy that followed. Stigmatizing nonmarital births frightened young girls into being careful. This had the effect of keeping out-of-wedlock births within bounds. Ill-considered niceness, in contrast, multiplied the number of lives injured by casual sexuality. The choice between stigmatizing illegitimacy and accepting its reality had not been one between good and bad. It was a choice between two evils. The question was which of these was the lesser evil. Liberal smugness tilted society in the wrong direction without an acknowledgement that this had occurred.

On a great many issues, liberal compassion is not what it seems. Take the matter of being egalitarian. Liberals are fond of depicting themselves as kindly because they promote equality. As they tell it, their desire to share social benefits stems from a bottomless concern for the welfare of others. But wait. Many liberals are not equal. Just as in *Animal Farm*, they are more than equal. The bobos, in particular, live the good life. They may anguish about the disabilities under which others labor, but are not about to redistribute their own material goods. Paradoxically, their purported compassion elevates their status. As good people, they are morally superior. Their compassion may not help the weak, but it demonstrates their own moral fiber. Unspoken is the fact that moral superiority translates into social superiority. Morality is a potent source of interpersonal power. People who are regarded as better than the common ruck are treated with deference. They receive respect for their kindliness. As long as they can convince others they are nicer than most, they get to bask in social admiration. In other words, being acknowledged as more compassionate means that you are more than equal. You may be egalitarian, but then again maybe you are not.

Similar considerations apply to being more democratic. Democracy means rule by the people—all of the people. Nevertheless no large society can be a participatory democracy. Given that it is physically impossible for everyone to partake equally in making joint decisions, this task is ceded to duly elected representatives. These individuals therefore get to exercise more influence than do others. Liberals may subscribe to democracy, but this does not mean they intend to allow others to rule over them. Rather, they hope to use democratic institutions to make the decisions. Indeed, they are fond of promulgating rules others are expected to follow. In this, they can be quite dictatorial. Forget about the majority rules, with minority rights. When liberals are in charge, free speech is something that applies to them, not to their critics. When they are in control, political correctness prevails. Men lose their jobs because women are offended by sexist jokes. Whites are not promoted so that blacks can gain equality. Homosexuals march in favor of gay marriage, while Mormons lose their positions because they donated to the wrong cause.

Liberals say they are compassionate, but they do not demonstrate compassion toward those with whom they disagree. They pride themselves on being nice, but they can be vicious toward their opponents. Should they disagree with a public speaker who defends traditional ideas about marriage, they have no compunctions about shouting her down. They claim to be exercising their right to protest, while they simultaneously refuse others the right to be heard. Nor is their language tame. The N-word may be taboo when issuing from a lily-white mouth, but the M-F word is brazenly hurled at George W. Bush. It seems that niceness depends on the context. Conservatives, especially religious fundamentalists, are undeserving of respect or even decency. Retrograde opinions earn them the derision of their reputed betters. Concern for hurting their feelings is beside the point. They have no feelings worthy of respect.

Amazingly, the litany of areas in which liberals have failed to demonstrate compassion is quite long. Thus, they remained unaffected when two million Vietnamese were killed after the American military withdrew. They were also unruffled by Pol Pot's killing fields or the tribulations of the Boat People. Likewise, decades earlier when Stalin starved millions to death, they awarded a Pulitzer Prize to the reporter who wrote that this was a myth. Nor did they sympathize with the victims of Stalin's Show Trials. As counterrevolutionaries, these persons deserved their fate. Similarly, business people who defied Roosevelt's NRA deserved to be sent to jail. As to the workers who lost their jobs, this did not matter so much as the fact that Roosevelt tried to help them. Moving forward, liberals shouted Daniel Patrick Moynihan down when he sounded the alarm about the decline of the black family. Instead, they responded by extolling the virtues of serial monogamy. Nor did they warn that welfare was creating an unhealthy dependency among the poor. Jimmy Carter called welfare "a disgrace to the human race," but that was about all. Rather, it was the insincerities of Joseph McCarthy that liberals hated. Oddly, at the same time they were indifferent to the damage done by communist spies such as Alger Hiss. They were also indifferent to the damage done by precipitously banning DDT. That millions of African children died a painful death from malaria on the mistaken theory that this saved birds, was out of sight and therefore out of mind. Closer to home, they ignored the plight of the victims of crime in their rush to protect its perpetrators. As far as the police were concerned, they were less than human and therefore exempt from sympathy. Nor were the mentally ill regarded as fully human. Simply expelling them from the mental hospitals fulfilled the requirement for compassion. What happened afterwards did not count. More recently, the killing fields of Rwanda came into focus only after it was too late to save the victims. And as far as Iraq went, what mattered is that the Americans killed Iraqi civilians, not that Saddam Hussein murdered hundreds of thousands of them.

Indeed, liberals yawned as mass graves were dug up in the desert. Nor was there adulation for George W. Bush as he increased the funds sent to Africa to fight AIDS and malaria. Given that he was a bad person, anyone saved by his compassion could be ignored. To do otherwise suggested that someone other than a liberal cared about the suffering of the downtrodden.

Particularly revealing about the nature of liberal compassion is the story of Israel. When this state came into existence under the auspices of a 1948 United Nations mandate, most liberals rallied to its support. They marveled at the miracle of a tiny people able, by dint of their own efforts, to hold off aggression launched by tens of millions of Muslims. But when the Israelis defeated Arab armies decisively in two wars, the roles were reversed. Now the Palestinians became an object of sympathy. They became the underdogs. When they sent suicide bombers into Israel or lobbed rockets across the border, they were only defending themselves. But when the Israelis responded by sending in tanks, they were bullies. Didn't they understand that their response was disproportionate, that they must allow the Arabs to kill a respectable number of Jews in order to keep the balance of terror?

This switch exposes a crucial aspect of liberal compassion. It is reserved for the little guy. Whatever the misdeeds of the poor or the vanquished, they deserve support. To do less is not nice. Since these folks cannot protect themselves, good people must come to their rescue. The rich and powerful, in contrast, can take care of themselves. So can members of the middle class. They do not require compassion because they are not suffering. In other words, people are not treated equally. They are not all regarded as comparably human. Liberal compassion is thus skewed. It looks in some directions, but not others. It seeks credit for defending the defenseless, not people in general. Nonetheless, this goes counter to the Liberal Dream—which is supposed to serve everyone.

Less Greedy. Liberals also like to portray themselves as less greedy than conservatives. They may not be living in hovels—the bobos are certainly not, but neither do they organize their lives around the accumulation of material goods. Everyone knows capitalism is founded on greed. All thinking people realize that those at its helm are consumed with avarice. This, of course, is the engine that drives the expansion of market-based prosperity. It is the *reason d'etre* of the system. Liberals, however, are different. They are humanists. They are more concerned with promoting human needs than fabricating physical objects.

Liberals want to cultivate universal love, not build yachts or dress up in furs. They understand what is truly important and intend to further its expansion among the masses.

The trouble with this is that it does not accord with reality. Once it was taken for granted that the rich voted Republican, while the poor voted Democrat. The Democratic Party unquestionably pandered to the less well-off. At least since the New Deal, it has specialized in making promises to lower class voters. Nowadays, although this image has not changed, the facts on the ground have. The proportion of the electorate that votes for each party is nearly identical. Moreover, the wealthiest members of congress are no longer Republican. They are Democratic. Likewise the biggest contributors to national elections come from the left, not the right. Without the likes of benefactors such as the billionaire George Soros, organizations such as MoveOn. org would be out of business.

Nor are wealthy liberals shy about flaunting their assets. Thus, during the Obama inauguration an entire runway at Dulles International Airport was reserved for the arrival of their jets. Similarly, Al Gore, who made millions since his retirement from the vice presidency, continues to use his private jet, despite preaching against atmospheric pollution. He also draws about twenty times as much energy for his Tennessee home as the average American. This, however, is not regarded as hypocrisy. As he tells it, since he is buying carbon credits, he is energy neutral. Of course, most left-wing plutocrats are more discrete. They play with their toys out of the public limelight. Still, they are not shy about making the money. Money is apparently bad only when it is in the hands of capitalists. Warren Buffet, although one of the richest men in the United States, is exempt from criticism. Because he advocates increasing taxes on the wealthy, he is allowed to multiply his fortune as fast as he can.

But it is in the lifestyles of the bobos that we perceive the customary attitude of liberals toward wealth. They enjoy it, yet are vaguely embarrassed by it. While they happily accept millions in bonuses from their jobs, and seek the most lucrative investments for their savings, they pretend money does not matter. They would never think of purchasing a Cadillac, whereas buying a Humvee is acceptable. Because this over-built vehicle might be used to ride up Pike's Peak, it is an environmental investment. Similarly, a home at Newport, Rhode Island, would be gauche, but one in Vail, Colorado, is not. After all, a person can go skiing in Vail and skiing is good exercise. Likewise, building one's own tennis court, learning to fly a plane, or taking a whale watching vacation cost money, but they are not evidence of greed because they promote health and adventure. Greed, it seems, depends more on a person's political allegiances than his/her income.

More Moral. Liberals are particularly proud of their moral stature. After all, they are nice people who care about the welfare of others. Some years ago I had a conversation with the husband of a colleague that confirmed this. A self-proclaimed liberal, he knew I was not. This puzzled him. He did not understand how a decent human being could be insensitive to the needs of others. Liberals, he informed me, wished to make a better world, whereas conservatives did not. They only sought to hold on to what they had. How could I be on the side of people like that? When I told him I too wanted a better world, this came as a surprise. From his perspective, only the good guys, which is to say those on the left, were concerned with social improvements. Only they were moral.

What is remarkable about this attitude is that it is displayed by the very people who claim "everyone lies and everyone cheats." Liberals came to this conclusion in defense of Bill Clinton. He had obviously been caught in misrepresentations about his relationship with Monica Lewinsky. He had even lied to a Grand Jury. But these slipups did not matter. His lies concerned sex and everyone lies about sex. Further-more, cheating with regard to sex is normal. Most men do it. Certainly most presidents do it. This defamed dozens of chief executives, includ-ing George W. Bush, his father, Jimmy Carter, and Harry Truman. But not to worry; Clinton had to be defended. When I ask my liberal students if they lie and cheat, most are less brazen. They know that an affirmative answer would reflect badly on their integrity. Yet in the political sphere, anything goes. As long as an advocate can get away with something, it is not really wrong.

In fact, research shows that liberals are more likely to lie and cheat than are conservatives. Much-maligned religious conservatives are actually the least likely to engage in immoral behavior. Yet instead of earning respect, they are disparaged for their naiveté. Sophisticated people understand that bending the rules in favor of a good cause is socially justifiable. But the question is this: How does this make them more moral? They may not be worse, but why are they better? They might argue on their own behalf that their compassion makes the difference, yet compassion devoid of concern about consequences is hardly moral. The best explanation of liberal self-righteousness (which incidentally is similar to religious self-righteousness) is ethnocentrism. Most people consider themselves better than others. They are certain that their beliefs and actions are superior to outsiders. Liberals are no different.

Yet how sophisticated is this? Shouldn't people who tell us they are among the best and brightest be aware of their frailties? Shouldn't they realize that their moral superiority is in the eye of the beholder? If they are going to offer recommendations about how society is to be reformed, shouldn't they understand their place in the scheme of things?

The Liberal Attack Machine

Hillary Clinton famously defended her husband's honor by bewailing the attacks of a "vast right-wing conspiracy." Her husband had not done wrong. He was merely the victim of power hungry reactionaries who sought to topple him. Like those he devoted his life to protecting, he was a little guy being maligned by the big boys. He too was a "victim" of the system. Right-thinking people should therefore rally around him. They had to make certain he could continue his good work. What Hillary left out of her analysis was the "vast left-wing conspiracy." In her universe, *The New York Times*, *The Washington Post*, *The Los Angeles Times*, *Time* magazine, *Newsweek* magazine, CBS, NBC, ABC, MSNBC, and CNN never ganged up on right-wing politicians. The *NY Times* never published classified documents in order to embarrass its enemies, and *Time* magazine never featured Obama on its cover dozens of times. Nor had she and her husband ever done opposition research in the hopes of destroying the reputations of opponents. They would never hire private investigators to dig up dirt on their adversaries. Bill and Hillary were against sleaze. After all, hadn't Bill declared he was opposed to "the politics of personal destruction?"

The problem with this "who me?" defense is that it rings hollow. It reminds one of the old-time movies in which the hero kicks his opponent in the groin and then says "we'll have none of that." Kenneth Starr, the independent counsel who investigated Clinton's wrongdoings, found this out the hard way. Before he assumed this role, he had an impeccable reputation. Afterwards, he was widely regarded as a religious fanatic who indulged in neo-Nazi tactics. Even as normal an investigative technique as questioning Monica's mother was characterized as brutal. This occurred because once the stain on Lewinsky's dress was identified as belonging to Clinton, he decided that the best defense was a good offense. He would push others off balance before they could do the same to him. In this, he was on familiar ground. Clinton had earlier adopted a similar strategy. Thus, a series of women with whom he had sex, groped, or in one case purportedly raped, were vilified as liars. Clinton, however, was always portrayed as the innocent victim. Even when caught distributing pardons to felons in return for financial considerations, he was the one unfairly assailed. One reporter captured this attitude when she opined that she would gladly engage in fellatio with such a sexy president, especially one who had performed so many good deeds.

To hear liberals like Obama tell it, they believe in bipartisanship, whereas their opponents do not. What they apparently mean by this is that doing things their way is bipartisan, whereas doing it the Republican way is not. This would be terminally confusing to a disinterested observer were it not evidence of liberal desperation. The concentrated vituperation emanating from the left is the equivalent of the frantically flapping wings of a dying bird. It is indicative of death throes of a failed ideology, not of an assured ascendancy. To blame George W. Bush for all the nation's woes years after he left office is more than disingenuous. It signals a fear that the next election will not go as desired. Clearly despite his vaunted ability to work across party lines, Obama has been the most partisan president in living memory.

Ironically, the very energy with which liberal accusations are hurled reflects on their lack of confidence. The weakness of their case, not its strength, impels them to overstate it. Thus, Obama's economic policies not only worked, they saved the nation from a second Great Depression. Meanwhile, his energy policies were not only going to protect the atmosphere, they would create millions of good paying jobs that could not be exported. (But, shhhh—don't mention Solyndra.) This weakness also prompts them to lie, cheat, and steal. Thus, Obama's was going to be the most moral administration in American history. He, for instance, would not hire any lobbyists for his team or condone earmarks—except that he did. Nor would his cronies benefit from special treatment—except when he funneled money and contracts their way. And, of course, he would balance the budget—except for the fact that he never submitted one that reduced spending by a single cent.

Liberals are not stupid. They know that their promises have not been fulfilled. Nor are most liberals immoral. The majority of them genuinely want to do the right thing. Indeed, it is a disquieting awareness of their failures that drives them to deny their fiascos. It is an underlying desire to do good that impels them to protect unsuccessful policies by attacking their opponents. To this end, a whole series of liberal pundits gloated about the possibility of sending Karl Rove "frog-walking" his way to prison for the offence of leaking materials he never did leak. Some, like John Conyers, actually threatened presidential impeachment and, even after Bush left town, promised investigations that would lead to the imprisonment of his staff. Like the president they so admired, these nonpartisan partisans believed the best defense is a good offense. They, who declare that they abhor enemies lists, want to make sure that their enemies pay. When in power, they, like Nixon, use the IRS to do their dirty work. But when they get caught in irregularities these are described as forgivable oversights—such as those of Tom Daschle in not paying over a hundred thousand dollars in taxes.

One of the ways liberals fight back against conservative critiques is by increasing the number of promises they make. Clinton told the country that the era of big government was over, but with the rise of Barack Obama it returned with a vengeance. According to Politico.com, Obama made no less than 510 distinct promises during his campaign. This was an incredible spectacle, one John McCain could not hope to match. Obama's campaign was a virtual promise machine. He knew—he must have known—that no one, not the most effective politician, is capable of accomplishing as much as he vowed. Obama himself signaled as much by later indicating that there was a difference between governing and campaigning. When a person ran for office, he said what he did to in order to garner votes. This was normal. It need not get a politician in trouble. As long as people believed in him, he would be okay. Only if he lost, would he have to apologize.

Some members of Obama's party were equally carried away by success. Although they denied being socialists, they perceived his victory as an opportunity to dramatically expand government programs. As Obama's chief of staff, Rahm Emanuel, put it, "a crisis is terrible thing to waste." Since the economy was going south, Democrats would revive it by spending trillions of dollars. This was described as a stimulus, but it included billions for pet projects to be spent in the out-years. The unemployment rate had only recently climbed to over 7 percent, but congress proceeded to act as if it was as critical as the Great Depression's 25 percent. This made it reasonable to go into as much debt as the government did during WWII. It also gave liberals a license to take over the nation's health-care system, increase the federal stake

129

in education, and boldly attack Global Warming by intruding further into the private sector. Some actually talked about the government taking over the banking system, while still others sought control of the automobile industry by specifying mileage standards or demanding managerial participation in return for bailout monies. At minimum, they would reinflate the unions by eliminating the secret ballot. In general, federal largesse would be distributed to as many Democratic constituencies as possible so as to maintain political control.

But overblown promises of the utopian future were not thought sufficient. The enemy had to be demonized. It did not matter if the accusations were true, as long as they seemed plausible. Hitler's propaganda minister Joseph Goebbels long ago demonstrated that repeating lies convinces most listeners they are accurate. One of the consequences of this was what Bernard Goldberg called the Bush Derangement Syndrome. The hatred of George W. Bush reached such extremes in some quarters that people spent more time bad-mouthing him than promoting their own issues. He was a stupid liar. He was the next Hitler. As the man who single-handedly engineered the Iraq War in order to obtain revenge for an attack on his father, he was determined to deprive Americans of their civil rights. He obviously used the excuse of a war on terror to amass as much power as he could.

Of course, in order to achieve this impression, a few distortions, if not outright deceptions, were necessary. Bush was accused of being a liar because after the American Army took over Iraq no weapons of mass destruction were found. Bush obviously invented these as an excuse for war. But this was nonsense. Bush believed they were there. He had been told as much by the CIA and almost every other intelligence agency in Europe and the mid-East. He had not lied. He had been mistaken because they were mistaken. Indeed, evidence emerged that Saddam was laying the groundwork to reestablish his nuclear and poison gas programs once the UN inspectors left. This, however, was not enough to vindicate Bush. He had evidently strong-armed the CIA into providing phony data. There was no proof of this, but he was Bush—so it must be so. The same was true of reports that Saddam sought to purchase yellowcake uranium in Africa. The British told Bush this occurred, and he said as much in congress, but when Joseph Wilson, the man sent to investigate the matter, changed his story and claimed this was not the case, the testimony of this single inexperienced individual was enough to convince the Bush-haters the president had been caught red-handed. Wilson was a liberal whose wife Valerie Plame engineered his appointment in order to achieve this result, but this was discounted. Bush was a liar. Indeed, he had to be a worse hypocrite than Clinton in order to balance the moral accounts.

Bush was also alleged to be stupid. His college grades might have been better than those of Al Gore or John Kerry, but he was a religious fanatic—hence dumb. He was also power hungry. Although he sought, and obtained, both congressional approval and funding for the Iraq War, this did not count. The liberals in congress were bamboozled. Bush might not have been misled, but they were. And all that wiretapping clearly transgressed civil rights. Not a single case of domestic eavesdropping was uncovered, but this didn't matter. Bush was Nixon reincarnated. He too spied on his political enemies. As for water-boarding members of al Qaeda at Guantanamo, the government claimed this policy thwarted further attacks on the United States, but this was self-serving. It was a rationalization for torture. Michael Moore even made hay by implying that Bush killed innocent children. Liberal audiences flocked to his movies, their eyes glowing with adulation, as they witnessed distortions piled one upon another. Served red meat, they consumed it with relish.

As for the media, its anti-Bush, pro-Obama, bias was breathtaking. Year upon year reporters badgered Bush to admit he had made mistakes. They promised all would be forgiven once he did, but this was disingenuous. Happy to pounce on his every mistake in pronunciation, they rarely admitted their own errors. No doubt, as liberals, they never made any. And make no mistake—they were liberal. Most claimed not to be. They argued that as professionals, they were even-handed, but this was laughable. Although 90 percent of Washington-based journalists voted Democratic, this was irrelevant. Left-wing reporters insisted that they kept their preferences out of their stories. Except that they did not. By the time Obama ran for president their cheerleading was so blatant few could deny it. Chris Matthews famously admitted that a thrill ran up his leg when he contemplated an Obama victory. And once Obama became president, embarrassing reportorial questions were as scarce as hen's teeth.

The reality was that, as card-carrying liberals, most reporters believe they know best. They are merely educating the public as to their interests. So partisan are they that they were not scandalized when Democratic operatives were discovered to have engaged in voter fraud. After reports came out of fraudulent registrations sponsored by ACORN, they accepted this as the price for ensuring minority representation. Eight years earlier, however, they had been outraged by erroneous reports that Bush stole the Florida vote. Weeks and months were spent investigating how conservatives achieved an ill-gotten victory. But once it was determined Bush would have prevailed even with a one-sided recount, they did not make an issue out of left-wing machinations. To the contrary, accusations that Bush cheated continued to surface and were treated with respect.

In this, reporters are much like other liberal interest groups. For years advocacy organizations have sought to promote their causes by any means necessary. Almost second nature has been the manipulation of statistics to elicit unwarranted alarms. Consider the homelessness agitation. As Joel Best has documented, the media routinely repeated a number disseminated by Mitch Snyder, a national spokesperson for the homeless. Snyder claimed there were three million; hence so did they. Fortunately, Snyder was an honest man, thus when a reporter asked where he got this figure, he answered candidly. He admitted he made it up. Journalists had badgered him for numbers, so he gave them one. Regrettably, other advocates have been less forthcoming. It took over a year for Naomi Wolf to admit that the 150,000 women she said were dying of anorexia were not. She had confused the total number of cases with the annual deaths. The latter number was approximately 150. This happens because liberal activists know low figures do not generate excitement. They claimed, for instance, that two million children are snatched annually from their families. The actual number of stranger abductions is less than five hundred, but this was not sufficiently shocking. It had to be supplemented by including runaways and children purloined during divorce disputes.

But when it comes to distorting the truth, few have been able to outdo President Obama. Hardly a day went by without a whopper issuing from his lips. Thus, he promised his administration would be transparent, but it specialized in sponsoring legislation no one read. He said his health-care program would be revenue neutral, while an honest accounting showed it increased the deficit by trillions. He vowed to keep lobbyists out of his administration, then hired them by the dozens. He told the nation that there was no more oil left to drill in the United States, but that was because his administration forbade drilling where there was. He insisted he would never raise taxes, then promoted programs that required the states to do so. He vowed to decrease the national debt, but then increased it by trillions. And when Republicans offered a plan to control spending, he remained silent as members of his party accused them of seeking to kill grandma. Even with respect to foreign policy, he lied. He maintained he would be a friend of Israel, but regularly left it to hang out to dry when Islamic countries objected to its policies.

This may be putting matters a bit strongly, but liberals frequently engage in con games. They stoop to egregious manipulations because they have made so many promises, for so long, that they are now being asked to produce results. As a consequence, they manufacture them. In a mass society where most people do not have access to all the facts, they can be hoodwinked. This is especially so if they want to be misled. Yet this is the situation among the true-believers. Their commitment to the Liberal Dream is so ironclad they cannot let go. The upshot is that they thrash about, attempting to disguise unpleasant truths. This, however, is a major reason liberalism is destined to perish. It has to. It is not possible to fool all of the people all of the time. Sooner or later the honest ones catch on. If nothing else, a new, less corrupt generation eventually comes on the scene. Its members, having a smaller investment in the old hypocrisies, have less difficulty relinquishing them.

A Front Row Seat

When I began writing this book, I asked my wife Linda to review the manuscript. She considers herself a liberal, so even though I warned her she might not like what I had written, when she returned the first chapter her face was screwed up in an expression of disbelief. "Do I know you?" she asked. "I thought you were a nice person. How could you be so mean to liberals?" The answer is that I have seen liberal hypocrisies up close and personal. Having myself been fooled many times, I am now predicting the death of liberalism partly in reaction to being deceived. Strange to say, I began my career as a socialist. I too was a true believer. I thought liberalism was the real deal, yet I was subsequently betrayed by what I learned over the course of five decades. The dreams I once shared turned to ashes as I dug into liberalism's dishonest foundations. Linda told me I sounded angry—and I guess I am. The answers I counted on to organize my life turned out to be lies. And these from people I assumed were "the best and the brightest."

In many ways I have had a front row seat in observing liberal failures. Because I took its promises seriously, like many of my contemporaries who became neoconservatives, I was deeply disappointed. My road to disillusionment began in high school. The Brooklyn, New York, into which I was born was uniformly liberal. In fact, I never met anyone in its Jewish community who was not. Most came by this conviction honestly. Their socialist ideologies were imported from Europe. Back in the old country, Jews were outcasts. Only recently released from the ghettos, they were politically handicapped and socially despised. Although many made money by obtaining secular educations, they continued to identify with the downtrodden. As they saw it, socialism was about making everyone equal. Once no one owned anything, no one would be better off than anyone else. Discrimination would then be impossible. In essence, everyone would belong to a single extended family.

My high school teachers, most of whom were Jewish, taught the honors classes where most of my fellow students were also Jewish. All of us, therefore, shared the same political allegiances. We called ourselves liberals, but were actually socialists. Of course, we couldn't say this out loud because the larger community would not understand. They thought socialism was the same as communism. Not as smart as we were, they did not make such fine distinctions. In any event, all of my teachers indoctrinated me in left leaning ideologies. They never suggested that other points of view merited consideration. Moreover, only liberals were intellectuals. Only they wrote books worth reading. If I wanted to do something of value, I would therefore dedicate my life to pursuing public administration. If I could invent new ways of delivering government services, this would be as great a boon to humanity as Edison's taming of electricity.

Not until I got to college, and associated with economics majors, did I learn about people like Edmund Burke, Friedrich Hayek, or Milton Friedman. Earlier they had not merely been dismissed, they were utterly invisible. My teachers assured me they believed in a marketplace of ideas, but it was a depleted market. This was my first hint that liberals might not be completely trustworthy. It was also my first indication that liberals were not as economically astute as they claimed. Having always boasted that their policies worked, it did not occur to me that their depiction of the business practices was self-serving. Nor did I realize that business people were not always a pack of ravening dogs.

Among my best friends as an undergraduate were Benjamin Klein and Walter Block. Both eventually became professional economists, one teaching at UCLA and the other at Loyola University of New Orleans. Indeed, after we graduated, we became roommates. For me this was one of the most intellectually stimulating periods of my life. The three of us would stay up, sometimes all night, arguing about ideas. Because both Ben and Walt had become conservatives, and I remained liberal, we fought about politics with gusto. At first, I considered their views treasonous. They were letting down our ancestors by going over to the enemy. Nevertheless, I had to admit that a lot of what they said made sense. A particular bone of contention was rent control. Rent control had existed in New York City since WWII. It was supposed to protect tenants from rent-gouging landlords and I was sure it did exactly this. My father hated our landlord, Mr. Hertzbach. The man was regarded as a vampire who needed to be resisted at all costs. Had not the government limited what he charged, he would surely have jacked up the rent to whatever the conditions would bear.

Ben and Walt contended that this was untrue, that the market determined what was feasible. But they went further. They claimed that by limiting rents, the law deprived landlords of the funds needed to maintain their properties. If this continued, these owners would be forced to abandon unprofitable buildings. I scoffed at this, but events proved me wrong. Years later when I worked for the welfare department, each day I trekked up to the Tremont Welfare Center. Whether I took the Third Avenue El, or on snowy days walked under it, I was required to pass through devastated areas of the South Bronx. Block after block of rubble stretched out as far as the eye could see. The neighborhoods looked just like pictures of bombed out German cities. The difference was that this devastation had been caused by rent control. As my friends predicted, the landlords abandoned buildings that cost more to salvage than they earned. Vandals then stripped them of everything of value. Next, the weather and drug addicts finished the job.

Working for welfare was a revelation on many levels. To begin with, as a caseworker I was obliged to enter the homes of poor people in places like Harlem, Bedford-Stuyvesant, and Brownsville. Most of their apartments were dismally kept. There was urine in the hallways and trash everywhere. But it was the people themselves who were the most depressing. Most of them had given up. They had become dependent upon a system they despised. Very few sought work—at least honest work. The teenage girls wanted to get pregnant so they could get welfare cases opened in their own names. The little boys emulated the pimps in the hope that some day they would be rich enough to afford velvet hats and pink Cadillac's. For the first time in my life I encountered families where all of the children had different fathers, some of whom they did not know. This was social disorganization in the raw. It could not be sugarcoated as "diversity."

The welfare authorities told us the department was there to help people, but the actions they sponsored belied this assertion. For instance, they were dishonest about the degree of welfare cheating. They insisted that no more than 2 percent of clients did so. Yet we caseworkers were skeptical. Every month we watched clients drive up in taxicabs to collect their checks, knowing full well that we could not afford to do so. Only years later did research indicate that almost half of our clients cheated. We also learned that the poor, in general, spent more than they supposedly received. Nevertheless, liberal idealism was rife back in the 1960s. Among the proposals for reform was an honor system. Instead of investigating to see if applicants were eligible for payments, we were to take their word for it. All they had to do was sign a piece of paper asserting they were destitute. The experts told us this would increase cheating from two to 5 percent, but that this was acceptable given that the system would save more on administrative costs.

Something we actually implemented were directives to distribute pamphlets that alerted the community to the fact that welfare was a right. This so increased the demand for services that welfare centers citywide were swamped. But the city fathers had a solution. Previously three clerks staffed the reception desks. Instead of being increased, however, this number was reduced. A bottleneck quickly ensued. The lines immediately stretched around the block. As a result, those not in acute need became discouraged and melted away. Another response to the war on poverty was loosening welfare standards. Mayor Lindsay told administrators that he did not want "long hot summers" punctuated by urban riots; he did not want unhappy citizens shouting, "burn baby burn!" One consequence of this was that I was told to authorize a check for several thousand dollars to replace the furniture of a woman who had summarily thrown out her perfectly good furnishings. When I ultimately switched from being a caseworker to employment counseling, I found that most clients never reported for job interviews. What was more, whatever their excuses, these were accepted. Never, in my experience, did anyone suffer a significant penalty.

At one point, the caseworkers decided to go on strike. They wanted larger salaries. I knew this, because I was part of the discussions. I also knew that our union leaders claimed the strike was intended to gain greater benefits for our clients. None of the employees I knew cared about this, but they agreed it was good propaganda. I, however, was young and idealistic. I worried that if we all went out on strike, there would be no one left to serve those in dire need. After much soul-searching, I therefore crossed the picket line. This was a frightening experience. The strikers were loud and vulgar. For my trouble, people I thought I knew cursed and spit upon me. They would not countenance a scab—for whatever reason.

During my twenties and well into my forties I went from one social service job to another. At the time, I considered this my duty. One of the places I worked was the Gold Star Mother Methadone Clinic. Heroin addicts were long considered among the lowest of the low. They were literally killing themselves in the streets. The situation was so horrific, someone had to care—and that was going to be me. If I showed that I was genuinely concerned, most of these hopeless souls would surely come around. Only they didn't. Deeply injured by life, in their defensiveness they struck out at others—often violently. Much to my surprise, I found myself in the middle of several knife fights. Far from being nice, my clients engaged in robberies, carried guns and razor blades, and committed murder. Many died, one sitting right in front of me. It was here that I learned niceness has its limits. It was here I discovered you sometimes had to stand up to people in order to persuade them to do the right thing. In one case, a client asked me to okay additional drugs so he could attend his grandmother's funeral in South Carolina. Unfortunately for him I had been counting and realized that this was his third grandmother. When I said no, he got toe to toe with me and demanded that I change my mind. Since he was about six foot two and I am only five six, he had the physical advantage. Nonetheless I did not back down. Ultimately, he turned and walked away, but then returned two hours later to apologize. This taught me that quiet strength can, in fact, earn respect.

My social service career, it must be said, was interrupted by a stint as a newspaper reporter. I was hired by the *Hudson Dispatch* in northern New Jersey. One of my assignments was to cover organizing sessions sponsored by the war on poverty. These were supposed to mobilize poor people to fight for their rights. Nevertheless, that is not how things went down. Usually very well attended, these meetings typically degenerated into free-for-alls. People who were not accustomed to exercising power attempted to out-shout each other. As a result, no one could be heard. In the end, middle-class do-gooders such as myself, and later that more famous community organizer, Barack Obama, controlled these programs. The poor were simply too disorganized.

I also learned something about reporters from my stint at the paper. A fellow student, who had herself been a reporter, a few years earlier warned me that reporters were neurotic. I, however, dismissed this as sour grapes. Yet she was right. The folks that I worked with were not nearly as well informed or levelheaded as I imagined. Indeed, some of our newsroom discussions were peculiar. They featured the kind of BS I had formerly experienced during drinking sessions with friends. The difference was that these uninformed speculations often made it into the paper, which gave them an air of authority. Much to my surprise, being a reporter turned out to be a passive activity. Outsiders assume reporters are active because they provide accounts of others doing exciting things. They, in reality, are spectators. More wannabes than doers, this tended to produce an impractical streak. I also learned that many politicians were not what they seemed. Thus, when I interviewed Senator Harrison Williams, who was at the time running for reelection in New Jersey, I discovered he was a florid alcoholic. This, however, did not make it into my story.

Returning to graduate school in my thirties was another exercise in idealism, but it was also a corrective to unrestrained romanticism. The sociology department of the Graduate Center of the City University of New York was a hotbed of neo-Marxism and feminism. At least one third of the students were self-described Marxists. But this was not how the discipline characterized them. They were called "conflict theorists." Just as in high school, all those concerned understood that a Marxist designation was not socially palatable. Meanwhile, I got to participate in a massive study of prison rehabilitation programs. This determined that the percentage of recidivism was about the same whether criminals were exposed to treatment or not. While a variety of interventions seemed to work during their try-out phase, they were less effective when generalized. Once those committed to making them work departed the scene, routinization sapped them of their corrective properties. I likewise got to conduct an observational study at an elementary school on the Upper West Side of Manhattan. For the better part of a year I sat in on open classrooms. These revealed that children of different social class backgrounds did not benefit equally from the project method of learning. Upper middle-class kids, whose parents taught them self-direction, did much better. They were able to organize their own work, while the children of welfare parents could not.

Moving ahead after I had earned my PhD, I still had a dilemma. I was not sure what to do with my life, so I accepted a position working in a psychiatric hospital in Rochester, New York. One of my goals was to determine whether I was crazy. My father always told me I was, and I knew I was different from many people. Although my psychotherapist assured me I was sane, she was paid to be nice. Now I wanted to compare myself with the real thing. Working at a traditional psychiatric hospital would allow me to do this, as well as to help the oppressed. The good news was that I soon realized I was not mentally ill. I did not experience the delusions or hallucinations many of my clients did. I might be a little strange around the edges, but was firmly in touch with reality. The bad news was that schizophrenia was more intransigent than my idealized graduate school education indicated. Like many of my colleagues, I experienced "reality shock." I was ultimately forced to admit that I was going to do less good than I hoped. Perfection was not in the cards. Human malleability had its limits. More specifically, personal change was far more difficult than I assumed. Although having been in therapy should have convinced me of this, being able to examine the nature of "resocialization" from the outside made me aware of the reasons many people stay the same. Neither being nice, nor attempting to educate my clients, could substitute for the painful emotional experience of relinquishing dysfunctional social roles.

Nevertheless, my worst instance of disillusionment grew out of the process of deinstitutionalization. Looking around me, I could see that mental hospitals were the total institutions Erving Goffman described. They attempted to control every aspect of their patient's lives. I also became aware that long-term patients became institutionalized. The spark left their eyes and in the worst cases, they seemed robotic. Yet the hospital was not a snake pit. It could be dismal. It was surely regimented. Nor was the staff as expert as I hoped, while therapy was almost nonexistent. Still, abuse was rare. Not all of the attendants and social workers cared, but many did. The central problem was that mental illness, especially schizophrenia, was debilitating. Not even the highly touted psychotropic drugs then being employed actually returned patients to normality. The mentally ill could cope better with medication than without, yet not well enough to sustain themselves on their own.

Nonetheless, deinstitutionalization was grounded on the premise that drugs and therapy would allow former patients to participate fully in society. They would no longer need to be hospitalized and could be set free. This, however, was wildly optimistic. The psychologists and social workers delegated to create discharge plans frequently found that there was no good place to send the seriously impaired. Often their families were as crazy as they were, while most of the group homes were full and the boarding houses were zoos. Patients sent to the available referrals generally returned to the hospital in worse shape than when they left. This created caution in framing discharges, which, in turn, slowed down the release process. As a result, the hospital population was not being reduced as quickly as planned.

Soon the officials in Albany were expressing dismay. They wanted half the patients in our thousand-bed plus facility to be released by a date certain. The hospital administrators were consequently warned they would lose their jobs if they did not comply. As a result, the staff began authorizing discharge plans everyone understood to be impractical. Within weeks, I noticed a new phenomenon. The Rochester papers were suddenly reporting dozens of people living under the bridges over the Genesee River. This was attributed to homelessness—that is, to a lack of adequate housing. The connection to deinstitutionalization was nowhere in sight. Nor were the politicians and administrators responsible for this debacle prepared to admit there was one. After all, they were doing good. They were freeing people from oppression. Why would they acknowledge that their humanitarian endeavors backfired? This might cast doubt on their intentions, not to mention their ability to control events.

Although I was stationed at the psychiatric hospital, I was officially employed by the Office of Vocational Rehabilitation. Yet this organization also had its problems. One was an instance of theft perpetrated by a counselor. He created dummy clients, then channeled funds into his own bank account. The solution had been to create an additional level of management. This was supposed to provide oversight, but it merely established another level at which dishonesty could occur. No one admitted this, because the senior administrators loved the idea. It improved their opportunities for promotion. Whatever the pamphlets they created claimed about the mission of the agency, their personal agendas centered around feathering their own nests. They were empire builders. The larger the agency grew, the more prestige they garnered. Similarly, the greater the funds they could expend, the greater their power. These were the issues that mattered.

The central importance of large budgets was also revealed on other occasions. During one economic downturn, for example, our administrators claimed they would have to cut the services most in demand. But they were essentially "gaming the system." The point was to manipulate their bosses by threatening disaster. During another downturn, counselors were merely asked to limit the funds spent on client services. We were to engage in triage, setting strict priorities on what clients received. In fact, we did this so effectively that within months our administrators were back with a different message. It now seemed we had a surplus. Accordingly, the goal changed. At this point, we were asked to spend everything the agency had been allocated before the end of the fiscal year. If we did not, we would be apportioned less money next year. The question was not what worked best for our clients. The real concern was how we could maintain the size of our organization. The bottom line—the real bottom line—was power, not altruism.

As for using my PhD to improve government services—that was not desired. My high school teachers thought devising innovative practices a good idea, but my bosses and colleagues did not. Their watchword was CYA (cover your ass). Most resented my education. It made them feel inferior. When I published my first book, this only made things worse. No one came to me to ask about the methods I was developing. It was almost as if they did not exist. Indeed, my immediate boss told me to stop doing what I was doing. When I asked why; he at first balked. But I was persistent. Was it because my techniques weren't working? At this, he decided to answer truthfully. He said my methods might be succeeding, but he couldn't tell. He insisted that I stop because he did not understand them. Nonetheless, he never expressed the slightest interest in my explaining my innovations.

As might be expected, this encouraged me to move on. Someone somewhere must be interested in my findings. Now I pursued an academic career. This would provide a platform for disseminating my discoveries. I subsequently began teaching at Kennesaw State University, then a commuter institution in suburban Atlanta. As a relatively new regional college, it was growing rapidly. Soon, I found a comfortable niche in which to pursue my studies. The trouble was that I was out of sync with many academic customs. However competent my teachings and writings, they were not always politically correct. As I discovered, most contemporary universities do not encourage intellectual diversity. They claim to be advancing knowledge, but liberals dominate them both administratively and academically. Dissenting ideas are sometimes tolerated, but they are never promoted. My own discipline of sociology is among the worst offenders. It is notoriously narrow-minded. Since its ratio of liberals to conservatives is thirty-to-one, only one side tends to be heard. While most sociologists insist that sociology and socialism are distinct, many openly argue that the discipline is inherently collectivist. Because it focuses on social factors, it inevitably militates toward group-based solutions.

As a New York Jew by origin, most strangers assume I too must be liberal. Unfamiliar sociologists likewise make this assumption, therefore, many are candid in expressing their biases. On literally thousands of occasions I have been treated to vulgar put-downs of people and positions I admire. By the same token, when I open my mouth, I am usually the only conservative voice in the room. At moments like this, I discover that liberal tolerance does not extend to me and my ilk. We tend to be excluded from panels, journals, and books. Our opinions are not refuted; they are merely left out. Thus, one nationally known author confided to me that his publisher forced him to make his social problems text more liberal on the grounds that only this would sell. Other colleagues have secretly told me they sympathized with my views, but could not say so in public. They remained in the closet, because they feared doing otherwise would ruin their careers. Indeed, one nationally known sociologist wrote me that although he admired my book on race and morality, it was not a "good career move." It would make more enemies than friends. Much of my subsequent e-mail demonstrated exactly this.

Liberals say they do not believe in censorship, but academic liberals clearly do. Thus, the president of an organization to which I belonged, and for which I organized several national conferences, refused to let the editor of its newsletter publish a piece by me. Since he disagreed with my thesis, he was going to write a counterpiece, but then he decided to excise my contribution completely. Similarly, on my own campus, although I was the only faculty member to have published a book on race, I was never invited to participate in campus-wide events dealing with the subject. Although I volunteered to do so and was told that I would be asked to participate, I never was. With respect to outside speakers, such as Charles Murray, they were invited only when a counterbalancing liberal voice was also asked to speak. In Murray's case this was the Harvard physiatrist Alvin Pouissant.

Sociologists, in particular, claim to be social scientists, but this is misleading. A significant proportion of them are more moralists than scientists. In fact, most of those who enter the discipline are intent on reforming the world along lines to which they already subscribe. They are " social movement" people. Some years ago I asked dozens of my colleagues what our discipline had added to the store of social knowledge over the last twenty-five years. The most common answer was that it improved our understanding of social movements. Moreover, they said this with pride. This, after all, is what they cared about. I am always surprised by how many of my peers are more interested in improving the human condition than in investigating how our social world works. Since they believe they already understand what needs to be done, they are eager to set about doing it. Only this attitude makes them feel like good people.

5

Ties that Bind

Stranger Anxiety

It is a cliché for good reason. Fish are said not to notice the water in which they swim. Since they are always surrounded by this medium, they apparently take it for granted. From their perspective, it does not require an explanation. It is simply part of their world. Something similar applies to human beings. We, however, do not swim in water. We swim in a sea of humanity. Everywhere we look, there are other human beings. There are many thousands of them, and in the United States over three hundred million of them. This is normal. It is the way things are—the way they have always been. As far as we are concerned, this is how they will always be. For us, people are a part of our natural world; hence this does not require elucidation.

Modern Americans encounter other human beings whenever they step out their front doors. Our fellow citizens are ubiquitous. We ride alongside them on superhighways, shop next to them on supermarket aisles, and take vacations to Cancun in their company. Whether at home, work, or the movies, there they are. But more than this, most of them are strangers. A huge majority of those we encounter are unknown to us. We have never previously met or been introduced. Nevertheless, we greet them, speak to them, and shake their hands. We do not run from them in fear—except perhaps on a dark night in an inner city neighborhood. More usually, we assume they are safe and trustworthy.

As importantly, we depend on these strangers. They provide us with food, shelter, and clothing. They also protect us from dangers—both foreign and domestic. Although they may not care about us personally, they furnish the innumerable services that enable us to survive. Some live on farms thousands of miles away, others drive trucks along highways we never traverse, and still others work the night shift in factories we never enter. Yet we trust them. Some crazies have been known to conceal poison in over the counter medications, but they are the exception. Others engage in drive-by shootings, but they too are a tiny minority. In any event, most of the time we do not worry about these possibilities. To the contrary, we expect other people to do their jobs and to do them well. Furthermore, we assume they will continue to report for work and will perform their tasks with diligence. We surely do not expect a knife in the back as we walk past them on a crowded street.

Another contemporary cliché, albeit not as valid as the fish in water truism, warns that life is dangerous. Journalists, for instance, tell us that, "if it bleeds, it leads." Stories about violence make the front page because people are transfixed by blood and gore. If someone has been killed, they want to know about it in all its gruesome details. Indeed, sometimes violence seems to be everywhere. The body count keeps piling up. But once more this is misleading. Stranger on stranger violence occurs, but homicide is not the norm. Nor are premeditated assaults. In fact, the level of violence is now less than at most previous points in history. The butter knives we today use at our tables are evidence of this. Louis XIV of France decreed their rounded points. He was tired of his nobles stabbing one another at the dinner table. But who today has such a concern? Who fears that going to a restaurant will invite an attack with a steak knife?

For some reason, we imagine that at the dawn of time people were more temperate than now. Rousseau even speculated that our remote ancestors were "noble savages." In his view, they lived in harmony with one another, as well as with nature. This, however, was pure fantasy. Based on the behavior of contemporary hunter-gatherers, the homicide rate among them must have been greater than today. In many ways, life then was similar to how we imagine the Wild West. The movies and television have conditioned us to believe that cowboys routinely engaged in shoot-outs. They didn't, but when they did, this captured the public imagination. Among hunter-gatherers, the equivalent of shoot-outs were more common. Potential weapons were everywhere. After all, these were the tools of their trade. Hunters required spears and knives. Their wives likewise required cutting and scraping implements. These were thus close at hand should people get angry—as they often did. Jealousies and disagreements were as prevalent among them as us. But they had fewer protections against random aggression. Unlike the Wild West, there was no sheriff to keep the peace. Our remote ancestors were on their own. If they could not control their passions, they were in trouble. No wonder that rivalries over women and hunting rights frequently resulted in bloodshed.

The violence back then was even worse between competing communities. Because hunting bands were small and widely separated, the number of strangers personally known was limited. In addition, because hunting territories were jealously guarded, poachers were unwelcome. If a group allowed outsiders to hunt their lands, these others might take food out of the mouths of their own family and friends. Outsiders were therefore suspect. They were rarely received with joy and often murdered on sight. Consequently, people did not wander onto unfamiliar territories. They tended instead to stay close to home. As a result, their knowledge of others was restricted. They may have had relatives in nearby bands or boast a few distant trading partners, but that was about all. Theirs was a small world. It was far removed from the mass society we inhabit.

This introduces an interesting question. How did we go from where they were to where we are today? How, in the space of twelve thousand years, did we make the journey from small bands of intimates to teeming cities filled with strangers? This is not an academic matter. It is directly relevant to our day-to-day experience. Although our ancestors evolved to fit the world they knew, we must accommodate a very different one. While our genes are the same as theirs, we have to cope with vast numbers of unknown others. How do we do this? How is this accomplished without our becoming terrified?

Thanks to John Bowlby, we today know that children have a fear of strangers built into their genes. From about the age of seven months to three years, they are uncomfortable when exposed to people they do not know. At such moments, they cling to their parents for protection. Mothers and fathers frequently become impatient with this lack of manners, nevertheless it persists. We, however, should not be surprised. Adults too experience anxiety when confronted with unknown others. People who dress differently, speak differently, or pray differently leave us uneasy. Indeed, if we do not understand what they are saying, they appear less than human. Since we are unable to decipher their motives, we suspect the worst. As a consequence, we revert to ethnocentrism, not only assuming that the way we do things is better, but that their ways are worse. Who knows, they might be plotting to kill us. In the United States we applaud diversity, but the political scientist Robert Putnam has indicated this multiplicity increases distrust. Most people, even in a diverse society, are wary of those they do not understand.

According to the Bible, God prevented the completion of the Tower of Babel by generating linguistic confusion. By decreeing that the workers speak in different tongues, He ensured that they were unable to coordinate their activities. Worse still, they became frightened by their differences and scattered to the ends of the earth. How then is it possible for us to live and work together? Given that so many different cultures, religions, and races gather together in modern nation-states, how do we live in productive harmony? We know it can be done, because we do it daily. Nevertheless, what are the mechanisms that make this possible? What prevents us from running away?

Indeed, our difficulty with strangers is not uniquely human. It also occurs among chimpanzees. These, or closest biological relatives, subsist in small jungle bands. This is not news. What is rarely noticed, however, is that there are no chimpanzee cities or nation-states. In fact, chimpanzees wander around restricted territories much as our hunter-gatherer ancestors formerly did. At about fifty-to-sixty members, their groups are smaller than those of our forebears, but they are even more hostile toward their neighbors. Once the conventional wisdom held that only human beings went to war, but today we know that chimpanzees do as well. When their territories are encroached upon, they organize hunting parties to murder their rivals. They do not sit down to parley with their enemies or agree to create a larger political entity. Instead, they stealthily sneak out to beat them to death.

We human beings, in contrast, have mechanisms for integrating larger assemblages. In recent times, folk migrations allowed millions of strangers to gather into single political units. The United States is such a nation. It is composed of immigrants from every corner of the globe. Although these émigrés began suspicious of one another, most overcame their doubts. At first merely accommodating each other, a majority eventually assimilated into a shared civilization. More than this, nowadays many have biologically amalgamated. They entered marriages with partners whose ancestors had no contact with their own and then produced offspring unsure of their ethnic heritage. In the end, many simply refer to themselves as American. They have no clue as to the efforts their predecessors put into overcoming their differences, nor of the creativity required to forge a common culture. For them, getting along seems natural.

Most of us take this camaraderie for granted. We believe in tolerance. We take pride in the breadth of contributions that made the United States what it is. We have been described as a "universal nation" in the sense that our culture includes elements from around the world. Whether eating a slice of pizza, chomping on a bagel, or consuming Chinese take-out, we consider these diverse cuisines part of our heritage. That Santa Claus was purloined from the Dutch and the Christmas tree from the Germans is considered irreverent. Even non-Christians enjoy Christmas. We, as a nation, are a potpourri and glad of it. From our perspective, diversity makes us richer and more cosmopolitan.

But how did this happen? And what makes it possible? What enabled us to overcome our normal human anxieties regarding strangers? This is an important question. More than this, it is a vital question. If we are going to understand what is possible in our future, we must begin by understanding what permitted us to get to where we are. The mechanisms that enabled us to knit contrasting legacies together hold the key to how we can deal with the conflicts that lay ahead. Liberals tell us they want us to be kind to one another. They also ask us to treat each other as equals. They even denounce property ownership. But can we achieve these things? Will the means that permit us to live together allow us to accomplish these ends? Perhaps there are limits to togetherness. Perhaps the instrumentalities that allow us to overcome stranger anxieties constrain the ways we can work together. If so, this is crucial information. It may dictate our futures in a way the Liberal Dream cannot.

That we made the transition from small to large societies is something of a miracle. That we take it for granted makes it no less so. No other large animal has ever made this journey. Some social insects have, but the mechanisms ants and bees adopted clearly differ from our own. To repeat, if we are to understand ourselves, we must understand this difference. It is what makes human societies special, but also what limits our options.

Social Limitations

Liberals are fond of telling us that we can be whatever we choose. We are alleged to represent the ultimate in biological flexibility. Other species have little choice in how to live, but not us. Humming birds are condemned to flit from flower to flower sipping nectar, while tigers are forced to wander through jungles stalking game. We, however, are different. We are born blank slates. How we live is up to us. The ways in which we are raised, and the choices we make, decide what we become. The briefest review of the thousands of cultures inhabiting our globe confirms this proposition. The foods people eat, the clothes they wear, and the governments they create are so diverse as to reveal a startling plasticity. Our big brains and unmatched manual dexterity allowed this wealth of opportunities. It is thus up to us to take advantage of this gift. Such limits as we have are imposed strictly by a lack of imagination—that is, according to the liberals.

Thomas Sowell has described this liberal attitude as the *unconstrained vision* of humanity. Liberals themselves sometimes sum it up by asserting that "if you can dream it, you can do it." Because the sky is allegedly the limit, the Liberal Dream is unquestionably feasible. Thus whatever conservatives say, we can be equal if we so decide. We can likewise share our love with every other human being if we so choose. There is no need for war or conflicts over material objects. If we use our heads and decide to be moral, we can overcome our petty differences. What is more, this is the decent thing to do. In fact, it is the only rational thing to do. It is up to us to dissolve the borders separating nations, races, genders, classes, and religions from one another. We can do it. We merely have to make the effort.

The *constrained vision* of humanity, the one Sowell associates with conservatives, is not as sanguine. It declares that there are limits to human plasticity. According to most conservatives, people cannot be whatever they imagine. Both their personal shortcomings and a variety of social constraints narrow their options. Moreover, because we are not completely rational, we can never be sure what is best. Nor can we ever fully resolve conflicting interests. Just as people cannot fly unaided, we can never be completely equal or universally loving. Limited perspectives, exorbitant passions, and inescapable selfishness prevent this. While people are capable of love, no one is capable of infinite love. Nor is anyone so brilliant that he or she always has the right answers. People make mistakes; they are shortsighted, and sometimes mean. These limitations need to be considered, and their negative impacts controlled, in any realistic human society.

Liberals are more optimistic. They believe in human perfectibility. While they admit people are not currently perfect, they assume that they are capable of being much better. While they are aware that their contemporaries squabble with each other, liberals have a solution. They assure us that some people are more advanced than others. These special individuals are smarter and more moral than the mass of humankind. They are also nicer, more rational, and more loving. As a result, they have a responsibility for the welfare of others. Essentially philosopher kings in embryo, it is their duty to teach others to be better. Once these lesser mortals realize it is in their interest to support that which is beneficial for all, their selfishness will melt away. Once this happens, people will become equal. Their conflicts will dissipate and love will become the norm. It is merely a matter of learning. This, however, is not a problem. Because we human beings can learn almost anything, we can learn this. Just as Rousseau and Marx predicted, it is merely a matter of raising children properly. Indeed, if people are forced to conduct themselves as they should, the proper ways of behaving will eventually become natural.

Nonliberals are not so sure. When they look at the history, they conclude that it supports a different conclusion. They are unaware of any time or place where complete rationality or universal niceness prevailed. Liberals retort that this might be so, but there was also a time when no one could fly in heavier-than-air machines. They insist that just because something never was does not mean it never can be. It is therefore time to try something new. Being hidebound and paying unwarranted respect to tradition is a formula for failure. Change needs to be embraced. Progress has to be celebrated. To this, conservatives reply that they too want change, but prudent change— change tested in reality. They allege that liberals are intoxicated with their own talents. They point to Socrates who, when described by the Delphic oracle as the wisest man alive, responded that if he were, it was because he knew how much he did not know. Those who hold the constrained vision of humanity suggest liberals could do with a little more modesty—that they ought to begin by acknowledging their own ignorance.

This conflict of visions is one of both values and beliefs. The parties differ in what they consider best, but also regarding how they think the world works. Liberals believe that they can calculate and control events well enough to secure the results they deem moral. If they are utilitarians, they assume that they can figure out what will bring the greatest happiness to the greatest number. If they are neo-Marxists, they are convinced that central planning will produce greater efficiencies than an unregulated marketplace. Liberals like to view themselves as social engineers. They hope to use their knowledge, logical abilities, and good intentions to design ways of life that work for everyone.

Neoconservatives, in contrast, do not believe anyone has the ability to calculate and control events to this degree. They maintain that crucial factors are always left out of these computations and that unintended side effects have a way of upsetting the best-laid plans of mice and men. While they too believe in planning, they also believe in the marketplace and tradition. They assume that the best answers emerge gradually through a give-and-take process to which millions of people now, and in the past, have contributed. Their favored model is economic negotiations. They point out that when it comes to what is produced, it is supply and demand, as mediated through prices, that decides. No supreme leader, no committee of the best and brightest, compares with the wisdom of millions of decision makers determining what is personally best for them. Although no one controls this process, and mistakes are made, the result is preferable to outcomes that are dictated by the hubris of self-designated intellectuals. For evidence, they cite the bungling of Soviet central planners.

What this translates into in political terms is that liberals, given their unconstrained vision, favor centralized institutions, whereas those with a constrained vision prefer decentralized ones. The irony here is that neoconservatives are usually more dedicated to democratic processes than liberals. Although liberals trumpet their democratic intentions—after all they want everyone to be equal—in practice they wish to dictate events from above. They insist, for instance, that experts in Washington, DC, are better able to decide how to spend the nation's wealth than are individual citizens. This, of course, is described in paternalistic terms as to everyone's benefit. Nevertheless the decision-making championed by liberals is not that made by ordinary people.

Meanwhile conservatives, though described by their rivals as oligarchic hegemonists, favor local governments and small business owners. They understand that while some government services are needed, they insist these should be limited. They also realize that centralized systems are good at coordinating complex activities and imposing uniformity, but they are nonetheless convinced that decentralized systems are more flexible and responsive. Because widely dispersed decision-makers are closer to where people live, these are believed superior at discerning what is required. This clash of perspectives is exemplified in the difference between local school boards, teachers, and parents deciding what students are taught, as opposed to federal authorities imposing identical lessons for everyone. In this sense, the constrained vision is more democratic.

Another of the ironies of liberalism is that its advocates are prepared to undermine the very laws they depend upon to impose their vision.

Western democracies have labored long and hard to develop a rule of law as opposed to one of men. Ancient empires were often at the mercy of the arbitrary decisions of autocratic rulers. Whatever the emperor desired was going to happen, did—by force if necessary. Only gradually did modern nations substitute standardized statutes for personal caprice. While it is true that written laws require interpretation by jurists before they can be applied, these judges are expected to follow the regulations as written. They are not supposed to substitute their personal judgments for those of the legislators. This way, everyone can be equal before the law. For this reason, people can know what is expected of them and not be blind-sided by the spontaneous impulses of their rulers.

Nowadays liberals tell us this rendering of the law is not quite right. They favor the notion that a constitution and the statutes flowing from it are living documents. These, we are told every time a Supreme Court justice comes up for confirmation, need to be updated to accord with developing conditions. Simply following the pronouncements of our ancestors would tie us to outmoded standards thereby introducing superfluous rigidities. What is needed instead are judges who exercise discretion. They must be moral agents willing to apply the law in a manner that achieves desirable results. Liberals insist that results must supersede processes. They argue that the latter can go wrong, whereas the former are more concrete. Thus, if a process does not lead to a moral consequence, they want the outcome to be adjusted. The trouble with this premise, at least according to conservatives, is that not everyone agrees as to what is best. Not all judges, left to their own devices, come to the identical conclusions. In contrast, following the appropriate processes is more apt to result in favorable results. These may not always get it right, but they have a better track record.

But not to worry. Liberals assure us that they do know what is best. Thus, they understand that laws against hate crimes must be applied to whites who injure blacks, but not the other way around. Because they are uniquely rational and moral, they understand what these regulations really mean. Unfortunately, we are required to take their word for this, which means that under their auspices the laws are what they say they are. In other words, liberals hope to reinstate a rule of men rather than laws, but only that of liberal men and women. This does not bother them because they are confident they will make the right decisions. Moreover, they believe that this is fair, because like Rousseau they are sure that they embody the General Will.

Nonetheless, this is not democratic. Nor is it safe. It is a path to despotism, to a world without checks and balances. When individuals personally decide what is best, should they go astray, they can go far astray. As Lord Acton sagely warned, "Power corrupts and absolute power corrupts absolutely."

But there is another profound irony in this. Many liberals tell us they believe in ethical relativism. They claim that moral rules are socially constructed; hence every society creates its own values. These are automatically valid for them because they define them. But liberals go even farther. They assume they can construct moral rules any way they desire. As the best and the brightest, they understand when traditional standards are obsolete and must be updated. They also understand how to update them. The rest of us are consequently asked to stand aside and allow them to make whatever modifications they deem necessary. The irony here is that if they were consistent relativists, they would acknowledge that when traditionalists are in charge, whatever they consider moral must be moral for them. It would then be up to the liberals to stand aside and allow their adversaries to do as they wished. This, of course, is not how liberals operate. They believe they are right. They also believe others should allow them to decide. If nonliberals differ, they are regarded as obstructionists, not collaborators. Accordingly, they are pushed aside so as not to derail the required alterations.

Meanwhile, the supposedly mean-spirited adversaries of the liberals are less confident. They look to the past for guidance, but they also encourage a panoply of voices in what amounts to a moral marketplace. They assume that human interests always conflict, and must therefore be controlled by a variety of balancing mechanisms. So far as they are concerned, it is a bad idea for any specific group to be in charge, not even themselves. They further assume that if ordinary people are allowed to advocate what they believe, this will produce compromises that, in general, serve the needs of all. Neoconservatives are often depicted as fascists, although their actual practices point in the opposite direction. They do not wish to be social engineers who dictate to others. To the contrary, they prefer processes in which all participate. In this, they tend to be less self-righteous than their liberal adversaries.

The bottom line is that there is a deep-seated moral difference between those holding the unconstrained and constrained visions of humanity. Whereas the former believe people are primarily good, the latter find them meaningfully bad. For the former, they are fundamentally unselfish, while the latter perceive them as frequently otherwise. Likewise, for the unconstrained theorists, people are rational, whereas for the constrained theorists they are not. Yet paradoxically it is the constrained thinkers who trust ordinary people more. They are willing to allow them to make a greater number of decisions, even though they recognize many will be mistaken. They are also more comfortable with selfishness. While they do not recommend egotism, they accept human imperfections. Convinced these are inevitable, they do not seek to remake the world along utopian lines. Satisfied with incremental improvements, they are the antithesis of revolutionaries.

The battle lines are clearly drawn. There are plainly differences between the two sides. Yet neither may have it quite right. Because both tend to moralize, they depend upon simplified conceptions of our human and social natures. This should not be astonishing because moralists have a way of abridging reality. The world upon which they build their recommendations is generally a mere shadow of the one we inhabit. Their visions not only leave out subtleties, but vital building blocks of human societies. This is inevitable, given the nature of morality. As we shall shortly see, the way moral rules are created and enforced guarantees they ignore bewildering complexities. This is especially true for liberals. As moral entrepreneurs dedicated to reorganizing our moral commitments, they emphasize sweeping generalizations. Although they claim to be intellectuals, they are not objective scientists. Not so much concerned with understanding how the world works as with modifying it, they are the opposite of neutral empiricists. Transfixed by an idealized dream, they employ it, rather than disinterested observations, to assemble their conceptions of the sorts of creature we are.

If we are going to understand why the Liberal Dream is beyond redemption, we must do better. We cannot take on faith that people are good and therefore capable of universal love and total equality. Nor can we assume that exceptional individuals possess insights and commitments denied others. Rousseau's noble savages existed only in his mind's eye. Marx's communist man resided only in his fertile imagination. But what of real people? Of what are they capable? Does their nature, or the ways their societies are put together, limit what is possible? If so, these constraints must be understood before theorizing about a better future. True intellectuals are careful observers of the human condition. If, as suggested above, there are unique mechanisms that allowed human beings to move from small to large-scale communities, these must be perceived for what they are. Moreover, if such mechanisms limit the ways in which people interact, these too must be understood. To ignore them in the name of niceness is a prescription for disaster. It guarantees that events will not live up to expectations.

If liberal idealism can be a trap, so to a lesser extent is the constrained vision. Liberalism tells us there are no limits—which is absurd—but many versions of conservatism do little better. They assure us there are limits, but are not specific as to what these are. Merely to describe human beings as selfish or incompletely rational may be correct, but it is a condensed version of human nature. It is less idealized than that of the liberals, but scarcely more precise. What is needed instead is a generous dose of what liberals claim to provide. Genuine science must be brought into play. If we are to safeguard our futures, we must use our intellects to investigate the ties that bind human societies together. Although value neutrality is difficult to achieve, we must pursue it. Instead of jumping feet first into the moral dispute between the constrained and unconstrained camps, we must stand back and put the human condition into better focus. This said, let us take our promised look at Social Domain Theory.

Social Domain Theory

If we are to discover what is socially possible, if we are to determine why and how we are constrained, we must first break free from the myths cobbled together in the fevered imaginations of thinkers such as Jean-Jacques Rousseau and Karl Marx. The contemporary versions of these fictions are not a realistic guide as to what the future is likely to hold. The actual social world that we inhabit is far more complicated than the one imagined by these philosophers. It too holds pitfalls, but they are not necessarily the ones of which the Liberal Dream warns. To the contrary, the political fairytales that liberal activists hold so dear divert us from the actual problems with which we must grapple. They divert us from exploring the actual constraints that limit our options.

It should be obvious. Human beings and human societies are enormously complex. It takes decades for the human brain to absorb enough of their details to function in an adult manner. Even so, honest adults recognize that they understand a tiny fraction of what might be understood. Many, especially nowadays, correctly think of themselves as superannuated children long after they are responsible for managing their own affairs. As a result, people often comfort themselves with edited versions of reality. They pretend to know what is going on when they are almost as clueless as they were in elementary school. To admit otherwise might make them look foolish.

Our need to reduce reality to bare bones is one of the basic aspects of human nature. As a college professor, I see this whenever I enter the classroom. If I am too abstract in the manner I convey a lesson, it goes straight over the heads of my students. Their eyes glaze over and their attention wanders elsewhere. If, on the other hand, I want to keep them interested, I tell stories. Students love stories. Indeed, everyone loves stories. Fortunately, I have lived a varied life and have a large stock of experiences upon which to draw. When I explain what it was like to work in a psychiatric hospital, they perk up. When I share the particulars of being caught in a knife fight or climbing the steps of a Harlem tenement, they pay attention. Moreover, they remember these accounts when test time comes around. This is the way we humans think. Anecdotes, myths, and just plain gossip form the frameworks around which the most intelligent of us build our understandings of the world. Abstractions are regarded with suspicion, whereas dramatic narratives are thought to provide a direct connection with reality.

The difficulty with stories, however, is their very concreteness. In their particularity, they cannot apply to all relevant cases. They mislead, not by being wrong, but by oversimplifying. We humans can apparently hold only so many elements in our minds at any given moment. As a result, we look in some directions, but not others. This would not be a problem, except for our concurrent tendency to discount that which is out of sight. The upshot is that many of the theories we employ are incomplete. It is not that we are incapable of understanding complexities, but rather that we choose not to. Seeking the complete picture is too difficult. It takes effort. All of those niggling exceptions feel inconsistent. They produce a mental overload not unlike Festinger's cognitive dissonance. As a consequence, we turn off our brains and cling to favored simplifications as if they were the whole story.

At this point, I must beg the reader's indulgence. I am about to introduce a host of technicalities. To begin with, we human beings are not infinitely plastic. We have a wide range of abilities, but these are not unlimited. There turn out to be a large but finite number of mechanisms through which we construct our social world. Although these allow a great deal of latitude, they permit some ways of life but not others. It is therefore essential to comprehend their extent. Individually, these mechanisms are not difficult to understand. The problem is keeping them all, and their copious interactions, in mind. As I say, life is complicated. Pretending otherwise does not improve the situation. Understanding what it takes to keep mass techno-commercial societies together may be laborious; nonetheless, it is worth the attempt.

Which brings us to Social Domain Theory. This conceptual perspective begins by distinguishing two super-domains. These are respectively the *cultural* and the *structural*. Every human society possesses both elements. Some social scientists emphasize one rather than the other, but the two are always present. Moreover, they always interact. A society's culture helps shape its structure, whereas its structure determines how its culture is transmitted. Culture, in its simplest form, can be defined as "a learned and shared way of life." It includes many aspects, such as language, social norms, and art, which determine how people behave. We human beings like to believe we spontaneously decide what to do, but this is not entirely true. Each day when we wake up we brush our teeth, take a shower, then put on our clothes. In none of these instances do we invent our conduct. The toothbrush in our hand is not an inspiration of the moment, nor is the idea that we should use it in conjunction with toothpaste. To the contrary, we learned these things from our parents. Moreover, our situation is not unique. Other parents convey similar lessons. They too belong to the culture in which we participate. This is what it means to say culture is learned and shared.

Social structures are a bit different. They are "persistent patterns of interpersonal behavior." Social structures are essentially the social networks in which we participate. They are composed of a variety of positions, which are occupied by a revolving cast of characters. A social role is an example of such a position. A "teacher," for instance, has structured relationships with "students." These individuals interact with each other according to patterns neither invented. The teacher is thus responsible for teaching and the students for learning. When they meet in the classroom, each knows what is expected. The parts they play, however, are not identical with the persons playing them. Another teacher might replace this one, while the students can be exchanged with other students. It is the relationship between the parties and not the individuals that constitutes the structure. As with cultures, structures are not invented by the people who occupy them. Nor need they disappear when these individuals move on. The

Atlanta Braves will still have a first baseman, even when the current one is traded. Structures persist. Thus, a teaching relationship does not exist at only a specific time and place. It recurs in ways that make it readily identifiable.

To simplify matters a bit further, cultures tell people how to conduct themselves, whereas structures tell them with whom to interact. Cultures give us particular ways of behaving, such as shaking hands, whereas structures direct us to shake hands with some persons, but not others. Within cultures there are a variety of subdomains. We have met some of these social orders already. In chapter 1, we were introduced to the normative, cognitive, symbolic, emotional, aesthetic, material, and ritual orders. We will shortly examine their specifics. In the meantime, suffice it to say that every society contains all of these elements. As for the structural sub-domains, these include personal relationships, social hierarchies, social exchange relationships, social roles, reconciliation communities, and spatial and environmental orders. These are also represented in every society. They too will shortly be discussed in greater detail.

The social domains and their various orders are abstractions, but they enable us to identify patterns of human conduct that might otherwise remain invisible. The language in which they are communicated may be unfamiliar, but their referents are the stuff of everyday life. Once we get down to particulars, these will seem less daunting. The reason for engaging in this unnatural exercise has to do with the ways the social domains operate in different sorts of societies. The manner in which they are expressed in small societies is not the same as in large ones. This is because the ties that bind small numbers of people together cannot be the same as those that bind large numbers. We will see that something called the "inverse force rule" determines what works and what does not. Its operation reveals why some ways of organizing mass societies are possible, whereas others are not. This, in turn, explains why the Liberal Dream is destined to remain unfulfilled. Social Domain Theory may appear to be needlessly conceptual, but its abstract qualities enable us to unravel social dynamics that have weighty implications.

The Cultural Domains

Let us go through the various cultural domains one by one. There is some overlap between them, but there are enough differences to make meaningful distinctions. In general, the clusters of mechanisms through which they operate distinguish the domains from one another. The territory is thus divided up according to the causal elements via which they function. There is, in this sense, an empirical basis to their classification. It is not arbitrary. Rather it is grounded in observations of how people behave, and more specifically of the learned and shared ways in which they conduct themselves.

The Normative Constraints. Children like to brag that America is a free country. In reality, no society is ever completely free. A thicket of rules that shape what we are allowed to do always hedge us in. Just try walking down Main Street in the buff. One of my psychiatric clients in Rochester did exactly this and was promptly hospitalized. In fact, we human beings live in a world brimming with norms and values. These tell us how to conduct ourselves and which goals to choose. In a sense, norms and values are like means and ends. They provide templates on how to operate in a world replete with so many options that we would be paralyzed if we had to choose entirely on our own. As importantly, they standardize our conduct such that it is predictable to those with whom we interact. If we continuously made arbitrary choices, our social world would be so chaotic that individual behaviors would inevitably collide. If I drove my car on the right side of the road, while you drove on the left, not only would we total our vehicles before the week was out, but we would never get anywhere because the gridlock would be so acute.

The predictability thus provided is so crucial that these patterns are rigorously enforced. Norms are not average behavior; they are socially sanctioned behavior. We are punished for violating these standards and rewarded for following them. This is a ubiquitous social phenomenon. It is evident in every society. Moreover, we do not require police officers to keep us from running stark naked in the streets. Our friends, neighbors, and even strangers do an effective a job in keeping us within bounds. A raised eyebrow, a smile of derision, or an angry rebuke can be as potent as the threat of jail. Sometimes all people have to do is stiffen their bodies to communicate the message that we are out of line. As significantly, norms and values are internalized. We become our own control agents once we learn what is required. The mere thought of stepping outside in the buff arouses feelings of shame that keep us clothed.

A particularly important part of the normative order is the moral order. Every society has one. They need to. Without rules against murder, theft, or rape, life would be unbearable. Our conflicting interests would cause so much harm that a Hobbesian war of all against all would be a reality. Similarly, societies, whether small or large, require trust. If people are to live side by side, they cannot subsist in constant fear of each other. Nor can people be dependent upon others if they are constantly prone to lying, cheating, and stealing. Were this the case, we could not be sure that they would provide what we expect. Moral rules are more strictly enforced than so-called folkways precisely because they are so vital. Our neighbors become understandably upset when these are broken. More than this, we internally enforce such rules. We subject ourselves to serious internal sanctions when we go astray. Guilt, shame, and disgust arise within us to warn against doing "wrong." We call this phenomenon a conscience and all but sociopaths possess one.

It is for this reason that we must understand how morality operates. Unfortunately, both liberals and conservatives are more concerned with enforcing their version of what is right than with standing back to investigate the enterprise. As a result, both sides often go wide of the mark. While liberals insist morality is relative and conservatives counter that it is absolute, both are mistaken. Morality may be socially constructed, but it is not open to unimpeded manipulation. Morality is essentially a social process that creates and maintains important rules. Rather than a compendium of specifiable regulations that are open to conscious substitution, it is a malleable means of social control in which we all participate. None of us is in charge of morality, but all are concerned with its outcome. Moreover, because we all sometimes seek rules favorable to ourselves, we frequently attempt to drive communal standards in directions we desire.

To begin with moral rules are *informal*. We may think they are clear and precise, but they are rarely written down. Thus, while we usually assert that there is a rule against lying, its dimensions are inexact. Almost no one believes every falsehood is forbidden. Most allow for exceptions such as "white lies." But which lies are of this color? People disagree. Some say it is okay to lie about sex, whereas others do not. Moral rules are always qualified by a penumbra of modifications that are hardly ever specified. The way we learn them is through example. It is not so much what people say as what they punish (or reward) that alerts us to their dimensions. Unfortunately, paradigmatic learning is never exact. It is subject to interpretation, yet interpretations differ. The upshot is that there never is, or can be, complete agreement about what is moral. The best that can be achieved is a loose consensus.

The way this consensus is achieved is through *polarized negotiations*. People generally divide themselves into two camps to fight over what is right. A salient example of this phenomenon is found in the abortion controversy. Some folks identify themselves as pro-life, whereas others claim to be pro-choice. Members of each faction are certain they are right, whereas that the other side is wrong. What emerges is a good guy–bad guy mentality. Each party regards him/herself as on the side of the angels, while those on the other side are castigated as in league with the devil. As a consequence, the parties talk past each other. Neither side listens to the other, lest it be corrupted. Likewise, each demands orthodoxy of its allies. Simplified catechisms become the order of the day. At the same time, the leaders of these factions tend to be extreme. Frequently more Catholic than the Pope, in order to be effective spokespersons, they are both energetic and emphatic. As a result, they tend to speak in absolutes. In a sense, the flag-bearers of their respective parties, they must make sure the streamers they fly are brightly colored and distinct from those of their opponents. Accordingly, they are not subtle. Nor can factional leaders afford to be generous. Their enemies must be characterized in shades so repellant that no decent person would care to be decked out in their insignias.

This is why the Culture Wars have been so fierce. Neither side wants to give an inch. Liberals, in particular, because they rest their case on their alleged moral superiority, like to portray conservatives as retrograde villains. Remember, those to their political right are characterized as stupid, mean-spirited, and greedy. They are also routinely described as racist, sexist, ageist, and elitist. They are, in short, bad guys. Who, accordingly, would want to emulate them? Who would even want to read their tainted books? Obama, as a liberal team leader, is therefore obliged to defend his programs by asserting that they are designed to help the American people, whereas the Republicans are devoted to "business as usual." While he is "bipartisan," they are more concerned with defeating him than doing what is right.

Lastly, morality is deeply emotional. Its rules are both negotiated and enforced by way of strong feelings. Partisans represent their positions as supremely rational, but this is propaganda. More often it is their anger, gussied up as moral indignation, that is used to bludgeon others into submission. Moral partisans also use shame, disgust, and guilt in order to discipline wayward troops. By the same token, they try to attract people to their respective positions by eliciting sympathy.

162

This is why extremists are always trotting out individuals as examples of the damage done by their opponents. Do they want to outlaw poverty—well, here is a person starving to death. Do they support same sex marriage—well, here is a couple whose love has been thwarted by hard-hearted reactionaries. Their rights—their fundamental human rights—have been trampled upon! For the same reason, liberals portray themselves as the party of "love." They care, whereas their opponents do not. They can be trusted because they—and only they—want the best for everyone

The Cognitive Constraints. Human babies are born less mature than other creatures. With their heads barely able to make it through the birth canal, it takes time for their brains to mature. The glory of our species is that we are more intelligent than any other animal on the planet. So proud are we of our mental acuity that we have character-ized ourselves as "rational animals." This may not be an idle boast, but it is far from ensuring an unwavering allegiance to logic. We may be smarter than other creatures, but we often act as if we were not. The primary reason for this is that as members of cognitive communities, what we believe depends upon what others believe. Instead of using our brains to evaluate matters, we frequently cede our conclusions to the opinions of our fellows.

Once upon a time, educated people sought to be "Renaissance Men." Those days, however, are long gone. Nowadays, there is so much to learn that no single person can grasp more than a fraction of it. In many ways, this too is one of the glories of our species. As members of cooperative communities, we can know far more than any isolated individual. By learning from one another, as well as from preceding generations, our stock of knowledge has become impressive. Much as honeybees working in concert can fill a hive with honey, we in concert have filled numerous libraries and computer memory banks. In part, this is because we listen to each other. When others share information to which we have no personal access, we take advantage of their observations to enlarge our own store of insights. Indeed, they can communicate what happened out of sight and long ago or far away.

So far so good, but there is a downside to this practice. Thus, we often depend upon the authority of other persons, rather than decide questions for ourselves. We take what they say on faith, rather than in-dependently validate its truth. Years ago, Solomon Asch demonstrated a phenomenon he called "consensual validation." In an extensive series of experiments, he showed that people will agree with a group even when it contradicts the evidence of their eyes. Rather than trust their senses, they feel more confident accepting the collective judgment. The same applies to our attitudes toward authorities. Individuals thought to be smarter or more powerful than ourselves are ceded the right to decide what is correct. We accept their word on the assumption that they know better. Hence, if they tell us the world is flat—or round—we agree without checking its shape for ourselves. This works well when the authorities are accurate, but can be dangerous when they are not. To illustrate, Hitler was mistaken when he told the German people they were the master race. Nevertheless, they agreed and ultimately acquiesced in genocide.

Liberal opinion leaders also assure us they are worthy of being cognitive leaders. They promise us, for instance, that they are smarter than others. It follows that they are better situated to decide what is true. Also more moral than the rest of us, they can be trusted to make important decisions. Although they typically validate their observations only within their own intellectual circles, these are portrayed as authoritative. There is, of course, little modesty in this. To the contrary, liberals assert that they are able to calculate *all* of the factors that go into deciding what is best. After all, they are experts. They are the best and brightest. Liberal leaders likewise seek a bandwagon effect. If they can convince the undecided that everyone believes as they do, those on the fence may join the crowd. In the end, fifty million Frenchmen cannot be wrong. We saw this strategy employed in the global warming craze. Advocates of this belief assured us that all competent scientists endorsed their position in the hope of making it seem inevitable. If everyone agreed, how could less well-informed holdouts remain in opposition? They must be Global Warming deniers.

The Symbolic Constraints. We human beings are also symbol users. Recent research has indicated that many other animals possess sophisticated ways of communicating with their own kind, but these pale in comparison with the complexities of how we exchange information. Human language is a marvel. It enables us to coordinate extremely intricate forms of behavior. So adept are we at doing this, that we can explain to complete strangers what is needed to construct a skyscraper or to send people to the moon. Merely by stringing sounds together or making squiggles on a piece of paper, we can direct these others to do things they never previously considered. We can even get them to visualize things they have never previously thought or seen.

We human beings take our language skills for granted. We learn them when we are so young and employ them so habitually that they seem part of the natural order. And yet there is no other creature capable of human language. Some of the great apes have acquired vocabularies in the hundreds of symbols, while others have mastered rudimentary syntactical skills, but none have come close to our versatility. Linguists cite the following example because it is so revealing. What other animal, they ask, could communicate the sentiment, "My father was poor but honest." Even children understand this sentence, but how could a dog—or chimpanzee—convey this information? How would they handle possessives, the past tense, or conditionals? By what means would they express a concept as subtle as "honesty"? Moreover, merely by rearranging words, we transmit messages never before uttered. Our inborn syntactical abilities enable us to pass along an infinite number of meanings. That which our ancestors never even conceived is effortlessly communicated to others, even when they are not especially gifted. We say, "Bring me that laptop," and a child does as directed.

Nor are our symbols limited to language. We utilize all sorts of nonverbal cues. Our facial expressions, manual gestures, the clothes we wear, the automobiles we drive, and the homes in which we reside are all organized to send messages. The sociologist Erving Goffman alerted us to this by stressing the importance of what he called the "presentation of self" in ordinary life. As he indicated, we routinely manipulate each other through a myriad of visual and auditory signals. Thus, we smile at each other, make the okay sign, or (if we are lucky) flash a Super Bowl ring when seeking cooperation. Dressed one way, we convey the message that we are bankers who can be trusted; dressed another, we reveal that we are outlaws who ought to be feared. In many cases, these messages are unintentional. Nevertheless, they regularly determine how others treat us.

But just as there are cognitive communities, there are symbolic communities. People belonging to different populations communicate by utilizing common symbols. Speak a different language or dress in a different lexicon and outsiders are confused. If one's symbols are sufficiently different, one may not be regarded as fully human. Indeed, a mere shift in the accent can provide the difference between receiving deference or being dismissed as a fool. We brag that we deal with others equally, but if their symbols differ from our own, we are liable to erect impenetrable barriers. Anyone who believes in universal love

165

or complete equality must understand that these distinctions are not epiphenomenon. They cannot be eradicated by the simple expedient of teaching people to be more tolerant. Culturally based symbols ensure that we are more comfortable with some people than others. Those with whom we can communicate always seem more human.

The Emotional Constraints. Of not quite the same importance as the symbolic order, but easily underestimated, is the emotional order. Emotions are often thought to be personal and thus completely private. But this is untrue. Our feelings, in a sense, are located within ourselves, but they are also transmitted between individuals. Emotions communicate. They likewise motivate. What we feel influences what others feel. That which makes us uncomfortable may make them equally uncomfortable. Take fear. A frightened person is generally responding to a perceived danger. But if he feels fear, those with whom he is in contact will probably feel it too. They will suspect that there is a danger in the neighborhood and look around to determine what it is. Yet this is not the end of the matter. A frightened person is also motivated to seek safety. It is not enough to recognize there is a danger; it must be avoided. The classic response is fight or flight. The goal (albeit often unconsciously) is either to distance oneself from the danger or to neutralize it. This is also the objective of persons to whom fear has been communicated. They too are impelled to fight or flight, for the very same reason. A community of fear is thus one in which everyone is simultaneously impelled to seek protection, often precipitously.

Emotions can be contagious. As a result, they are able to push crowds one way or another. When thousands of spectators attend sporting events, the joy of participating is transmitted to those assembled. One of the reasons people take pleasure in attending football games is that it enables them to partake in this emotional intensity. It makes them feel good. They feel part of a larger, more powerful, entity than their isolated selves. Yet emotional contagions can mobilize people for more serious matters. In the political arena, they are routinely employed to energize a candidate's supporters. This is the purpose of political rallies and nominating conventions. It is also why politicians, including liberals, precipitate crises. If they can frighten people into believing as they do, these others may respond to the presumed danger as hoped. This was why Obama began his administration by repeatedly declaring the country faced an economic catastrophe. If a large enough segment of the electorate was sufficiently alarmed, it might put pressure on congress to vote as Obama desired. Liberals, in general, like to portray capitalism as a disaster in the making. They also like to depict the rich as selfish bogeymen who deserve to be loathed. Moderates are therefore urged to embrace the Liberal Dream on the assumption that poverty, discrimination, and an environmental catastrophe will otherwise engulf us. There is no time to waste. We must act now!

The Aesthetic Constraints. John Keats is often quoted as saying, "'Beauty is truth, truth beauty'—that is all ye know on earth and all ye need to know." He also wrote that "a thing of beauty is a joy forever" and to a friend opined, "What the imagination seizes as Beauty must be truth—whether it existed before or not." Keats died while he was still in his twenties so he may be excused for his youthful exuberance. Yet he was representative of a Romantic movement that celebrated art above all other human activities. Art was for him, and his compatriots, the primary reason for living. They regarded it as the essence of humanity. In this, they overestimated the importance of art—it is not the equivalent of truth—but they were correct in depicting it as distinctively human. More than this, art is one of the factors that create social cohesion. Communities are characterized, and in part held together, by what their members consider beautiful.

Anyone living in the Western world cannot help but notice that styles change. A person does not have to subscribe to fashion magazines to realize that skirt lengths go up and down, ties get thinner and wider, and hats go in and out of style. Dress in a manner totally at odds with what is believed attractive and passersby stare goggle-eyed at the temerity of your bad taste. There is, in essence, a revolving consensus as to what looks (or sounds) good. As with morality, aesthetic values, although regarded as absolute by some, are demonstrably transient. What people during the Middle Ages considered the height of elegance today strikes most of us as over the top. As with the vernacular in language, being *au currant* with the latest variations in taste is a ticket to social acceptance. If you dress the way others do, or use the latest idioms, you will be perceived as a member of the in-group. If you do not, you are rejected as gauche. With respect to liberalism, it must be remarked that there are political styles. The latest political cause—as witnessed by the peregrinations of Hollywood personalities—may be worn almost as if it were a fashion accessory. Repeat the up-to-date political mantras and you are obviously both well informed and astute.

The Material/Technological Constraints. We human beings are also tool users. It is not our physical strength, or even our unaided intelligence, that enables us to master our environment. Were we unable to apply these capacities via the manipulation of physical objects, they would go for naught. This said, despite Madonna's self-congratulatory depiction of herself as a "material girl," nowadays the in-crowds tend to look askance at unvarnished materialism. Bobos imagine themselves to be too intellectual and aesthetically sophisticated to tie their self-images to their possessions. They are presumably so knowledgeable, and tasteful, that the automobiles they drive cannot possibly characterize their essence. Of course, this is not entirely true. If you happen to drive Prius or a Ferrari, this is perceived as evidence of an elevated sensibility. Moreover, a great many material items surround even nonmaterialists. Despite their denials, the cognoscenti too pride themselves on their nice homes, art collections, and electronic gadgets. In this, however, they are only human. People have always liked to possess things. Indeed, we frequently do define ourselves by what we own.

Sociologists often refer to a given society's material culture. By this they mean the inherited objects with which the group conducts its business. Whether discussing the automobiles people drive or the chairs in which they sit, these physical things allow individuals to accomplish tasks they could not otherwise manage. An object is a tool to the degree that it can be employed to achieve designated purposes. Hammers help drive in nails, knives enable us to cut pieces of meat, and light bulbs permit us to transform darkness into light. Nevertheless, not every society possesses the same tools. Americans use airplanes to fly across the country, whereas many of our ancestors did not even possess the shoes needed to walk over sharp stones. We did not personally invent these tools; they are part of our heritage. Our parents and role partners introduced us to them. We then employed them to engage in a variety of activities in conjunction with other members of our community.

Nowadays we often refer to new and exciting tools as technology. The automated machines that keep our factories humming, the computers with which we write memos, and the cell phones used to call fiends and relatives all qualify. They enable us to produce goods and services more efficiently than ever. Paradoxically, the huge quantity of these items and the complexity of the techniques needed to produce them has fostered the equality so vehemently demanded by liberals. The sociologist Gerhard Lenski argues that an increased surplus of goods allows these to be more broadly distributed. Thus, when automobiles were new, they were the almost exclusive preserve of the wealthy. These days, thanks to Henry Ford and mass production, even working people own such vehicles. Indeed, Karl Marx himself speculated that the wonders of industrial productivity would allow communism to come into being. Its plentitude would give everyone access to what they wanted. Lenski has also claimed that complex technologies facilitate a reduction in social distance between the top and bottom of a given society. Because more people have to be skilled at creating, maintaining, and operating complex tools, they must be rewarded for doing so. Why study to be an electronic engineer, if one will not earn more for doing so? Similarly, why apply oneself to interpreting the results of an MRI, if there are no additional dollars in one's pay envelope. Marx thought people would contribute these services out of the goodness of their hearts, but the real world is not constructed this way. In the real world, complex activities command greater remuneration and, in the process, redistribute wealth without government intervention.

Material cultures also organize societies by coordinating the activities of their members. They connect large numbers of people by facilitating their interactions. Of particular note are technologies that ease communication and transportation. A continental nation, such as the United States, would hardly remain a single entity if it still took months to journey from one coast to the other. In this case, the decisions of politicians in Washington, DC, would be irrelevant to highway builders in California. Those on the spot would need to decide matters for themselves, which would foster an independence of spirit similar to that asserted by American colonists vis-à-vis their English overlords. But not to worry. Once upon a time telegraphs and railroads provided the glue holding our country together. Today jet planes and cell phones do an even better job.

Common carriers, such as radio and television, but also the Internet, similarly contribute to maintaining our collective culture. The dialects in which Americans speak are more homogeneous than previously because children coast to coast model their accents on the Standard English spoken on television. Watching the same movies, listening to identical news reports, and cheering interchangeable entertainers, recruits them to common moral, cognitive, symbolic, emotional, and aesthetic communities despite living thousands of miles apart. As a result, they can talk to each other—and be understood—when they

169

meet. They need not be complete strangers because much of their culture, including how they dress and the songs they sing, are acquired by way of shared media.

The Ritual Constraints. Lastly, societies share a ritual order. They use stereotyped methods of accomplishing certain acts. Shaking hands is an example. This is a standardized method of greeting in Western societies. In Japan, bowing once performed the same function. Other, extremely important rituals are associated with religion. Folding one's hands in prayer, making the sign of the cross, or kissing the Torah qualify as means of demonstrating allegiance to particular beliefs. Likewise specific liturgies, icons, and incenses are deemed spiritually efficacious. Bells and smells matter. So do vestments, the various stages of the mass, and baptismal ceremonies.

Almost all social organizations have unique rituals that solidify membership. Moreover, only identifiable sequences of behavior, elaborated in the requisite manner, are considered valid. Only they confirm group membership or deliver the appropriate magic. Thus, business corporations organize pep rallies to mobilize the troops, armies stage parades to demonstrate their strength, and colleges hold commencement ceremonies to launch their graduates. Even superstitious acts, such as tossing salt over one's shoulder when it spills, count as private, albeit shared, rituals. As a result, these customs, not just personal decisions, serve to maintain social solidarity. Because they are mutual, they elicit interpersonal sympathies that go beyond conscious decisions to be each other's keepers.

The Structural Domains

Now we turn to the structural domain. The distinctions between its various orders are also empirically based. And as with the cultural domain, these overlap. Nonetheless, the causal mechanisms that create and maintain enduring patterns of interpersonal behavior are sufficiently well-defined as to make these distinctions useful. Moreover, identifying them makes it obvious that there are limitations to the manner in which societies can be organized. The patterned ways in which humans interact permit some ways of living, but not others. It is absolutely not the case that if we can imagine something, we can always achieve it.

Personal Relationship Constraints. We human beings are not interchangeable. We cannot be perfunctorily substituted for one another. Furthermore, people play favorites. We treat some individuals better than others. Likewise, we engage in activities with some, but not others. The notion that one day all humans will love all other humans is absurd. The only way that this can happen is if we are genetically altered. In the meantime, we notice differences between people. When we look into their faces, we do not see an undifferentiated mass. To the contrary, this one is John, while that is Mary. Nor do we react to them the same way. He may be a friend with whom we enjoy playing basketball, while she is a notorious gossip to whom we do not tell secrets. With one we are pleased; with the other we are not.

Several decades ago the psychiatrist John Bowlby introduced us to the concept of personal attachment. In studying the nature of motherhood, he noticed that children bonded with those who take care of them. Their mothers, in particular, became persons to whom they were steadfastly connected. It mattered to the young who fed and nurtured them. A mother's smiling face brought comfort, whereas a stranger's elicited fear. Mother essentially served as a home base that assured a child of safety. On the other hand, an encounter with a stranger sent the same child scurrying to her side to wipe away the tears. What was more, when mother unexpectedly departed her child became disconsolate. He raucously cried in an effort to bring her back. But if mother did not return, he became depressed. Her presence, and not just that of any concerned adult, mattered. She, and only she, conferred consolation.

The tight bonding between mothers and infants develops early in their relationship. A mother's touch and warm smile elicit a predictable response in a neonate. It is not by accident that the child looks into her eyes and returns her smile. This genetically programmed reaction then melts her heart and motivates her to love this, and not just any, infant. Wide eyes, a high forehead, and a small nose look cute to adults, but they are not sufficient to cement the relationship between a particular adult and child. For this to occur, they must interact in a manner that allows them to bond. Only then does love flow between them.

Something similar occurs between adults. They too bond to form emotionally attached couples. Indeed, the courtship behavior that establishes this connection has been rigorously studied. Science has developed a good understanding of how it unfolds and why most men and women do not promiscuously swap sexual partners. The process through which these attachments arise begins when the parties come to each other's attention. In societies where marriages are arranged, others, usually their parents, set up these encounters, whereas in modern Western communities individuals themselves make plans to meet members of the opposite sex. Whether they get together at a bar, church, or work, they then take the time to get to know each other. Initially, they rate potential mates. Is this other attractive, successful, or intelligent, enough to be considered for a lasting alliance? If so, the two must get to know each other. In so doing, they eventually go beyond their natural inclination to put their best feet forward. Only after they reveal their actual selves do they learn if they are suited to each other.

One of the early stages of courtship is therefore biography swapping. Starting as strangers, the parties must eventually disclose who they are. What they have done, with whom they interact, and their dreams for the future are the stuff of their conversations. If this information is exchanged in a balanced manner, the two may continue their explorations. At the same time, because intimacy can be dangerous, they must find out if this other is trustworthy. Living in close proximity permits people to inflict serious physical and emotional injuries. Such propinquity allows them to discover, and take advantage of, each other's vulnerabilities. As a result, during dating most parties keep their eyes open. Thus, if a potential mate routinely lies to outsiders, it is a good bet that he or she will eventually lie to a loved one. Yet this is not enough. Trust is so important it must be tested. Circumstances are arranged so as to allow the other's natural impulses to emerge. This is why courtships take time. It is why it may be months before the parties let their guards down. Thus, only on an automobile trip may his impatience rise to the surface or at a fancy restaurant does her tendency toward self-indulgence become evident.

Should all go well, should the parties both like and trust one another, the next stage of courtship transpires. At this point, the two become infatuated with each other. After they do, the prospective mate seems special. He or she glows with a magical radiance. Indeed, when most people think of love, it is of the all-consuming delight of this period. Under the influence of infatuation, people feel as if they are walking on air. Now nothing the partner does seems wrong. Now his or her slightest touch sends a thrill charging through one's body. Suddenly the clouds part and one's hopes seem destined to come true. Intoxicated by passion, lovers are convinced they can live on love.

In fact, what occurs during the infatuation stage is that the parties emotionally build each other into their respective lives. They become a couple rather than separate individuals. In a sense, they develop the same sort of attachment that arises between a mother and child. Once it does, many of their plans become joint plans and their independent futures are transformed into a shared future. So entangled do their destinies become, that when they differ—as they are sure to do—they stick around to work out their differences. What at the beginning of their relationship would have prompted them to move on now motivates them to seek an acceptable compromise. At this point, they have entered the negotiation stage of courtship. Intimate couples must discover how to work out their disagreements such that both are reasonably satisfied. There needs to be a give and take during which both receive sufficient gratification to make their alliance worthwhile. If not, it is liable to dissolve.

Ironically, it is when marital bonds are torn asunder that the strength of a couple's attachments is revealed. There was a time when people thought divorce should be a civilized parting of the ways. In fact, it typically elicits an emotional firestorm. People at first refuse to believe someone who promised eternal love has betrayed them. When this realization sinks in, they are apt to be furious. They may even seek revenge. Consequently, if efforts at bargaining do not repair the damage, they separate. At this juncture, they do not experience elation. To the contrary, they feel depressed. Whereas infatuation brought the couple into emotional alignment, sadness seals their disconnection. Their misery is, as it were, the mirror image of their joy at coming together. The pleasure they experienced back then rearranged their priorities so that these melded together, while their sorrow modifies their allegiances such that they become independent. Only when this occurs—and it can take years—will they be emotionally free to enter other intimate relationships.

Personal relationships are a fact of human existence. They occur between parents and children, husbands and wives, and, to a lesser degree, between friends and associates. Human beings live in families, participate in acquaintance groups, and interact with colleagues. Moreover, they normally do so on the basis of attachments of varying intensity. What they do not do is relate to others disinterestedly. People are never completely objective. They may be told they should love their neighbors as themselves, but they do not. Proposed social reforms based on universal love are therefore destined to fail. However much people pledge themselves to be completely fair and cosmically empathetic, they never live up to this promise. Nor can they as long as they remain human.

The Hierarchical Constraints. We human beings are also hierarchical animals. We invariably rank ourselves relative to others. Who is "higher" or "lower" matters to us. Moreover, we want to be better than at least some others. We hope to be special. This is true of everyone. Not just the rich and powerful, but the poor and impotent crave what they perceive as success. None of us want to be losers. We all intend to be winners. In this sense, we all contribute to the final outcome of our ranking systems. Because all—top and bottom—compete to be better, we all help to establish, and maintain, the hierarchies in which we participate. Nor is this a human failing. Our desire to be more than equal is our best defense against mediocrity. In individually striving for superiority, we collectively insure that our species achieves remarkable results.

Many liberal theorists assume that complete equality is the natural human condition. Because most people are envious of those who outrank them, these thinkers conclude that were it not for the selfish desires of the powerful everyone would be on the same plane. This, however, is specious. In no society—not in the entire history of the world—has any society been completely equal. Empirical observations reveal that all societies, including hunter-gatherers, distinguish between the more and less powerful. It would therefore seem that hierarchy is the natural human condition. If so, it is the possibility of complete equality that must be demonstrated. Instead of assuming that parity will one day arise of its own accord, the mechanisms through which it can need to be established.

As for hierarchy, the mechanisms through which it is produced and maintained are readily observable. People, all people, behave in a manner that creates ranking. They engage in "tests of strength." They literally compete to determine who is better in particular dimensions. Whether they engage in wrestling matches, beauty pageants, or commercial ventures, the object is to see who is more potent. Once this is established, the winner acquires a reputation for being stronger, while the loser is regarded as weaker. The parties—and those who witness their contest—then relate to the contestants on the basis of the reputations thereby acquired. Winners are regarded as superior and hence receive deference, while losers are regarded as inferior and are required to supply deference to the victor. The parties do not immediately engage in a rematch, but honor the results of their encounter—at least for a while. In this, the losers, because they are shaken by their loss, behave in a manner that sustains their comparative status.

174

Given that types strengths vary, human beings can belong to a variety of hierarchies. In one context, they come out as superior bowlers, whereas in another they are relegated to low-level employment. One of the reasons contemporary societies are so complex is that they are composed of multiple intersecting hierarchies. This is confusing, but it also enables people to go "hierarchy shopping." In college, for instance, students shuttle between majors looking for one in which to excel. These matters are further complicated by the size of modern societies. Because they are so populous, it is impossible for everyone to take everyone else's measure. As a result, people often judge other's relative standing by symbolic means. The way they speak, the clothes they wear, and the neighborhoods in which they reside are treated as evidence of relative power. Instead of literally fighting to see who is best, the players are intimidated by the appearance of greater power.

Another complication in how hierarchies are established is that victories in tests of strength do not have to occur mano-a-mano. We human beings are expert at creating and utilizing alliances. We often work together in coalitions to defeat other coalitions and in the process obtain our personal status from the positions we hold within these alliances. This is what politics is about. Thus, someone who is effective in assembling and leading a dominant political combination may be regarded as personally dominant. If he or she is president of the United States, it will not matter whether he can best others in a wrestling match. Similarly, if he or she is the CEO of a successful corporation, the resources and decision-making opportunities this provides result in greater social respect. Such persons are regarded as leaders and allowed to make choices that bind others. Their opinions are received as expert such that a halo effect surrounds them with an aura of supremacy.

Hierarchies, of course, are unfair. They enable some people to win, while others lose. Moreover, the winners obtain advantages. They generally live more comfortably. That their inferiors envy them makes sense. Nevertheless, a belief that all hierarchies will eventually be dismantled does not. Ranking systems are too functional to disappear. They organize complex activities, motivate difficult tasks, restrain interpersonal and inter-group conflicts, allow for sexual selection, and distribute scarce resources. Individuals may suffer from the way power is distributed, but the groups to which they belong usually benefit. In any event, we humans are biologically programmed to create hierarchies. Their shapes vary, for example, the distance from a top to the bottom may be greater in some than others, but their incidence is universal. The question is thus not whether we will decide to have them, but rather how they will be organized. The strengths over which people compete, the alliances in which they participate, and the rewards they obtain can be modified, whereas complete equality will never come to pass. If liberals offer this as a possibility, they are promising the impossible. Then again, since they personally expect to be the first among equals, they almost certainly know the truth. In their heart of hearts, they too want to be more powerful than others.

The Social Exchange Constraints. Have you ever tried to take candy from a baby? It is supposed to be easy, but is not. Babies generally hold on to sweets with an unexpectedly strong grip. Likewise, once they learn to talk, they warn off potential thieves by declaring, "Mine! Mine!" Parents do not need to teach their children to defend what belongs to them. They do this on their own. As with hierarchy, the impetus to do so is genetically determined. It has been part of our biological heritage since before we were human. We are, in short, property-owning creatures. Rousseau believed property was the arbitrary invention of a single, supremely selfish individual, but he was wrong. Property ownership arose from our hunting heritage. Many hunting animals, such as chimpanzees, do not distribute the outcome of the hunt by chance. Those who participate in the chase have a superior claim to the resultant meat. They, as it were, own the carcass. By the same token, because hunters depend on their weapons, these are not communally owned. Tools that are difficult to produce, but essential for survival, are jealously guarded. They are, in essence, property.

Once property rights are established, their corollary is property exchange. This sort of transfer of ownership rights can also be traced back to prehistory. Thus, we know that our remote ancestors traded precious materials, such as flint, over long distances. That we continue to engage in trading today should therefore come as no surprise. Indeed, we live in a society dominated by commerce. People today buy and sell almost every commodity and service necessary for survival. So competent have we become at exchanging a plethora of goods, that we are far more prosperous than our ancestors. By utilizing money and credit, we have discovered how to transfer valued items so effortlessly that we do so on a daily basis. Indeed, it is difficult to imagine how we could carry on otherwise.

Commerce, however, has rules. Economists may not understand all of the variables of the marketplace, but they know enough about supply and demand to predict many outcomes. They know, for instance, that wealth is not created when governments transfer resources from one individual to another. Liberals who ignore economics thus do so at their peril. Those who expect ownership to disappear or who urge people to relinquish the results of their labor for no return are deluded. Once more they are expecting human beings to cease being human. An idealized world in which people simply take what they need, as they need it, is a pipe dream at best; a nightmare at worst. It does not factor into our impulse to protect, and compete for, what we desire.

The Social Role Constraints. Over the past several decades sociology has seen a changing of the guard. Where once structural-functionalists were dominant, today conflict theorists have displaced them. As a result, one of the chief insights of the functionalists has dropped from view. Investigators such as Herbert Spencer and Emile Durkheim stressed the importance of a division of labor in understanding human societies. They noted that people perform different jobs and, furthermore, that as societies grow in size, these jobs become more differentiated. Today our vocational division of labor is so extensive that the Department of Labor's *Dictionary of Occupational Titles* is as large as a telephone book. It enumerates literally hundreds of thousands of different jobs.

There are also divisions of labor within our personal lives. Within families and friendship groups, people specialize in performing different tasks. One daughter, for instance, will be regarded as the family's beauty, while another is deemed its athlete. There are an almost unlimited number of such niches available; hence all of us occupy several. But not all roles, whether personal or impersonal, are created equal. It is usually more rewarding to be a doctor than a ditch-digger; more satisfying to be the smart one in the family rather than the dumb one. The question therefore becomes who will occupy which role. Since there are a finite number of slots on offer, there is usually competition over them.

Generally speaking, specific divisions of labor are socially negotiated. Thus, children squabble over who will do the dishes or take out the garbage. On a larger scale, adults compete to see who is admitted to medical school or hired to be a sociology professor. Once occupying a role, however, the division of labor is further specified by negotiations between the partners. A husband demands that his wife perform her duties in a particular way, while she returns the favor. The pair, in fact, learn the details of their respective roles from one another. The demands they make may not always be fair, or sensible, but it is from these that they weave the fabric of their daily lives. The fact is that we human beings do not do whatever we like. More usually we do what dovetails with what our role partners do, and therefore what we mutually expect of one another. This results in the dentist taking care with how he drills our teeth, while we adjust the angle of our head to make his job easier. Each party responds to the other in a series of corrections from which they modify their own dispositions.

A particularly important sort of role in the modern world is the professionalized one. Whether on the job or at home, more people than previously are required to be self-motivated experts. Be they engineers designing a bridge or parents raising a child for vocational success, they must know what they are doing and do it without external prompting. As we transformed into a middle class society, decentralized roles became the norm. These roles were required to keep complex a techno-commercial society operating. The odd thing is that many people do not realize they are in the midst of this fine-tuned network even as they adjust their activities to accommodate it. Nor do most realize they are part of a professionalizing society. More to the point, liberals remain oblivious to it. Instead, they continue to think in terms of bosses and workers. Trapped in a mindset derived from nineteenth century Marxism, they do not urge people to hone their professionalized skills. Rather, they advise them to throw off their oppressors and act spontaneously.

Reconciliation Community Constraints. The primatologist Frans de Waal noticed something surprising while observing the daily life of chimpanzees. These, our closest relatives, were a contentious lot. They were forever fighting for hierarchical supremacy or access to favored food items. As described in his book *Chimpanzee Politics,* they regularly raced up and down howling at each other or engaging in the equivalent of fisticuffs. But then things would quiet down. Eventually one of the lower ranking animals approached a higher-ranking individual requesting what amounted to forgiveness. A hand might be reached out, which was then reciprocated with a gentle touch. The two animals might even hug, and then settle down to grooming one another's fur. What essentially occurred is that they kissed and made up. De Waal called these occurrences reconciliation ceremonies. They were pre-patterned mechanisms for reducing interpersonal tension and allowing the group to continue functioning as a whole.

Mechanisms of this sort may seem relatively unimportant among human beings. We do kiss and make up, but this is not necessarily a daily event. Nevertheless, we too live in conflict-saturated communities. Personal relationships go awry, hierarchical positions are contested, business deals fall apart, and role partners disagree about a particular division of labor. There is, as a result, a great deal of ill-will that needs to be overcome. We cannot afford to hold grudges lest it become impossible to work together. Reconciliation communities are therefore more common than might be imagined.

For many of us, church services provide this function. When we pray together, we symbolically assert that we are part of the same family. Although we have had disagreements during the week, we put these behind us as we bow before a common deity. For others, business meetings provide this function. When they listen to pep talks or cheer the latest sales figures, their shared objectives are reasserted. Something similar occurs at college graduations. Parents, students, and professors gather under one roof to display their loyalty to a common institution. They ritually sing songs, walk down an aisle, and applaud award winners as a token of their devotion to shared values. At the end of the day, they leave feeling better about themselves and those with whom they might have had a quarrel. Reconciliation ceremonies are part of our common heritage. Even liberals avail themselves of their power during political rallies. Sadly, they neglect them when contemplating a utopian future in which people can do whatever they please.

Spatial Constraints. Other social structures entail spatial constraints. How people relate to each other is often determined by the physical spaces in which they gather. Praying together is thus facilitated by doing so in a church. The way its seats are arranged and the colored light filtering in through stained glass windows create an ambiance in which interpersonal piety is possible. Classrooms, on the other hand, provide a different sort of ambiance. They are designed to promote teaching and learning. Were they too loud, or cold, it might be difficult to pay attention. Different sorts of atmosphere are likewise provided by public parks, factory buildings, or clothing boutiques. In all of these, the goal is to enable people to interact in some ways, but not others. Indeed, the ability to organize such spaces is the stock and trade of architects.

Oddly, when Rousseau described the idea of property as created by a person who arbitrarily fenced in a piece of land, he was talking about the spatial order, not just of property ownership. We human beings have long been territorial animals. As hunter-gatherers, we did not own personal strips of land, nevertheless we protected tracts of ground as part of our band's hunting territory. These regions were our shared home base. They were where we felt comfortable. Moreover, they were places from which we excluded others, especially if they had designs on its wildlife. This feeling for home is still with us. It may not be expressed in the same terms, but is built into our bones. As with property, it is part of our genetic heritage and as such must be factored into our dreams of a better future.

Environmental Constraints. Lastly, the environments we inhabit shape the nature of our interpersonal relationships. Things like climate help determine the food we eat, the sorts of houses we construct, and the clothing we wear. In so doing, they determine who will work with whom and how. They even constrain the sorts of family we construct. Like the spaces we occupy, an environment can determine how many people may reside comfortably together. It may even determine whether hierarchical mechanisms are needed to distribute scarce resources. Similarly, the surrounding landscape influences how far we travel and with whom we trade. Thus, the ancient Greeks became traders in part because they were bounded by the Aegean Sea and favored with numerous good harbors.

Putting all these cultural and structural pieces together, the nature of what is socially possible—or probable—depends on far more than people deciding to be nice to one another. Nor can the leadership of a particularly talented and well-meaning band of mentors shepherd us in the direction promised by the Liberal Dream. Neither complete equality, nor interpersonal love, nor peace, nor wealth are in the cards. The factors that make human societies possible decree that these are not—and never will be fully realized. As we have seen, who we are, and what we must do to ensure our shared survival, relegate the liberal vision to the realm of fantasy. Specific cultural and structural constraints restrict what we can do. They place boundaries on what is feasible, not because we humans are inherently immoral, but because we are inherently social.

Social Change

When structural functionalism reigned supreme, its chief American advocate was Talcott Parsons. He set the standards for what was expected of scientific sociology. When, however, the conflict theorists challenged his eminence, one of their complaints was that he did not allow for social change. As neo-Marxists, they believed only class conflict determined social progress. Yet in this, the Marxists misinterpreted Parsons. He too believed in change, but of a different sort. In fact, both were correct in emphasizing the importance of social change. Societies are not static. They are modified over time. The question is how. Conflict theorists, and to a lesser degree liberals, favor dramatic change. They hope to foster revolutions in which there are quick and decisive adjustments. Those who disagree with them prefer slower transformations. They favor evolution. Which of these is liable to occur is an empirical matter. Still, it is one upon which Social Domain theory can shed light.

The content of the cultural domains varies enormously. The norms and values to which people are committed, the beliefs they hold, the symbols through which they communicate, the emotions they feel, the things they consider beautiful, the technologies they employ, and the rituals they create differ over time and from place to place. Societies can be so diverse in their ways of life as to be incomprehensible to one another. Nevertheless, individual cultures do not change over night. Far from it, they tend to be conservative. Even people who scoff at tradition have a habit of honoring it in their daily activities. For the most part, the way people interact is based on what they have learned from members of their community. These seem natural; hence are performed almost reflexively.

William Ogburn gave us a name for this phenomenon. He called it "cultural lag." He noted that people tend to get attached to familiar modes of behaving and thinking. Conversely, that which is new or different feels uncomfortable. It takes time to assimilate. Consider the humble cell phone. Members of the younger generation treat these items as a necessity. They often walk down the street with them attached to their ears. Most older folks (such as myself) take a different tack. We use cell phones when necessary, but do not regard them as essential. As a result, cultural changes are often generational. Thus, the slang of one generation is gibberish to the next, while the next generation in turn invents newer forms of jargon to distinguish itself from its predecessors.

As to the structural domains, they too are modified with difficulty. The personal relationships in which people are entangled, the ranks they hold in specific hierarchies, their trading networks, their social roles, the reconciliation ceremonies they favor, the spatial and environmental orders in which they operate tend to be sticky. These are, as their definition implies, *enduring patterns* of interpersonal relationships. Once established, they are apt to follow familiar pathways. Lovers do not instantly cease being lovers and members of the upper class do not instantaneously become members of the lower class, while the family clown does not, in flash, transform into the family genius. Changes do occur. Social mobility, for instance, is possible, but it generally takes time and effort. Even after making oodles of money, ambitious persons may find this is insufficient to accomplish a desired makeover. Thus, the *nouveau riche* normally discover that they are not readily accepted by the existing elite.

Structural changes, in fact, entail losses of varying degrees. For the most part, before new relationships can be established older ones must be relinquished. As with failed marriages, the equivalent of a divorce must occur. But divorces are rarely easy. They are not merely a matter of saying "I divorce you" three times. What is usually needed may be compared with grieving for a loved one. A period of mourning is generally required to cut our ties to the deceased. Whether these internalized attachments are personal relationships, hierarchical positions, or social roles, once they have become parts of our lives, we must reorganize our inner commitments before moving on to new patterns. We have to engage in "resocialization." To do less is to remain bound to forms of interaction that no longer serve our purposes.

Resocialization, however, takes time and can be painful. People do not put aside old attachments as if they were worn out shirts. As with moving from an old love to a new one, both social mobility and role change can be wrenching experiences. They routinely entail angry protests, destabilizing anxieties, and anguishing periods of sadness. As a result, the people who are the loudest in their desire for something different often hold on to the past with the greatest tenacity. They may even disguise their conservatism by camouflaging it under a cloud of optimistic verbiage. They assure us they are in the process of change, whereas all they are doing is modifying how they describe their behavior. Too afraid of transformations to engage in them, they attempt to convince themselves, and others, that they are suffused in them.

This is the situation with liberals, especially extreme liberals. They are enormously vocal in demanding a social revolution, whereas many are closet reactionaries. They do not want to adopt new ways of interacting so much as hark back to idealized versions of the past. Despite their bluster, they are terrified of genuine change. Trapped in cultural lag and petrified by the prospect of resocialization, they pretend to be what they are not. Despite what they say, few of them are progressives. Genuine progress would entail moving toward a professionalized society, whereas the Liberal Dream is committed to establishing a fantasized version of a society-wide family. Its projections will never occur because they cannot. They simply do not fit the needs of mass techno-commercial societies.

6

Back to the Future

The Inverse Force Rule

Liberals tell us they believe in rational change. They assure us that they have intelligently analyzed the possibilities, and in the light of their superior moral and intellectual qualities, have decided what is best. Nevertheless, rational social change is the exception rather than the rule. Examining all of the facts with disinterested objectivity, then carefully calculating what is best, rarely occurs on this level. Liberals further tell us they are predicting a future that is sure to come about, whereas they are actually attempting to dictate a way of life that can never be realized. If we are to understand what is truly possible, we must examine real-life societies. But in order to do this, we must first appreciate how the various social domains have been actualized at different points in history. This was why we devoted so much space to Social Domain Theory. We had to discuss it before we could make sense of the social organizations appropriate to different types of society.

Liberals take pride in being progressive. They believe they are forward looking and hence their opponents must be the opposite. The truth, however, is that the Liberal Dream is based on very old ideas grounded in even older ones. Some conservatives may be reactionaries, but this does not relieve liberals of their burden of obsolete proposals. As we have seen, their worldview derives not only from Rousseau and Marx, but also early Christianity. Its notions of universal love and equality are hoary parables that first captured the human imagination in societies very different from our own. Moreover, the appeal of these fables goes back to social circumstances more ancient than the long-ago empires of Rome, Persia, or China. They hark back to the dawn of human experience.

To see why this is so, we must look at Social Domain Theory from a slightly different angle. As we have seen, its cultural and structural orders are the mechanisms through which human societies are

185

organized. Nevertheless, not all societies rely equally on each of these. The emphasis differs depending upon their respective natures. Thus, the ways in which a domain is expressed vary with factors such as size and technology. We human beings may be social animals, but our ability to live together in both tiny and immense communities stems from the plasticity with which the various domains can be instantiated. They may constitute ties that bind, but how they do depends upon how many of us need to be connected. Huge societies, in which millions of strangers are dependent upon one another, require different adhesives than small numbers who cooperate face to face. Emile Durkheim recognized this over a century ago and his insight is no less valid today.

If the various social orders are conceptualized as social forces, their relationship to social size quickly becomes apparent. Upon close inspection it develops that they are arranged according to an "*inverse force rule.*" The comparative strengths of the physical forces that bind the universe together provide a useful analogy. Physicists have described four such forces. These are gravity, electromagnetism, and the strong and weak nuclear forces. It might be supposed that gravity is the most powerful of these. It, after all, helps hold the universe together, whereas the nuclear forces only make themselves felt at the center of atoms. This, however, is wrong.

As counterintuitive as it may seem, the nuclear forces are the strongest. Even electromagnetism is stronger than gravity. The relative potency of the two can be observed by the simple expedient of allowing a cup to drop to the floor. Upon letting it go, it falls downward under the influence of gravity. But it does not continue falling forever. Long before it reaches the center of the earth, it is brought to an abrupt halt by crashing into the floor. What has occurred is that the electrons of the atoms on the surface of the cup have encountered the electrons of the atoms at the surface of the floor and they repelled each other. The force of this repulsion turned out to be stronger than gravity; hence gravity's influence was canceled out. The cup stopped moving and was held in suspension by the continued operation of electromagnetic repulsion.

The simplest way to describe what occurred is to recognize that weaker forces, such as gravity, operate over longer distances than do the stronger ones, such as electromagnetism and the nuclear forces. The weak ones have an effect that traverses the galaxies, whereas the nuclear ones are confined to neutrons and protons. Something similar appears to be the case with regard to the forces holding societies together. As strange as it seems, the ties that bind large-scale societies are weaker than those that bind small-scale communities. Put another way, the social orders most important in holding massive societies in place are less potent than those uniting small ones.

Personal relationships and face-to-face hierarchies turn out to be very potent, whereas social roles, cognitive information, and material technology are less compelling. Somewhere between these lie normative rules and social exchange processes. Still, what does it mean to say that some forces are stronger than others? The answer is simple. The way their comparative force can be calculated is in terms of their emotional potency. The stronger forces tend to be more emotionally compelling than the weaker ones. To begin with, they are more powerful personal motivators. They can impel us to action despite our desire to behave otherwise. Secondly, strong emotions are also potent interpersonal motivators. Although feelings are often regarded as private, they are essential in organizing interpersonal relationships. They not only provide vital information about the world; they can impel people to act in conjunction with one another. Thus, both personally and interpersonally, strong emotions govern much of what we do. They are almost impossible to ignore. The weaker ones, however, are easier to overrule.

But how do these various forces motivate us? Let us start with personal relationships. The emotional attachments we form with other human beings are enormously powerful. People will literally sacrifice their lives to protect those to whom they are bonded. Mothers have been known to starve themselves in order to make sure their infants are fed, whereas loving husbands have physically interceded to save their wives. Similarly, were it not for the potency of these personal relations, armies could not be persuaded to protect their homelands from invasion. Told their families were at risk, the soldiers would shrug their shoulders. Likewise, were it not for the power of personal attachments, divorces would not be the melodramas they are. The parties would simply go their separate ways. Love matters. Sex matters. Caring matters. These are not myths. They may falter, in which case they leave us cynical, but the degree to which we become disillusioned underlines the importance of what is lost.

Next let us deal with face-to-face hierarchies. As hierarchical animals, we human beings take ranking systems seriously. No one—I repeat—no one wants to be a loser. We may not all rise to the top, but we certainly do not want to fall to the bottom. The efforts expended in preventing this can be enormous. Just how huge is visible in childhood. This is what sibling rivalries are about. When brothers and sisters fight over who will receive more ice cream, it is not the volume of ice cream that is at issue. What matters is who gets more, for this is interpreted as an indicator of comparative parental love. Consequently, siblings can be cruel in their efforts to come out ahead. So can athletes and business rivals. Football players are even prepared to sacrifice their bodies to prevent a loss. Being the goat is utterly unacceptable. It is tantamount to losing a test of strength. For the same reason, people hate to play games against more skilled rivals. Rather than suffer a crushing defeat, they confine their competitions to those with similar abilities. The same sort of motivation is evident in the classroom. Poor students tend to keep their distance from the good ones. They may even decide to skip studying so as to have an excuse for doing poorly.

Moving to the opposite end of the spectrum, most social roles are clearly less involving than personal relationships. While it is rarely painless to move from one paramour to another, it is far easier to transfer from one job to another. Even though the tasks we perform constitute part of our identities, we know they are distinguishable from who we are. Thus, I do sociology. But it is a task I perform rather than the essence of my being. More significantly, when we interact with strangers in terms of our roles, we remain relatively detached. Students sometimes hate their teachers, but this passion is dwarfed in comparison with their attitudes toward their parents. Similarly, when people interact with a clerk at the supermarket, their relative social status is not on the line. Even though the shopper and clerk are performing an activity vital to both, they remain emotionally separate. Each is motivated to do what is required, but they are not so involved that a miscalculation inspires ferocious anger. Customers who become irate under these circumstances are regarded as overinvolved. Their emotional outbursts are viewed as disproportionate, whereas anger at a sexual betrayal is not so regarded.

The technological means that keep us in touch with members of our community are similarly of less emotional import than personal relationships or hierarchical rivalries. When an e-mail is not returned, we get annoyed. When the highway on which we travel to work is tied up with traffic, we curse under our breath. These snafus can be a serious inconvenience. Yet they are about things rather than people. We may want to punch out a television set that unexpectedly goes blank, but it is only a television set. Indeed, we frequently take out our anger at objects as a means of deflecting our wrath from other human beings. Thus, a traffic tie up is more aggravating if our boss has just chewed us out. We displace interpersonal anger onto inanimate objects precisely because these are less emotionally involving. Some people, it is true, fall in love with the objects they own, but most of us feel pity for those who substitute fast cars or baseball card collections for loving relationships or hierarchical success.

The knowledge that keeps us on the same page as other members of our society is of even less emotional consequence. The fact that we believe germs cause disease facilitates sympathy for a sick colleague, but it does not dominate our life space. I say this as a college professor who has devoted his life to becoming knowledgeable. If I did not believe the information I impart is of value, my job would be far less satisfying. Furthermore, I love learning. Nevertheless, I cannot imagine swapping my wife for an informative book. Nor does the pleasure I receive in working through an idea compare with my need to be good at my job. Being successful, that is, being hierarchically superior is more essential to my well-being. This said, most others are even less involved with their cognitive accomplishments. They are generally indifferent to the acquisition of huge quantities of knowledge. Indeed, most prefer to watch an adventure movie than read a book on the settlement of Australia. They readily cede the latter to the eggheads.

Somewhere in between the strong forces represented by our personal relations and face-to-face hierarchies and the weak ones epitomized by social roles, technological ties and cognitive knowledge lie the intermediate forces embodied in the normative order and exchange relationships. The normative order, especially as represented by moral rules, can be compelling. Injunctions against murder, rape and pillage are, for the most part, seriously sanctioned. People rarely allow significant violations to go unremarked. In fact, they may punish murder with death. This would seem to make moral rules a potent force in controlling unwanted behaviors, which, of course, they are. People grow enormously angry when crucial regulations are violated. At such moments, they express "moral indignation." They may also experience crippling guilt or shame when they break such rules. On the other hand, folkways entail less passion. When a friend dyes her hair green, we are thrown off stride, but we probably will not condemn her too harshly. Normative standards are intermediate precisely because, although they can be potent, their effects are uneven. Sometimes they engage people, whereas at other moments they are almost invisible. For example, telling lies is sometimes treated as a critical fault, while at other times it is shrugged off as irrelevant. To illustrate, the Republicans sought to impeach Clinton for perjury before a grand jury, whereas Democrats asserted this was no big deal because everyone lies about sex.

As to exchange relationships, modern commercial societies could not survive without them. Billions of people would starve were the wheels of commerce to grind to a halt. Calvin Coolidge told us the business of America was business and he was not far off the mark. Buying and selling goods is so important to our way of life that Thomas Jefferson almost included property ownership as a right in The Declaration of Independence. Most people fight for what they own and grow despondent if they heedlessly squander their wealth. Likewise, if they are cheated in a business deal, they get upset. Even so, exchange is about things. What we own may symbolize our status, but the status matters more. Still, the exchange of property has other implications. In a sense, it forms the substrate of modern techno-commercial societies. The consequences of commercial activities have emergent properties that deserve recognition. The growing importance of professionalized social roles is one of these. Professional roles could not, and would not, exist without the presence of trading relations. Nonetheless, these roles insert adhesive qualities above and beyond what commerce provides. They are about more than an exchange of goods. They also imply collaboration on joint tasks.

At this point, our discussion has cited only seven of the fourteen social orders previously enumerated. Left out of our account have been several cultural orders, including the emotional, aesthetic, and symbolic ones. Also slighted were several structural orders, such as reconciliation communities and the spatial order. These are no less important in holding societies together, but they are less helpful in distinguishing between why societies vary by size. How these orders are expressed also differ from small to large groupings, but these differences do not have as much impact as the ones emphasized above. Thus, what societies consider beautiful is modified as technologies change; nevertheless the effects of the technological developments themselves have greater consequence. Romantic theorists would disagree, but the evidence goes against them. Likewise, reconciliation communities vary in how participative they are, with large societies involving more spectatorship, yet this is more a matter of style than substance.

Hence, let us return to the inverse force rule as it applies to human societies. Its import is that it explains why personal relationships and face-to-face hierarchies are more important in holding hunter-gatherer communities together than in mass techno-commercial societies. It is not that they are absent in the latter: they are not. It is rather that their influence is more restricted. They contribute to keeping these societies together, but they do so over less inclusive distances. Conversely, social roles and technical knowledge grow in significance as societies grow in extent. They enable millions of strangers to interact, without resorting to violence. Indeed, the increased prominence of roles and knowledge is one of the primary reasons large-scale societies emerged. These mechanisms provided a means by which strangers could act as if they knew each other. As to normative rules and exchange relationships, had universal religions and monetary exchange never developed, human societies would never have grown beyond the agricultural stage. Moreover, they provided the economic resources and interpersonal trust without which professionalized societies would be impossible.

The Liberal Dream, as we shall see, is grounded in an exaltation of personal relationships and face-to-face hierarchies. It tends to dismiss social roles as of little import and even though it pays lip service to our "information age," it is apt to be anti-scientific. Liberalism cannot supply the blueprint for our shared future because it violates the inverse force rule. It is riven with contradictions and saddled down with failures precisely because it seeks to organize a mass society with forces that cannot do the job. Instead of honestly assessing what is needed to keep people working productively in a techno-commercial world, it wallows in fantasies derived from long ago and far away. As a result, its devotees make egregious mistakes. With their eyes closed to reality and their hearts committed to ancient fairy tales, they stumble over hard truths. While they assure us they are super-moral intellectuals, their leaders act like spoiled children. Although they tell us that they hope to share marvelous treasures, they essentially predict that candy will one day rain from the sky. They may believe what they say, but some of us remain skeptical.

If the inverse force rule is correct, then liberalism's unconstrained view of our future is profoundly wrongheaded. If large-scale societies are to survive, they must endure constraints on what is possible within them. Conservatives may be vague as to these limits, but we should now have a better grasp of their extent. Social Domain Theory describes our human and social natures in greater detail than is customary. As such, it tells us who we are and what we can become. Thus, those who attempt to prophesize the future must respect these restrictions. Every potential society has to account for all of the cultural and structural orders. Each must also respect the inverse force rule. Predictions that do not include mechanisms for allowing large numbers of people to interact harmoniously are implausible. Such prophesies are bound to fail because they are out of sync with how societies develop. We currently belong to a techno-commercial civilization that is likely to grow larger and more technological; hence idealized improvements that do not accommodate these facts cannot come true.

A History Lesson

When I teach social change at Kennesaw State University, my students generally have less to say than in many of my other classes. Because social change involves history, and they know precious little about the past, they are usually too uncomfortable to participate. In this, they are like most Americans. Chiefly concerned with the here and now, a majority are blissfully unaware of George Santayana's dictum. Santayana famously cautioned that those who do not remember the past are destined to repeat it. Of course, many of my students never learned history, never mind forgot it. Back in high school the lessons taught were so bland and uninformative, they were considered irrelevant. Why, they asked, should they commit to memory names and dates that had nothing to do with the lives they would eventually lead?

At this point, I must once more beg the reader's indulgence. History may not be everyone's favorite subject, but it is time for a short history lesson. The particulars of how the various social orders have expressed themselves in different sorts of societies must be reviewed. Before we can examine what is possible in our future, we must familiarize ourselves with what happened in the past. Indeed, evidence confirming the inverse force rule is only obtainable by looking backward. Only this can provide tangible examples of how small and large societies have been constructed. These instances also allow us to understand how and why communities transform over time.

Hunter-Gatherer Societies. Hunter-gatherer societies were family-based. Not only were they small, with most of their interactions face-to-face, but a majority of their members were biologically related. When anthropologists began to study so-called primitive societies, their kinship bonds transfixed them. Accustomed to Western societies in which kinship categories are fairly restricted, they were unprepared for the distinctions these peoples made. They not only spoke of cousins, but distinguished cousins on their mother's side from those on their father's. They often did the same for aunts and uncles. Where we tend to consider ourselves members of both our mother and father's families, they frequently counted themselves as belonging to one or the other. Indeed, many of these societies were patrilineal, whereas others were matrilineal, that is, they figured descent from the father's line or the mother's. Some were likewise patrilocal, whereas others were matrilocal. In these cases, married couples were expected to reside either near the father's or the mother's family. In other words, it mattered more to them than us with whom they associated on a daily basis.

There was a reason for this. Different behaviors were associated with different family relationships. The way you greeted your father's sister might not be the same as how you greeted your mother's brother. If you made a mistake in these matters, it was considered a grave error for which significant reparations were in order. Nor were the duties assigned to particular relationships neglected. These too were highly differentiated and strictly enforced. For instance, it might not be the father who was required to support his biological children. It could be the mother's brother. Not his own children, but hers received the fruits of his labor. Food acquired in the hunt or grown in a nearby garden was not distributed willy-nilly. Who was entitled to get what was determined by how people were related to each other. Accordingly, one relative might be entitled to the liver, while another received the tenderloin. This meant there were fewer disputes about who got what. Personal relationships were important among our hunter-gatherer ancestors thanks to the fact that carefully specifying obligatory interactions helped reduce potential conflicts.

Because these distinctions were crucial, family counted for far more among them than us. Families back then provided emotional support for their members, but much more. They were not merely expressive institutions, but economic, political, and religious ones. Members of a family had to work together to support themselves. Without supermarkets, they were forced to hunt and gather with relatives. They also fashioned their tools and prepared their meals in the company of relatives. They likewise participated in shared decisions about where the group would travel. Were they to have split up and journeyed around their territory as independent agents, they would soon have perished from starvation. In addition, everyone played a vital part in praying to the gods. The ceremonies in which they participated depended upon all concerned upholding their designated roles. Family members were even vital in providing medical services. The band might boast a shaman, but individual appeals to one's ancestors were integral to maintaining health.

Obviously, with no one else to provide sustenance but themselves, they had to make certain family relations were dependable. Theirs, we tend to forget, was a world fraught with uncertainty. Both figuratively and literally, they clung to one another for aid and comfort in a hostile physical environment. In this sense, the family was the center of their universe. Their need to rely upon it was so imperative that a longing for closeness became part of our biological heritage. We human beings still crave closeness to a few well-known others. Even though our circumstances are profoundly different, without this we feel lonely.

On the other hand, one of the pervasive myths of contemporary social science is that small-scale hunter-gatherer societies did not have hierarchies. They are often depicted as completely egalitarian. Because people knew each other intimately, it is scarcely imaginable that they would have lorded it over one another. It was true, of course, that hunter-gatherers did not live in palaces. Everyone resided in correspondingly modest huts. Similarly, no one had retinues of servants. Each was required to work to provide for the community. In fact, all ate the same things and shared similar dangers. No one patronized fancy restaurants or stood aloof from animal attacks. Thus, they all knew first hand that they were vulnerable. As a result, extreme deference was unknown. Hunter-gatherers did not bow to one another. Nor did they kiss a leader's feet. If one became too pretentious, he or she was taken down a peg. Teasing a person who acted superior typically served to enforce humility. It informed the braggart that self-importance was unwelcome.

This, however, does not demonstrate an absence of hierarchy. Inequalities were indeed present, albeit in a form different from our own. We know this because the archeological record is filled with indicators of unequal status. One is the presence of beads. These tiny adornments were difficult to produce in pre-industrial communities and therefore served as a mark of respect. Only a group's leaders, not its novice hunters, were allowed this sort of decoration. We also find differences in burial goods. Respected leaders were sent to the afterlife accompanied by tools and ornaments that honored their standing. Moreover, in life, hierarchy was generally expressed through deference to the group's elders. Their words were listened too more carefully than those of callow adolescents. They were also addressed in a manner consistent with their status. If for no other reason, they elicited awe as the band's long-term memory bank. In an era filled with physical hazards, life expectancy was short, ergo those who survived to a relatively great age were unusual. This meant that they experienced things younger persons had not. They recalled, for example, when a drought forced game animals to move down river. They also remembered how the band survived this and other dangers. As a consequence, their opinions were valued. When they recommended that the group travel in one direction rather than another, their advice was usually decisive. They therefore exercised greater power than others. Their wisdom, in essence, ranked them higher than their band-mates. Their strength was thus not physical, but was expressed in greater knowledge and measured judgment. These allowed them to defeat lower ranking individuals who challenged their primacy.

Another form of hierarchical dominance also existed among them precisely because they were hunters. We human beings are effective carnivores because we are group hunters. We are able to bring down large animals because we cooperate in the attack. Nevertheless, cooperative assaults necessitate coordination. Much as football teams require a quarterback to call the signals, so do hunting parties. They need someone to plan the attack and signal who should do what. As a consequence, the hunt leader needs to be good at what he does. He also needs to command respect. If he does not, others may defy his instructions. How then did a person achieve this status? It must be remembered that members of hunter-gatherer bands lived with each other day in and day out. They therefore had many opportunities determine who was better at particular skills. Years of hunting in concert provided what were essentially extended tests of strength. In the end, the best hunters were known and esteemed. They received deference because they had earned it.

Lest it be forgotten, such tests were face-to-face encounters. They consequently possessed the potential for face-to-face violence. Hierarchy was present, but had to be handled with care. A comparable situation existed among horticulturalists. Small-scale farmers, such as found in the New Guinea highlands, are often led by individuals described by anthropologists as "big men." One of the ways they obtain their status is by providing sumptuous feasts for the community. In order to achieve this they must be good farmers. But this is not enough. The only way to collect enough food for a major banquet is to induce others to contribute to the venture. Big men generally obtain these donations, not through violence, but via their diplomatic talents. They are invariably good talkers and accomplished students of human nature. They know what to say and how to act in order to assemble winning coalitions. In command by virtue of their superior aptitudes, they also depend on their greater political acuity. Leaders among hunter-gatherers must be similarly skilled. If they are insensitive bullies, they are unlikely to receive deference, despite their hunting prowess. People who know them intimately would become resentful and look elsewhere for guidance.

Women too have unequal status in hunting communities. As with the men, age matters among them. Older women have more experience with midwifery and health concerns than younger ones. As a result, they are listened to with greater respect. Similarly, the most influential gatherers are usually more politically astute. They too must be good with words and diplomatically savvy, otherwise they cannot acquire the alliances needed to obtain superior status. Putting these pieces together, it becomes plain that our remote ancestors, even though they resided in small and relatively impoverished societies, lived in a hierarchical world. The difference between their situation and ours was that theirs more often involved face-to-face arrangements. As a result, they had to be more careful in how they asserted priority. It was also more difficult for them to pretend to be what they were not. They did not have to promise "transparency" because they could scarcely avoid it.

Agricultural Societies. When climatic changes forced our ancestors to grow their own food, this transformed their way of life. Instead of participating in small nomadic groups, they settled down in villages and towns. At first hundreds of people, but eventually many thousands, became neighbors. No longer was it possible for everyone to know everyone else. This was especially so when towns consolidated into nations and nations joined together to form empires. Peoples who did not even speak the same language might thus find themselves part of the same political entity. As a consequence, they did not, and could not, work together as if they were literally members of the same family. Of necessity strangers to many with whom they had to cooperate, they required different sorts of attachments.

Nonetheless, the family did not disappear. It still existed within the local village. It also persisted among the governing elites. Now it was transformed into a hereditary principle within the ruling class. Leaders did not have to prove their individual merit in order to exercise sovereignty. If they were born to the right parents, they could succeed despite their personal limitations. This placed the emphasis on lineages. Familial aristocracies became the norm. Some people were deemed to have bluer blood than others because of their biological connections. As a result, they inherited the land, titles, and prerogatives of their parents. Family connections remained important, but their influence was exercised over a more restricted sphere.

Similarly, hierarchies did not disappear. In fact, the distance between their apex and base grew. Instead of face-to-face hierarchies in which people assessed their relative power in actual tests of strength, they now depended on symbolic indicators of power. Eventually, empires were ruled by sovereigns who lived under different circumstances than the peasants over whom they reigned. Now the emperors resided in palaces where they were fawned over by legions of retainers. Many were even considered Gods. For a peasant to approach an emperor might therefore be considered an act of defilement, which was subject to the death penalty. Under these conditions, it was impossible for lower ranking members of the community to evaluate the strengths of their leaders directly. They had to depend on roundabout evidence. Being able to command the construction of a massive pyramid or decorating a temple with mysterious hieroglyphics served as proof of a monarch's strength. This is why rulers regularly burnished their images via efforts at conquest or in elaborate building projects. These, not their individual qualities, were used to impress others.

Still, something else was needed to hold millions of subjects in quiet submission. Terror sometimes worked, but it also bred rebellion. Another sort of adhesive, one that could connect huge numbers of strangers, was required. This mechanism, this interpersonal force, was found in religion. The Pharaoh was not only a king, he was a God. Not only a great general, he was the empire's supreme religious leader. Religion provided a cosmological explanation for why the existing order was what it was. More importantly, it also furnished supernatural sanctions to defend it. People who broke the rules, including the prescription demanding obedience to the supreme leader, were deemed immoral. Hence, they deserved to be punished for their insolence. If they did not follow the rules, they would not go to Heaven, but be sent to hell. This was frightening, but also alluring. It gave people a reason to be obedient. Moreover, it motivated people who might differ from one another. If they believed in the same Gods, they could be induced to live up to the same standards. Unable even to observe the Beings from which the sanctions flowed, their unpredictability made them more threatening.

Thus, with the advent of agricultural societies, first national religions and then universal ones arose. Egyptians were Egyptians, in part, because they honored the power of Isis and Ra. They likewise followed the Pharaoh's directives to build an enormous pyramid because after his death this edifice would facilitate his mediation with the other Gods. This would ensure that the annual Nile flood fertilized their fields and kept their bellies full. They therefore obeyed a unified leadership because it was in their interest to do so. When empires succeeded nations, the same principle applied, but over wider areas. It was at this point that universal religions arose. Gods who were not national, but international, became prominent. In the case of Judaism, then Christianity and Islam, this was a single deity. Monotheism made it possible to postulate a Supreme Being who was both omniscient and omnipotent. As the creator of the universe, He decreed how people—all people—should live. Moreover, he had the power to enforce his commands. More potent than any emperor, He could ensure that disparate peoples complied with their ruler's directives. Constantine the Great understood this when he promoted Christianity in the Roman Empire; Clovis the Frank understood it when he converted to Christianity upon conquering Gaul; the great Indian emperors understood it when they endorsed Buddhism. What is more, this strategy succeeded. It made different peoples feel as if they were part of a single extended community.

The Classic Civilizations. The Bible says that the love of money is the root of evil, which makes it sound as if money has always been with us. In fact, fungible currency is a relatively recent invention. Indeed, its advent, like agriculture, was one of history's momentous turning points. It changed the way our ancestors lived and made possible advances that could not otherwise have occurred. In the West, coinage was invented in roughly 650 BC. Starting in what is today Turkey, it quickly spread to places like Greece and Rome. These became powerful commercial entrepots only after a reliable means of exchange enabled them to do business in every corner of the Mediterranean. Athens, for instance, could scarcely have assembled a mini empire had it not been able to sell wine, olive oil, and pottery far and wide. Its own impoverished soil could never have sustained its opulence were the Athenians forced to consume only what they produced. It was by exchanging their goods for the grains and lumber of others that they established their power. Money facilitated the trade in which they engaged by making it possible to do business with those who did not possess the products they desired. The coins these others proffered were accepted because these could be used to purchase desirable goods elsewhere.

Money-based societies quickly became city-based. Commerce was centered in municipalities because these were convenient places to do business. Their compact size brought buyers and sellers together in face-to-face marketplaces. Cities were also convenient places to manufacture items for exchange. Athenian artisans, for instance, developed highly coveted forms of pottery. These utilitarian objects, originally needed for the transport of wine and oil, became valued in themselves as intensive practice perfected the skills of their makers. But city life had its own imperatives. The Greeks and Romans came to think of themselves as civilized precisely because they resided in these locales. Residence within them altered the ways people governed themselves, the way they produced wealth, the manner in which they amused themselves, and even how they thought. Ultimately, it made them more sophisticated and self-reliant.

In the commercial city-based societies of the classic Western civilizations families continued to exist, but their shape and functions were again modified to fit the evolving conditions. Literal families could no more hold city-states together than they could agrarian empires. What now supplemented them were artificial families. Thus, successful Romans were not only the heads of biological families, but of patronage chains. They doled out benefits to clients who treated them as quasi-fathers. This arrangement was something like that found in Mario Puzo's *The Godfather*. Here too the patron held a mini-court attended by clients in search of favors and instructions. On a larger scale, granting citizenship to a broad constituency encouraged family feelings among disparate peoples. Tribes that had not been Roman were allowed to join the nation, that is, to enter its quasi-extended family. This gave them a say, if a limited one, in the community's affairs.

As to hierarchy, the arrangements of the classical civilizations varied wildly. The Athenians are still celebrated for their participatory democracy, whereas the Roman Republic was a casualty of its own success. Rome ultimately became an empire, not entirely unlike its agrarian predecessors. Some emperors actually styled themselves Gods and lived far more opulently than plebeians. Nevertheless, electoral office survived in Rome even at its imperial peak. Who got to vote differed with the sort of election, and both politicking and bribery were rampant; nevertheless, the opinions of ordinary Romans influenced the policies of their rulers. If nothing else, bread and circuses were required to keep the rabble content, while ordinary soldiers were rewarded with plunder and land.

The hierarchical spoiler in this otherwise more egalitarian order was slavery. Indeed, Marx was so impressed with its prominence that he characterized the classical civilizations as "slave societies." Paradoxically, this form of submission became widespread thanks to their commercial underpinnings. Slaves are not very useful in agrarian societies. When most production is for local consumption, surpluses are of relatively little value. When, however, these can be marketed in exchange for other products, they increase in worth. As the human tools that produced these surpluses, slaves also increased in usefulness. Consequently, capturing enemies in battle and forcing them into bondage became a source of wealth. The result was that as the Roman Empire expanded, it expanded in prosperity.

Although the Romans possessed advanced technologies, their industrial capacities were grounded in slave labor. The Romans were indeed great engineers. Had they not possessed the technical capacity to build durable roads or construct enormous aqueducts, they could not have fed or watered their cities. Nevertheless, their commercial greatness depended on an institution contingent on military expansion. Once this growth came to a halt, once vast resources were required just to keep potential invaders at bay, the logic of Roman commerce turned on itself. As a result, the classical way of life was no longer self-sustaining. Business became ossified and wealth more land-based. When this occurred, the most critical adhesive holding its society together failed. Peoples who previously cooperated because there was a profit in it, lost the incentive to join forces. Conflict became endemic, which was bad for business. Eventually, desperate emperors resorted to price and job controls in order to keep the creaky edifice intact. This, however, had the opposite effect. In undermining the flexibility of the marketplace, it reduced trade and the tolerance that comes from it. What had been a cosmopolitan world soon became a parochial one ripe for invasion. No longer able to muster sufficiently loyal armies, the Barbarians came crashing through the gates.

Industrial Societies. When modern Western societies arose from the ashes of the Roman Empire, they did so on a different industrial basis.

A machine-based economy ultimately replaced the old slave-based one. At first this did not seem likely. Early Medieval Europe was poor and local. Having reverted to its agricultural roots, a family-dominated political system reasserted itself. Feudalism was much like the earlier agricultural empires in depending on family lineages to organize interpersonal relationships. Hereditary principles once more became prominent, with estates and titles being handed down from father to son. Hierarchy was thus linked to biology, while the symbols of power were embodied in the castle and military prowess. These unfortunately had centrifugal properties. In glorifying conflict, they made it difficult for leaders to assemble large political entities.

Things began to change when commerce revived. It did so under the patronage of kings and embryonic nation-states. Once these could protect trade by means of new inventions, such as the cannon and stirrup, they could command revenues that further enhanced their ability to enforce a centralized peace. And, as had happened earlier, once commerce accelerated, the demand for additional articles of exchange also grew. This time, not slavery, but mechanical means came to the fore. Nonhuman sources of energy were ultimately harnessed to produce unprecedented volumes of merchandise. At first water wheels and windmills did the job, but eventually steam engines took over. When teamed with spinning jennies, power looms, and railroads, they flooded the market with higher quality goods than previously. Entrepreneurs grew rich, not because they conquered foreign territories, but because they mastered ingenious technologies. In this respect, Marx was correct. Those who controlled the means of production, now concentrated in industry, acquired the ability to grow fabulously wealthy.

The growth of commerce was also abetted by monetary innovations. The invention of coinage was a seminal event, but so was the advent of credit. The creation of banks, checking accounts, and stock markets made it easier to buy and sell goods. In due course credit cards, computer transfers, and brokerage houses furthered this process. Added to this was the invention of the modern corporation. Its bureaucratic machinery allowed hundreds of thousands of individuals to work in concert on extremely complex tasks, such as producing automobiles. This resulted in a deluge of material products that enabled even relatively poor workers to live more lavishly than the kings of yore. Commerce became a way of life. Almost every article needed for survival arrived by way of the marketplace. Technology also became a way of life. New and better techniques developed so quickly that adjusting to their increased tempo became an integral part of modern societies. This accelerated change—now called progress—continued to contribute to the comfort of ordinary people.

Under these circumstances, the family retreated, not to insignificance, but a secondary status. It became, in Christopher Lasch's pregnant phrase, "a haven in a heartless world." After a hard day of competing in an economic system located outside the home, men and women sought protection among individuals to whom they were emotionally attached. As desirous of such bonding as their remote forebears, these ties were now of more personal than social significance. Connections such as these did not so much hold society together as create pockets of affection within it. Families also served to socialize the next generation. With no other institution capable of furnishing the sort of love and lessons available from parents, children were unlikely to grow into the self-directed adults necessary to manage a complex techno-commercial civilization without them. In this, families provided the community with vital benefits, but not the extensive economic, political, or religious services of the past. Families were instead transformed into isolated nuclear units. No longer extended as they were centuries earlier, their members frequently resided at different ends of the country.

With respect to hierarchy, the face-to-face contests of old also retreated in significance. People still engaged in athletic events in order to test their mettle, but these were more for fun than social standing. The more serious competitions occurred in the economic and political realms. Making money or rising to prominence in major bureaucracies became the ticket to higher social standing. In a world were more people than ever were strangers, individuals often introduced themselves by announcing their occupational titles. These, along with the clothes they wore and the cars they drove, indicated their relative power. But this was not the end of the story. Society also became more democratic. Some people still had greater clout; yet lording it over those with less power became almost as gauche as among hunter-gatherers. Every one was to be regarded (at least in theory) as entitled to equal opportunity and equality before the law. In this respect, hierarchy too became more confined in its influence.

Religion too declined in significance. No longer was there an established faith to which all subscribed. Indeed, many people regarded themselves as secular. A majority maintained a loose belief in a deity, but most were vague about the details. Many, in fact, saw their religious sentiments migrate to an allegiance to universalistic ideologies. They were still true believers, albeit in communism, liberalism, or libertarianism. This is not to say that arguments over political allegiances could not grow heated. Nonetheless, they were less likely to be violent. Democratic institutions fostered a commitment to compromise and tolerance. Except for aberrations such as Nazism, modern Westerners preferred nasty words and protest marches to civil wars or duels to the death.

As a consequence, commerce and its accompanying technological developments became a more important source of social solidarity. Today, people get along with one another because they realize they are dependent upon each other. As in all trading societies, it does not make sense to insult, never mind to injure, one's customers or suppliers. It is far more important to understand them so as to make profitable deals. Some say ours is an Information Age. If so, this is partly because people profit from knowledge of each other. In this regard, it is no accident that the most advanced industrial communities are the one's that most value knowledge and tolerance.

Often overlooked as ties that bind are our social roles. We may identify ourselves with the jobs we perform, but these seem more private than social. We know such tasks are part of a complex division of labor, yet we perceive them from our personal points of view. Even less visible is how often we deal with others in terms of our respective roles. Especially when encountering strangers, we cannot rely on knowledge of who they are. Instead we recognize their roles. Is this person standing behind a glass window in front of a movie theater, then we understand why she is asking which film we wish to see. We in turn answer her question, tender our money, then receive tickets we shortly hand to a ticker-taker. It is all so straightforward that we forget there was a time we had to learn these operations. Now they are so reflexive it does not occur to us that these procedures regulate our relationships with unfamiliar persons. It is as if these others were well-known because we are comfortable with their parts. We, and they, all know what to say and do. There is no need to fear the unexpected because there is no unexpected.

Social roles form the woof and warp of contemporary social life. They are the most extensive element in organizing our relationships with strangers. Whenever we enter a shop, walk down the street, or participate in a business transaction, we do so on the basis of our roles.

Whenever we drive an automobile, ride on an airplane, or attend a baseball game, we follow role-based templates. Everywhere we turn there are roles to be played, even at home with our spouses and children. Erving Goffman claimed that, as per William Shakespeare, all the world is a stage—and he was not far wrong. We do regularly perform for one another. Indeed, we often recognize one another through these performances. Not only are they the masks we wear; they are also who we have become. These may be parts we play, but they are also part of us. Moreover, as we shall shortly see, professionalized roles occupy a more prominent position than previously. No longer is it sufficient to play roles; we are now required to perform more complex roles ever more competently. Our personal happiness and social integrity depend upon it.

Summing Up. At this point it should be clear that the inverse force rule is reflected in our history. The stronger forces were, in fact, more prominent in binding small societies together, whereas the weaker ones have increased in salience in the larger ones. While all of the social orders are visible in every society, the family and face-to-face hierarchies were most potent among hunter-gatherers. Conversely, social roles, as well as both knowledge and technology, occupy more prominent positions in industrialized societies. Meanwhile the intermediate forces, namely morality as exemplified in religion and social exchange as embodied in commercial transactions, grew in importance as communities grew in size. The pattern is clear. So is the rational for this progression. Strong feelings have the greatest influence among people who know each other well, whereas strangers must rely on lesser passions. Because strong feelings are most likely to arise between intimates, they are available to regulate how they interact. It would be difficult for these to do so among people who do not know each other. By the same token, were intense passions to arise between strangers, they would be difficult to contain. People who do not care about one another can go to extremes. They can engage in cold-blooded murder precisely because they are operating in cold blood. The Holocaust was a modern phenomenon because bureaucracy was used to treat human beings as objects of commerce. Likewise Genghis Khan casually annihilated millions of Chinese peasants because for him they were the equivalent of draft animals.

On the other hand, social roles and technical knowledge work well among strangers because these do not require people to know each other. The same applies to business transactions. These mechanisms can be applied dispassionately. While they are no substitute for strong feelings, they reduce the likelihood of casual violence among those who do not, and cannot, personally care about each other. There may be nothing romantically satisfying about a world in which humans treat each other in terms of what they do, rather than who they are, but this is the world in which we live. It is also the one in which we have to live—that is, as long as billions of us continue to occupy this planet.

Conservative Ideals

Conservatism is widely reckoned to be retrogressive. It is generally assumed that conservatives wish to return to an earlier, more idealistic era. They presumably want to go back to a time before the modern hustle and bustle of industrialization and our massive exposure to untrustworthy strangers. There is some truth to this—but only some. It represents what certain conservatives want, but not all. For simplicity's sake we will distinguish between religious conservatives, traditionalists, and neoconservatives. As we shall see, their goals are related, but not identical.

But first, from whence do our political ideals derive? When people conjure with the possibilities, where do they draw their inspiration? By and large, political theorists assess them in terms of their purported end-point. But where is their actual starting point? Ideals do not descend from heaven, nor are they snatched from thin air. More usually, they are grounded in one or another of the social orders. Idealists usually look toward the mechanisms that keep societies together and then romanticize them. In their imaginations, they push these to extremes. They typically fantasize about their perfect incarnations and assume that once these arrive people will be totally happy. Moreover, because ideals are inherently moralistic, that is, because they embody highly valued behaviors, their most vociferous partisans tend to be radical. As the flag bearers of moral factions, they are apt to be simplistic, enthusiastic, and intolerant. They know that in order to be persuasive, they must paint idyllic pictures of the future. That these are based on inflated illusions bothers them not a whit. They do not prize accurate roadmaps because their goal is to lead people to the Promised Land, not to take them over the river.

Among religious conservatives, the social orders found most salient are personal relationships as exemplified in the family and hierarchy as instantiated in face-to-face relationships. In accord with the assertions of their enemies, the religiously devout essentially want to go back in time. As astonishing as it may seem, they would like to return to an idealized version of hunter-gatherer bands. In their mind's eye, however, they do not perceive us as scratching out a living by slaying antelopes or digging for roots. Rather, their vision returns us to an idealized vision of these activities. They would like to revive the Garden of Eden. In their ideal, we are projected as living in a lush setting where all of our needs are provided. All we will need to do is take what we want, without killing or grubbing in the dirt. Actually, the place they have in mind has a name. It is called heaven. In heaven, we will no longer have any cares. All of our needs will be provided by supernatural means; hence we will be eternally content.

In heaven, we are also told that we will be reunited with our loved ones. They will be resurrected in perfect bodies and perfect spirits. All of the old arguments that once divided us will evaporate in a bacchanal of love. We will then embrace each other and luxuriate in a conflict-free environment. More than this, love will be universal. We will share it with every other being that has similarly arrived in heaven. They too will be embraced as if they were members of our immediate family. Moreover, no one will be treated badly. No one will be rejected because of any imperfection. Indeed, there will be no imperfections. Consequently, everyone will be equally respected. Having been scrutinized at the entrance gate, no one need be judged any further.

Our love will also be directed toward God. If every other resurrected spirit is regarded as a sibling, God will be looked upon as our common father. Having created us from the dust of the earth and then elevated us to everlasting paradise, He is deserving of unconditional love. He is the perfect father. Both omniscient and omnipotent, He will provide whatever we need. An unparalleled protector who always wants the best for us, He is essentially a flawless village elder writ large. Back among the hunter-gatherers real leaders were fallible. As a faultless sovereign, however, He is not. He is the ideal hierarchical superior. Better than any mere human, it is impossible for Him to lose a test of strength. His authority is thus absolute. We, in turn, must worship Him and provide unqualified obedience. His will is to be done, not ours. His is in command, not us.

This then is an idealization of both family and face-to-face hierarchy as integrated into a seamless whole. It takes what we once were and converts it into the perfect realization of our deepest hopes. We are essentially being told that our genetic biases toward personal attachments and face-to-face ranking systems will be gratified to the

206

nth degree. This ideal is attractive precisely because it indulges our long-standing biological dispositions. A desire for a close-knit family and fair, protective leadership is our birthright. It is a genetic heritage derived from a long hunter-gatherer apprenticeship. As a result, we will be infinitely happy.

Religious conservatives are also reactionary in idealizing universal religiosity. They are the legitimate heirs to the great religions that arose during the heyday of the agrarian empires. As a result, their fantasies of a better future tend to be modeled after what was then considered ideal. God, as portrayed by most monotheistic religions, is not merely a father, but a mighty emperor. He is described as sitting on a throne surrounded by sycophants continually praising His virtues. Moreover, like the emperors of old His word is regarded as law. God is thus the perfect emperor, the lord of lords; and we His subjects are idealized peasants, always obedient to his every whim and grateful for His favors. As far as fundamentalists are concerned, both God and the Bible are infallible. The word of the Lord, as handed down by the Church, is to be accepted literally. Whatever questions we may have must be submerged in our adulation of our Creator.

Religious conservatism also seeks to cultivate a universal community of believers. Just as with the Great Religions, everyone is supposed to belong to a common church. Contemporary American evangelicals pay lip service to the need for tolerance, but they secretly long for nonbelievers to come to Christ—that is, Christ as they understand Him. If we will all just believe what we are supposed to, then we will all love each other as we were commanded to, and the millennium will finally arrive. Protestantism encouraged people to read the Bible for themselves, but it also encouraged conformity and submission. Saints are to be emulated, preachers to be admired, and the word of God obeyed.

In this sense, most religious conservatives are not conservative. They are reactionary. They do not want things to remain unchanged. They want to return to an idealized version of the long ago past. Unfortunately, their conception of the future cannot be actualized—unless there is a literal millennium. As long as people are what they are, familial and hierarchical perfection are unattainable here on earth. These principles cannot hold large-scale societies together because universal love and total hierarchical fairness cannot emerge when billions of people are, and must remain, strangers. Furthermore, favoritism and deception will persist as long as our genetic legacy is what it is. For thousands of years religious activists have sought to convert humanity to their ideals and at times have imposed theological supremacy. As often, they have found willing converts who pledged to live up to their vision. Nevertheless, they have never come close to achieving universal love. People have always played favorites and/or cheated in their struggle to get ahead. Moreover, it is safe to predict they always will.

The traditionalists, unlike religious ideologues, are genuinely conservative. They honor religion, but their passion lies in preventing change from overwhelming their comfort zones. Traditionalists believe in preserving the customs and beliefs bequeathed them by an older generation. They too favor obedience, but it is obedience to what has long been the norm. Thus, if the standard has been hierarchical absolutism, this is what they desire. As a result, when monarchies gave way to democracy, they remained ardent monarchists. They fought as cavaliers for Charles I against the parliamentarian roundheads. Later in America, they encouraged George Washington to accept a crown transferred from the head of George III. Traditionalists also honor long-established family customs. They believe the father should be the undisputed head of the household. Women are correspondingly supposed to be submissive and children obedient. Their roles have presumably been laid down from time immemorial and hence are regarded as the foundation of domestic happiness. Unfortunately, this pattern fit the farm-oriented lifestyles of centuries past better than the professionalized needs of a techno-commercial society. It celebrates obedience, as opposed to collaboration or self-direction. For them, what was, is best, irrespective of social advances.

Nonetheless, traditional ideals, although sometimes intransigent, are useful in cautioning us to be vigilant before we make dramatic changes. Before kicking over the traces and discarding the past, we should be sure a projected future does not harbor unwanted side effects. Still, traditionalism does not serve us well in formulating novel approaches to unanticipated challenges. Thus, in looking toward the past, it does not foresee the challenges involved in becoming professionalized. Traditionalists rightly alert us to the fact that our ancestors were as human as we are and therefore faced problems not unlike the ones we face. They are also correct in asserting that our forebears were as intelligent as we are and therefore made discoveries potentially relevant to our situation. Where they are less helpful is in examining the implications of developing events. The past cannot be ignored, but neither should it be slavishly followed.

The neoconservatives, in contrast, are not particularly conservative. Nowadays they find themselves aligned with the religious and traditional conservatives, but this is more in opposition to radical liberalism than in allegiance to the past. Most neoconservatives are comfortable with what liberals believed a hundred years ago. They too want progress, albeit slow and measured progress. They agree that some government services are essential, but are convinced that a healthy market-based economy is likewise critical. As fiscal conservatives, they favor sound spending policies, while as social moderates, they want a safety net for the disadvantaged. Moreover, the neo-cons tend to be internationalists. They do not support isolationist policies, nor fear international competition. While they insist on protecting America militarily, this is because they believe democracy must be defended against its enemies.

Nor are the neocons opposed to a professionalized society. They have not explicitly sponsored one, but that is because professionalization is rarely recognized as pervading our techno-commercial society. They should, therefore, not be blamed for missing what most people miss. Nor are the neocons opposed to knowledge or technology. They do not look toward the past for inspiration in the manner that religious and traditional conservatives often do. To the contrary, they tend to be passionate intellectuals. Many, in fact, are displaced academics who became disillusioned with the authoritarian streak of liberal scholars. Although sometimes dismissed as not very bright, today they are liable to be more intellectually adventurous than their rivals. Absolutely *not* afraid of new ideas, neither do they distrust new-fangled machines. To the contrary, they champion technological solutions to environmental problems. They also support technological improvements in our way of life, including in communication, transportation, information, and production. Despite their name, the neocons are fond of change. They also appreciate democracy, fairness, freedom, and prosperity. Thus, their ideas, though in some quarters reviled as mean-spirited and authoritarian, come closer to suiting the demands of modern mass living.

Liberal Ideals

Liberals assure us they are progressives. Indeed, nowadays many prefer this designation. They claim to be the wave of the future, but when their ideals are analyzed in light of the inverse force rule, they fall far short of what is advertised. Recall the major elements of the

Liberal Dream. Liberals believe in (1) universal love, (2) as mediated by government programs, (3) designed and administered by the best and brightest, such that (4) war, poverty, and discrimination are eliminated, and (5) full equality which (6) protects the underdog emerges. They also intend to (7) liberate people from oppression by encouraging self-actualization, and by (8) getting everyone to be nice to everyone else. This is the future as they see it. This is the vision of progress for which they are prepared to fight. The question is this: Is it viable? As good as it may sound, is it feasible for a mass, techno-commercial society?

Let us start with universal love. Liberals believe in love. They believe in it as ardently as any religious conservative. Liberals want all human beings to belong to a single planet-wide village. Our common humanity is to be acknowledged and the barriers to cooperative action torn down. We are essentially asked to join a global family. Every other human being is described as deserving of the same love we bestow on our friends and relatives. To favor just those we know personally is regarded as parochial. It is thought to exemplify an outmoded prejudice. Just because our grandparents were jingoistic is no reason we should be. We must, in contrast, look outward to embrace diversity in the sense of loving those different from ourselves. Merely being human is the only qualification they require for joining in their crusade.

Since many people are reluctant to follow these prescriptions, liberals turn to the government to enforce their ambitions. Not the Church, but the power of the state, is to be employed to obtain compliance. Liberals may believe in equality, but they also believe in centralized authority. That this authority is based on hierarchy is not, however, part of their mantra. Determined to be nice (as opposed to coercive), they have an odd vision of government. They officially believe it must persuade rather than command. Although they have no compunctions about forcing recalcitrant souls into submission, they imagine that most of the people, especially the oppressed, will accept the truth as they see it. Others will also welcome government leadership and follow its mandates once they realize this is in the common interest.

In addition, the liberals who design and administer these beneficial programs will receive respect for their aid and compassion. Smarter and more moral than the bulk of humankind, lesser mortals will not resent their authority. Overflowing with saintly love, liberal leaders will be perceived as doing what is right. That this admiration implies hierarchy is not, however, acknowledged. Since the compliance of ordinary citizens will be voluntary, the best and brightest assume that this entails appreciation rather than obedience. After all, they do not ask for submission, only a rational acceptance of the truth. Except, of course, that in being respected, they will be esteemed to a greater degree than other folks. These others will listen and comply because they recognize the superior qualities of their mentors.

In essence, liberal leaders perceive themselves as an updated version of the elders who once held sway among hunter-gatherers. They believe that they too deserve respect as an outcome of their superior knowledge. Theirs is thus the equivalent of a face-to-face demonstration of transcendent ability. Essentially best because they will prove stronger in intellectual/moral tests of strength, this does not imply coercion. Rather, they will command deference by gently leading the less gifted to recognize what is best. Their strength is therefore not that of bullies, but of concerned father figures. Although they may not be older than those they govern, it is as if they were. As a result, their intellectual and moral, rather than chronological, age must prevail. Still and all, whatever they say, this is hierarchical deference. Liberals often portray the government as impersonal and devoid of overbearing status. They depict it as a collection of rules and programs, rather than of people. Nevertheless, governments are composed of individual humans; hence to the extent that its leaders make decisions others must follow, they exercise power over them.

Liberals tell us they hate oppression. Their goal is to rescue the little people from exploitation by the powerful. In their best of all possible worlds, they will transfer resources from the wealthy to the poor so that everyone is on the same plane. But to do this, they must first confiscate the resources of the wealthy. Since few people willingly surrender their property even for the greater good, they will have to be forced to do so. The government must take the excess they presumably do not need. It must, in short, tax them. But to tax them, it has to possess the clout to enforce submission. And herein lies the rub. Enforcing a tax code is not nice. It is inherently coercive. As many conservatives are fond of pointing out, a government strong enough to give people everything they want is strong enough to appropriate everything they have. Indeed, it will wield more power than the emperors of old. By concentrating the apparatus needed to govern in a relatively few hands, it bestows an authority far greater than that possessed by the Egyptian Pharaohs or the Persian emperors. As a consequence, these leaders become oppressors—or at least they possess the potential to be oppressive. No longer equal, they may pretend to be like everyone else, but they are not. Nor can they be entirely nice. Given that there will be some opposition, they must crush it to maintain control.

The liberal vision is therefore grounded in hunter-gatherer principles, as supplemented by the machinery of empire. In complete disregard of reality, it posits a way of life that is no longer viable. Liberals say they are progressive, whereas they are retrogressive. Like religious conservatives, they are reactionary. They, in effect, wish to reinstall ways of life that existed millennia ago. Theirs, to be sure, is an idealized version of our nomadic past, but so is that of the fundamentalists. The difference is that whereas Christian idealists look forward to entering heaven in Heaven, liberals seek it here on earth. Paradoxically, the reason the two hate each other is that they are so alike. They are basically competing for the same constituency. Thus, both liberals and religious conservatives promise perfection. Both also pledge absolute security and total well-being. They consequently appeal either to those who aspire to be village elders or who are resigned to needing their protection.

The trouble is that in subscribing to an unconstrained view of humanity, the liberal ideal ignores the way social domains operate. It pretends that people can be whatever they desire, without acknowledging that they must sometimes be pressured into respecting each other's interests. Liberalism advocates total love, whereas it pays no attention to how actual human beings develop emotional attachments. The liberal ideal does not appreciate that the bonds that held hunter-gatherer bands together were not intellectualized commitments to universal love. People held fast to particular others because their personal feelings produced this outcome. When liberals recommend that we act as if we belong to a single village, they forget that we do not belong to a common village. Villages are small. Their inhabitants know each other. Gossip travels from house to house with alarming speed because it is about people with whom all are familiar. Villagers care about each other and their children (or conversely hate each other), because they are close enough to form intimate bonds. Yet these feelings only emerge with time and proximity. When Hillary Rodham Clinton told us that it takes a village to raise a child, she meant it takes a government. She knew—she had to know—that most people never even meet, never mind look after each other's young as if these were their own. She exploited the emotional connotations of village life, whereas most of us live in a less personal world. We do not, and cannot, interact based on the close attachments that operate over shorter distances. Once more, we may claim to love everyone, but cannot.

Something similar applies to hierarchical relationships. Face-to-face ranking systems in which status is acquired by slowly and carefully assessing comparative strengths depend on individuals being in direct interaction over considerable periods of time. But this is generally not possible in mass, techno-commercial societies. People still compete for hierarchical priority, but usually by symbolic means. Liberals tell us they are the best and brightest, but how do they prove it? For the most part, we are asked to accept their promises on faith. We are told about the miracles we should expect, but when do we see them delivered? We get speeches, see awards presented by liberals to liberals, and are offered extensive legislative programs, but when do we obtain universal love? Similarly, when do we acquire complete equality? If being the best and brightest means your predictions come true, perhaps liberals are not so wonderful. If being superior means you are more moral, liberals may not qualify in this dimension either. Verbal claims are symbols—not actualities. They may be attractive, but they do not possess independent substance.

Meanwhile, the liberal ideal does not stress either knowledge or technology. These two social orders are either assumed or denigrated. This is especially odd given that liberals fancy themselves intellectuals. Often themselves professionals, they prefer a romanticized version of the future to the one they are charged with achieving. This bias is visible in the three greatest strongholds of contemporary liberalism, namely the university, the media, and the entertainment industry. These institutions are cultural leaders, but they are also preeminent symbolic deceivers. The universities boast of being receptacles of knowledge, whereas many have become apologists for liberal causes. Instead of educating students, a majority of professors in the humanities and social science prefer to indoctrinate them. Grades are disseminated, not for what students know, but according to whether they agree with their instructors. Far from being marketplaces of ideas, contemporary higher education perpetuates the received wisdom of the ideologues who control them. At the same time, reporters and editors, who revel in their liberal credentials, dominate the media. They hope to educate the public as to their best interests by writing stories favorable to these causes. Although they insist they are objective, they happily editorialize on the front page. As to the entertainment industry, it glorifies liberals as heroes while shunning conservatives as villains. It likewise distributes glorified visions of a liberal future as if these were achievable. This, however, does not constitute knowledge. It is a pretense of

213

knowledge. It does not seek truth so much as portray its prejudices as factual. More about rationalization than insight, its self-congratulatory tenor masks a procession of shortcomings.

By the same token, technology is relegated to secondary status as compared with all things "natural." Among liberals environmentalism is all the rage. They are therefore skeptical about using technology to achieve greater wealth. Much like John Kenneth Galbraith, they believe an affluent society should devote its resources to helping people, rather than creating things. Besides, producing ever more objects defiles the environment. It pollutes the air and water. As a consequence, we must return to a simpler time when we lived in harmony with nature. Once more the hunter-gatherer lifestyle emerges as the liberal ideal. Many on the far left literally want us to return to the woods. They ask us, for instance, to use less electricity and exploit fewer mineral resources. Their goal is to conserve, rather than misuse. Nuclear reactors are thus out, whereas recycling is in. Cell phones are acceptable, but wouldn't it be better if we abandoned the suburbs so that the forests could regrow? And as to automobiles, there are far too many of them. We need mass transportation not unlike that which existed a century ago. Either that or we should walk to more places. And, oh yes, more front porches would be nice.

Liberals are also uncomfortable with social exchange. They distrust this social order because they associate it with the wealthy, and the wealthy are the enemy. Although most liberals earn their livelihoods in the marketplace, they scorn commerce. It is regarded as grubby and anti-intellectual. So far as they are concerned, making money is about cheating people. The operative word here is "greed." Capitalism is despised because it is presumably grounded in greed. Liberals assume that they themselves are not avaricious. Because they are nice, they are only interested in helping others. Thus, when Obama became president, like many of his predecessors, he bashed business. If the economy had gone South during the Bush administration, it was because Wall Street was dominated by cupidity. Bankers made bad loans, not because regulators told them to, but because they hoped to make a quick buck. They lacked restraint. The government had to tell them to whom, and at what rate, to lend. Industrialists were likewise led astray by self-interest. They too required government administrators to dictate their energy policies. The government always acted responsibly, whereas business people did not. It was therefore up to the government to protect the little people from market driven excesses.

Years earlier, FDR set the tone by declaring during his first term in office that "the forces of selfishness had met their match," while in his second he hoped they would "meet their master." He would impose the correct standards. He would tell business people how much to charge their customers. Oddly, this meant raising prices so that workers could be paid more. Of course, it also meant there were fewer workers and higher unemployment. Senator Charles Schumer recently declared that Roosevelt ended the Great Depression, when, in fact, his policies extended and deepened it. Because Roosevelt distrusted the marketplace, he hoped to dismantle it. The price he paid for this hubris was that the marketplace was no longer available to regulate interpersonal transactions. The glue it provided in a techno-commercial society was diluted and ordinary people bore the brunt of this failure by being unable to find jobs.

As to the normative order, liberal idealists neglect it too. Being secular types, most distrust religion. They regard it as a superstition and therefore as anti-intellectual. In its place they recommend ethical relativism. Every person must be free to define morality as he or she sees fit. Were this the reality, however, the upshot would be chaos. Morality secures individual interests by imposing common standards. Without a consensus as to what these should be, they remain unenforced and therefore nonexistent. Fortunately, liberals are not so foolish. As idealists, they are committed to a host of shared standards. Among these, of course, are universal love, equality, and niceness. But being relativists, they disdain the task of defending these values. Instead of analyzing them, they are assumed. They do not ask, for instance, if a total equality of results is possible. Nor do they question the efficacy of niceness in controlling untoward behaviors. Meanwhile, they are vague as to the meaning of personal responsibility or individual freedom. These tend to be redefined according to the needs of the moment.

The bottom line is that liberals assure us they have banished, or are about to banish, war, poverty, and discrimination. For some reason, they believe that an emphasis on social orders more applicable to hunter-gatherers will bring harmony to a techno-commercial society. In fact, their policies have resulted in nothing of the kind. As we saw several chapters ago, the strong forces they favor have not achieved the goals they prefer. Liberals did not win the war on poverty or end the cold war. Nor did they avert the Great Disruption. Crime and incivility did not disappear under their tutelage. To the contrary, they became more prevalent. Nor have liberals been tolerant of dissent. They claim to hate censorship, but promote a fairness doctrine designed to silence the voices of their critics. Oppression, it seems, is in the eye of the beholder. Liberal policies have also failed with respect to education, welfare, and racism. In none of these cases has an appeal to interpersonal love, total equality, or wholehearted niceness proved effective. In none has the celebrated intellectual prowess of liberals solved the problems as promised.

Contrary to the much-vaunted liberal niceness, this record of failure has elicited dishonesty and massive corruption. Trapped by the contradictions implicit in attempting to create social solidarity via mechanisms unsuited to the task, liberals fall back on deception and manipulation to preserve their reputation for effectiveness. With their caps set on defying historical trends, they seek to obscure their errors. Thus, they ask for greater civility, then defame their opponents. Next they insist they are not greedy, but then provide special benefits to the unions and their crony capitalist friends. Liberalism is dying, and must die, because it cannot furnish the means of maintaining the integrity of massive commercial societies. It can only pretend to. It can twist arms in an effort to force people to agree with its prescriptions. What it cannot do is change reality. Its advocates may ignore the inverse force rule, but that does not mean it will cease to operate. Unfortunately, there is a price to pay for defying reality. Sadly, it is innocent bystanders who usually pick up the tab.

When Barack Obama became president of the United States, he promised an end to politics as usual. He would be honest, direct, and principled. He delivered on the latter pledge only in the sense of being a consistent, far-left ideologue. From his first months in office it became clear he would divert people with a blizzard of lies. Almost immediately he rescinded promises made during the campaign. Obama promised an administration that would be transparent, then sponsored a monstrous stimulus package written in a congressional back room and enacted into law without anyone, including the legislators, reading its eleven hundred pages. He said he would be bipartisan, then told the Republicans they must accept the bill as written. More than once he proclaimed he would banish lobbyists from his administration, then almost immediately made exceptions to this rule. He also swore that there would be no tax hikes on the little people, then proposed a regressive carbon tax. Amazingly, after vowing to eliminate earmarks, he presided over the greatest increase in "special projects" in American history. Nor was he finished with the lies. The biggest whopper was that he was against "big government" and deficits. In fact, in the name of fighting a recession, he planned the largest increase in government spending since the Revolutionary War. In support of reform, according to some calculations, he charted education, energy, and health programs that would spend over twenty trillion dollars. That is trillion with a "t." After having assured the nation he was against waste and budget deficits, he proposed the largest deficits and greater waste than any president before him. By comparison, he made FDR look like a piker. Nor was he above making sleazy deals to pass his programs in the dead of night. Nebraska, Louisiana, and several unions got special considerations to make sure they came on board. Meanwhile Arizona was sued for attempting to enforce immigration laws that Obama would not. The president even claimed the country had run out of oil, when it had only run out of places that could be legally drilled.

Liberals claim to be truth tellers, but they are not above manipulating words to their advantage. One way they attempt to disguise their duplicity is via Newspeak. They use familiar words, then give them a spin opposite the conventional one. Hoping to piggyback on the connotations of the originals, the objective is to entice people to agree even if they do not understand that to which they are consenting. A simple example is "socialism." For years this word was taboo. Because the communists championed it, Americans were wary; hence liberals preferred "social democrat" instead. The result would be the same, namely government control of the economy, but the latter term was more palatable to squeamish voters. Only after Obama won a decisive electoral victory and began to promote the nationalization of the banks did *Newsweek* screw up the courage to crow "We are all socialists now." Evidently the goal had not changed—only the means by which it was sold to the public.

Other examples of liberal newspeak are legion. Thus, Obama sought to disguise his spending bill by calling it an "investment." With investments, however, one expects a return on one's money; with spending it is merely gone. Obama told the American people that they needed to be more "responsible," then took the responsibility out of their hands by concentrating further power in the federal government. He also spoke of "bipartisanship," by which he meant doing as his party wanted. After all, as Nancy Pelosi explained, they had won the election. Even "earmarks" ceased to be earmarks. They became "special projects." And of course, the "fairness doctrine" was never meant to be what most people call "fair." Sad to say, this is a time-honored liberal policy.

217

Roosevelt engaged in it when he redefined "freedom *from* want." Before this, freedom meant the freedom *to* do something, such as to exercise free speech. Clinton followed suit by manipulating the definition of sex to suit his purposes and, of course, by being uncertain about the meaning of "is." Earlier he even seemed unsure of what it meant to "inhale." Time and again the objective was to throw up a smoke screen so as to obscure reality.

As for corruption, liberals seem unconcerned when the rules are bent in their favor. Since the underlying goal is to win rather than be consistent, they had no trouble defending the right of ACORN to buy elections. This was rationalized as an effort to protect minority rights. Years before the mere suspicion that not all of their Florida votes had been counted sent them into paroxysms of righteous indignation, but when extra votes were found for their candidates in Washington State and Minnesota, they were pleased. By the same token when Republicans got into sex trouble they were outraged, whereas when Democratic congresspersons and cabinet nominees were revealed to have tax problems, they shrugged. Worst of all have been the goodies placed into legislation for their friends. These were rationalized as constituent services, even when they enrich the families of legislators. Asked to defend these practices, the response was, "The other side does it too." Perhaps, they do. But one wonders if their mothers taught them that two wrongs do not make a right. Do they seriously believe corruption in the furtherance of their objectives is no longer corruption?

To sum up, liberals and the liberal ideal are not pure. Despite all of the posturing about moral superiority, they cannot be superior because their prescriptions are subverted by the contradictions inherent in their principles. In defying the inverse force rule, in attempting to bind a massive techno-commercial society with forces suited to small face-to-face societies, they seek the impossible. Destined to fail by the nature of their objectives, liberals are forced to deceive themselves and others. However noble their ambitions, they descend into squalid subterfuges in an effort to rescue their project. In the end, they cannot succeed. The nature of the society in which we live will not let them.

Other Ideals

The multiplicity of the social orders allows for a variety of ideals beyond those discussed. Aside from liberalism and the various conservative ideals, other visions enticing followers are anarchism, libertarianism, and romanticism. Their supporters may be small in number, but they remain vocal. Each of these factions relies on a different order to bind society together, or in the case of anarchism not to bind them. Because these ideals continue to command respect, their roots need to be examined. To what extent are they possible?

The anarchists tell us government is unnecessary. Adamantly opposed to hierarchy, they favor a more consistent brand of equality than liberals. Where liberals want to guide less enlightened souls toward a more perfect world, anarchists leave people to their own devices. Even more confident in the goodness of ordinary persons than Rousseau, they are certain everyone can get along without external controls. From their perspective, leadership of any sort is oppressive. The trouble is that anarchists do not offer a believable alternative. Primarily oppositionalist in temperament, their practice has been to tear down rather than build up. Often literal bomb-throwers, they agree with the revolutionary cliché that "you can't make an omelet without cracking a few eggs." Though skilled at breaking things, they have yet to offer a credible recipe for an omelet. How indeed can large societies be held together? What noncoercive mechanisms can keep people from flying apart? The anarchists do not say. They are much better at telling us what they don't like as opposed to what can work.

The libertarians are not so softheaded. They are not thrilled with hierarchical controls either, but they offer an alternative. Most libertarians are fascinated with economics. Where liberals distrust the marketplace and are apt to be economic illiterates, libertarians have inordinate faith in the free market system. They are confident Adam Smith's invisible hand is all that is needed to keep industrial societies intact. If people are allowed to buy and sell unfettered by artificial restrictions, their independent choices will generally add up to what is best for the whole. Reasonable libertarians know there must be safeguards against cheating. Along with Milton Friedman, they also recognize that community effects must be considered. Nonetheless, the emphasis is on free enterprise. As a result, their recommendations usually entail deregulation and divestment. Whether discussing education, transportation, or communication, they assume independent entrepreneurs can do a better job than government apparatchiks. Left to their own instincts, the former are inevitably more efficient and innovative. Consequently everyone benefits, especially their customers.

The difficulty with the libertarian vision is that it has blinders on. Utterly transfixed by the virtues of the marketplace, it neglects other social orders. Rarely mentioned are the moral imperatives required by commercial societies. Also left out is the impact of social roles. The libertarians are aware of the importance of knowledge and technology, but assume that entrepreneurs can take care of these. As to the realities of family and hierarchy, they are almost silent. The family is not their concern, except to indicate that it too should be free, while hierarchy is apt to be treated superficially. Libertarians understand that some government functions are essential, but because they hope to see it decline in importance, they rarely study their implications. In the end, they make useful contributions to our understanding of the boundaries of social exchange. Still, what they offer is incomplete.

Finally, there are the romantics. Back in the nineteenth century these were primarily bohemians, while nowadays bourgeois bohemians dominate their ranks. They are fascinated by the importance of art. It is the cynosure of their existence, their reason for being. Up to this point, we have said little about the aesthetic order as a mechanism for bonding peoples together. This is because most contemporary ideologies also say little about it. Yet almost no one hates art. Conservatives treasure the artistic legacies of their cultures, while liberals assume that people free to be themselves will fulfill many needs through artistic pursuits. All the same, it has been the romantics who have focused on this area. They, and probably only they, agree with Keats that "beauty is truth, truth beauty." As such, only they put art at the center of human endeavors.

To begin with, the aesthetic order translates into a weak social force. Even though some people are willing to die for their art, it does not possess the emotional clout of personal relationships or face-to-face hierarchies. This being so, it would seem a likely candidate for bonding large-scale societies together. And indeed it does perform this function. Like social roles, technology, and knowledge, art crosses borders. So permeable does it find national frontiers that an international aesthetic has emerged. People the world over today watch the same movies, listen to the same music, and read the same books. Similarly, fashions established in New York or Paris turn up in China or South Africa. As a result, people everywhere feel part of an international community. When they meet, these others are not surprised by how they dress or by the tunes playing on their iPods.

Fashion has long been with us, as has keeping up with the latest fashions. So constant is this human imperative that archeologists can distinguish particular communities by the style of pots they produced. Conforming to the most recent stylistic innovations is nothing short of a means for proclaiming that one belongs to an identifiable group. In the present context this generally involves adopting the fashions of the dominant players. This is why so many people attend American films, adopt American slang, and listen to American music. This said, such practices do not make these others American. They can communicate with Americans, but are not bound to them as if to the same society. A shared aesthetic makes them part of a common lifestyle, not a common community.

Art holds disparate peoples together, but not with a force sufficient to keep them from engaging in mutual slaughter. It is important, but not as important as social roles, technology, and knowledge for keeping techno-commercial societies intact. Indeed, romantics can engage in their esoteric concerns largely because the other weak orders do so well in providing social solidarity. On their own, aesthetic forces are insufficient to maintain this integrity. They provide a "we" feeling, but not much more.

7

The Professionalized Ideal

The Jazz Band

If the liberal, conservative, or other enumerated ideals are inadequate to bind modern techno-commercial societies together, what is? As we have seen, liberals favor family ideals and philosopher king style hierarchies. Strangely, many conservatives also emphasize personal relationships and face-to-face hierarchies. Religious and traditional conservatives, of course, add a candidly normative dimension in stressing religious values. Meanwhile, libertarians look to the marketplace to obtain social solidarity, while romantics place their faith in the arts. None of these, however, is up to the task. Each has limits in what it can accomplish. All are partially correct however. Family relationships continue to be imperative for our mental well-being, as well as for the socialization of children. Similarly, hierarchies not only survive, they thrive. Now tamed by the checks and balances of democratic governments and bureaucratic organizations, they nevertheless preside over huge swaths of our lives. Needless to say, the marketplace remains prominent. We could not feed or clothe ourselves without it. Even the arts continue to influence our lives. Indeed, with more spare time than ever, we devote long hours to aesthetic pursuits.

Still, there is something vital missing. The importance of social roles, and to a lesser extent knowledge and technology, has been underplayed. This is unfortunate because in combination these provide an alternative better suited to a mass techno-commercial society. And make no mistake—a plausible alternative is needed. However flawed a belief system, people are disinclined to give it up if they cannot identify a superior substitute. As long as nothing better is hovering over the horizon, they cling to what they know. Thankfully, there is an appropriate replacement. It is the *professionalized ideal*. Of course, few people as yet recognize this possibility. Nonetheless events are pushing us in this direction. As long as the demands of our

223

large and enormously complex society are what they are, people will be confronted with the need for something of the sort. In fact, they are likely to become more professionalized before they perceive the ubiquity of professionalization.

The nature of modern life is such that it must inevitably become more decentralized and expert-driven. As a consequence, visions that depend on central coordination are more limited than is recognized. There are simply too many factors that need to be meshed together for a fully top-down approach to be effective. Even so, an awareness of this remains limited. Partisans of both the constrained and unconstrained visions often assume that hierarchical leadership is essential to maintaining social equilibrium. Those who favor the constrained view look to authority figures to reduce violence and harmonize competing interests, whereas those who favor the unconstrained view assign themselves the role of social tutors. Although they deny a desire for superiority, they envisage themselves in this position by default. In any event, both sides are partly correct. Centralized leadership is required to accomplish many complicated activities, and probably for reasons they cite. But it is insufficient. No individual, or group, can come close to covering of the necessary ground. No one, or group, is smart, knowledgeable, or flexible enough to adjust to all of the contingencies that arise.

A simple analogy is in order. The difference between what is envisioned and what is needed is similar to the difference between a symphony orchestra and a jazz band. Most people conceive of society as like the former, whereas it grows closer to the latter. A symphony orchestra is a traditional means of organizing complex musical performances. It is a mechanism for coordinating the contributions of many individuals to a common objective. The members of the orchestra do not decide what to play on their own. The conductor provides this from above. The score comes in the shape of sheet music to which they are expected to comply. Composed by someone they may not know, they are required to follow it note by note. Interpretative adjustments are made, but the conductor imposes most of these. Indeed, he (or she) can be imperious in demanding compliance. It is almost as if the orchestra was a mechanical device designed and directed from above.

Jazz bands are different. They are smaller, but also more flexible. They too have musical compositions from which they commence their performances and experienced guides from whom they take their lead, yet these are looser in application. Jazz musicians are expected to improvise. Under ideal circumstances no two performances are exactly the same. It is assumed that the individual players are sufficiently skilled to make modifications in the text as they go along. When they play riffs of their own devising, the other players do not respond with anger. Nor does the bandleader ridicule the innovator for breaking a sacred rule. To the contrary, the other members of the band are likely to respond with improvisations of their own. What develops is a kind of musical conversation during which the creative impulses of the ensemble are given wide latitude. The players, as it were, negotiate the final performance between themselves as they go along. In the end, what emerges is a vibrant presentation that would not otherwise have existed.

Contemporary Western societies have much in common with jazz bands despite their enormous difference in scope. The division of labor in large-scale communities is much greater than in musical groups, but these assemblages also depend on the spontaneous coordination of multiple players. Although they too have leaders, they are more than ever dependent on contributions from below. So pervasive has this need become that authority figures are oftentimes unaware of what their subordinates do in order to achieve what is expected. The fact is that many role contributions have become so complex that those responsible must be professionalized. Like members of a jazz band, they have to be skilled at what they do, as well as capable of independent initiative. By the same token, they must be able to coordinate their contributions with those of their colleagues. This means they have to be sensitive to what these others are doing and flexible enough to make the appropriate adjustments. They too, as it were, engage in an on-going conversation with their role partners. Yet if this is successful, the final product is superior to that which would have emerged from a rigid arrangement. It is more creative, more effective, and more satisfying.

To repeat, if a techno-commercial jazz band is to be successful, it must be professionalized. A larger proportion of its members have to be self-motivated experts. They need to be competent at complex tasks that often necessitate working with data and people. Besides being intelligent and well educated, they must be mature enough to engage in self-direction and interpersonal negotiations. Often required to make independent decisions, they need to be capable of doing so. Likewise, they cannot be one-man bands. They have to be aware of what their role partners are doing and be prepared to make changes as necessary. This, of course, entails being able to deal with diversity and opposition, which in turn requires genuine political skills, as well as a capacity to cooperate with others. Merely being a self-involved technocrat serves useful purposes, but a broader social competence is also essential.

What then makes a person professionalized? As importantly, how do people become professionalized managers, engineers, financiers, social workers, or educators? To repeat, professionalized persons are *self-motivated experts*. They are people who are both skilled at difficult tasks and able to supervise their own activities. In other words, professionalized individuals combine knowledge, technical capabilities, and internalized impulses into an integrated social role. It is their job to do so. They thus occupy positions that call upon them to apply insights and proficiencies most others do not possess. But more than this, they do so willingly. Their personal motivation is such that they do not need to be coerced into performing their parts. As self-directed adults, they possess an intrinsic desire to be competent and the courage to deal with uncertainties. When unanticipated problems arise, they do not flee in a panic, but remain on the scene to address the issue at hand. Although they are capable of taking advice, they do not always require a superior authority to direct their contributions.

This may sound like a tall order, but it is one more people than ever find congenial. They, to be sure, do not suddenly wake up one morning as professionalized experts. It takes time and effort to acquire the requisite components. Much like members of a jazz band, they must internalize what amount to social scripts. These are not as exact as the musical arrangements of symphony orchestras, but they do provide information about how important tasks are to be accomplished. The knowledge, values, and techniques necessary are learned, practiced, and adjusted to serve as guides on how to behave. The ways people think, feel, and decide are literally altered such that they spontaneously conduct themselves as required. Much of this is obtained via interactions with role partners. The give and take of their mutual demands alters what the parties do. They become more skilled, more flexible, and, in combination, better able to achieve what is necessary for themselves and society. As a result, social negotiations, which often occur outside of the awareness of higher authorities, frequently produce results that would not have emerged otherwise.

If this seems obscure, it is actually as familiar as what millions of middle-class Americans do every day. Indeed, it is fast becoming the norm in all advanced industrial societies. Many people continue to think of themselves as bound hand and foot by hierarchical imperatives. Despite their desire for independence, they assume that they are imprisoned by restrictions they cannot evade. Yet while there are many such restrictions, there are also vast areas of latitude. Most people are both more and less free than they suppose. The point is that many would be even more free were they to embrace the requirements of professionalization. If a larger number decided to function as self-motivated experts, they would be less dependent on the whims of authority figures. The guidance of pseudo-village elders or would-be philosopher kings would no longer be required. Nor would people need to submit to the imaginary families that liberals and conservatives posit. As such, they would make more decisions for themselves—and better ones into the bargain. What is more, the result would redound to the benefit of all. Techno-commercial societies not only fail to profit from the solidarity-providing mechanisms that worked for our ancestors, but a community of expert role players is more effective at cementing them together.

Social Ecology

So far so good, but more needs to be said about the nature of professionalization and a professionalized society. In order to achieve this, we will require a different metaphor. Nowadays, given the popularity of environmentalism, most of us are aware of ecological concerns. We have learned that plants and animals are joined in a complex web such that what happens to one organism has an impact on others. No individual is totally independent of other living things. The destruction of a single species may therefore result in the destruction of others far afield. This interdependence has become a contemporary cliché, yet it is based on fact. The more we learn about nature, the more it becomes clear the welfare of particular organisms is conjoined with the welfare of a myriad of ostensibly separate others.

An example of this is found in the life history of the Brazil Nut tree. Found in the Amazon and other South American jungles, this plant's ecological connections were long a mystery. Despite the worldwide favor its fruit achieved, the way it grew made no sense. As a huge tree that sometimes achieves a height of 150 feet, it apparently flourishes only in pristine forests. Generally isolated from others of its kind, some individuals live to be over five hundred years old. As peculiarly, its nuts are encased in a hard shell that does not allow for germination

227

if they merely fall to the forest floor. Together, these factors seemed to conspire against the tree's perpetuation. It was so finicky about where it thrived and so difficult to implant that the question which arose was this: How did the species survive?

Ecological detective work eventually discovered that undisturbed forests were required because these were the home of the large bodied bees that pollinated the tree. Only these insects could open its flowers to fertilize them. Yet the plants in which these pollinators resided were only found in pristine places far from where the Brazil Nut trees stood. As to the bees themselves, they required the tree because the scent of its nectar was necessary for their mating practices. Meanwhile, the nuts were only opened by sharp-toothed rodents such as the agouti or by capuchin monkeys wielding rocks. The agoutis subsequently buried the seeds. Then once these sprouted, they remained small for many years. Only when the trees surrounding these saplings died did they receive the sunlight necessary to grow to their full height. Together these factors explained why the tree was distributed as it was. In concert, they constituted an integrated network of connections upon which all of the constituent elements depended.

So delicate is this balance that the next question that occurs is how did it come into being. The most reasonable explanation is that its disparate parts evolved in conjunction with one another. As each adjusted to the requirements of the others, they were progressively modified to fit more closely. In the end, they formed an improbable ecological community. Improbable, that is, if one assumed it was designed in a single brilliant stroke. It is less peculiar if one accepts evolutionary tenets. In this case, it makes perfect sense that the pieces fit together because they developed in combination with one another. They mesh because a complex series of adjustments took place in the light of what was needed to make them interconnect. An awareness of only the end product might make it seem too contrived to arise, whereas the many steps along the way dissolved this mystery.

Social ecologies are similar in their operations. The social roles of which they are composed fit together in a comparably decentralized manner because these too evolve to fit together. Societies do not appear full grown from the head of Zeus. They develop slowly over time. Not only years, but centuries and millennia go into shaping what they become. This was certainly true for Western societies. The complex techno-commercial communities in which we reside are the product of a vast series of adjustments. So too are the many roles that today constitute their divisions of labor. These evolved gradually in conjunction with a multitude of other roles such that they today mesh in a manner that might otherwise seem improbable. Social roles, and more particularly professionalized roles, constitute an ecosystem. They can interact independently of higher authority because they evolved to do so. The role scripts that guide their operation and the negotiation processes that adjust how they coordinate their activities developed in much the same manner that genetic modifications shape plant and animal bodies and behaviors. The primary difference is that one is biological, whereas the other is social.

Not many years ago, large numbers of people believed that consciously controlled processes were required to maintain modern complexity. They were certain that rationality, in the form of scientific management and centralized planning, was essential for industrialized efficiency. Mesmerized by the idea that intelligent creatures operated best within intentionally designed organizations, they assumed that someone super-intelligent deliberately put these concerns together and that other clever individuals purposively directed their continued activities. Without this, they would obviously be chaotic and inefficient. What the conventional wisdom had not reckoned with was the social and commercial nature of human communities. Industrialized societies are far from logical machines. They are more organic. Almost as complicated as biological ecologies, their innumerable segments must constantly be fine-tuned to match one another. This means that there is, and can be, no super-intelligence guiding the overall process. Nor is there an identifiable assemblage of the "best and brightest" available to control every event. The truth is that no one person, or group of persons, is in complete control. There is not even an invisible hand to make sure things always turn out right. Only continual efforts at repair keep the whole functioning. Only the inputs of millions of individuals enable these organizations to operate with reasonable effectiveness.

The old scientific management model depended on strict authority. Everyone theoretically knew who reported to whom. It also depended upon precise rules and procedures. Managers presumably devised exacting methods for achieving precisely defined endpoints and then made certain that their subordinates conformed to their directives. In this top-down arrangement, there was very little discretion. Decisions were made by the relatively few individuals capable of making them, whereas the majority of workers simply followed instructions.

This pattern worked reasonably well when most industrial activities were routine. Predictable technologies could, in fact, be directed in a predictable manner. When, however, the work to be done became more complex, too many adjustments had to be made for them all to be anticipated in advance. Issues came up that no one foresaw, but that nevertheless had to be managed. A machine broke in a way no one expected, a customer's needs shifted with unplanned rapidity, or a new international development changed projected outcomes. In these cases, someone had to recognize what had gone wrong, and why. Some individual, or individuals, on the spot, had to do what no physically absent boss could do. What was needed was therefore discretion. Accordingly, decision-making had to be more widely disseminated. As a consequence, greater numbers of participants were required to be capable of expert discretion.

Professionalization is about competent discretion. It does not rely exclusively on hierarchical predictability, but on the dynamic flexibility of a community of colleagues. Professionalization is inherently decentralized. Not dependent on one—or a few—brains, it is contingent upon widespread intelligence and initiative. Unless professionals are self-directed experts who know how to make their specific contributions mesh with those of their role partners, unless they have their eyes and ears open and their motives engaged, this arrangement can not work. A professionalized model is relatively egalitarian. It distributes authority very broadly. As a result, it is dependent upon numerous players who are capable of exercising authority. This sort of model also forms an interlocking community. The participants must know how to respond to one another in a manner that produces a reasonable result. Although they are separate human beings, they must behave as part of an interconnected whole.

The sorts of discretion that are necessary vary widely. With modern communities more like lush jungles than desiccated deserts, there are hundreds of thousands of roles to be played. Unlike hunter-gatherer bands where people were either hunters or gatherers, today they are oncologists, patent lawyers, mechanical engineers, tax accountants, computer programmers, advertising copywriters, marketing managers, psychiatric social workers, and kindergarten teachers. The number of options is staggering. So great is the diversity of specializations that few people appreciate the details of jobs other than their own. They cannot exercise competent discretion with respect to these others because they cannot fathom their full dimensions. Only those who occupy them can. These persons must therefore be both self-directed and proficient in making choices.

To illustrate, as college professor, I design and conduct my own courses. The chair of my department knows a lot about technology, but relatively little about social change. Thus, when we agreed that I would teach our social change course, he did not specify the details it would cover. He depended on my knowledge of the subject when it came time to develop the syllabus. Nor did he come into my classroom to advise me on pedagogical techniques. These too were left to my discretion. Indeed, there was not much guidance he could provide. Both he and I knew that when students ask embarrassing questions, a professor must be prepared to handle them on the spot. My own store of knowledge and classroom poise had to be up to the task. Similarly, I do not interfere with my wife's classes. Her specialty is medical sociology. She has read far more extensively in this area than I have. Moreover, her many years of working as a nurse provided experience I do not possess. As a result, her decisions about how to organize her classes are much better than mine would be.

Years ago, when I was a clinician providing the equivalent of psychotherapy, my need for discretion was as great. When clients came to me for help dealing with personal problems, we were sequestered in a private room. If a client discussed a matter I found disquieting, it was up to me to maintain my composure. If asked for advice on a question of which I was ignorant, it was likewise up to me to address it. I could not seek the assistance of my supervisor while actively engaged in a counseling session. Were I incompetent, my clients would quickly become aware of my inadequacies and the trust upon which our collaboration rested would have evaporated. I, to be sure, had limitations, but these had to be handled in an open and honest manner. There was simply no substitute for personal competence and a dedicated performance.

To cite one more example of personalized discretion, my brother is a lawyer who runs his own law firm. Yet, years ago, while still a novice attorney, he confessed to being intimidated by the judges and competing attorneys. These days, of course, his trepidations are long gone. He could not have survived in the courtroom had he not found the means to think on his feet in the midst of the adversarial process. There, in the act of attempting to be persuasive, he could hardly have turned to a superior to provide a predigested script. This he was required to devise for himself. Similarly, he had to prepare his own briefs, and when he began to employ subordinate attorneys, he had to learn how to supervise them so that they, in turn, could operate as competent professionals. Had he not acquired these skills, his juniors would scarcely have developed into valued colleagues.

But this is not the end to our growing need for professionalization. As a college professor in a department that includes criminal justice, I see the same sorts of competence developing in occupations where they were once absent. A century or so ago, police officers were expected to be physical toughs who could keep others in line. Their chief aptitudes were a large size and a willingness to mix it up. Today, however, bullyboys need not apply. Self-restraint and practical intelligence are more sought after. Police officers are expected to be respectful of the public. They are required to deal with diversity and impertinence in a manner that keeps the peace. Much of the time, they achieve this independently. Alone on the streets or with a partner, they cannot always expect immediate supervision. Correspondingly, they must know the law. If they do not, they will make arrests that do not stand up in court. Were they unable to understand the exclusionary rules that make some pieces of evidence invalid, they would fall down on the job. They would not be professionalized and therefore would make inappropriate choices.

Even nursing has become more professionalized. Not long ago my wife informed me that our university's nursing school was about to obtain approval for a doctorate in nursing. As she explained, if nurse practitioners are to hold their own relative to medical doctors, they require a stronger credential than a master's degree. If they too are to diagnose patients and make treatment recommendations, they require the knowledge and respect to do so. The days when nurses only emptied bedpans are past. With medical technology and medical knowledge having become increasingly complex, nurses must be capable of implementing these. Were they empty-headed helpmeets who always needed detailed instructions, many tragedies would ensue. They too must therefore be professionalized, lest modern medicine return to a dark age.

Then too, professionalized persons must exercise discretion in collaboration with others, many of whom are also professionalized. Thus, college professors must be able to work with both colleagues and students. If they were unable to respond appropriately, the resulting conflicts would make their assignments impossible. Prima donnas, who assume they always know best, usually meet a bad fate. If their role partners refuse to cooperate, they find the isolation debilitating. Not only do they fail to benefit from the information others might provide, but they create problems via gratuitous insults. Even college professors need to be sensitive to other human beings. They are no longer intellectual gods who hover above mortal concerns. As university employees, they are responsible for sustaining these institutions, not just their own research agendas.

By the same token, therapists must collaborate with both clients and colleagues, while lawyers must do the same with theirs, and police officers and nurses with theirs. However professionalized persons become, they are integrated into larger communities and therefore are dependent upon the contributions of numerous others. They are, in this sense, part of a social ecology to which their own roles are inherently linked. What they do was not invented in isolation, nor is it performed in seclusion. The roles they play evolved in the hands of the countless practitioners who preceded them. Many of the techniques they use and attitudes they adopt have thus been bequeathed them from previous generations. While they modify these plans as they go along, their overall outlines were acquired from others. An extensive give-and-take slowly shaped, and continues to shape, what the players do—even as they are called upon to exercise independent discretion.

To be blunt, professionalized persons must be socialized to be professional. They need to be educated to perform the parts they play. The knowledge they require, the skills they employ, and even the emotional reactions they experience are imparted via lengthy apprenticeships. Nowadays, this often entails a formal education. Potential doctors, lawyers, college professors, as well as police officers, nurses, and accountants spend years acquiring the appropriate degrees. But they also require informal socialization. Many of the lessons learned are imbibed unconsciously. Their role partners do not intentionally set about imparting them, but do so in conjunction with their ongoing interactions. A casual remark, a furrowed eyebrow, or a visibly successful role performance by another can all influence how an individual constructs his or her role persona. The professionalized skills that today permeate our private lives are especially likely to be informally acquired. How to be a competent husband, wife, or parent is not generally taught in an official way. These abilities tend to be absorbed almost by osmosis. Thus, we often model our behaviors after people we know and admire. They instruct us as to the possibilities without ever sitting down to tell us what they believe. They simply are who they are and, in playing close attention, we become apprised of information that changes how we behave.

Professionalized persons are also socialized by way of the cultures in which they participate. Once they graduate from school, their learning is not finished. Now they must deal with reality shock. Idealized lessons quickly become modified by practical contingencies. To begin with, they will have colleagues who have strong opinions and who make insistent demands. These others possess standards they use to evaluate the newcomer and sanctions they apply for failures to behave as expected. There are also journals to read, conferences to attend, and professional societies to join. Sometimes formally, but sometimes while playing a round of golf, expectations are communicated and judgments are rendered. Because we human beings are social creatures, these exchanges matter. They influence us. They alter who we are and what we do.

But still other pressures mold also our professional skills and attitudes. Clients and coworkers likewise function as role partners. So do our various opponents and enemies. Wherever we turn, there are people with opinions as to how we should comport ourselves. Not just supervisors, but subordinates and complete strangers seek to modify how we act. They too have ideas about what is best and are not shy in expressing them. Social roles inevitably elicit reams of feedback. Because they are embedded in networks of partnerships, the impact we have on others elicits a myriad of responses. A division of labor is exactly that: a division of labor. It divides into parts operations that belong to a larger whole. As a result, when individual segments evolve, so does the whole in which they fit. As an ecological system, it develops into something it was previously not. A massively complex techno-commercial society is therefore different from a tiny hunter-gatherer band. The roles composing the former are far more convoluted and are therefore more fluid.

Nor should we leave out the impact of competition. Professionalized communities are not wholly cooperative. Role partners may collaborate, but they also compete. A desire to be better than others often results in efforts to outdo one another. This may be harsh, but it provides an incentive for improved individual performances. People consequently become more skillful in an effort to surpass their rivals. In the process, they also benefit. But so does the larger community. If the changes that occur are genuine improvements, others too may live better. As crass as this sounds, just as with tropical jungles human ecologies flourish through the survival of the fittest. When the best come out ahead, the less successful are pushed aside. This is not nice, but it is reality. As Darwin taught us, within biological systems new innovations ultimately lead to the extinction of less suitable designs. It is the same with social systems. This is not to say, however, that Social Darwinism is inevitable. People do not compete solely as individuals. They also vie for supremacy as teammates. As such, they can help their partners become winners. They can also be kind and altruistic, and by so doing enable their team to surge ahead. This too is natural. It too is one of the mechanisms that allow some societies to become more dominant than others.

The Professionalized Economy

The best place to begin a discussion of the implications of professionalized ideal is with the economy. It is certainly here that professionalization began, at least with respect to the service aspects of how people make a living. For most of history, professionalization was meager or nonexistent. Hunter-gatherers might be good at what they did, but they were not professionalized. Their level of knowledge and technological prowess did not rise to the level of specialized expertise. Virtually all of the men were expected to be accomplished hunters and all of the women proficient gatherers. Indeed, they had to be competent or they would have perished. Nevertheless, they were generalists, not specialists. This lack of differentiation did not change appreciably with the advent of agrarian empires. Craft specialties abounded, whereas the theoretical knowledge required of them was limited. So was the motivation. People worked to earn a living, not because they pursued a calling. They might have conceived of themselves in terms of their occupations, but they did not regard these as missions to which they were dedicated. A silversmith was a silversmith, not a person upon whom critical social functions were dependent.

In preindustrial times, most craft persons worked independently. If they were masters, they owned their own shops in the back of which they fashioned their products and in the front of which they sold them. A few journeymen, as well as apprentices, might work for these entrepreneurs, but that was about all. Many craft-persons were thus their own bosses. This changed when steam-powered machinery took over. It was at this point that factories came to the fore. More people began to work away from their homes, often in large establishments centered around heavy equipment. With technology having become more complex, so did the division of labor. As a consequence, workers became more interdependent. What they individually did had to be coordinated with their coworkers. Accordingly, someone had to indicate who would do what—and when. The role of coordinator usually devolved to the factory owner or someone he appointed. In fact, because these enterprises entailed the management of a relatively small number of operations, a single person could generally understand all the various functions. His mind could encompass the entire operation and plan the best ways to improve productivity. He was therefore the boss and his underlings were essentially tools at his disposal.

Soon, however, industries grew. They metamorphosed into gigantic corporations. Instead of employing hundreds of persons, they employed hundreds of thousands. Now it was impossible for a single person to govern the entire conglomeration. However energetic or intelligent he might be, he was not, and could not be, everywhere or comprehend everything. Too much was going on; often in widely separated places. The operations were also too technical. There was not one kind of machine to master, but many hundreds. In order to maximize their performance, each had to be understood, as did the ways they interacted. Karl Marx believed the industrialist and a small group of front-office workers could manage this complexity. This capitalist, and his while-collar employees, would be sufficient to maintain peak efficiency. Yet this quickly proved wrong. The job was too big for a band of amateurs. As a result, it was not long before professionalized managers and engineers controlled these massive companies. Marx mistakenly thought of capitalists as parasites who feasted on the labors of their subordinates. He did not recognize how difficult it is to coordinate the efforts of thousands of people doing different things. This is where bureaucracy came in. It provided the means of mastering what amounted to industrial armies.

At this point, Max Weber codified our understanding of bureaucracies. While he was not fond of their rigidity, he believed them essential to managing modern commercial ventures. Deriding them as an "iron cage" that kept workers in virtual submission, he nevertheless praised them for institutionalizing rationality. Unlike the nobility of old, their managers were not arbitrary despots. They had clear organizational goals that were achieved through a sophisticated division of labor. Individual workers were assigned identifiable tasks that were supervised by identifiable superiors. As such, there was a chain of command in which authority was clear, albeit limited. There were also rules and procedures intentionally designed to produce efficiency, as well as files and records aimed at keeping track of what was going on. What was done would not be left to chance, nor be dependent on the whims of a single individual. The bureaucracy was a huge team. It was brilliant because it relied on numerous knowledgeable heads. While it was centralized, the senior bosses did not have to understand everything that went on. The intelligence, and motivation, of the business was lodged in the organization itself. The way it was put together focused the contributions of a host of individuals on the larger project. A bureaucracy thus functioned as a complex whole, where none of its human elements exercised total discretion.

Professionalization, however, was not part of the Weberian vision. Professionals historically operated outside large organizations. Their history goes back to the Middle Ages. Initially there were only three professions. These were the clergy, physicians, and lawyers. It was they who were educated at the medieval universities and they who boasted of a divine calling. Because their missions entailed responsible discretion, they had to be dedicated to what they did. This was why God had selected them for the tasks they performed. Furthermore, in a world where only the church and a few governments were comprehensively organized, physicians and lawyers were largely independent practitioners. Most were self-employed individuals who rendered their services to a variety of clients. Of necessity supervising themselves, they had to be personally motivated to do what they did. In an era of belief, this is why religion was used to certify individual commitment. By our standards, of course, their expertise was minimal, whereas in their own context it was substantial. Not yet major players in a society where the aristocracy was still dominant, they nevertheless pioneered a trajectory that would eventually shape our era.

Given what Weber knew about the emerging corporations of his time, he did not put much stock in the role of professionals within bureaucracies. He continued to think of them as independent of organizational control. For him doctors and lawyers remained well-educated specialists who rendered private services. Although Weber did not fully recognize the relationship between bureaucratically defined offices, hierarchies of authority, and role specialization, such a connection was developing. Like Durkheim, he understood the power of a functional division of labor, yet he had not conceptualized the parallels between professional roles and the various positions within the bureaucracy. More concerned with understanding how large organizations could be centrally controlled than with their lower level operations, he was less aware of their potential for decentralized discretion. From his perspective, the iron cage limited individual decision-making; it did not facilitate it.

In fact, the defined offices of which Weber spoke were social roles. Nowadays, we usually refer to these as "jobs," and they have become ubiquitous. A job is, after all, a specified package of duties. Positions such as this exist when a particular person is delegated to perform a limited number of tasks. In contemporary corporations, he or she probably has a "job description" in which these assignments are enumerated. In the Weberian model, however, these tasks were relatively simple. A job might be something as modest as operating a particular machine. Nevertheless, this is not the only possibility. A job can also be complex. It may even be professionalized. If what needs doing requires self-motivated expertise, there is no reason it cannot be occupied by a professional. Nor is this a theoretical option. Modern hospitals could not operate without such assignments. Their physicians and nurses are nothing less than professionalized jobholders. No longer self-employed independents, they too are bounded by bureaucratic restraints and detailed job descriptions.

The difference between Weberian style jobs and professionalized jobs is that the latter must incorporate considerable discretion if they are to be effective. Physicians who are not allowed to make independent diagnoses or treatment recommendations are useless. Their self-motivated expertise would go for naught if they were not permitted to make autonomous choices. No hospital administrator can supersede their know-how. No one whose skills lie primarily in management can make better medical decisions than those intensely trained in making them. Those organizationally superior to physicians are therefore not necessarily their functional superiors. Despite their many misgivings, they must defer to their medical subordinates, lest the hospital's goals go unfulfilled. Like it or not, this is decentralized professionalization in action.

Oddly, role professionalization permeates bureaucracy via the hierarchy of authority itself. Weber described the motto of bureaucracy as *sine ira et studio*. This translates as "without fear or favor." As a student of history, he was aware that medieval authority was steeped in blood and favoritism. The noblemen who held society in their grip frequently resorted to violence and nepotism to enforce their will. For them, coercion might be expressed at the tip of a lance or in a favorable marital treaty. Successful leaders were not squeamish when it came to dispatching rivals or brutalizing the peasantry. This tended to reduce their own life expectancy, as well as that of those they coerced. Still, after a fashion, these policies worked within the agrarian societies they controlled. Weber himself, however, recognized that this would not do in a complex techno-commercial society. Industrial workers forcibly tied to their machines tended to be sloppy at what they did. Similarly, employees denied advancement in favor of the boss's relatives grow restive. Instead they demand fairness, consistency, and decency. They will accept supervision, but not if it is arbitrary or brutal. One way or another, the medieval reign of fear and favor had to come to an end.

Earlier eras might not have thought it possible, but the modern bureaucracy accomplished exactly this. It was not perfect, but was an enormous advance. People continued to cheat and bully, but not nearly as widely as was once the case. Bureaucracy achieved this miracle by institutionalizing a "hierarchy of authority." Hierarchies, as we have seen, go back to the dawn of human communities. Ranking systems are part of our biological heritage. The difference comes in how they are constructed. Among hunter-gatherers, they were created in long-term face-to-face tests of strength that were handled with care because they were between intimates dependent upon each other for survival. Later, in larger agrarian societies, symbolic, and often cruel, acts of violence became common. Military aristocracies did not hesitate to torture thousands in order to send the message that they must not be defied. In a world filled with unsophisticated strangers, this was often the only way to ensure dominance. While these efforts generally succeeded, the side effects were such that they are not appropriate to complex divisions of labor.

Contemporary organizational hierarchies of authority are different. They are more closely defined and effectively constrained. Contemporary bureaucracies attempt to be clear about who is subordinate to whom. They boast chains of command, such that each person knows to whom he or she is to report. Where once the relationships between Barons and Earls were a fluid muddle where relative dominance was often decided in battle, today's workers and bosses are hired to fill particular organizational ranks. Before they walk in the door, they know where they stand vis-à-vis those with whom they will interact. They also know—more or less—what is required for promotion. There are usually explicit procedures for moving from one rank to another. The tests of strength involved are likely to be politically mediated, but are not physically violent. Proving that one deserves to move up can be a matter of demonstrating functional competence or tactical acumen. Sometimes being good at what one does impresses others, whereas at other times back room political maneuvers do the trick. These contests can be jarring, but are rarely deadly.

There is another aspect of modern hierarchies of authority that must be noted. In particular, the authority assigned to particular slots is limited. A boss may be the boss, but he or she is not an absolute boss. The authority that goes with a specific position is circumscribed. Orders can be given, and enforced, but not just any orders. These directives must be within the superior's sphere of influence. If he is in charge of the loading dock, he does not have the right to order a worker to report to the advertising department as an office boy. If she is a marketing manager, she cannot demand that a subordinate marry a man of her choice. These commands are not part of their responsibilities. And this is the point. Bureaucracy incorporates specific areas of authority into the job. Being able to give only certain orders is part of a person's role. Under the best of circumstances, this authority becomes professionalized. Those who exercise it develop into self-motivated experts in managing others. They are not impulsive oppressors who arbitrarily impose spontaneous caprices, but self-controlled individuals whose directives are in the interest of a shared objective.

Bureaucratic jobs and positions of authority also differ from familial roles. People do not occupy them because they are related to other people in particular ways. Nor are they militarized roles. People do not acquire them because they have demonstrated martial prowess. Neither are they religious roles. No supernatural moral mandate bestows a corporate niche. These slots are earned via strengths relevant to our techno-commercial society. They are, in short, techno-commercial roles. The social orders that are operative in establishing them are not about personal relations or norms, but concern knowledge and technology operating within social exchange processes. Bureaucracy represents the triumph of the weaker forces over the stronger ones. It lashes large economic organizations together via the means suited to doing so.

This process has been enhanced by the increased professionalization of bureaucratic concerns. As jobs requiring a self-motivated expertise have become prominent, large organizations have, of necessity, become more decentralized. The functions covered by techno-commercial roles have therefore expanded. With more people capable of supervising themselves, organizational power has become less arbitrary. The old notion of top down control is being replaced with collegial control. Individuals competent at what they do are now able to coordinate their activities with others of their kind. This is a new development. What is more, it is a liberating one. Yet it has a long history. The professionalized dedication essential to make this system work has been centuries in coming. That so many people are today self-motivated experts, in such a wide diversity of specialties, has taken a long time to evolve. The learning curve has been slow, but steady. Fortunately, we are the beneficiaries of millions of small innovations. We are therefore unlike our ancestors. Although we too are human, more of us are professionalized. As a consequence, we are better able to take advantage of self-direction on the job.

This does not mean that traditional bureaucratic constraints will suddenly disappear. Some tasks must be centralized. The strategies that armies follow to defeat their enemies require coherent organization. If individual commanders cannot move their troops where they desire, it is impossible to mass forces where they are needed for a breakthrough. Similarly, the design policies of automobile companies must be centralized. Since the resources at the disposal of even the largest corporations are limited and customer demands are fickle, it is essential to concentrate on a few product lines. Supply chains must also be rationalized, machine acquisitions coordinated, and marketing plans synchronized. To do less, entails wasted motion and contradictory procedures. In general, centralization is suitable where complex coordination and uniformity are at a premium. Hence the bigger the assemblage, the greater the need for centralized planning and consistent management. These, however, place discretion at the apex of the organization.

Nonetheless, although it is commonly thought that a large organization must either be centralized or decentralized, it can be both. This is true in the military where the overall strategies come from the generals, but tactical modifications depend on sergeants and privates. Often it is only those in the field who recognize the need for a locally altered application of forces. The same applies to automobile manufactures. The design of an automobile may be centralized, but its manufacture takes place on the shop floor. This has led to the realization that individual workers must be delegated the right to halt the assembly line. If something goes radically wrong, they need to act promptly lest millions of dollars of damage occur. Nowadays front-line workers are also encouraged to participate in quality circles. Their ideas about how to improve operations are sought because they are aware of problems and opportunities their distant bosses may not recognize.

Decentralization based on techno-commercial role specialization has other virtues. A professionalized workforce is thus a less volatile one. The potential for conflict is greatly reduced in a clarified chain of command. When limited authority is incorporated into roles, there is less to fight over. Industrial barons and factory floor foot soldiers may lust after enhanced power, but their appetites are constrained by the role structure in which they are incorporated. While they may lobby for additional responsibilities, these are conferred by altered job descriptions and political machinations, not military victories. People still talk about "blood on the floor," but it is not literal blood. The competition for superiority is more controlled and far less destructive than previously. Role negotiations provide order, whereas unregulated tests of strength between strangers might not.

Decentralized role-based organizations also tend to be more flexible than absolute forms of control. When lower level individuals are delegated to make changes, their decisions can be diverse and responsive. Thus, a teacher in Minnesota does not have to use exactly the same examples as one in Hawaii. Because her students are familiar with snow, it makes more sense to use this as an illustration than it would in a tropical climate. In the old Soviet model of industrial efficiency, by contrast, variation was not allowed. Central planners devised five-year programs that were supposed to be followed to the letter, whether in the Urals or the Ukraine. Unfortunately, when these went awry, as they frequently did, production could grind to a halt. In the end, a system intended to be efficient was barely able to manufacture a decent ballpoint pen. Shortages were everywhere, as were shoddy merchandise and featherbedding workers.

Nor is centralization conducive to innovation. When all of the organizational brains are concentrated at the top of the food chain, their utilization further down the line is discouraged. New ideas are routinely squelched so as not to confront the top bosses with their limitations. In fact, much of the innovation in the American economy has come from small business. Apple, not IBM, pioneered the personal computer. Breaking up AT&T, not sustaining its monopoly, initiated an explosion in telephone services. Because top down managers favor stability, few are keen on change. Uncomfortable with unanticipated challenges, they prefer known products and procedures, rather than untested ones. A case in point: when General Motors was relatively small it introduced a range of new products such as the self-starter, but after it dominated the market, it became a massive ocean liner that could not be turned around, even as foreign competition punctured its hull.

Professionalized roles celebrate intelligence. They bring a greater store of knowledge and technological competence to the table than the most principled philosopher kings. Ordinary people may not be at the same level as the best and brightest, but when they adjust what they do in conjunction with others of their kind, they are a potent force. If allowed appropriate discretion, and not unduly hampered by self-important superiors, they possess untapped potentials. Moreover, they are far better at reconciling competing interests than detached leaders. They can because they are able to engage in a give and take of which their bosses are liable to be unaware. As a result, decentralized professionalization fosters freedom and progress. And with respect to economics, it is the key to further techno-commercial advances.

A Professionalized Political System

Professionalized decentralization is also crucial to the preservation of our democratic institutions. The American experiment is over two centuries old, but when it began many sage heads wondered if it would survive. Most of them had read Montesquieu; hence they were aware that he believed a republican style of government was appropriate for small political entities, not large ones. They were also aware of the fate of Athens, the Roman Republic, and more recently The United Netherlands. Each of these had dissolved under the pressures to protect themselves from external enemies. The United States, it seemed, would have similar difficulty in implementing an integrated defensive policy. Westerners would worry about trade on the Mississippi, Easterners would fret over fishing rights on the Grand Banks, while Southerners would demand protection of their slave system. Shared political agreements would consequently fall apart in a welter of parochial interests.

This was no vain worry. Within a few short years, the dangers of centrifugal political forces were revealed in the fate of the French Revolution. France had long been governed through familial and absolutist mechanisms. The nation was first and foremost a monarchy. Little more than a century earlier, the Sun King Louis XIV had declared that he was the state. He clearly believed in ruling over the land as if it were a family enterprise. Having inherited it from his father, he would bequeath it to his great-grandson. Indeed, the various Louis's were proudly Bourbon. They believed their family possessed a Devine Right to rule. As a result, they had few compunctions about drawing on dynastic connections to provide governmental functionaries. Beyond this, they dramatized their right to rule in a panoply of state ceremonies. The principal symbol of their power was Versailles itself. This immense palace served as a stage upon which aristocrats could prance so as to demonstrate their dominance. Endless rituals, such as the levee and coucher, were enacted in elaborate costumes for the sake of the players and distant members of the third estate. Ordinary citizens looked upon these performances with awe. In this, they confirmed the enormous social distance between the rulers and the ruled.

Far less important in maintaining political stability were social roles and role negotiations. Ordinary people were so hierarchically inferior that the makeup of most of their jobs did not include the prerogatives of authority. They were expected to do what they were told and do so gratefully. Political and hierarchical nonentities, all of this changed after the Revolution. With the minor aristocracy and bourgeoisie already growing restive, economic hard times lit a match that ignited a political explosion. The gunpowder that gave this blast its intensity was provided by the sans-culottes. These ordinary working men and women rose up to march on Versailles and take the king and queen prisoner. Later, when the royals tried to escape, they demanded and received their heads. Along the way, regularly whipped into a frenzy by revolutionary agitators, they often lost personal control. Not only did this occur when they stormed the Bastille, but also when they decapitated officials who had surrendered. Worse still, they were the audience for, and provocateurs of, the Terror. Once freed from the familial and symbolic bonds that previously kept them in place, they went wild, murdering hundreds of thousands. Absent internalized political roles to keep them civilized, they heeded the encouragement of journalistic rabble-rousers, such as Jean-Paul Marat, to dispatch those who defied their whims. Politically and hierarchically unsophisticated, they lacked the knowledge or the skills to create the democratic society for which they clamored. In the end, they did not get it. Within little more than a decade, a man on a white horse, that is, Napoleon Bonaparte, appeared to restore order—this time also based on familial and authoritarian principles.

Across the Atlantic things were different. The American Revolution did succeed. And it created an enduring democracy. The leaders of this rebellion were almost as skeptical of the mob as the French ruling classes, but their qualms about democracy were soon overcome. Americans had experience at self-government. With the king and parliament an ocean away, the colonials had overseen many of their own affairs. This provided practice in political responsibility and in negotiating differences between rivals. The parties may have disagreed about fundamental matters, but they nevertheless developed the internal controls to arrive at agreements without resorting to violence. This was put to the test in the Constitutional Convention, where the delegates worked out differences between the small and large states and between the slaveholding and Free States. Their compromises were not perfect, but they held for nearly a century, despite occasional threats of secession. Gradually, the country became more democratic as the franchise was expanded to include all males, even if they did not own property, and eventually all females as well. Over the centuries, the right to be self-governing was conferred on virtually all adult citizens.

What was it that made this possible? Why didn't Americans go wild and require external controls, as did the French? The answer was that the abilities that made this feasible had been incorporated into their civic roles. A Frenchman, Alexis de Tocqueville, provided insights into these developments. Visiting the young nation in the 1830s to see why democracy worked in the United States but not his native land, he arrived at a series of astute conclusions. Thus, he realized that Americans had learned to honor democratic institutions, as the French had not. When their candidates lost an election, they ceded government to the winners. The unhappy losers did not take to the streets and raise barricades. Americans believed in compromise. If they could not get the whole cake, they settled for a part of it. They realized that an all-or-nothing attitude generated enmities and violent outcomes. It was therefore more sensible to make deals by negotiating with rivals. These others did not have to be destroyed; all that was necessary was to work out a *modus vivendi* with them. From experience, they found that a little tolerance went a long way. Thus, not only was it acceptable that these others had different role commitments, but an interplay of these differences created emergent solutions from which everyone benefited.

Americans were also egalitarian. They believed people had equal rights. While individuals might not be hierarchically equal, the same laws applied to all. Furthermore, everyone was allowed an opportunity to succeed. Hence, those who were commercially successful were accorded a right to their success. If this also provided them political clout—then Godspeed to them. Some day the current losers might strike it rich and then they too would be permitted to enjoy their good fortune. Also widespread was a belief in personal responsibility. Americans were individualistic. They had faith in their know-how. In a large nation, where difficulties with communication and transportation introduced decentralization, members of local communities were required to solve their own problems. They could not wait for the federal government to come to their rescue, but had to develop workable solutions on their own. This produced habits of independence. As a result, many ordinary Americans participated in the political process. They became members of local school boards and ran for positions on the town councils. Even if they did not, almost everyone had opinions on how the nation's business should be conducted, and expressed them at the polls.

Much of this presupposed political knowledge. Voters and local office holders had to be reasonably well informed about the issues they helped decide. Fortunately, the media provided this information. Unlike many of the French, most Americans were literate. Benjamin Franklin was able to accumulate a small fortune in the publishing business because he found thousands of customers for his almanacs. Similarly, Thomas Paine was able to light the fire of revolution because his pamphlet *Common Sense* became a runaway best seller. In time, Americans also pioneered public education and penny newspapers. They thereby encouraged every citizen to become politically aware and competent at decentralized citizenship.

What did not occur in America was a resurgence of familial forms of political control. George Washington did not accept a crown, but preferred the role of a Cincinnatus. He would be the general who returned to plowing his field after saving his nation from destruction. Nor would absolute symbolic power dominate. Washington did not allow himself to be called His Excellency or His Majesty. He was simply Mr. President. While he held numerous public receptions, there were no fawning legions of grandees. Yes, there was ceremony, but it was modest. The American political system was also to be based on defined offices and elections. Starting with the Constitution, the jobs of officeholders were carefully circumscribed. Those in authority were to have power, but limited power. There would, in short, be checks and balances. Washington might be the best—if not the brightest—but even he was not granted free reign. Moreover, when the spoils system came to an end, appointments were to be distributed on the basis of merit, not cronyism. Just as in bureaucracies, positions were to be awarded for competence, not because of favoritism. Needless to say, lobbying and partisanship survived these reforms, but in a truncated fashion. The exceptions that managed to endure were nowhere near as blatant as under France's *ancien regime*.

In order to sustain democratic decentralization, American children were taught more than reading. They were also provided lessons in civics. As early as grade school, they were instructed on American history and the nature of the country's political institutions. They were also encouraged to keep up with current events. Sometimes these lessons were idealistic, yet they served to instill a commitment to fundamental ideals such as freedom, equal rights, and fairness. Perhaps less well appreciated in sustaining a decentralized and professionalized polity was the role of prosperity. People who were economically well off were unlikely to be envious or unruly. Having a stake in the benefits of the existing system, they sought to perpetuate it. Moreover, prosperous people had the time and inclination to become politically sophisticated. Educated to perform complex techno-commercial roles, they also became more subtle thinkers. Accustomed to responsibility on the job, they transferred this attitude toward politics. They got involved. They read. They watched the television news. They even argued about current policies with their friends and associates. In short, they were politically engaged. Unwilling to cede total authority to anyone, they jealously guarded the prerogatives of citizenship. In the process, they became politically professionalized in the sense of being self-motivated experts in participatory government.

The enemy of decentralized professionalization is demagoguery. Demagogues hope to concentrate as much power as they can in their own hands. What is more, they are eager to do so by whatever means seem necessary. Demagogues attempt to be all things to all people. They say whatever they need to say and do whatever they must do, in order to maintain control. If they have to lie, they lie. If they have to mislead, they mislead. Promises are thus made to all and sundry. The objective is to seduce vulnerable hearts and minds. If the rabble can be persuaded that the demagogue is their savior—and there is no other potential savior—he/she may be given a *carte blanche*. Instead of making decisions for themselves, these are delegated to him. He becomes the ultimate father figure—the supreme elder.

Demagogy works by persuading ordinary people not to be self-motivated. It denies them the knowledge they need to make competent political decisions by pulling the wool over their eyes. It likewise robs them of personal motivation by making them emotionally dependent. Demagogues both frighten people and offer them protection. When journalists become partisans and conspire to distort the information provided to the public, they conspire to promote such manipulations. Likewise, when politicians become addicted to hypocrisy and emotional exploitation, they pave the road to demagoguery. False idealism and ideological purity are the mother's milk of antidemocratic institutions. They hide important truths and make unsupportable guarantees. To the degree that liberalism engages in these practices, it is the foe of widely dispersed political institutions. When it emphasizes centralization as opposed to political discretion, it undermines democracy. It is not enough, as is often claimed, to declare an allegiance to "rule by the people." If government of the people, by the people, and for the people is to survive, the intelligence and initiative of ordinary citizens must be encouraged. They cannot be told they are responsible, but then deprived of responsibility. Even if they make mistakes, they must be allowed to learn from these. This is the essence of professionalization with respect to politics.

The Professionalized Family

Liberals have little confidence in the family. Many of them believe it is an outmoded institution. Indeed, they describe it as oppressive and authoritarian. The husband, as the traditional head of the household, is depicted as a tyrant. He ruthlessly controls the lives of his wife and children for his own benefit. A bombastic exploiter, he happily enslaves those subject to his hegemonic domination. Meanwhile, his wife is a meek house-frau. Thoroughly intimidated by her overlord, she losses the ability to pursue her own interests. His will, not hers, becomes the focus of her duties. As to the children, their duty is obedience. As the property of their father, they are his to order around. If a heavy hand is employed to keep them in line, then so be it. Order and hierarchical stability must be maintained. After all, this has been dictated by hallowed custom.

The above is, of course, a caricature. Nowadays, it is encountered more in fiction than reality. Some households, to be sure, are characterized by physical and emotional abuse, but they are a minority. In fact, the police routinely intervene in these matters. They do not stand idly by to allow intrafamilial violence. Nor do they condone male supremacy. There may have been a time when men were reckoned to own their wives; nevertheless those days are far behind us. Once men were even encouraged to strike recalcitrant wives and children. A few whacks of the hickory stick were said to go a long way toward beating the devil out of them. But that was then; this is now. All the same, for many liberals, the past remains operative. They know the contemporary family is not what it once was, but they are eager to tar it with a brush appropriate to very different times. The evident goal is to delegitimize the family. This is conceived of as the first step toward liberating women from its deadening grip. If women are to be emancipated and their children relieved of oppression, the family must lose its aura of inevitability. Ancient myths have to be punctured so that equality and decency can become the norm.

From the liberal perspective, people are perceived as isolated individuals (save for their participation of the family of all humankind). They are not naturally bound to nuclear families, but must be permitted a choice regarding how to live. In the 1920s the ideal was "free love." Both men and women would be allowed to engage in any romantic liaisons they desired. As long as these were voluntary, people were encouraged to enter, or leave, them. Most importantly, no one must be "owned" by anyone else. This was equivalent to slavery. Everyone therefore had the right to change his or her mind, whenever this occurred. Anything less was not love. Genuine love could not be constrained by artificial means. Moreover, women must be as free as men. Gender-based distinctions were anathema. They were vestiges of a dreaded "double standard."

Today, family diversity has become the watchword. However people choose to construct their families is up to them. There may be cultural differences between groups, but all cultures are inherently equal. Thus, if some individuals prefer single-parent households, that is their business. Or if they are divorced, or remarried, or divorced again, this is also their choice. So is their decision to enter same sex unions. Even swinging alliances are permitted. As long as a couple agrees to tolerate partner swapping, who is to say this is not their right? Years ago, Cole Porter wrote a catchy tune called "Anything Goes." These days what was once an amusing conceit has become a politically sponsored reality. If anything, it is the traditional family that is now under siege. Even "shacking up" is preferred to a "piece of paper" that submerges a person's individuality under arbitrary restraints.

This liberal ideal is especially odd given the concurrent idealization of universal love. How can liberals be skeptical of family-based love when they are enamored of love in general? This paradox is resolved when one realizes that the universal family so adored by liberals is a fiction. A global village, in which everyone is related to everyone else, has nothing to do with how actual people live. Nor does substituting the government for the family correct this miscalculation. As an emotionally indifferent institution, the state cannot provide the expressive ties that bind individuals to one another. Relying on a pretend version of personal relations to supply social attachments is to place one's faith in a fairytale. It thoroughly misunderstands the nature of personal attachments. Love—genuine love—not free love, or diverse love, is part and parcel of family living. It is in families that people obtain the ability to care deeply about one another. It is within them that they acquire much needed human support and where children can obtain a protected socialization.

A massive techno-commercial society is supposedly emotionally cold—and in many respects is. A world in which most people are strangers is also one in which they care relatively little about a majority of others. The irony of this is that it makes emotional closeness all the more important. Attachments to particular others become increasingly salient when a preponderance of people are acquaintances—or less. The problem is that dependable emotional attachments are difficult to achieve and maintain. Isolated individuals find it problematical to discover one another, never mind to create reliable bonds. They have a tendency to bounce around like rubber balls in a Chucky Cheese pavilion. People meet, warily interact, and then depart for points unknown. Who will turn out to be Mr. or Ms. Right is the mystery of the age. Most men and women dream about finding true love, but they are less sure of where to locate it than their grandparents were in an era when people married the boy or girl next door.

This is where the professionalized family can come to the rescue. It has two primary components: the professionalized relationship and professionalized childrearing. In a techno-commercial society, a self-motivated expertise not only applies to economics and politics, but to our personal lives. If people are to find love, if they are to raise happy, successful children, they must know what they are doing. Trusting to luck or instinct is rarely effective. There was a time when marriage and family were expected to come naturally. People fell in love and then conceived children because that is what people did. Whatever their own confusions or insecurities, they plunged ahead, no doubt using their relatives and friends as models for how to proceed. The notion of being expert in personal relationships seemed a contradiction in terms. Love was something that just happened; it was not learned.

It must be admitted, of course, that there is something peculiar about the concept of a "professionalized" relationship. Professionalization is associated with occupational roles, which are usually impersonal. An occupational expertise also implies detached knowledge and skills. In theory, competent professionals coldly, and meticulously, assess a problem and then systematically go about solving it. They do not tumble head over heels for their role partners. Romance is different. It is mysterious. Eyes meet across a crowded room and suddenly two strangers realize they are fated to be soul mates. What is professionalized about this? Moreover, wouldn't professionalization deprive it of the inscrutability that makes love exciting? Love turned cold and calculating scarcely seems like love at all.

And yet professionalized relationships are essential in mass techno-commercial societies. The mistake is in assuming a self-motivated expertise in matters of the heart is devoid of emotion. Needless to say, this sort of expertise differs from that of a physician or engineer. Given that the skills and knowledge required are not technological, but personal, they are intrinsically emotional. Nor are these competences acquired in school. There are no degrees in love. What is needed is on the job learning. People hone their competences by reading, talking to friends, going to the movies, making mistakes, and then practicing and practicing some more. The only advantage we have over our ancestors is that we, as a society, have learned more about relationships. We understand, for instance, that successful relationships must be worked at. They do not grow like Topsey from thin air. We have likewise discovered that divorce is no cure-all. Some marriages may be destined to fail; yet failure is not always a gateway to future success.

Unlike the caricature of the traditional family peddled by the skeptics, the contemporary family is evolving in new, more professionalized, directions. Grounded in the isolated nuclear family, it does, however, lack many supports, just as its detractors complain. Because it is more

251

decentralized than its antecedents, those who embark on it are more dependent on their own resources. They have to know what they are doing and be prepared to do it without external pressures. To begin with, the contemporary marriage is based on "voluntary intimacy." People no longer get married because they have to. Both men and women are today capable of supporting themselves without the assistance of a mate. Nor do they have to stay together after they have married. Our postindustrial prosperity is such that they can reestablish separate households, even if they have children to support. Not even the opinions of friends and relatives need keep them together. With moral standards having loosened, they can leave their partners without fear of social repercussions.

The modern marriage is also companionate in that a husband and wife are regarded as moral equals. No longer is he the undisputed head of the family. She too is presumed to be an active participant. Their union may similarly be described as collaborative. Nowadays the parties are supposed to be a team. When they make decisions the needs of both, as well as of their children, are to be considered. It will not do for him to impose a unilateral decision, nor for her to manipulate him into doing as she alone desires. Both are to be up-front and honest in negotiating their differences. Under the best of circumstances, there exists a give-and-take intended to maximize the interests of both. The very notion that one person should be subservient to the other flies in the face of larger social trends. In a professionalized society, where more people exercise decentralized discretion, that either a husband or wife is denied a freedom of choice is unthinkable. It is inconsistent with our other liberties and hence is considered oppressive.

As it happens, both voluntary intimacy and collaborative marriages require professionalized abilities in order to function. In establishing and maintaining appropriate emotional attachments, both men and women have to be self-motivated experts on the nature of intimate relationships. They must personally understand how people fall in love if they are to choose the right partner. They must likewise comprehend how to negotiate differences if they are to resolve their inevitable conflicts. On top of this, they must be emotionally mature. Unless they are grown-up, they will not be motivated to work through the many issues that accompany marital life. A childlike selfishness is inimical to teamwork. Only if both parties are allowed to be winners, will they be able to sustain their union. Only if they are both capable of self-restraint, and generosity, can either be satisfied.

Nowadays personal relationships begin with courtship. There was a time when many marriages were arranged. The parents sought an appropriate partner and facilitated a union that was as much a family alliance as a love match. Today, people select their own mates. Out of millions of potential candidates, they decide on someone with whom to share a lifetime. This is a serious question. In the movies, people just gaze at each other—and know. In real life, they test things out. They have to. They cannot possibly enter the process knowing where it will end. Indeed, young people are still trying to figure out who they are and what they want. Deciding whom another person is, and what he or she offers, is even more of a challenge. At first, it may seem as if good looks and a stylish demeanor are sufficient. Experience, however, usually indicates otherwise. Getting out into the world and interacting with a series of strangers helps the parties understand themselves, as well as these others. The rating-dating game reveals facts previously not known and improves the judgment of the players. Growing both older and wiser, they eventually narrow their options.

As suggested earlier, courtship itself follows a predictable pattern. First, two strangers must come to each other's attention. Something about how the other looks, sounds, or behaves must be attractive. If this person reciprocates, the two then explore their respective attributes. They talk. They engage in biography swapping. Each tells stories about the past, the present, and an envisioned future. If they do so in a balanced manner such that both remain interested, they may decide to continue. If so, they must determine if this other is trustworthy. Intimacy is dangerous. It enables another person to get close enough to inflict damage. Intimates come to know each other's secrets and weaknesses. Moreover, their proximity provides an opportunity to do harm. Any sensible person must protect against this. As a consequence, their respective dependability must be tested. How this other operates needs to be observed first hand. Does he or she lie or bully? Is he or she inordinately selfish? These facts have to be ascertained. The parties must interact in a number of circumstances—some of which are stressful—to determine the other's internal dispositions. Professionalized relationships thus begin with interpersonal knowledge. An expertise in establishing an emotionally fulfilling attachment starts by being a good judge of character. Those swept away by unexamined appearances only court trouble.

Assuming the parties continue to regard each other as potential mates, they enter the infatuation phase of attachment formation. This period is crucial for emotional bonding, but it too holds dangers. During an infatuation a person's judgment is impaired. He or she "feels" in love. The other person now seems perfect. To examine him or her at this point feels tantamount to betrayal. It would be questioning the other's suitability. Instead there is wholehearted belief and complete devotion. More particularly, this is the phase during which both of the couple's motives are reorganized. What they want out of life changes. Where once their plans were indistinct, these now come into clearer focus. This other person—the beloved—enters the picture. Making him or her happy becomes a topmost priority. This is not an intellectual choice. It is not rationally decided or coolly enforced. This is passion. To this extent, it is anything but professional in character. Nevertheless, this is the basis of being self-motivated in the subsequent relationship.

Eventually, of course, the aura of undiluted love wears off. At this point, the parties become aware that their paramour is imperfect. Despite their previous estimations, this other always is. What results is the lover's quarrel. This becomes the anteroom to the negotiations through which the couple resolves their differences. And there are always differences. No two people are perfectly matched. Their interests and hopes never fully coincide. They therefore have to make deals in which they give up something in order to get something. Unprofessional persons do not realize this. They expect to live on love without making compromises. Emotionally mature individuals, however, know better. Having previously learned something about human nature and intimate relationships, they are not surprised by the concessions required of them. At least moderately expert regarding personal relationships, they are prepared to learn how to negotiate differences. They understand that this is a major challenge thrown up by marriage, but also that it is the foundation of interpersonal equality.

To cite a timeworn cliché, marriage is not a placid pond upon which a couple sails unimpeded into an untroubled sunset. There are always troubles. Voluntary intimacy is about sticking around to work these out. Among the skills needed is an ability to engage in dual concern negotiations. If the two are to arrive at acceptable compromises, a husband and wife must perceive their own interests, and those of the other, and then factor these into a joint solution. They must also be problem solvers who innovate when necessary. The objective is not to defeat the other, but arrive at a place where both feel like winners. To do otherwise sets up grievances that will fester until the couple separates.

Moreover, marriage entails a division of labor. If they are to function as a collaborative team, the roles of a husband and wife will not be identical. The tasks in which they specialize may differ from those of traditional couples, but will diverge nevertheless. Nor can their assignments be completely interchangeable. Were this so, it might well be fatal for their collaboration. When a husband and wife are responsible for the same tasks, they are liable to become competitors. Instead of complementing each other, they compare who does what better. Were this to occur, one might be perceived as the winner and the other the loser. One would thus be regarded as better and the other inferior. On the other hand, if they concentrate on different tasks, both can be expert at what they do. They can therefore be individually professionalized in what they bring to their union such that both benefit from their respective contributions. In this case, they need not feel envy, but can take pride in each other's accomplishments.

An effective marital division of labor does not, however, have to follow conventional patterns. In modern professionalized marriages, the partners can work together to develop roles unique to themselves. Because marriage has become decentralized, being collaborative entails delegating tasks in a manner that works for the parties. She does not have to do the cooking, nor he mow the lawn. If they decide to do the reverse, there is no one to stop them. In fact, as marriages become more professionalized, the participants can engage in all sorts of experimentation. As knowledgeable, self-directed individuals, they possess the sophistication and confidence to take chances their ancestors did not. Far from being trapped in the past, they are free to develop supportive lifestyles consistent with a techno-commercial context.

Implied in the above is that androgyny is not the answer. Unfortunately, liberalism has become associated with feminism, and feminists interpret complete equality as meaning that gender differences must disappear. They argue that unless a gender division of labor is totally eradicated, the inequalities between men and women will persist. Contending that there are no biological differences between the sexes, they insist that any remaining disparities are illegitimate. If these are perpetuated, it is only because boys and girls are raised differently. Once this inequality is ended, males and females will do exactly the same things; including in the marital bed. They will thus be interchangeable. Once our ancestors proclaimed "*vive la difference*," but feminists spurn this as unjust.

But the feminists are profoundly wrong! There are gender differences. These are biological facts. To claim otherwise is to deny empirical realities. Feminism is not scientific, but ideological. It promotes moral goals by falsifying the data. Feminism is deeply antiprofessional because it is opposed to the development of legitimate expertise. Nor does it allow men and women to be personally motivated. Men and women, in fact, tend to be competent in different areas. Their abilities overlap, but are concentrated differently. Thus, women are better with words, while men are superior with numbers. As importantly, women are more sensitive to emotions, while men are more competitive. Yes, men can be sensitive. Yes, women are also competitive. Even so, this usually means that more women are comfortable working with young children, whereas more men are driven to achieve hierarchical supremacy. There are exceptions. And there is no reason why there should not be. But the fact remains that men and women tend to make different choices in what to specialize. Yet if they do, the roles they develop within the family are likely to differ. Furthermore, to be genuinely professionalized, that is, to be self-motivated experts, they must be allowed to make independent choices. Were this not so, people would not be bound by roles with which they personally identify.

On top of this, a voluntary and collaborative intimacy must allow the partners to be themselves. If they are to negotiate compromises that succeed in meeting their needs, they must understand themselves and each other. Ideological fantasies will not do. Vital to dual concern bargaining is an ability to engage in role-taking. If the two are to understand each other, the partners must put themselves imaginatively in each other's shoes. Only if they recognize what the other wants, will they come up with practical solutions. Whether or not their individual selves are politically correct, it is they who must implement what they decide. Attempting to fulfill impossible dreams is therefore not the best way to accomplish what will work for them.

The second major constituent of the professionalized family is professionalized childrearing. Not every couple has children, but if they do, they need to know how to raise them. Once upon a time this was considered unproblematic. No longer. In times gone by, children were allowed to raise themselves. They had chores to perform and rules to obey, but much of the time they were unsupervised. Unless apprenticed or in school, they spent hours playing with and learning from one another. Among the lower and working classes, this was considered sufficient. Because the jobs that they later occupied were not intellectually or emotionally demanding, they did not have to acquire professionalized skills. Such controls as kept them civilized were imposed from the outside. Even as adults they were expected to be obedient to authority figures, usually from a higher social class. They did not themselves need to be self-directed.

Times have changed. Economic and political imperatives today dictate a more intense period of socialization. If children are to grow to be successful adults, they must develop professionalized competences, that is, they must be able to operate as self-motivated experts. But this has to be learned. Some authorities insist that the best place to do so is in school. They claim that the only way to generate an egalitarian society is for all children to receive exactly the same lessons. Yet because parents have different abilities and connections, they provide their offspring with dissimilar opportunities. Like it or not, the children of successful middle-class parents have an unfair advantage over the children of working-class parents. Exposed to more stimulating conversations, able to visit more exotic places, and provided with more demanding reading materials, they learn more. They also have access to more valuable social networks.

All of this is unfair. But then, life is unfair. Radical egalitarians would correct this imbalance by equalizing opportunities. And they would achieve this by raising children outside their families. This would presumably deny higher status parents the opportunity to provide unearned advantages. In doing so, however, it would also deny many children the opportunity to become professionalized. The fact is that the skills needed to become self-directed experts are best instilled in close emotional relationships. It is parents who love their children who most effectively implant the necessary internal controls and wide-ranging knowledge. But since professionalized parents are more likely to possess the information and skills needed to do so, were they prohibited from helping their young, there would be fewer professionalized adults. If this is true, an artificially enforced equality can only be achieved at the price of mediocrity. In this case, the self-motivated expertise necessary to sustain a techno-commercial society would be virtually absent.

That said, professionalized childrearing is a skill. Merely being middle class does not automatically bestow an ability to raise self-directed youngsters. How far this is from being reflexive was demonstrated by the permissive parenting styles of a half-century ago. The newly-minted middle-class parents during the Eisenhower era

257

assumed that letting their children have whatever they desired would produce happy, successful adults. It did not. Their offspring grew up to be spoiled hippies. But neither is the rationalized coercion of tough love the answer. Something else, something informed by an understanding of the nature of childhood and maturation processes, is required. Expert parents must know how children learn, as well as what they need to learn in order to be successful. They cannot blindly do what feels right. Nor can they mechanically interact with their offspring. They must be human, but intelligently human.

What is needed is *limits with latitude*. If children are to become self-directed, if they are to be capable of independent decisions, they must first acquire self-control. Those unable to manage their impulses do not so much decide what to do as spontaneously act. Nonetheless, internal controls begin with external controls. Young children have neither the knowledge, nor the mental acuity, to make the best choices. They must therefore be protected from mistakes they do not recognize as mistakes. Parents do this by setting and enforcing limits. They provide boundaries that are ultimately internalized, assuming their children are allowed to adopt these on their own. Yet the young also require an opportunity to practice decision-making. They must consequently be provided with the latitude to make choices. Even if they fall into error, they must be allowed to discover that errors can be corrected. Unless they are, they never develop the courage to become self-motivated experts.

The full dimensions of professionalized childrearing are too complex to be detailed here, but suffice it to say these too are decentralized. They likewise depend upon the implementation of complex parental and childhood roles. All in all, the professionalized ideal is not for the faint of heart. It does not delegate responsibilities for economic, political or familial tasks to external authorities. If professionalized adults are to exercise personal discretion, they must grow to be mature adults. If they are to coordinate their activities effectively, they must acquire the judgment, the wisdom, and the courage to do so. Asking to be saved by the best and brightest is not a viable alternative. Quite the contrary, it is a prescription for retrogressive policies. It begs to be returned to the bad old days of poverty, absolutism, and superstition. The professionalized ideal may be a frightening, but the liberal option is more so.

8

Post-Liberalism

Cultural Lag

Liberalism has been lingering on for some time. There is no doubt about it; it has been dying a very leisurely death. The patient has been coughing blood for decades; nonetheless, it has not yet been fully consumed by its illness. The disease will eventually be fatal, but it has not yet run its course. The question is this: Why? Why after so many failures, after so many broken promises and blatant untruths, are so many decent people committed to its survival? Liberalism is clearly a case of a failed prophecy. All the same, tens of millions of intelligent people do not regard it as such. They still believe. They continue to await the fulfillment of its exaggerated claims. The flying saucers have not yet landed, but they remain convinced they will. In the meantime, they are prepared to justify whatever goes wrong. As with all true believers, they have ready explanations for why the millennium has not arrived. Thus, Obama's stimulus package might not have reduced unemployment, but things would have been significantly worse without it. Similarly, his budget deficits may be leading us over a financial cliff, yet they accept rationalizations about why spending more while simultaneously raising taxes will be the solution.

Again, why is this so? Why the apparent irrationality? There has to be a reason. Indeed, there are many. Part of the explanation is analogous to the persistence of the flying saucer cults. Most liberals are embedded in communities of like-minded souls. Almost everyone they know is dedicated to the Liberal Dream. This is part of belonging to a communal faith. Thus, their friends recount the latest conservative idiocy while their colleagues laugh at the simple-minded faith of right-wingers. Likewise, wide smiles of agreement appear whenever they reaffirm the current Democratic policy initiative. As with the Unarians, they are amazed, and a bit saddened, when outsiders refuse to recognize the validity of their vision. These others just do not understand. They

259

need to be educated. Perhaps in time, they will come to understand that liberals desire the best for everyone. And when they do, liberalism will finally be vindicated.

True believers also hang on because they have publicly committed themselves to the cause. Years ago social psychologists demonstrated that when people broadcast a position in front of others, they are reluctant to renounce it later on. Having staked their reputations on the correctness of their assertions, they are loath to admit errors. They fear that this would make them look foolish. Instead, they raise their voices and grow more emphatic. Of course, they are right! Every principled human being understands this! What is more, with a bit more energy, the opposition will fold like cheap suit.

Still, this too is not the complete explanation. Something more fundamental is going on. Almost a century ago, William Ogburn discussed a phenomenon he called *cultural lag*. He noticed that during periods of rapid technological advance many people grow uncomfortable. They cannot deny the automobiles on the streets, but wish them to disappear. When one breaks down, they advise the driver to "get a horse." Or, if they see a heavier-than-air machine, they shake their heads and mutter something about how if God intended people to fly, He would have given them wings. In Ogburn's time, these same people hated the modern corporation, distrusted huge banks, and were not sure women deserved the vote.

Ogburn, however, concentrated his observations on our resistance to technological innovations. Thus, had he lived today, he would have recognized the discomfort many people (like me) have with the cell phone. He was, however, less concerned with styles of life or belief systems. Yet these too tend to be conservative. Most people—even those who believe in change—maintain the values of their early adulthood. Hence, if at age twenty-five, they registered as a Democrat (or Republican), they remain one at sixty-five. Likewise, how they dressed, combed their hair, or danced still seem the epitome of good taste and sophistication.

If this sounds trivial, it can be deadly serious. People are often so dedicated to the ways of life with which they grew up that they kill to preserve them. The world witnessed this impulse with the advent of Hitler's Germany. Nazism appealed to the German people because most came of age in a nation ruled by the Kaiser. It, therefore, seemed natural to have a strong man as head of the state. That memories of Bismarck were still fresh did not hurt either. The Weimar Republic may have boasted an extremely democratic constitution, but most Germans were not democrats. Having had no experience with democratic institutions, they did not trust their messiness. Unlike Americans, they lacked an apprenticeship in self-government. As a consequence, when Hitler offered himself as their fuehrer, reverberations of a bygone stability attracted them. He would protect Germans from the uncertainties of modern living. Under him, the clock would be turned back to the halcyon years before World War I.

We recently observed the same dynamic in Iraq. One of the mistakes of the Bush administration was to underestimate the degree to which ordinary Iraqis were attached to totalitarianism. Bush and his advisers assumed everyone wants to be free. Accordingly, they imagined that when American forces toppled Saddam, ordinary people would joyously welcome their liberation. It came as a shock when many did not. It was also a shock that democratic institutions did not immediately take hold. Nonetheless, the Iraqis had never been free. Like the Germans, they never experienced democracy. It was not part of their culture; hence, they did not possess the aptitudes necessary to maintain democratic institutions. These had to be cultivated. In the meantime, many Iraqis hungered for a strongman. Be he an ayatollah or an al Qaeda commander, he would suppress sectarian violence and restore Iraqi glory. Indeed, many looked even further back. They sought to resurrect the glory of the Islamic caliphate.

Oddly, cultural lag does not always look like resistance to change. It can come clad in futuristic raiments. Reactionaries often portray themselves as the wave of the future. This is one of the secrets of the Communist appeal. Paradoxically, one of the more disquieting echoes of the past that roiled Bolshevik Russia was the collective farm. In an effort to create social solidarity, Stalin seized the holdings of small farmers, the so-called Kulaks, and forced them onto large, government-managed communes. If they resisted, they were regarded as counter-revolutionaries. Many millions were literally starved to death as a result of their stubbornness. And yet Stalin was reviving an ancient institution. His collective farms were nothing less than a reincarnation of the boyar estates. Once, not long before, most Russians were serfs who labored on these large-scale domains. The difference was that Communist Party apparatchiks, rather than aristocrats, now ran them. Otherwise, they were the familiar past restored to life.

John Bowlby gave us a hint of why the culturally familiar is so reassuring. In his investigations of the relationship between young children and their caretakers, he encountered the phenomena of attachment and loss. He realized that the very young have a deep-seated need to bond with their protectors. When feeling insecure, they assuage their fears through physical closeness. This was especially true when they are deserted by a parent. At such moments, they protest against the potential loss and cling desperately to those who seek to leave. Indeed, the less secure the relationship, the tighter their grip. The same is the case with familiar ways of life. The more insecure people feel, the greater their anxieties, the more they cling to old habits. Because they are afraid, they are disinclined to let go of the time-tested and well-known. These calm their doubts because they are predictable.

Liberals tell us they are progressives; nevertheless, their social solutions are of hoary vintage. In our techno-commercial society, where change is constant, their proposals hark back to the dawn of humankind. The social domains that worked best among hunter-gatherers are, for them, the most comforting. Likewise, the sorts of relationship that characterize an idealized childhood hold the greatest charm. In short, they want to be loved and protected. Thus, they imagine that if we live in a puffed up version of a hunter-gatherer band, watched over by communal elders who have our best interests at heart, all will be well. With everyone nice and part of a single loving family, there will be nothing to fear. The bogymen that haunt existence in a Gesellschaft society will thus be forever cast out.

Liberals do not ask us to become professionalized adults. Their dream is not about self-motivated expertise. Rather, it is about childlike dependence. Instead of looking the uncertainties of a mass techno-commercial society in the eye, they blink. Afraid they might not be up to the challenges, they retreat into a fantasy world grounded in ancient verities. And because they are afraid, they will not let go. To be sure, they loudly proclaim their courage. They shout out, often at the top of their lungs, about how brave they are. But this is sham. According to their propaganda, they, unlike their adversaries, are eager to explore the unknown. They alone are prepared to experiment with a future in which everyone can be a winner. The truth, however, is that they are disguising their fears in order to suppress them. Rather than leading us into the future, they are cemented to phantoms of a bygone era.

This attachment to the past is confirmed in the policies liberals favor. Somehow these always resuscitate proposals made decades or centuries earlier. For many, the central ambition is completing the Roosevelt agenda. FDR is their hero. In their view, he was the greatest champion against greed and oppression the United States has known. Unfortunately, reactionary capitalists prevented him from accomplishing his mission. If the New Deal was not fully successful, it was because he was only allowed to do "too little, too late." Had he been permitted to go full bore, freedom, equality, and prosperity would have been the consequence. The business cycle would have been abolished and the little people liberated from commercial exploitation.

Liberals not only maintain their faith in Keynesian economics, they retain an allegiance to nationalized health care, federalized education, and welfare on demand. They would also like to see the unions restored to a position of industrial dominance and bankers cast into a nether world of impotence. Liberals believe in class warfare. They favor a redistribution of wealth. They are also schizophrenic internationalists. On the one hand, they believe in a family of all humankind and deeply admire European social democracy. Many would even eradicate national borders and create a single world government. On the other, they despise free trade. They wish to erect protective tariffs so that work remains in the United States and ordinary people can find good paying jobs.

The bottom line is that liberals believe in centralization. The world may be becoming more decentralized as professionalization marches forward, yet they would halt this process in its tracks. Although they proclaim their devotion to freedom and democracy, they intend to reduce individual discretion. On their watch, more decisions will be made in Washington, DC. Despite their love of ordinary people, they do not trust them. They argue that universal love, niceness, and equality lie in our future, but are nevertheless wary of the person on the street exercising too much responsibility. They do not believe that he or she is sufficiently competent to be professionalized. For the time being, self-motivated expertise must be reserved for the best and brightest. These cognoscenti are needed to promulgate the plans that control how health care, education, energy policy, fiscal institutions, manufacturing priorities, and welfare are organized. Able to see the big picture as ground-level people cannot, a cadre of capable leaders should be delegated the authority to protect people from themselves. Only this will produce progress. Only this can safeguard justice.

The Professionalized Awakening

Liberalism is, in fact, desperately thrashing about. Ironically, its recent political efflorescence is evidence of this. As surprising as it seems, the radical left-wing tendencies of those recently elevated to power have demonstrated that liberalism is in deep trouble. Their very excesses highlight profound insecurities. Like the dying bird that hit my window, the energy with which they have pursued an ill-fated agenda confirms a struggle against death. Having proven wrong so often, they have sought to deny their continuing failures by asserting them ever more strongly. The problem is that what cannot survive, will not survive. Like a light bulb about to expire, it may flare up, only to be snuffed out.

When Barack Obama was first elected, most people did not know what kind of president he would make. He had a liberal voting record while in the Senate, but he promised bipartisanship and a pragmatic approach to national problems. It was obvious that Obama was very intelligent, and also that he was calm under pressure and supremely confident in his abilities. All told, there was reason to suppose he would be moderate. Yes, he claimed that he would bring change and end business as usual; nevertheless, he was a problem-solver. He would get the economy moving again and put millions of people back to work. Indeed, it was in his interest to do so, if he hoped to be reelected.

Within weeks, however, this hope evaporated. Obama quickly demonstrated his radical left-wing commitments. He was a true believer. Apparently, he was intent on being the second coming—of FDR. Unwilling to settle for talk, he would complete the New Deal agenda. And he would do this right away. Unlike others, he would be a consequential president, not a placeholder. At this, the country held its breath, while his liberal base was overjoyed. Most people wanted Obama to succeed. They felt pride in electing a minority president. Still, the less committed grew uneasy. Did it make sense to propose spending trillions of dollars during an economic crisis? Was it wise to increase taxes on those whose investments were more necessary than ever or to risk the hidden taxes of inflation and increased energy costs?

The question was thus, was this a bridge too far? Was there a limit to the degree a radically liberal agenda would be tolerated in a techno-commercial nation? Would a point arise where ordinary voters lost faith in the Liberal Dream? Furthermore, how many broken promises would it take before they decided there had been too many? President Obama seemed determined to find out. He bet his office on the dual propositions that he could enact the liberal agenda and that it would deliver on his grandiose expectations. If it didn't, if his proposals struck too many voters as extreme, there might be a reaction against him and his program. The person on the street might decide that for all its florid rhetoric, liberalism threatened his/her lifestyle.

And make no mistake—Obama's proposals were extreme. He intended nothing less than to remake the nation's economic and social systems. Traditional capitalism was to be dismantled, while the national government was to intrude itself into places it had never been. This was centralization on a grand scale. He, and his advisors, hoped to take their special expertise and moral vision and apply these to protecting people from themselves. After all, they were rational to a degree ordinary people were not and incorruptible as their conservative opponents never were.

One of the places the national government had, of course, been was education. It had long subsidized local school systems and in some measure set their standards. This was surely the point of the "no child left behind" initiative. But Obama wanted to go farther. He intended to funnel hundreds of billions of dollars into regional systems. These would provide the resources to offer quality education. Unspoken, but implied by previous federal actions, was that there would be strings attached. Local governments would have to abide by federal regulations and oversight if they wished to receive the allotted funds. The feds would impose uniform standards, which, because these were designed by experts, would be more effective than the decentralized alternatives. Accordingly, children would learn more, with less discrimination.

What Obama and his minions left out of their calculations is that previous federal expeditions into this area had not been notably successful. As early as the mid-1960s, James Coleman's research documented a disconnect between the dollars spent and the academic results produced. Higher paid teachers and a greater number of computers did not translate into improved learning. The correlation that mattered was the one between the value parents placed on education and the efforts their children expended. If parents didn't care, their children didn't—with the consequence that they did not learn. Moreover, decades of experience demonstrated that throwing money at schools was ineffective. Reduced class sizes, magnet schools, and fancier textbooks made little difference. Nevertheless, spending dollars was easy. As long as Obama and his cronies controlled the checkbook, they could direct massive spending where they chose. And one of these was toward teachers. In addition, because teacher unions were among his most reliable supporters, the political payoff would be substantial.

The federal government had also been involved in welfare programs before. From the war on poverty right through to the Clinton administration, most Democrats believed spending more on welfare was the way to end poverty. Jimmy Carter called welfare "a disgrace to the human race," but his party did not allow him to dismantle one of its signature programs. It took a Republican congress to put a cap on what welfare clients received. Critics predicted disaster, yet almost half of the welfare clients left the dole. They got jobs and reduced their incapacitating dependency. This seemed to be a success story. Even so, Obama decided to retreat to the old format. He would allocate billions of dollars for enhanced welfare payments. This was proposed in the name of justice. Poor people simply deserved more.

As to the health-care system, this was not virgin federal territory either. Nevertheless, according to the Obama team, Medicare and Medicaid were insufficient. With tens of millions uninsured, only a centralized system could cover all of those who required it. Medicine constituted more than a seventh of the economy, but, no matter, the national government was big enough to swallow it. Medicare and Medicaid might be riddled with corruption and inefficiency, but the new program would be different. It would be rationally designed. Other centralized health systems in places like Canada and the United Kingdom were plagued with long waiting periods and/or a lack of sophisticated equipment, but the American model would learn from their mistakes. It would be state of the art. Moreover, it would be affordable. By stamping out waste, many hundreds of billions would be saved and applied to the funding increases. Perhaps Medicare and Medicaid cost tens of times more than originally projected, but this program would not. It would come in under budget. Despite projections that the existing programs would bankrupt the nation, this project was doable. Obama and his advisors promised that it was.

As if this were not sufficiently ambitious, the Obama administration intended to solve the global warming problem by reducing carbon dioxide emissions. It, therefore, fought for a cap and trade program to decrease the use of dirty fuels. Even Obama's advisors calculated this would cost trillions, but they dismissed this as insignificant because the extra taxes would be directed toward the poor. The standard electric bill might increase, yet the persons least able to pay would be protected. That economic growth might be adversely affected did not trouble them. Siphoning dollars into health and energy merely removed funds from luxuries and directed them toward necessities. These were, in fact, investments. After all, the environment had to be saved. That there was no scientific consensus global warming was man-made, or that lowering American emissions could reverse it, did not disturb Obama. He knew this had to be done and those who disagreed were environmental counterrevolutionaries.

On a smaller scale, Obama intended to resurrect the union hegemony. Just as educators were among his most fervent supporters, so were labor unions in general. It was therefore his duty to increase their membership. The proposed method for doing so was to eliminate the secret ballot in the elections that designated unions as bargaining agents. This would allow their leadership to intimidate workers, but it was not antidemocratic because unions were inherently democratic. Nor was there a problem in paying off unions by refusing to endorse trade agreements with countries like Columbia and South Korea. It was even acceptable to abrogate trade agreements with Mexico and Canada. Although Mexican trucks were statistically no more dangerous than American trucks, they would not be allowed on American roads because the unions alleged they were unsafe. It did not matter that Mexico was likely to retaliate. Nor did it matter that the Smoot–Hawley Tariff was a major contributor to deepening the Great Depression. Obama was prepared to risk a trade war because his union allies believed this would create American jobs. No evidence was cited to justify this course. The political benefit was deemed sufficient to move ahead.

Even charity was not to be spared the Obama meat cleaver. He proposed to reduce the percentage of charitable contributions taxpayers could exempt on their tax forms. The effect of this would be to reduce the amount directed toward independent charities, while the funds received by the federal government would increase. Meanwhile, government-sponsored volunteer programs would expand. Private groups, however, were suspect. Many were not sufficiently liberal. Religions, in particular, were distrusted. They were apt to be conservative. On the other hand, the government could be counted on to favor liberal causes. It would reliably increase diversity and support for the poor.

As for the banks, in the past, the government instituted policies to prevent fiscal abuses. Now it would take a more active part in managing financial institutions. In many cases, it would own a majority share. Nor would it be a silent partner. As with the schools, there would be strings attached. The government, for instance, might mandate where loans were made. Favored consumers, such as the poor, would get the money they needed. Making profits was not the issue—doing good was. As to the administration of these institutions, early on the president decided to regulate matters such as salaries and bonuses. Greedy executives would not be paid more than they deserved. Again, it was not good business practices that mattered, but what was politically palatable. If the president's liberal base considered some expenditures unjust, they would be disallowed.

With regard to taxes, the rich were to be taken to the cleaners. Because Obama and his associates found it convenient to blame private greed for the economic downturn, the wealthy could be safely scapegoated. Even during the campaign, Obama declared that if raising capital gains taxes reduced investments, this still ought to be done because it was fair. Once in power, he lengthened his reach and contemplated confiscatory policies. For one thing, we would make the social security tax applicable to every dollar people earned. This alone would take 10 percent of everything the rich made. Under FDR, social security had been sold as an insurance policy. The elderly would take out of the system only what they put in. Under Obama, it was regarded as a payroll tax; therefore, he was unfazed by the prospect that the rich could never hope to receive back more than a fraction of their contributions. This was intended as a transfer payment where the poorest persons received the greatest subsidies.

Worse still were the monumental deficits Obama projected. Although he and his fellow Democrats for years complained about the Bush deficits, theirs were of a magnitude many times greater. Initially described as a stimulus to get the economy going again, it quickly became evident this was intended to continue into the indefinite future. John McCain characterized this as stealing from our grandchildren—and he was correct. Even more importantly, most economists predicted that massive unfunded expenditures would produce a rip-roaring inflation. If so, the victims were sure to be the poor. The very people Obama said he would never tax, would then be subjected to hidden expropriations. Even though their ostensible earnings might remain the same, they could afford to purchase less.

All of this was promised as a means of overcoming the financial emergency, whereas most economists believed it irrelevant to this purpose. The point, as Rahm Emanuel observed, was not to let a good crisis go unexploited. The liberal agenda had to be enacted while the iron was still hot. Even if the truth had to be manipulated, it was necessary to shepherd the electorate in the desired direction. In the long run, voters would not object since this was for their own good. Hundreds of billons of dollars might be expended in the dead of night without anyone reading the fine print, but the administration knew best. It would take care of people.

Voters also needed faith in the numbers the president bandied about. He claimed his policies would create or save three to four million jobs. He likewise promised his energy policies would generate five million unexportable jobs. Indeed, he repeated these figures many times. The interesting part is where he got them. He simply made them up. He plucked them from thin air and then depended on Joseph Goebbels' philosophy that if a pseudo-fact is repeated often enough, people come to believe it. The same strategy was used with taxes. Time and again Obama promised that 95 percent of the population would receive a tax break. Only the top 2 percent were to pay more. Meanwhile, the proposed taxes proliferated. Worse still, the administration did not mention where the money would ultimately come from. Increased business and energy taxes were likely to be passed along to customers in the form of higher prices, but this was not acknowledged. By the same token, fewer investment dollars would hold down economic growth, yet this too was left unsaid.

Instead Obama boasted of his sense of responsibility and recommended it for the nation at large. He was doing his level best to protect the public, but others needed to accept the shared sacrifices. Likewise, on his watch corruption would be eliminated and selfishness controlled. Only they weren't. Barack quickly rationalized going back on his word not to hire lobbyists. He similarly found a way to explain why he approved a spending bill that included over eight thousand earmarks. And as for "investing" a half a billion dollars in a solar panel company controlled by a political contributor, the money might have gone down the drain, but that was what happened in a market system. Left unexplained was why his friends, not the federal government, would be first in line to recoup their losses. Nor did the president seem perturbed when his union buddies, not the bondholders, were given priority protections when General Motors went bankrupt.

Even less savory was Obama's reaction to the AIG scandal. This insurance company had been bailed out to the tune of tens of billions of dollars in exchange for 80 percent of its stock. Thus, when it was learned that its executives received over a hundred and sixty million dollars in bonuses, the shock waves rippled across the nation. When this news got out, ordinary citizens were perplexed why executives who lost billions should be rewarded for their performance. But the legislators were even more incensed. They would not tolerate this malfeasance. Then it came out that the legislators, in collusion with the executive branch, had inserted a clause into the unread stimulus legislation that allowed these bonuses to be paid. Those responsible initially blamed the oversight on someone else; nevertheless, there was enough blame to go around for committee chairs and treasury officials alike. At this, the congress vowed to correct the error by enacting further taxes. Ninety percent of the bonus money would be returned to the government by this means.

Meanwhile, the president stood silently by. Despite his professions of responsibility, as was his wont, he took no action. Nor did he request any of his legislative allies. Congress essentially passed a bill of attainder in an ex post facto manner. Even though the constitution explicitly forbade punitive bills, the legislators needed a scapegoat. They had to find a way to divert attention from their ineptitude. As for Obama, this was a hot potato he tossed elsewhere. What made this particularly noteworthy was that the Democrats had for seven years pilloried George W. Bush for promoting legislation that allowed the government to wiretap overseas terrorists. This was said to violate civil rights. Although the practice was not expressly forbidden by the constitution, they insisted that it violated the spirit of the document. Here, however, the Democrats, with barely a murmur of dissent, violated constitution's exact words. What they referred to as a sacred text mattered not a whit when their own desires were involved. Nor did it to Obama. His sense of responsibility did not extend to defending the nation's fundamental law.

All told, this added up to a sorry record of dishonesty, hypocrisy, and inconsistency. The level of cynicism demonstrated by politicians who promised to clean up Washington was truly breathtaking. They, for instance, promised to reduce government expenditures by not spending a trillion dollars no one had ever intended to spend on the wars in Iraq and Afghanistan. The stated goal was to end business as usual; hence, it was astonishing that they were eager to use smoke and mirrors to disguise their cupidity. Liberals were determined to implement their dreams whatever the impact, which meant increasing the government's share of the gross domestic product. If what they delivered was not what had been promised, they would disguise this as best they could. As a result, they continued to impugn the Bush administration and Wall Streeters. They, the Democrats, were blameless.

Since their hearts were in the right place, the opposition was at fault. Retrograde conservatives were merely being negative. They always said no. Never mind that a supposedly bipartisan president dismissed their suggestions out of hand.

The paradox, and perhaps the undoing, of the resurgent liberal hegemony was that its ineptitude and deceitfulness were at odds with its self-image. Liberals constantly promoted themselves as the best and the brightest, but here they were being neither. Thus, they could not manage to put together a slate of competent officials to manage the treasury department during an economic crisis, nor devise a coherent policy to get credit flowing in financial markets. Indeed, they did not appear up to the task. They were particularly bad with respect to managing the economy. A penchant for over-regulation combined with runaway budget deficits threatened to produce long-term economic stagnation. Jobs were lost, while market-oriented innovations and private risk taking were discouraged. The result has been, and will be, that the American (not to say the Liberal) Dream is put on hold. Worse still, the prospects for our children and grandchildren are dim. Simply refusing to do anything about Medicare, Medicaid, and Social Security might be good politics, but it was not honorable statesmanship.

Nor have liberals been particularly moral. Routinely caught in misstatements and grubby deal making, they were hardly knights in shining armor. Obama himself attempted to stand above the fray. His inspirational rhetoric did not fail him, nor did his affable and easygoing style. People continued to like the man. Nonetheless, there was a problem. Liberal legitimacy depended on its advocates being superior human beings. They had to be smarter than conservatives, who now included Paul Ryan and Eric Cantor. They also had to be more compassionate. As importantly, their policies had to work. If they did not, what was the point of delegating them power? Liberals traded in hope. The Liberal Dream allegedly produced utopian endpoints. But if it did not, what then? Would its failures bring disillusionment? Would people caste about for a better alternative?

If cultural lag had kept liberalism from slipping into disrepute, will ever more glaring liberal failures convince people there must be a more viable option? Will they look elsewhere, or continue to rationalize its abortive prophesies? This experiment is currently being tried. Sadly, the Obama administration is working overtime to make liberal failures more obvious. The question is will these disappointments drive a stake through the heart of liberalism? Only time will tell.

In general, people make dramatic changes only when things get sufficiently unpleasant. This is what happened during the Great Depression. It is also what occurred during the French Revolution. The reason is not difficult to perceive. Among alcoholism counselors it is common to distinguish between high and low bottom drunks. The former decide to get sober when things have gone moderately wrong, whereas the latter require disaster before they reform. Will contemporary Americans be the one or the other? How bad do conditions have to become before they grow disenchanted with liberalism? There is no way to be sure. Of course, it is also possible that they will refuse to accept disagreeable facts. Some alcoholics drink themselves to death before they decide to make a course correction. The same has been true for some nations. They did not alter their directions until they fell into obscurity. Thus, the glory days of Spain came to an end when Spaniards decided to maintain their loyalty to a rigid Catholicism. Unwilling to become commercialized, they settled into being a European backwater. The glory days of China similarly came to an end when the Ming emperors decided that they had nothing to learn from the outside world and closed the nation off from barbarian contacts. Eventually they became so militarily and economically inept that a small seafaring nation from half a world away (Britain) easily defeated them during the Opium Wars.

Will this be the fate of the United States? Will it too fade into obscurity under the influence of a liberal opium pipe? If history is a guide, significant change generally comes under the auspices of a new generation. Clearly, the liberal mandarins are unlikely to awaken from their reveries. As true believers, their fantasies are too deeply entrenched. Many moderates are willing to entertain new ideas, but they need time to change. Comprehensive ways of life are never casually abandoned. Too much is at stake. People have to be sure that a new direction is an improvement. Moreover, they must understand this in their hearts, not just with their heads. To do otherwise invites tragedy. It allows people to embrace ill-considered chimeras. This is why ways of life tend to be conservative. Even when failing, they continue to feel appropriate.

If there is to be a professionalized awakening, it has to be cultural, not merely structural. People must not only adopt new political arrangements; they must change who they are. Novel government programs, even draconian ones, cannot accomplish this. Attitudes, beliefs, and emotional dispositions all have to be modified. How people understand their world, the norms and values to which they are dedicated, as well as their vocational and political skills, must all be reworked. In a more professionalized world, people themselves have to become professionalized. It is not enough to adopt professionalized roles; they need to become self-motivated experts. In order to be authentically competent, they must therefore undergo a steep learning curve. Responsible professionalization is a way of life, not a temporary political expedient.

If this is makeover to occur, the first step is for people to understand what is at stake. The implications of the inverse force rule must be recognized. This is merely an intellectual accomplishment; nevertheless it is essential. By itself, it cannot induce significant modifications, yet it can prepare the ground for them. The second step is to stop making the same tired mistakes. If you are digging a hole, you must stop digging it deeper. This means that current liberal policies have to be laid aside. Instead of socialism remaining a cherished ideal, it must die a definitive death.

Still, nature abhors a vacuum. There must be a replacement on the horizon. What is therefore necessary is a reorganization of current political factions. The conservative/liberal dichotomy seems mandated by heaven, but it is not. In fact, the US political alignment has undergone dramatic shifts. When the nation emerged, the divide was between Federalists and Republicans. Then it was between Whigs and Democrats, followed by Republicans and Democrats. Even after this last shift, the parties modified their platforms. Thus, at one point the Democrats were internationalists, whereas today Republicans are more likely to be so. Exactly what will happen next is unknowable, but people may again alter allegiances, perhaps in accord with the constrained and unconstrained model. As Thomas Sowell has observed, this is a longstanding divide. Perhaps it will become more consciously recognized.

Another possibility is a distinction between professionalizers and bureaucratizers. In this case, the fault line would be between those dedicated to decentralization and those who favor centralization. Another prospect might differentiate between Modernists and Traditionalists. Here the former would promote professionalization, while the latter remained conservative. In this case, the modernizers would be aligned with the inverse force rule. Or there might be division into collectivists versus free marketers. Here too the issue would be between centralization and decentralization, with the collectivists sponsoring greater governmental control. The former might therefore be designated the Government Party, as opposed to the latter's being the Market Party.

If any of this transpires, who will fit into which designation is uncertain. Would most liberals or conservatives opt to be centralizers or decentralizers? Oddly, it might be the center that coalesces against the extremes. If this arises perhaps neoconservatives and moderate liberals will make common cause. In this case, they might style themselves as "pro-cons," which could stand alternatively for "progressive-conservatives" or "professionalized-conservatives." Or they might describe themselves as "neo-neos," which would stand for "neo-neo-conservatives." Arrayed against them might then be the radical liberals and the radical conservatives. If this seems bizarre, it should be remembered that both religious fundamentalists and radical liberals promote universal family relationships and face-to-face hierarchies to maintain social solidarity. As much as they despise each other, the worlds they envision are strikingly similar. Since no one is in charge of how events will unfold, it will be fascinating to observe the choices people make.

Can We Become Professionalized?

Up to this point, it has been assumed that the professionalized ideal is possible, that it indeed provides a feasible way of life. But does it? Can real human beings in mass techno-commercial societies actually implement its projections? If they cannot, then all of our speculations will be moot. In this case, everything hitherto written will amount to little more than an intellectual exercise. Even though liberalism is fraught with defects, it may still dictate our future.

One of the criticisms that arises when the professionalized ideal is discussed is the claim that most people are incapable of becoming professional. They are neither smart, nor dedicated enough, to achieve a self-motivated expertise. Because a majority does not possess the talents to become doctors or lawyers, it is fatuous to expect them to become as competent as the traditional professionals. This then is a form of utopianism even more egregious than the Liberal Dream. Despite being clothed in a scientific-sounding "inverse force rule," it is a fantasy of epic proportions.

Well, is it? Is the professionalized ideal merely an intellectual whimsy? The answer, I believe, is no. Were it the same sort of abstraction as the Liberal Dream, it might be. Fortunately, it is not. Liberalism is extreme. It projects a future in which everyone is entirely equal, loving, and nice. But since total equality, universal love, and absolute niceness are impossible, it is utterly impractical. The professionalized ideal, by contrast, is not utopian. It does not project a future in which everyone becomes a traditional professional. Professionalization is a matter of degree. Not everyone needs to be equally expert or self-motivated for it to be implemented. Some people can, for instance, be semiprofessional. Like police officers, the sort of knowledge they master may not be as complex as that of physicians, nor need they be as dedicated in applying it. Even so, they may be capable of self-supervision to an extent that previous constabularies were not. Despite their limitations, they will be worthy of an authority they are capable of executing.

Nor need everyone become professionalized. Even as our society becomes more complex, some people may remain holdouts. Many, of course, possess neither the ability, nor the inclination, to become self-directed specialists. Some, for example, may prefer to eschew re-sponsibility and allow themselves to be governed by others. Content to be followers, they will submit to external control. The truth is that decentralization can proceed without becoming complete. Indeed, there may be some jobs where close supervision is preferable. Health inspectors, for instance, may need to oversee a variety of working con-ditions. Nor does professionalization assume total equality. Because some people are liable to be more professionalized than others, they will exercise greater power. In fact, superior authority is liable to be built into many roles. Thus, to cite a familiar example, this is likely to remain the case between doctors and nurses. As the dominant medical experts, physicians will probably persist in supervising nurses.

As to our political and personal roles, something similar applies. No matter how democratic a society becomes, not everyone will be equally involved in the political process. Fortunately, democracy does not depend on everyone running for office. Professionalized political systems require only that a large portion of the electorate become knowledgeable about political issues—not that they all participate to the same degree. It suffices that enough are concerned to keep the system honest. As long as they hold officeholders' feet to the fire, the decisions reached are likely to reflect larger social needs. This would represent, not an implementation of a Rousseau-style General Will, but of large-scale social negotiations. The goal is not to optimize, so much as satisfice. Under these circumstances, good enough is good enough.

275

On the private level, good enough translates into satisfactory personal relations and reasonably competent parenting. Indeed, in these matters a self-motivated expertise is always limited. To be professionalized in love relationships does not imply conflict free devotion. Real human beings have moods. They are sometimes selfish and at other times oblivious to the requirements of their partners. Moreover, actual humans often have interests that cannot be fully reconciled. To be professionalized in matters of the heart therefore entails putting up with imperfections. In some respects, being professionalized in intimate relations involves making the best of uneven conditions. Happy marriages are never trouble free. To the contrary, they manage to surmount their troubles. As a result, they produce greater happiness than the parties would experience had they remained apart. This is so because the self-motivated expertise required incorporates the motivation to resolve differences. The necessary expertise also entails a need to understand themselves and each other, but not so well that the two are conscious of every detail. Here too, good enough is good enough.

As to raising children, every parent knows mistakes will be made. Any mother or father who has ever sought to break up a fight between squabbling children recognizes that it is sometimes impossible to know who started what. Nor is it possible to fathom a child's every mood. Reactions will be misinterpreted and punishments are sometimes inapplicable. Research shows that one of the most important parenting skills is responsiveness; nevertheless, complete responsiveness is not humanly possible. Parents have lives of their own, while their children—because they are children—are defective communicators. Fortunately, once again perfection is not required. Loving and reasonably well-informed parents can do a satisfactory job. Intelligently applied love, though it sometimes goes astray, is accepted, and returned, by children who understand that their parents are well intended. Yes, there will be misunderstandings, and yes children can be unreasonable, but enough can go right for the outcome to be favorable.

None of this, however, should be taken to imply that professionalization can ever be complete. Professionalization is a process, one that takes time and effort to work out. It is never a matter of instant self-actualization. Moreover, professionalized roles can take years, decades, and, occasionally, centuries to develop and become internalized by a significant number of persons. Social roles evolve. The particular skills and motives necessary to accomplish specific tasks are negotiated over time. Individuals innovate various aspects of what is required, and then hone these modifications in interaction with their role partners. The parties make demands of each other, and subsequently adjust to how the others respond. There is no magic here, merely a slow progression toward improved—albeit imperfect—performances. Liberals imagine that when they provide the appropriate conditions, personal growth is automatic. They seem to think self-actualization is a matter of providing water for seedlings. Yet personal growth is nothing of the sort. It is always difficult, always takes time, and always entails complex interactions with other human beings.

An illustration of what occurs is provided by crowd control. Back in the 1960s when passions regarding the Vietnam War were afire, the Democratic nominating convention became a scene of widespread rioting. Peace groups came to Chicago intent on causing trouble—which they did. By such devices as calling the police "pigs," they were able to elicit over-the-top responses. Those charged with keeping the peace became so violent that their actions were later characterized as a "police riot." In this, the demonstrators intended to make the authorities look bad and succeeded beyond their expectations. Viewers watching the televised chaos sympathized with the activists; hence many approved of their purposes.

Years later, the Republicans held their nominating convention in New York City. Once more, left-wing partisans disapproved of a war then in progress. Aware of the innovations pioneered by their Chicago predecessors, they hoped to repeat the success. The objective was again to make the police look brutal and therefore the war, with which these were identified, would seem cruel and gratuitous. Only this time, things did not work out as intended. During the intervening years the police had improved their techniques. The rioter's roles remained what they were, whereas the police's "crowd control role" metamorphosed into something different. This time they were able to restrain themselves. Aware of what to expect, they were able to channel the demonstrators into areas where they did little damage. Also aware of what they might be called, they did not take these epithets personally. Instead, newly internalized controls made the protestors look impotent. Now more expert and better motivated, the authorities achieved what they planned. In so doing, they demonstrated that professionalization can be achieved where it was previously absent. The police were no longer an out-of-control mob, but had become a better-disciplined group of professionals.

On a personal level, professionalization also takes time to evolve. Skills are not instantly learned, nor motives instantaneously transformed. They do not automatically grow as if from germ cells. Personal development is not a matter of self-actualization. As we have seen in the case of occupational roles, a lengthy period of socialization may be required. People need to be instructed in particular skills, provided an opportunity to practice them, and embedded in a professional community that rewards competence, while punishing the opposite. In some cases, individuals must endure a rite of passage. Making the transition from one role to another can be so rigorous that a person feels different at the end of the process. Having expended a great deal of effort and suffered considerable discomfort, he or she now identifies with the new role. Thus, only subsequent to attending medical school, enduring an internship, and surviving a residency, does an individual begin to think like a doctor. More than this, he or she is now motivated to live up to the role.

Of course, most personal, political roles, and even occupational roles, no matter how professionalized, do not entail a socialization this rigorous. The requisite skills are frequently acquired in the doing. Likewise, the players' motives are only gradually transformed by informal sanctions. People become who they wind up being by incremental degrees. Thus, husbands become more skilled at being husbands by marrying and interacting with their wives, as, *mutatus mutandum*, do their spouses. In these cases, the lessons arise in the process of living. Moreover, the required sanctions, both positive and negative, come in the form of a wink, a frown, or an angry reproach. Assuming that what is demanded is attainable and that a person is ensconced in a viable emotional relationship, this liaison may not only change how he or she behaves; it can modify how he or she feels.

To illustrate with an occupational example, decades ago, specifically during the 1970s, as a member of the Army Reserve, I was trained in crowd control. The federal authorities were afraid that the urban riots then in progress might explode with such ferocity that military force would be required to subdue them. Yet this was after the Chicago fiasco. If we citizen soldiers were to go on the street armed with deadly weapons, the authorities wanted us to be under control. In order to achieve this, we engaged in role-playing exercises where some of us played rioters, while others sought to maintain order. As one of those whose head was enclosed in a gas mask and in whose hands was a rifle outfitted with a bayonet, I was required to stand in a well-ordered line as pretend rioters pelted us with physical objects and nasty words. Although this was a game, it was surprisingly realistic. Indeed, as the pseudo-rioters approached, the mood grew ominous. The rioters were genuinely frightening—at least to me. Nevertheless, we were obligated to maintain control. It did not matter if we were anxious; we could not lash out. This was emotional learning. I, and my fellow troopers, had to internalize the emotional controls needed to restrain ourselves, even in these dire circumstances.

These sorts of processes, both on the social and personal level, have been evolving for eons. We today are far more professionalized than our ancestors. We have acquired complex skills and internalized motives they did not possess. Abilities once considered beyond the capacity of ordinary people are now considered routine. The development of these aptitudes shows what is possible. They demonstrate that professionalized abilities are not beyond our ability. But if this is so, the professionalized ideal is not a chimera. People can move in this direction, despite the fact that perfection is not possible.

Consider the case of etiquette. During the Middle Ages, table manners were so crude they would offend most of us today. A majority of people ate with their hands for, among other things, forks had not been invented. Nor had butter knives. Diners simply tore off what they wanted and wolfed it down without ceremony. Then, when they were finished, they tossed the bones and leftovers on the floor. If their mouths were greasy, they wiped them on their sleeves. With napkins also not invented, there was little choice. Nowadays this would not be tolerated. Even working class folks have better manners. At their own tables, without external prompting, they use tableware. They eat off plates; wash their hands before sitting down, and clean up afterwards. Not only is this not considered an imposition; it is virtually automatic. They have, in this sense, become self-motivated experts in the art of decorous dining.

Ordinary people have also learned to take baths. Mind you, there was a time—not very long ago—when most of our forebears did not. Nor could most people read. Once only scribes were able to do so, and, in consequence, they were regarded as an elite. Indeed, in ancient Egypt it would have been considered absurd for common people to become literate. They were not believed to possess the aptitude. Obviously things changed. By and large, most of us have developed internal controls once thought impossible. In fact, words like "vulgar" and "churlish" still denote the coarseness associated with being lowborn. They imply that a person is so unrefined that he or she is incapable

279

of suppressing embarrassing gaffes. Nowadays, of course, few of us descend to the boorishness of punching others in the nose. We may think evil thoughts, but we hold back because we realize that acting on impulse would be inappropriate. Likewise, when we meet strangers, we greet them politely. We do not hurl racial epithets or make insulting comments. We are too self-disciplined.

How improved our controls are, and how valuable these are to maintaining social cohesion, is revealed by the violence of the French Revolution. As previously noted, the unruliness of the sans-culottes is almost unimaginable compared with our present orderliness. They cheered when heads were cut off. They rampaged through the king's palaces tearing servants to pieces. And when the king's Swiss guards surrendered under their sovereign's direct orders, the mob slaughtered every last one of them. There was simply no holding the perpetrators back. Out in the Vendee, when believing Catholics rebelled, they were put down so violently that one third of the population was murdered, often by being shot and then buried *en masse* in common pits. Women, children, and cripples all met the same fate. People did not stop to distinguish the guilty from the innocent. When their blood was up, everyone was considered guilty.

Consider how different we are. When the results of the Florida vote were disputed during the 2000 election, we submitted the issue to the Supreme Court. Then when a decision was rendered, we honored it. Partisans said vile things about the justices, but no one reached for a gun. There was no insurrection despite the fact that many Democrats felt cheated. For years thereafter, they regarded George W. Bush as illegitimate; nevertheless they abided by the judicial process. In so doing, they facilitated an orderly transfer of power. Stability was maintained because people could, and did, control themselves. In this sense, they acted as professionalized citizens. Indeed, the American democracy could not have persisted as long as it has had not disciplined citizenship become the norm.

In France, it took centuries to develop the controls that we institutionalized much earlier. In Germany, these same developments took even longer. Today, Germany is no longer ripe for a Hitler style insurrection because the German people have changed. Their attitudes are not the same as those of their grandparents. Having lost a devastating war, ordinary Germans became emotionally ready to experiment with democratic institutions. Average Germans are still more respectful of authority than Americans, but their attitudes have mellowed.

They have learned what elections are about and discovered they can tolerate the messiness of political partisanship. In other words, they have become more expert, and personally motivated, in operating as professionalized citizens. They too have incorporated controls once imposed from above.

All in all, professionalization has obviously moved forward. Those who believe further centralization is required to maintain social order are therefore wrong. On all fronts, whether occupational, political, or social, ordinary people are more capable of self-supervision than our ancestors. Moreover, there is no reason this development cannot continue. Centralized government is not about to wither away. There are some services it is best prepared to provide. Nevertheless, there are other services people are capable of providing for themselves. As long as they are equipped to continue negotiating, and modifying, their roles in conjunction with one another, they can adjust these to meet the needs of an increasingly complex techno-commercial society. The better they understand what is possible, the more effectively they will be able to evolve into self-motivated experts. The answer to the question, can we become professionalized? would thus seem to be as follows: Yes! Most of us do possess the requisite abilities and, if history is a guide, can develop the necessary motivation.

Limitations

Nevertheless, there are limits as to what is possible. Perfection is not in our future. Things have always gone wrong in human societies—and always will. To be more specific, not everyone will be equally happy. Nor will everyone make comparably good decisions. Spreading discretion may improve overall outcomes, but it will not eliminate conflict, foolishness, and downright irrationality. Normal human beings will continue to cheat, intimidate, and act against their personal interests. However civilized we become, there is no overcoming the limitations inherent in the human condition. These always create difficulties; they always prevent our dreams from being fully realized.

Just as Social Domain Theory alerts us to the means by which societies are held together, it also alerts us to the constraints imposed on social cohesion. Paradoxically, the same mechanisms that enable us to mesh our activities also drive us apart. Consider the cognitive order. We human beings have been described as rational animals. We are able to think logically and use facts to arrive at accurate understandings. But not always. We may be able to think, but we do not always do so.

In fact, part of being human is deferring to the beliefs of other human beings. One of the glories of our species is that we belong to cognitive communities. In fact, most of what we know is not learned first hand. Other human beings transmit reams of information to us. They tell us what to believe, after which we too believe. We do not check the facts for ourselves, but accept their words on faith.

This strategy sounds simplistic, yet is essential for social progress. If we had to learn everything for ourselves, our knowledge, both individually and communally, would be extremely limited. Instead, we borrow from one another. Moreover, we borrow quite liberally. What we are capable of seeing and hearing has thereby expanded to cover the entire globe—and beyond. Even what our ancestors learned is available to us. Their discoveries were passed along by word of mouth, and nowadays via books and computers. As a result, our knowledge is greater than any single human being could acquire in the longest of lifetimes. Operating as a community, our brainpower is multiplied in much the same way electronic computers obtain greater power by being networked. By tapping into outside databases, we, as it were, enlarge our own databases.

But there is a down side to this. Just as with computers, garbage-in can result in garbage-out. Depending upon the knowledge of others makes us vulnerable to error. If what they believe is untrue, then so is what we come to believe. This becomes increasingly probable when we add the fact that we treat some individuals as authorities. That which our parents, teachers, and political or religious leaders tell us is apt to be regarded as gospel. So automatic is this tendency that when they are mistaken, we may never realize that they are. Thus, if liberal (or conservative) officeholders assure us a program will work, we rarely demand proof. Rather we suspend disbelief. Likewise, if religious authorities insist that God created a flat earth, we punish those who disagree. Faith is faith. It does not demand evidence. It may not even be persuaded by contrary facts. As a consequence, when mistakes are made, they are perpetuated. This is true of the Liberal Dream, but it is equally true of other dreams.

Another aspect of belonging to a cognitive community is that we often have more confidence in what the group believes than in our own senses. Many decades ago, the social psychologist Solomon Asch taught us of the power of consensual validation. In numerous experiments, he demonstrated that people will agree with a majority opinion even if their own eyes tell them it is wrong. Instead of deciding for themselves, they check with these others, then go along with the crowd on the assumption that its observations are more reliable. This is one of the foundations of failed prophecies. Thus, when people belong to a community of believers, they are liable to be intimidated into agreeing with its convictions. It is why liberals check with other liberals to determine the correct political positions, whereas conservatives do the same with fellow conservatives. Still, this predisposition makes is likely that inaccuracies will be perpetuated. Even as people become more professionalized, they will continue to find consolation in conforming with community attitudes. As a result, they too will fall into as yet unimagined blunders.

Among the most common communal delusions are those dealing with religious faith and political ideologies. Liberals, as might be imagined, find it easy to recognize the intellectual rigidity of evangelicals and fundamentalists. They understand that religious zealots are stereotyped thinkers who derive their beliefs from a common source. What they fail to realize is that they do the same. Contemporary liberals did not create the Liberal Dream. It was bequeathed to them from their ancestors and then swallowed virtually whole. So, of course, are the beliefs of most conservatives, even though theirs are very different. In both cases, what people believe has been absorbed from others. So have their prescriptions for a better future. Liberals, in particular, though they pride themselves on "critical thinking," are rarely critical of their own ideas. To the contrary, these are reflexively celebrated. Only the offerings of their opponents receive a rigorous analysis.

We human beings are also led astray by our hierarchical tendencies. Because we rank ourselves relative to others, we fall prey to the irrationalities inherent in social stratification. For one thing, people do not always live up to their mental abilities. Instead, they are intimidated into what may be called "artificial stupidity." Since the central mechanism that creates inequalities is the test of strength, the losers of such contests are intellectually injured in the process of being defeated. When they are vanquished, they acquire reputations as losers. In this, they too come to believe in their inferiority. One of the reasons they stop thinking is that they consider themselves incapable of doing so. Their defeats have a halo effect that casts a shadow on their mental acuity. This explains why many members of the working class seem less intelligent than their hierarchical superiors. They don't use their brains, as much as they might, because they don't trust them. They literally don't regard themselves as smart enough.

Two of the well-documented characteristics of the lower classes are fatalism and oppositionalism. Relatively unsuccessful people typically believe that success is not possible—at least for them. They assume that those above them in the social spectrum simply have better luck. There is no point in trying harder or thinking more deeply because whatever they do, they are destined to fail. Nor is there a point in studying too hard. This too would be a waste of time. Even if they do well at school, no one will listen to what they say. As social followers, their opinions are fated for disrespect. Consequently, they find academic exercises boring. These do not attract their interest because there is no reason to remember information for which they will never find a use. Who cares which side won the French Revolution? The insights that might be acquired from this event will never be applied, so why bother?

By the same token, the lower classes are resentful of their betters. They may be forced to take orders from above, but they do not have to like it. In fact, they do not. Not surprisingly, they often consider the good fortune of social leaders illegitimate. Were life fair, they, the inferiors, would surely be on top. Although nicer and more down-to-earth, they have had their rightful deserts stolen from them. No wonder they begrudge the power of their superiors. But how to respond? Getting even with them might be agreeable, but oppositionalism is more reliable. Powerful people have to be resisted. What they desire must be thwarted. The problem with this strategy, however, is that it is negative. Instead of thinking through what is best, social losers often mechanically react to initiatives from above. Their first impulse is to say no rather than exercise independent thought. The upshot is that they can be foolishly resistant. They sabotage what would be in their own interests, rather than give their opponents the satisfaction of being right. An example of this is the opposition of unions to free trade. So intent are they in stymieing their bosses that they do not realize they may be throwing away their own jobs. So far as they are concerned, Smoot–Hawley might be the name of an ice cream chain.

The other side of the coin is the often knee-jerk obedience of the lower classes. Stanley Milgram's classic piece of research throws light on this disposition. He asked ordinary people to deliver an electrical shock to students who did not learn a required lesson. Even when the victims screamed in pain, most experimental subjects continued to inflict a punishment they believed dangerous.[1] Milgram's conclusion was that most people follow authoritative directives despite their personal feelings. In direct opposition to the evidence of their eyes, they do what authority figures require. The same is true in the political arena. Ordinary citizens, especially in the lower strata, assume their leaders know best. If the president assures them that trillions of dollars are required to avoid an economic collapse, they do not engage in independent research to determine if this is correct. They don't read books, investigate alternative opinions, or question the president's motives. They merely go along. This indeed is what the German people did when Hitler was appointed Chancellor. They went along—until it was too late to do otherwise.

Nevertheless, it must not be supposed that only hierarchical inferiors are vulnerable to irrational impulses. Those at the top of the food chain are as susceptible to their own versions of foolishness. As winners of tests of strength, they develop reputations for potency that are unwisely generalized. Thus, winners often conclude they are smarter than they are. They assume their victories were based on abilities and knowledge they do not possess. As a result, they are in danger of becoming arrogant. Like Napoleon, they invade Russia in the belief that since they have always been victorious, they will be once again. They do not worry about the Russian winter and linger in Moscow too long to extricate their forces. In other words, they are so accustomed to winning that they fail to use their heads. Rather than keep learning, they rely on methods that are no longer appropriate. Having grown conservative and lazy, they too do not alter course until it is too late.

When under stress, social leaders can even be tyrannical. They brutally enforce their will, in part, because they are betrayed by their insecurities. If members of the lower social echelons underestimate their abilities, those at the upper end of the spectrum often overestimate them. They smugly believe they will win no matter what they do, until challenges to their dominance come close to succeeding. They may then realize they are more vulnerable than they assumed and defend themselves by whatever means seem necessary. Tens of millions have been killed because "uneasy rests the head that wears the crown." On the assumption that the best defense is a good offence, potential rivals are tortured or put to death. Thus, for hundreds of years Turkish sovereigns ensured that none of their siblings would lead an insurrection by strangling them to death. For the same reasons, the French Revolution consumed its leaders. Each new cohort of dictators distrusted those who had preceded them; hence they introduced their rivals to Madame Guillotine. Many leaders know all too well that they have limitations and therefore seek to eliminate the competition. This was the point of the Soviet Gulag. Opponents enslaved in Siberia were no longer a threat to Stalin or his cronies.

Authority is absolutely essential to the working of human societies—whether large or small. Nevertheless, authority can be dangerous. For a variety of reasons, it is capable of leading entire nations astray. Furthermore, since many authority figures acquire their legitimacy by ideological means, they have a vested interest in perpetuating the idea systems that brought them to the fore. From their perspective, it does not matter whether these visions produce the promised benefits. What counts is that they help maintain their positions. As a consequence, the prevailing orthodoxy is enforced with a heavy hand. Dissent is not permitted, even if millions of lives must be sacrificed to protect the established wisdom. Likewise, if a few falsehoods must be employed to manipulate the masses, these are told—and then retold. Truth is sacrificed on the altar of a higher good, which is to say, the interests of the leadership. This is true of liberals and conservatives alike. And it will continue to be true into the indefinite future.

Nor is submitting to authority always fun. Few people enjoy being pushed around, even when this is in their interest. A professionalized society may be more free of harassment than an authoritarian one; nevertheless is cannot be completely free. Some forms of imperative coordination must be enforced. If large numbers of people are to follow a common plan, they must sometimes be compelled to subordinate their personal desires to a more comprehensive design. This, however, can be frustrating. It often produces a rebelliousness grounded in the discomfort of those acting against their own wishes.

Which brings us to the issue of moral irrationalities. Here too a socially essential mechanism can cause difficulties. Every society requires moral standards and adjustments to these when conditions change. Social conflicts would get out of hand were moral imperatives unable to thwart potential obstacles to efficient cooperation. Nevertheless, the machinery that creates, maintains, and alters moral rules can be destructive. When a society's rules are unduly harsh or out of harmony with its needs, tens of millions of people can be killed in order to maintain stability. Hearts are removed from living bodies, poison gas is released from phony shower stalls, or the rack is used to elicit confessions of imaginary sins. Almost no social institution is as depraved as morality gone haywire. It—not patriotism—is the last refuge of the scoundrel.

As may be recalled, moral rules are socially negotiated. Communities divide into competing factions to fight over the ultimate consensus. Moreover, true believers, which is to say extremists, typically arise to lead these parties. These partisans are not concerned with rationality. Nor do they fret over subtleties. Since their positions are dependent on being more Catholic than the Pope, they do not hesitate to go overboard. For them, the truth is an occasionally convenient tool; nevertheless if a canard is found to be more persuasive, it is adopted. Nowadays, it has become a cliché that politicians tell untruths. Liberals, in particular, shrug their shoulders when someone on their side is discovered in a dissimulation. Their primary concern is that their values prevail, not that the truth does. First things come first, and for them winning is essential. As a consequence, falsehoods often guide social choices. The extreme is confused with the ideal and is imposed no matter how many casualties litter the field. This unhappy outcome occurred when the Spanish Inquisition imposed the auto-da-fe; it recurred when liberals encouraged welfare dependency; it will surely intrude when future moralists decide it advances their causes.

Another social limitation surfaces from our social roles. These may be central to professionalization; nevertheless they too are imperfect. A division of labor is divided in the sense that not everyone gets to do everything. In choosing to perform one role, a person simultaneously chooses to decline others. Becoming an astronaut, for instance, precludes becoming a concert pianist. Each of these ambitions is so demanding that pursuing it reduces the time needed to pursue the other. In the real world, no one can have it all. Some aspirations must be sacrificed for the sake of realism. Thus, being a mother may require forgoing an opportunity to be a CEO. This means that people may harbor regrets no matter how successful they are. They will continue to wonder "what if" long after it is possible to become a major league baseball player. Nonetheless, when dreams are relinquished, it can hurt. The pain is genuine. Still, a complex techno-commercial society makes it impossible for anyone to become a Renaissance Man (or Woman). There is simply too much information to master.

Nor are all social roles created equal. Some are more satisfying than others. They allow for greater personal gratification and social respect. Like it or not, being a Supreme Court justice produces benefits that collecting trash does not. Yet not everyone can be a Supreme Court justice. There are only nine of them at a given time. The same is true for being a professional basketball player. There are only so many slots available in the NBA. Even the availability of medical and legal positions is limited. There are only so many openings at medical schools and so many legal cases to be argued. Who will get to do what is therefore subject to competitive pressures. As a result, some people fulfill their dreams, whereas others do not. They are never accepted into nursing school or if, they become attorneys, they never attract enough clients to support a viable practice. In this respect, life is inherently unfair. Talent does not always succeed and virtue is sometimes its only reward. Here too limitations prevent perfection. Not only does total professionalization resist fruition, it is impossible. Once more, complete happiness turns out to be a utopian whimsy.

Even love has its boundaries. Conventional wisdom has it that the course of true love never runs smooth. There are always snags along the way. Regrettably, some obstacles run deeper than others. Thus not everyone achieves love. People make mistakes in their choice of partners, become intransigent in negotiating differences, or experience the misery of an unexpected loss. In the real world, people get sick, die, lose their jobs, and grow in different directions. One way or another, the unexpected disrupts the intimate bonds that individuals crave. This is not fair, or fun. Ironically, those most in need of love are usually the least able to obtain it. In their desperation, they drive away those who could offer them the affection they desire. This too is part of the human condition. In pensive moments, many of us fantasize about receiving the attention we deserve, but this is not always possible. Liberals cannot provide it. Neither, of course, can conservatives. Sooner or later, we must simply accept the world as it is.

The plain fact is that we human beings make mistakes and fall short of our hopes. We always have and always will. Furthermore, we do so routinely. We are not thinking machines, nor infallible computers. The conclusions we reach, whether individually or communally, are not mechanically calculated via facts and logic. We have feelings, we are irrational, and we are competitive. This has always been so—and always will be. Our emotions, especially our fears, continue to influence our beliefs, whether these arrive by way of cognitive communities, hierarchical authorities, or moral negotiations. No matter whether the Liberal Dream or the Professionalized Ideal lies ahead, this will be the case. Then too, we human beings will always dissimulate, cheat, and steal. Jealousies will arise, insecurities will plague us, and ignorance will remain intractable. By the same token, people will always be attracted by false faiths and be seduced by false prophets. The demagogues and charlatans are always with us. As a consequence, we need to be vigilant. As imperfect creatures, we must guard against egregious mistakes. Woodrow Wilson wanted a war to end war. He failed. FDR intended to abolish the business cycle. He also failed. Adolf Hitler, who was, in fact, an idealist, intended to help the Aryan people rule the world. Mercifully, he likewise failed. We do not know what other pieces of nonsense may appear in the future, but whatever path we choose, we must remain on guard. To do less courts disaster, even as we become further professionalized.

On Being Responsible

Professionalization is not easy. It is not automatic or effortless. It may be possible, but has its limits and it requires sacrifices. People do not have to become super-human in order to function as self-motivated experts; nevertheless most of us cannot do so unless we work at becoming stronger than we are. A decentralized society, one that allows more people to exercise independent discretion, is contingent on the responsible use of discretion. People must be competent decision makers if they are allowed to make choices that impact the lives of others. Unless they are reliable self-supervisors, it makes no sense to delegate authority that is liable to be mismanaged.

This said, personal responsibility does not come easy. It depends on achieving a self-motivated expertise that is, in fact, both self-motivated and expert. Professionalized persons have to be capable of competent self-direction and internally disposed to doing what is required. A fraudulent professionalism is not professionalism. It cannot be relied upon. However good it looks at a distance, it disappoints in the application. Nonetheless, the real article takes energy and intelligence. It entails dealing with life's uncertainties in a serious, sensible, and reliable manner. Braggarts need not apply. Nor are self-interested opportunists welcome. What is required are not empty promises, but a genuine expertise and unwavering effort.

To begin with, professionalized persons must be emotionally mature. They have to experience intense emotions without succumbing to panic or retreating into impotent isolation. Specifically, they must be able to get angry, without tipping over into mindless rage. They also need to deal with their fears, without running away in terror. Likewise, they must be able to experience love without being blinded by it. Above all, professionalized individuals need courage. Despite their insecurities, they have to keep going. People who exhibit valor still have fears and misgivings; nevertheless they maintain their equanimity. In short, they demonstrate "grace under pressure."

Courage is essential if a person is to remain under control—and control is essential for self-direction. People who are afraid often react instinctively. They do not consider their options, but go on automatic pilot. Instead of controlling what they do, where they head is decided by emotional reflexes. For instance, if they are afraid, they either flee in haste or fight wildly. They do not calculate the best way to counter the dangers they face. Self-directed people, in contrast, are aware of their feelings, but not overwhelmed by them. They are not automatons; rather they are aware of their emotions and factor them into their choices. Though alert to dangers, they are motivated to act in an intelligent manner.

Courage is also essential for flexibility. Human beings make mistakes. Even the most expert of us do. As long as we have imperfect information and limited skills, these will occur. It is therefore crucial to recognize and correct errors. Unfortunately, frightened people close their eyes to what scares them. As a result, they keep doing what they have always done because they are uncomfortable with the unknown. Successful people, however, must be prepared to accept their limits and innovate when this is needed. To do less is inflexible, and inflexibility leads to unnecessary mistakes. Rigid people do not adjust and therefore lose. They do not understand the problem is not making blunders, but failing to fix them. Nor are they sufficiently vigilant in dealing with social limitations. Because they find these overwhelming, they take refuge in comforting fantasies. They become hidebound ideologues or quasi-religious disciples.

Professionalized persons also require authentic knowledge. They have to be competent learners who expand what they know to fit their needs. If they are too afraid to explore the unknown, or too insecure in their mental abilities, they hold back and embrace their ignorance. Instead of reading, experimenting, or consulting better-informed friends, they insist they already know the truth. They are particularly set on avoiding opinions that differ from their own. Because these might undermine their worldviews, they remain within narrow boundaries. If liberal, they read only what other liberals write; if religiously conservative, they listen only to sermons from the faithful. They are convinced that they are experts, but never allow their convictions to be tested by reality. Yet facts are facts, and bite people in sensitive places when ignored.

Then too, professionalized persons need social skills. If they are going to lead others who differ from themselves, they must understand them. Those who give orders without being aware of the needs and abilities of others invite disobedience. Their insensitivities encourage disrespect and oppositionalism. Similarly, if professionals are to participate in successful alliances, they must engage in role-taking with potential allies. If they cannot imaginatively put themselves in the place of their partners, they make inept negotiators and unreliable collaborators. They thus prove unable to make necessary adjustments. Part of being a self-motivated expert is being a competent role-partner, which in turn presupposes social adroitness. Successful persons are rarely introverted isolates.

It may sound unsophisticated to the cognoscenti, but successful professionalization includes a moral dimension. People who are relied upon to perform difficult tasks must be trusted. If they are delegated authority, others must have confidence in their ability to perform. This depends partly on their expertise, but also on their trustworthiness. If they are treacherous, if for instance they do not keep their promises, few others will rely on them. Whatever they say is suspect. The same is true for people who are dishonest. Their assurances carry little weight and hence are unpersuasive. Fairness too is an asset in dealing with others. Most of us are reluctant to make deals with selfish persons. We rightly fear they will cheat us if they can get away with it. But since professionalized individuals must regularly negotiate with role partners, if they are distrusted, they will be incompetent at this. However much they know, they will be ostracized and denied the right to exercise discretion that impacts the welfare of others.

Being responsible thus includes a large number of competences. Some of these are biological in origin, whereas others have social precursors. The ways people are raised influence whether they have the courage, emotional maturity, flexibility, knowledge, moral integrity, or social dexterity to operate as self-motivated experts. Because their social scripts shape the ways they behave, if these are inadequate, they can be trapped in rigid incompetence. They may be hierarchically inept, socially repulsive, or intellectually bereft. Although they long for professionalized success, it eludes them as they either avoid competition or jump into the fray with uncivilized obtuseness. Often unconsciously reproducing the lessons of their childhoods, they keep making the same mistakes in the same old ways.

For many people, adopting more responsible, professionalized roles requires them to become stronger than their origins prepared them to be. If they are to be emotionally mature, socially adept and morally reliable, they have to overcome the dysfunctional social scripts they embraced when young. They must save themselves from these earlier impediments. If they are to be social winners, they need to develop the strengths and insights to win. Freedom does not come free. It has to be earned. So does professionalized success. If there are obstacles to achieving it, individuals must dedicate themselves to overcoming these. They must, to paraphrase the old army slogan: be all they can be.

The good news is that ordinary people are capable of personal growth. They, and society as a whole, can benefit from becoming stronger. They do not have to be dependent on the good will of the best and brightest. If they desire, they can acquire the skills and internal abilities to exercise greater control of their destinies. But first they must free themselves from ancient instruments of bondage. They must, for instance, relinquish dysfunctional roles if they are to adopt more professionalized ones. The decision to do so, however, must be theirs. Only they can change what needs to be changed. Only they can do what needs to be done.

Liberals routinely promise to save us, but they cannot. Their dream has helped us arrive at where we are, but it has become an albatross around our collective necks. Because its assurances are inconsistent with decentralized professionalization, it hinders our moving forward. Human progress is possible, but so-called progressivism is antithetical to genuine improvements. Ours must therefore become a postliberal world. Our personal and collective happiness depend on it.

Note

1.　In fact, the victims only faked their pain. As experimental collaborators, it was their job to provide as realistic an impression of distress as they could.

292

Epilogue: Saving Ourselves

Dreams of Salvation

Life is frightening. None of us survives it fully intact. Indeed, in the end, none of us survives it at all. Nor is life fair. We are all cheated some of the time, and many of us are cheated a great deal of the time. So much goes wrong and so much of this is not what we wished for when we were young, that it should come as no surprise that many of us have dreams of salvation. When we were small and relatively impotent, we, from time to time, hoped for someone to come along to save us from a dismal fate. In my case, this person was my grandmother. I often daydreamed that she would protect me from an undeserved beating from my father. For others, daydreams of wealth or power serve the same function. For many more, contemplating divine deliverance achieves this effect. Visions of heaven and a righteous God assure them that some day they will be compensated for current indignities.

The Liberal Dream serves this same purpose. Its promises are every bit as much about salvation. The liberal prescriptions will supposedly deliver not only us, but everyone, from the hell-fires of an unjust social system. The devil, in the form of unrestrained capitalism, will be tamed. It and its greedy minions will be ejected from what would be, save for them, a terrestrial paradise. Rather than oppression and avarice characterizing the human condition, equality, love, and niceness will prevail. Everyone will then be happy. Conflict will be banished and all of our problems, such as war, poverty, discrimination, and ecological degradation, will be eliminated. Led by what is essentially a band of terrestrial angels, we will enter this Promised Land right here on earth. The best and brightest among us will use their superior intelligence and dependable moral compasses to guide us. Asking no reward, they will organize a system of governmental programs that save us from ourselves. Then they will oversee these institutions to make certain they perform as intended. As a result, theirs will be the escutcheon behind which we huddle. Their strengths and insights will guarantee our well-being.

For many people the liberal siren song is irresistible. Its promises are so congruent with their dreams of salvation that they want to believe. Unsure of their own abilities, and confused by their failure to achieve long cherished goals, they hunger for someone stronger than themselves to provide the answers. They do not mind becoming dependent because they have faith in the pledges of their would-be saviors. When assured that these gurus are the best and brightest, they assume they are as smart and well intentioned as they claim. No one wants to pray to a God with feet of clay. And so liberalism has installed itself as the secular religion of choice. Its dictates are not questioned because the answers might prove embarrassing. Instead, the faith is renewed and intensified. Failures are overlooked or rationalized. As a result, there are no disappointments in the liberal world—only promises that will shortly be kept.

In a sense, people cannot be blamed for wanting to believe in so immaculate a prophecy. Life can be unsettling. So much is happening, so much of which is beyond our control, that the best of us long for certainty. Most people know they have limits. They know that their knowledge is incomplete and their powers imperfect. They also realize that on their own, should things go wrong, they might be unable to cope. They might, for example, lose their jobs, contract a deadly disease, or be brought low by marital strife. No wonder they crave protection. No wonder they give credence to promises of security. It is these desires upon which liberals rely. It is these that allow them to get away with pretending to have powers they do not possess.

The frightening truth is that, in many respects, only we can save ourselves. Despite our personal weaknesses, we must, on our own, guard ourselves from a multitude of potential difficulties. This means that if we throw up our hands in abject surrender, we make ourselves more vulnerable. Likewise, when we become dependent on the good-will of self-appointed authorities, we expose ourselves to deception and exploitation. People who refuse to protect themselves, who are content to remain weaker than they need to be, have only themselves to blame. Well, not only themselves. Those who make the inflated promises to which they succumb also deserve reproach. As smart as they believe themselves to be, these erstwhile saviors should know better. They should be honest enough to admit what they do not know and courageous enough to recognize their own limitations.

This is not to say that we need to become isolated supermen. Friedrich Nietzsche's worldview, where only the strongest prevail, does not have to be endorsed. Life need not be cutthroat and friendless. People can cooperate with one another and benefit from the leadership of competent authorities. But they must nevertheless rely on themselves for a great many things. Salvation is one of these. If people are to be winners in a world where winning matters, they must be strong enough to win—at least some of the time—and fearless enough to make the attempt. When Obama was nominated for president, some people, with tears in their eyes, told television reporters that now all of their bills would be paid. The new president would see to that. Similarly, after he became president, during his first trip to Europe, a commentator opined that ordinary Europeans were acting as if he were about to buy them all puppies. These Obama-maniacs gloried in their personal weaknesses. They were overjoyed to place themselves under their hero's protection. But the sad fact is that not all of their bills would be paid and there were no puppies waiting under the Christmas tree. In refusing to rely on their own strengths, they opened the door to a multitude of disappointments.

If people are to obtain hierarchical success, they must be able to win tests of strength. If they rely on others to provide all their needs, they thereby cede superior status to their benefactors. In celebrating their weaknesses, they publicly admit to being inferior to those who exhibit greater courage. They do not even put up a fight. Nor can superiority be bestowed from above. If one's strength depends exclusively upon the strengths of one's patrons, then sooner or later others will recognize one's powerlessness. Some people believe that in associating themselves with potent sponsors, they enhance their personal strength, but this is only partly true. As the teammates of their heroes, they do obtain benefits, or at least bragging rights. Nonetheless, their situation is comparable to that of sports fans. When their side wins, they feel as is they too have won. They, as it were, imagine they are as powerful as the athletes for whom they cheer. But they are not. A vicarious victory is not an actual victory. If anything, total dependence on second-hand triumphs is feeble. It reveals to anyone with a middling understanding that one's social status is modest.

Nor can love be obtained secondhand. Liberals claim to love everyone, but anyone who depends on their affection is bound to be disappointed. Obama may, in fact, be a humanitarian; nevertheless his love does not extend much beyond his family and friends. He cannot feel bona fide affection for people he does not know. When he smiles at his supporters, his emotion may be genuine, but it is a pale facsimile of love. It cannot assuage a hunger for tenderness. This can only be achieved by authentic intimacy. Only people who know and care for each other can provide this. Some people, however, are so inept at creating interpersonal attachments that they swoon over pictures of celebrities. Others are so desperate for affection that they stalk the objects of their desire. They convince themselves that a relationship exists where none does. Needless to say phony interpersonal bonds cannot provide a gentle embrace in the middle of an anxious night. Nor can they offer a caring word when a job is lost or a term paper receives a failing grade.

As almost everyone knows, love cannot be achieved by proxy. Individuals must do this for themselves. Matchmakers can get the ball rolling, but they cannot complete the deal. Even more than social status, there is a personal aspect to love that cannot be replaced by others. Parents may hope their children will one day be loved, but they cannot ensure this. Potential Cyranos can put words into the mouths of the lovelorn, but not reciprocal affection in the heart of a paramour. Only individuals can engage in the courtship process—and they must do so directly. Only they can participate in biography swapping, reciprocal infatuation, or dual-concern negotiations. Others may provide advice, but not the necessary performance. They must furnish this themselves. Yet this entails risk. It invariably allows for rejection. Nonetheless, there is no choice. Those who hope for love must expose themselves to a potential loss. When it comes to love, only they can save themselves from loneliness.

With respect to professionalized roles, the risk is not nearly as great. While it is true that a person's identity may be bound up with a job, the emotional exposure is not as huge. Even so, the expertise and self-motivation required for competent professionalism are significant. People do not master difficult skills without effort. Nor do they become dedicated to what they do by going through the motions. Self-directed specialists must commit themselves to achieving an expertise in which they take pride. They cannot delegate this to someone else. If they do, this other will receive the credit. As a consequence, those who are unwilling to grow strong enough to become competent role players obtain neither the authority, nor the esteem, that comes with professionalization. If they assume someone in Washington, DC, can compensate them for their ineptitude, they will find they are mistaken.

Words of impersonal encouragement, or even financial support, cannot substitute for vocational proficiency. This latter must be earned if it is to be satisfying.

People who depend on weakness as a means of obtaining respect find their prospects narrowed. Shelby Steele has eloquently argued this with respect to race, but the lesson applies more broadly. Anyone who relies on helplessness in order to extort protection from others may achieve some rewards, but not social preeminence. Relative helplessness imposes a ceiling beyond which a person cannot rise. To the degree that an individual is perceived as impotent, he or she thereby eschews leadership. Who, after all, wants to be led by someone who advertises his ineptitude? People who demand salvation are not looked to, to provide it themselves. As a result, they are not respected. They are neither feared nor admired. If so, the mechanism they employ to obtain security ensures that much of what they desire is never attained. They are always perceived as second rate and therefore subject to the whims of those willing to risk being worthy of responsibility. They, in short, become social losers. Whatever their personal virtues, in the larger scheme of things, they remain nonentities.

On top of this, a world in which most people elect to be dependent on would-be saviors is an impoverished one. Were a majority of individuals to select weakness as a way of life, they would deny the community the benefit of their abilities. Having decided, in effect, to be dropouts, they would be free riders sponging off the efforts of their betters. Too extensive a hunger for external salvation reduces the innovation, initiative, and intelligence available to the larger society. The upshot is that the community too is less effective. This disadvantages it with respect to other societies. Groups that do not harness the potential of their members are liable to be defeated by those that do. They become less prosperous, less powerful, and less respected. Those who believe that national prestige is trivial fail to recognize that communal weakness translates into personal weakness. Countries that are less influential tend to have citizens who are less potent. Both at home and abroad, they become timid nonachievers. Far from being saved by promises of protection, passivity condemns them to continued failure.

This being so, our shared future depends on larger numbers of people becoming further professionalized. Liberal promises notwithstanding, more of us must dedicate ourselves to saving ourselves. Despite our insecurities, we must find the wherewithal to risk becoming personally stronger. One difficulty is that many people do not know where to begin. They would like to be more competent, but fear that they do not possess the relevant resources. Having accepted the canard that they are more limited than they are, they assume that they will fail if they make the attempt. In this, most are mistaken. We human beings may not be perfect, but most of us can be more than we imagine. The questions, therefore, are these: How do we make this happen? What must those of us trapped in powerlessness do to become self-motivated experts?

Growing Up

Oddly, one of the things that liberals celebrate is youth. Even as the average age of Americans creeps up, they recommend the spontaneity and idealism of the young as a model for everyone. The old are said to be fixed in their obsolete ways. They rely too much on tradition and not enough on progress. No longer capable of having fun, their pessimism casts a pall on society. Because they are too concerned with being responsible, they need to lighten up. They should sing and dance, and allow the federal experts to guard their future. If only they will emulate the young, they will live longer and enjoy it more. The real object in life, after all, is to be happy. Too much brooding about work and relationships is counterproductive. Whatever feels right is what should be pursued. The old should allow their instincts to take over because these are more reliable guides than their heads. Intuitions are in better touch with reality than artificial social constraints; hence they are also more dependable.

Years ago, the hippies warned that people over thirty were not to be trusted. Apparently, they never expected to grow old themselves. As a consequence, they would not have to worry about supporting a family or paying a mortgage. Even as the years passed by, they assumed they would be listening to rock music, while puffing on weed in a crash pad. The irony is now that many decades have gone by, these ex-hippies are well past thirty. Indeed, those who survived their wild youth are liable to be considered old by their grandchildren. But thanks to cultural lag, their minds and hearts remain in their glory days. Determined to be eternally young, many look to liberalism to keep them so. Its ideals continue to be their ideals. Its promises of salvation allow them to transfer their responsibilities to an all-knowing federal government. This way they can cast off their burdens and have fun, fun, fun.

The endless summer of the surfers has likewise been glorified. Life, according to the Peter Pan set, ought to be a never-ending day at the beach. It should be carefree and filled with sunshine. Only it isn't. In the real world, there is work to be done and problems to be solved. People need the courage to grow up so that they can do what requires doing. Instead of being afraid of maturity, they must accept its inconveniences. But this is not so terrible. There are compensations. Maturity is not an unrelieved cloudy day. The sun shines on grown-ups too. There are actually satisfactions in being responsible. Work can be work, but achievement is achievement. As importantly, respect is respect. Those who carry the world on their shoulders do not necessarily collapse under the burden. If they succeed, and many who become professionalized do, one of the rewards is higher social status. Those who are competent problem-solvers are also apt to be social leaders. They thereby obtain power—and the trappings of power. Others look to them with admiration and defer to their authority. They become winners, who enjoy the benefits of winning.

There is also much to be said for controlling one's own fate. People who are strong enough to fight their own battles are strong enough to make decisions for themselves. Instead of someone else pointing them in a direction that may not serve their interests, they can select their own course. No one, to be sure, is in complete control. Life is filled with too many uncertainties. Nevertheless, being self-directed improves the odds. Professionalized adults do not have to worry as much about the hidden agendas of others. Children, on the other hand, are forced to respond to external demands. They do not so much participate in mutual adjustments, as furnish these. This is why the early twenties is a crucial time of life. It is the point where many people stop making choices in response to what their parents want. This is when they become independent adults with minds and futures of their own.

Independent-minded adults are also more capable of participating in sound interpersonal relationships. Adult love is, in fact, for adults. Many people—especially those who believe love will save them—assume that true love can come to anyone. It is presumably a magical gift that is bestowed on those worthy of it. In reality, genuine love depends on an ability to give and to take. Two adults can let down their guard because each is capable of caring and being cared for. The very young, in contrast, are specialists in the latter. They are better at taking than giving. Because they need so much, but remain limited in what they can offer, they are dependent upon caretakers. This means

299

that if they were not loved, they may desperately seek love later on. Unfortunately, desperation is a turn off. As a sign that a person is a taker rather than giver, it warns off those capable of both. Only adults who are genuinely capable of taking care of themselves can enter into a balanced, and therefore satisfying, intimate partnership. Only they have the strength to care for themselves when this proves necessary and the flexibility to care for a partner whose needs have increased. The upshot is that it is they who receive the benefits of mutual affection.

To this, the advocates of eternal youth have a rejoinder. They assert that there is something more important than adult responsibility, something that encompasses both love and personal control. This something is creativity. Creativity supposedly breaks new ground. It discovers what was thought impossible and makes it available to everyone. Responsibility, in contrast, is conventional and uninspired. It is oriented toward what is and is therefore plodding and melancholic. Given the choice, who would prefer it to creativity? Who but those who have given up on life would gravitate to the deadening hand of the past as opposed to the undiscovered glories of the future? To its partisans, creativity is synonymous with life. The young revel in it because they are intensely alive, whereas the old spurn it because they are closer to the grave. Any society that hopes for improvements must consequently tilt toward creativity.

One of the reasons that bobos prefer creativity is that in addition to the Liberal Ideal, they are committed to the Artistic Ideal. As eternal students, they think of themselves as forever young and also as potentially great artists. Having thoroughly internalized the values of the universities that provided their professional credentials, they assume aesthetic pursuits are the most satisfying. Because creativity is so highly valued in the arts, they too endorse it. Mere economic and political pursuits leave them cold. These are regarded as humdrum and intellectually undemanding. Creativity, on the other hand, holds surprises. It stretches a person to the limits and makes him or her a better person. Creativity is even a boon to love. Because passion is interpreted as creative, it is thought of as a mechanism for keeping intimate relationships vibrant. Without it, partnerships grow stale and fall apart as the parties grow bored with each other.

Art-oriented extremists, however, fail to reckon with the possibility of responsible creativity. The two are not mutually exclusive. To develop new ideas does not imply that one must be irresponsible. The very young may, to paraphrase Robert Kennedy, ask "why not?"

300

but there often is a why not that is discovered from living. To follow a path merely because it is new, without checking where it leads, is dangerous. It can be the royal road to tragedy. Conversely, keeping one's eyes open and aware of consequences does not imply an inability to innovate. The difference between the two approaches is that one is careful, whereas the other is not. The creativity of youth is often too daring, whereas that of adulthood is tempered by experience. Responsible creativity can explore what is new without falling off a cliff. As a result, it is capable of restraining those with less experience, while at the same time evaluating novel suggestions.

The point is that responsible adults are realistic. They can tell the difference between dreams and facts. They measure ideas against the real world before they attempt to implement them. The problem with many who support the Liberal Dream is that they do not think through the implications of their visions. They imagine a world in which everyone is equal, but do not ask how this can come about. Transfixed by images of universal niceness, they leave out the steps needed to get there. Matters of mundane cause and effect are treated as irrelevant. Novelty thus overrides achievability. In a sense, immature innovators care more about aesthetic concerns than actualities. Their visions, like Edward Bellamy's novel *Looking Backward*, are fascinating to contemplate but impossible to realize. Because they lack responsibility, they leave out essential elements and never discover their mistakes because they are not looking for them.

To be both effective and successful, it is essential to be realistic. Those with their heads in the clouds run out of oxygen. Successful people; people capable of protecting others, tend to be responsible. What they start, they are apt to finish because they are concerned with feasibility. In other words, they are not merely about making promises, but keeping them. They are distressed when their predictions do not come true, and as a result do not merely intensify the same old forecasts. They are adults in the sense that they acknowledge their errors and seek to correct them. For them, rationalizations are insufficient. They do not run from the truth because they are strong enough to tolerate it. Nor do they resort to fabrications in order to prevent others from discovering their limitations. They know they have limitations and prefer to work at overcoming them.

So what does it take to become a grown-up? Many of these qualities have already been discussed. First and foremost is emotional maturity. People who cannot cope with intense emotions cannot apply their intelligence consistently. They are apt to resort to primitive defense mechanisms to protect themselves from harm. Individuals who are wracked by fears or imprisoned by rage are poor decision makers. This is why General George Patton advised his officers not to take the counsel of their fears before going into battle. He knew that frightened men, such as the Civil War's George McClellan, make terrible decisions. Blinded by their apprehensions, they overestimate dangers and remain oblivious to potential solutions. He might have said something similar about anger. People consumed with fury are poor planners. They rush ahead mentally unprepared for action, only to be cut down by adversaries who have calmly assessed their vulnerabilities. As a consequence, Patton advised his soldiers not to die for their country, but to make the enemy die for his. They were asked not to be wild, but emotionally stable in the face of danger. This is the essence of courage, which is primarily the domain of the emotionally mature. They become winners because they can take calculated risks without succumbing to panic.

Grown-ups are also knowledgeable. Before they charge out into the world, they survey the lay of the land. This begins by looking inward. Before they interact with others, they acquire an accurate assessment of their own strengths and weaknesses. In interactions with others, whether these are tests of strength, role negotiations, or intimate collaborations, the starting point is their own abilities and motivations. Without a realistic understanding of these, a person is apt to try to do too much or too little, or sometimes the wrong things altogether. Because no one's resources are unlimited, it is essential that these be accurately evaluated. This entails knowing what one knows, but also what one does not. Many people assume that by ignoring their weaknesses they can sidestep them. They cannot. Others notice and take advantage when they can. Similarly, some people fear their strengths. Rather than intimidate others, they hang back. These folks do not get what they want because they do not put forth the effort. Meanwhile, those unfamiliar with their deepest desires may not attempt to achieve them. They are more likely to pursue goals others prefer.

By the same token, it is essential to understand other people. Their strengths, weaknesses, and motives need to be evaluated as carefully as one's own. The outcomes of tests of strength, role negotiations, and intimate collaborations are dependent on the relative strengths of both sides of the equation. To mistake where an adversary is coming from is to fight the wrong battles. Sometimes it even assumes that a person is an enemy when he is a friend (or vice versa). Moreover, on a fundamental level, it is difficult to establish alliances without understanding what others want. If a person does not recognize what potential collaborators consider a reward (or punishment), it is hard to employ these successfully. As to strengths and weaknesses, these cannot be exploited if they are not recognized. What frightens the other person, and conversely what does not, determines another's vulnerable points. As any good general knows, it is best to hit opponents where they least expect it and are least able to defend themselves. This may sound callous, but those who eschew such considerations are liable to sustain more defeats than they prefer.

Grown-ups also know what they believe. They possess a sturdy moral compass that points in socially useful directions. If they do not, they are untrustworthy. Moral relativists sometimes make it sound as if whatever a person believes to be right is right for him or her. As masters of their own fate, they, and perhaps their closest allies, get to decide what is ethical. Were this so, however, social values would be kaleidoscopic. No one would know what to expect of anyone else because priorities might change at any moment. There would be no consistency and therefore no predictability. Today a lie might be considered bad, whereas tomorrow it could be accounted good. The same would go for promises and sexual fidelity. Such a world would preclude cooperation because it would not be dependable. People, constantly wary of one another, would keep their distance. The only remedy for this state of affairs is a genuine commitment to stable values. Adults must be able to modify their moral allegiances, but not on a whim. They must carefully consider what they believe in response to their circumstances and the demands of their role partners, and then cautiously move ahead. Both steady and sensible, they must not fly off in unexpected directions. A flexible constancy is essential to being responsible, as well as to being fair and trustworthy.

Finally, mature adults have multifaceted social skills. Theirs is not the narrow world of the neighborhood in which they grew up. Because they are cosmopolitan, there are many arrows in their quiver. Having interacted with a variety of different people, they have developed mechanisms for coping with unexpected situations. Assuming that they are emotionally steady, they learn from these experiences. Instead of rejecting the unfamiliar, they become effective communicators. Responsive to the messages they receive, they adjust those they send. They also discover how to negotiate. Instead of just demanding what they want, they can participate in a give and take. Likewise, they understand how to lead and to follow. Capable of making independent decisions, they can also conform to decisions made by others. And because they can control themselves, they can figure out what is appropriate in a broad range of circumstances. This makes them better collaborators and more effective in their specialties. In short, they are likely to be winners. Highly effective in achieving their goals, they are helpful both to themselves and others.

Lest the implications of the above be overlooked, authentic grownups are competent learners. They become better at what they do because they are open to improving their skills. As a result, they benefit from interchanges with others. This is essential because life is filled with challenges. Things always go wrong. Self-confidence and flexibility are therefore essential to getting by. Genuine adults cope with stresses without being thrown off-balance. Psychotherapists sometimes describe this quality as being "centered." Put another way, mature human beings know who they are and are comfortable with this. They do not have to pretend to be other than they are, nor refuse to make necessary adjustments. To repeat, they are learners. They get better as they go along. They have to, that is, if they are to operate as self-motivated experts. Should they fail at this, their expertise would be counterfeit and their self-motivation captive to the demands of others. Superannuated children, on the other hand, no matter how creative, are limited. Unworthy of professional authority, they are apt to abuse their power. Living as they do in private worlds, they cannot be trusted to make decisions upon which others must depend.

Personal Scripts

No one invents the world on his or her own. Even the most flexible adults require guidance. The choices that we make have histories. Lessons learned in childhood and adulthood are internalized so as to regulate our conduct. Rather than invent what we do on the spot, we develop repertoires of behaviors upon which we later draw. If these are appropriate, we prosper. If not, they create problems. History, as had been said, is prologue. But not merely for societies. It is also decisive on a personal level. The foundations upon which our personalities rest are invariably established when we are young. But alas, unfortunate histories have unfortunate consequences. They can deprive a person of the opportunity to become professionalized. For those who do not acquire emotional maturity, genuine knowledge, dependable values, or social skills, becoming a self-motivated expert is problematic. Serious errors are made and damage done.

Like it or not, we human beings are often captive to personal scripts developed while we were growing up. If these scripts were functional, they prove helpful; but if not, they are the reverse. Instead of allowing us to grow into flexible adults, they trap us in a rigid childhood. When this is the case, it is difficult to win tests of strength, negotiate satisfying social roles, or participate in rewarding intimate attachments. Both on a personal and social level, success does not come easily. Should this be so, a person may need to modify scripts that interfere with moving forward. If he or she wishes to be saved from a deplorable fate, customary ways of dealing with life have to be confronted head on. They must be seen for what they are, and, if unsatisfactory, changed. This, however, is something that has to be done individually. Providential saviors, no matter how well-intentioned, cannot substitute for what persons must do for themselves.

As might be expected, the starting place for fixing damaged personal scripts is understanding them. These internalized plans may conveniently be divided into four sorts. These are respectively our cognitive, emotional, volitional, and social scripts. As with the various social orders, these may sound daunting, but are, in fact, familiar. We, all of us, deal with them daily. The only obstacle to comprehending them is getting past their labels. Once we do, it is relatively simple to recognize what needs to be altered. The real difficulty is in making the requisite changes—but that is another story.

Let us begin with our cognitive scripts. This is an enormous and confusing world, but as we have seen, we humans belong to cognitive communities. What we believe is often acquired from what others believe. Our cognitive scripts are thus the accumulated understandings that we have internalized. They are what we have come to accept as valid as a result of interacting with others and with reality itself. In a sense, these beliefs function as roadmaps to navigate around the world. They tell us, for instance, what is possible and what is not. As might be expected, accurate maps are crucial in avoiding missteps and noticing opportunities. Without them, we would not know what we were doing or where we were going. Nonetheless there is a potential problem here. What we come to believe may be wrong. W.I. Thomas advised us that what people believe real, is real in its consequences. Even when they are mistaken, their fantasies have substantial effects.

Should people, for example, believe that the world is flat, they do not sail across the Atlantic lest they fall off the edge.

Of particular note, what an individual believes true about him or herself can have immense implications. For each of us, among the most salient social facts are those regarding our personal characteristics. If we are mistaken regarding these, we may imagine there are things we can do which we can't, and conversely things that we can't which we can. Collectively, these ways of thinking are referred to as our self-image. For some of us, this persona is positive, whereas for others it is not. Included in such images are our understandings of our strengths, weaknesses, and motivations. Not surprisingly, if these are accurate, they pave the ways for successful choices, whereas if they are not, they foreshadow failure. None of us, of course, are completely correct in our assessments. Still, the closer we come to the truth, the more effective we are likely to be. Unfortunately, many of us receive defective messages in growing up. People close to us, typically our friends and relatives, transmit faulty information. Perhaps they tell us we are stupid when we are not. Or maybe they compliment artistic abilities we do not possess. We then, because our childhood standards of comparison are limited, come to believe these falsities. We too conclude that we are stupid, or artistic, and make vocational choices accordingly. Then we fail. We do not become competent decision makers, with the dire consequences this implies.

Clearly, people who are trapped in flawed self-images must discover that their beliefs are wrong if they are to live up to their potential. They must come to realize that what seemed to be a weakness is not, while a purported strength was a mirage. These insights, however, can only be achieved on a personal level. What is more, the truth is often discovered in the teeth of strenuous opposition. The authority figures that made the original assessment are likely to remain committed to it. It, therefore, takes courage to contradict them. Nevertheless, only by daring to defy the conventional wisdom can a person arrive at an accurate estimation. This, however, is vital before taking risks. People who wrongly imagine they are dumb refuse to go to college, or if they go, do not study as diligently as they might. Although perfectly capable of becoming engineers or accountants, they drop out.

Cognitive scripts can also be defective in their assessment of others. To cite an important example, many children assume their parents want the best for them without realizing that these adults are sometimes intimidated by a child's success. If a father or mother failed to live up to his or her potential, he or she may be envious of a youngster's accomplishments. Should this be the case, only an accurate assessment of parental motives can allow a child to recognize why she was berated. Only then may she realize that her strengths outweigh those of potential rivals. Unfortunately, without this insight, she is handicapped by defective baggage. As such, she may settle for less than is possible. Nevertheless, an awareness of the truth must be hers. It does not matter what others believe. She, after all, is the one who must act.

The same applies to dealings with others. Thus, if we imagine that government authorities are super-knowledgeable, we may be inclined to defer to them. Or if we assume that individuals who speak with strange accents are dim-witted, we may not benefit from their wisdom. So complex are other people, and so likely are they to disguise their weaknesses, that learning the facts takes effort. Mature adults must therefore move beyond their childhood categories. They need to work at developing a textured understanding and not depend solely upon what they were told.

So-called cognitive therapists assume that the most important factor in achieving social success are our belief systems. As a result, they attempt to correct problems by correcting the ways their clients think. In this, they provide a useful service, but it is incomplete. Accurate cognitions are enormously important, but they are not our only windows on the world. While the cognitivists tell us that what we feel depends on what we think, this is only partly true. We human beings have emotional scripts in addition to our cognitive ones. Sometimes what we feel depends on what we believe, but oftentimes our feelings precede our beliefs. The fears we experience, the furies with which we are consumed, and loves we cannot extinguish drive our behaviors every bit as much as our understandings. Indeed, in many ways, our emotions are the most basic parts of our experience. Who we feel ourselves to be is frequently grounded in these affects. Accordingly, when emotions go wrong, they can throw us off track. Particularly when they are immature, they can impel us in perilous directions. Fears that are not based on actual dangers, wrath directed at inappropriate targets, and loves that cling to lost attachments make life a misery. Even if these are properly directed, if they are too intense, the consequences are frequently regrettable.

This being so, uncontrolled emotions are the bane of our existence. The empty headed impetuosity of an immature passion does more than preclude sensible decision-making. It can precipitate disaster. Those individuals who are all primitive instinct are essentially babies writ large. Far from being responsible, their responses do not consider potential outcomes. Unthinking fears turn into panic, instinctive anger becomes mindless rage, while desperate love clutches the wrong persons. As a result, immature fear runs away with its eyes closed, immature anger commits murder at the slightest offense, while immature love sentences itself to a lifetime of frustration. Each of these is intent on making things happen, but, in their stupidity, they make the wrong things happen. In lacking controls, they lack measured reactions. Rather than rein in fatuous impulses, they do what momentarily feels right.

Marital therapists, when trying to sort out the juvenile fights into which some couples descend, warn against "gunny-sacking." They advise clients that storing up ancient grievances and then spewing them out is a recipe for interminable battles. This strategy ensures that no problems are ever solved. In the same way, immature adults may be the pawns of ancient emotions. These too can be stored up to spring out at inappropriate moments. Old fears are treated as current; ancient grievances precipitate contemporary animosities; and by-gone loves are held on to as if they were present-day realities. This makes it essential that a person distinguish the present from the past. If out-worn emotions are to remain dormant, they must not be confused with the here-and-now. To do so would prompt a person to address historical problems, rather than contemporary ones.

Consider our fears. All of us have many of these. They function as a kind of alarm system that warns of dangers. They also motivate us to fight or flight. In other words, they provide the energy to protect us from harm. As such, our fears are essential. Without them, we would walk into a lion's mouth without realizing this might not be wise. Nevertheless, our fears can be mistaken. What was once dangerous may no longer be. Conversely, what was once safe can turn hazardous. Obviously, it is important to recognize which is which. Regrettably, strong emotions can be both confusing and long lasting. Despite the fact that their alarms are unclear, they often persist for a lifetime. As a result, that which frightened us when we were small may continue to feel terrifying even after it is no longer harmful.

Take the case of a person who was beaten when he was young. Naturally, he feared his father's heavy hand. The pain of a strap across the buttocks felt dangerous because it was. Now fast-forward. Imagine the same person as an adult. No longer is his father able to put him across his knee. Nonetheless the old anxieties lurk only slightly below the surface. When he encounters his father, he still trembles at punishments that can no longer be delivered. What is worse, he may have the same reaction when he encounters authority figures that remind him of his father. In both cases, he defers to malicious demands as a way of propitiating a potential abuser. In this, however, he betrays his own needs in an attempt to protect himself from phantom dangers. Yet if he is to be potent, it is crucial to correct these misperceptions. He must be able to judge current dangers for what they are.

But this is not the whole story. Not only must a person be able to utilize his fears to assess current hazards, he must employ them to motivate an effective defense. Emotions both communicate and motivate. They provide vital information about the world, as well as impel us to achieve crucial objectives. In the case of fear, they alert us to danger and then help neutralize it. As a consequence, they must supply accurate information, as well as realistic plans of actions. Combating fears by hiding in a cellar is usually not effective. By the same token, jumping on top of a hand-grenade is not the best way to prevent it from doing damage. When people run blindly from fear, they tend to scurry to the wrong places. Likewise, when they rashly assault a danger, they can expose themselves to greater dangers. The objective is therefore to understand the nature of a fear, as well as the best ways to counter it. This takes emotional maturity. Yet the heads of people who panic are so filled with terror that they refuse to look a threat in the face. Nor do they prepare a skilled retreat. All they want to do is get away, while in the process they expose their flanks to the enemy.

Emotional maturity is about controlling intense emotions. With respect to fear, it entails developing the necessary internal controls. Emotionally mature persons are able to examine the past without blinking. They can also deal with the present without hiding under a bed. As should be obvious, this is critical for social winners. If they are to be self-motivated experts, they cannot be driven hither-and-yon by emotional tempests they neither comprehend, nor are capable of managing. More particularly, if they are to be self-motivated, they must control their emotions, rather than be controlled by them. Correspondingly, if they are to be genuine experts, they must be able to deal with reality as it is. Here too salvation is personal. No governmental expert can substitute for the calm judgment of someone tackling the challenges of his or her own life space.

Also fundamental to personal and social success is an effective use of anger. A person's emotional scripts may need to be revised so that he or she can express exasperation without it tipping over into rage. Here too irritants from the long ago past must be recognized for what they are and the means of articulating them scaled to meet current frustrations. As with fear, anger both communicates and motivates. Also, as with fear, what it says must be accurate and what it motivates effective. Otherwise it is an emotional tempest that is all sound and fury—as destructive, and indiscriminate, as a category five hurricane. The kinds of tantrums in which children engage are therefore anathema to professionalized adults.

Fear is about defending against dangers, whereas anger is concerned with overcoming frustrations. It rises to the surface when important desires are thwarted. Its message is that something vital has been denied a person. Ergo, the greater the disappointment, the greater the furor. Anger then seeks to obtain what was denied. It threatens others in the hope that they will provide what is desired. Unfortunately, if this tactic goes too far, it can backfire. Instead of cooperating, people may decide to fight back, in which case there can be blood on the floor. This makes it necessary for anger to be accurate in understanding what it wants and sophisticated in the manner it seeks to influence others. If it is too primitive, which is to say, if it is trapped in childhood frustrations and tantrums, it can make matters worse.

As with fear, intense anger interferes with a person's ability to reason clearly. Rage makes it difficult to determine whether a frustration is significant and even whether it occurred today or years ago. By the same token, an intemperate fury makes it difficult to plan an effective intervention. Merely shouting at or striking others can have an effect opposite the one desired. Impulsive rage is stupid. It fails to understand what motivates others and hence resorts to stereotyped outbursts. Anger is as vital to personal success as fear, but it too needs to be mastered. Incompetent anger management translates into a lack of self-direction. Rage goes where it wants and precipitates intended crises. Far from being professionalized, it impedes cooperative activities. And yet anger, like fear, lies within the personal realm. In this instance too, people who wish to succeed must work on their own impulses.

With respect to love, similar dynamics apply. In order to obtain a secure attachment a person must be capable of mature love. A desire for closeness cannot be so intense that it prevents accurate communications or motivates misguided actions. It must also be such that a person distinguishes between ancient attachments and current ones. Unless this is possible, a person may cling to abusers, while rejecting more suitable partners. Genuine love is not for adolescents. Only grown-ups can do the work of separating the sheep from the goats and engaging in dual-concern negotiations with comparably mature individuals. Anyone who believes a utopian political system can compensate for an inability to accomplish these deserves what he or she gets.

There is another emotion that must also be discussed. It too is a part of our emotional scripts and hence when mishandled can have unfortunate implications. This sentiment is sadness. Nowadays despair is considered abhorrent. It is so reviled that it is sometimes labeled an emotional disorder. People who are extremely unhappy are diagnosed as suffering from depression and prescribed medications to make them feel better. Instead of dealing with the feeling and attempting to understand how it operates, it is cast into a nether world of disease. This is unfortunate in that sadness is as crucial to our well-being as fear, anger, and love. Without allowing it to perform its services, we are destined for failure. Paradoxically, without unhappiness, there can be no happiness.

The goal of sadness is to separate us from our losses. It cuts our ties to that which we cannot obtain so that we can proceed toward what we can get. If we did not let go of attachments gone wrong, we would remain bound to decaying corpses. This is literally the case with respect to death. If we did not mourn those who died, we might be tempted to jump into the grave with them. Obviously, no matter how much they were loved, the time comes to grieve and move on. The same is true with respect to divorce. Yet a relationship that has gone awry can only be relegated to the past by undergoing a period of sadness. Failed marriages are not celebrated; they must be wept over. To a lesser extent, people feel sad when they have lost a job, failed a course at college, or had a manuscript rejected. In each of these cases, sadness prepares the way for letting go of what cannot be had.

The problem is that sadness is painful. We all hate to experience it. After all, who wants to hear that something vital has been irrevocably lost? As a consequence, many of us prefer denial. We pretend that all is well so we do not have to withdraw into a black shell from which we fear we may never emerge. In other words, sadness is for the strong, not the emotionally immature. People who doubt their ability to survive a loss prefer to act as if it never happened. They therefore believe potential saviors who assure them that they can return to the good old days. Thus, should they find a world filled with strangers daunting, they are comforted when told that they can join a single loving family. Or is self-direction intimidating? No need to worry; liberal authorities are eager to serve as surrogate parents. Each of us inevitably experiences losses, but if we do not develop the inner toughness to endure the pain of letting go, we thereby eschew the thrill of victory. Letting go, like history, is prelude. It paves the way for objectives that are not feasible while in the grasp of a departed past.

The next internalized patterns we must discuss are volitional scripts. These have to do with how we make decisions. The word volition is unusual, yet all it signifies is that we humans have free will. We are able to decide to behave in certain ways, rather than others. The question then becomes why do we choose as we do? Part of the answer is that our preferences are not made exclusively on the spot. Decisions arrived at in the past influence our current choices. Thus, we develop dispositions that push us in some directions rather than others. Part of what happens is that we develop habits. A variety of acts are performed so regularly they become automatic. Few of us, for instance, consciously decide to brush our teeth in the morning. For the most part habits are not problematic. Yet sometimes they are. Some people, for example, become caretakers. These folks were raised to take care of others. Their job in life was to wait on elderly parents or demanding husbands. So uncompromising were the demands to which they were subjected when young that they submerged their personal desires in favor of the wishes of others. They learned to comply with what was asked without thinking. If so, they got left out of the equation. Their own needs remained unmet because their volitional scripts never prompted them to consider these. In the end, they routinely decided against their own interests. The upshot is that they are unhappy. Thus, unless they modify their volitional scripts, they are destined for a second-class existence.

Two other aspects of volitional scripts deserve special attention. These are our norms and values. As may be recalled, norms are rules that guide our actions, whereas values are endpoints at which we aim. In the case of morality, both are obviously related, as it were, opposite sides of the same coin. Also as earlier indicated, morality is crucial for social harmony. Every society requires a fundamental suite of rules and goals that are internalized by a majority of its members. Where these are absent, chaos reigns. Nevertheless, moral systems can be out of joint. Under some circumstances, conventional rules interfere with achieving cooperative efforts. If, for instance, a totalitarian regime encourages people to spy on each other, the social fabric can be torn asunder. At the opposite extreme, crucial norms and values may be absent. If—for the sake of argument—enough people do not internalize the standards vital to a professionalized society, professionalization is difficult. Should they, for instance, not wish to become expert, they will remain unskilled.

As we have seen, one of the crucial commitments necessary for self-motivated expertise is a sense of responsibility. People who are allowed to make decisions that affect the lives of others must be dedicated to personal competence. They must be willing to put in the effort to develop a genuine skill, and they must also take the heat if they make a mistake. Indeed, responsible people need to be strong enough to deal with uncertainties and recurring defeats. In their minds and hearts, they must function as a locus of control. Responsible people are aware that decisions have consequences; hence they take them seriously. If, however, they are taught that nothing is their fault, if they are assured that whatever goes wrong is the consequence of a defective social system, then they are learning they are not responsible. Yet if they believe this, they will not be diligent, nor inclined to accept blame. As a result, such persons are not trustworthy. Their decisions are unreliable and hence do not elicit confidence.

Sad to say, the Liberal Dream discourages responsibility. One of its chief effects has been to encourage an excuse mentality. Liberals regularly seek to reduce personal guilt by assuring people that their limitations are someone else's fault. Thus, while Obama may mouth the word "responsibility," he does not ask it of ordinary people. Instead, he blames capitalism for their problems. Financers are said to be greedy. The bankers made predatory loans. The Republicans want to dismantle necessary regulations. It is their fault! Commonplace citizens who took out mortgages they could not afford were blameless. What is more, they must be rescued from the clutches of heartless business people. The government needs to help these "victims" pay their bills. Actually, everyone other than the capitalists is a victim. As such, they are never responsible.

Another value the Liberal Ideal cavalierly dismisses is honesty. There was a time when no one would have defended dishonesty, but those days are long gone. In order to guard the numerous lies they purvey in defense of a failed prophecy, liberals have sought to reduce the obloquy aimed at untruthfulness. The most vivid example of this was furnished during the Clinton impeachment. The president himself, of course, lied when he told the American people he did not have sex with Miss Lewinsky and he also dissembled when he testified before a Grand Jury. Nevertheless, these were not the most egregious offenses against honesty. This honor was reserved for the way the president's deceptions were defended. His partisans repeatedly declared that lying about sex was normal. They proclaimed that everyone does it; therefore it is acceptable. But they went further. They asserted that everyone lies—period! In particular, they affirmed that all politicians lie; hence Clinton was only doing what his predecessors had done. They had all lied and cheated. He should not be blamed for doing what comes naturally—nor by implication should anyone who does the same.

What was breathtaking about this performance, and should have discredited liberalism then and there, was that this dishonesty was endorsed with insouciance. Utterly no shame was displayed in defiling the reputations of countless others. If Clinton cheated, then all presidents did. If Clinton lied about sex, then Bush was worse; after all, he lied about weapons of mass destruction. So brazen did this vindication of deceit become, that bald-faced lies were described as truths. Bush, of course, was mistaken about the WMDs; he did not, however, tell a conscious untruth. Nevertheless, he was condemned as if he had. Liberal liars, in contrast, dismissed their own misstatements as inconsequential. Even ordinary citizens succumbed to the temptation of justifying deceitfulness. Suddenly, college students caught cheating defended their misdeeds as normal. Again, the excuse was that everyone does it; everyone cheats and lies. Some went so far as to argue that deception is a valuable skill. It enables ambitious people to profit in the real world. Clinton obviously did. In time, so would Obama.

This attitude is frightening. While it is true that anyone who believes virtue is always rewarded is hopelessly naïve, it is also true that anyone who believes dishonesty is without harm is more so. No society, much less a complex techno-commercial one, can survive unchecked fraud. Were volitional scripts that endorsed lying to become standard, no one could trust anyone else. Research has shown a majority does lie and cheat some of the time, but this is a far cry from universal duplicity. Most of the time, most of us are reasonably honest. Were duplicity to become the norm intimate partners could never rely on one another nor could commerce between strangers endure. In the end, our civilization would crumble as surely as that of the Mayans.

Finally, the last aspect of our personal scripts, the only one that is external in nature, are our social scripts. As we have seen, our most basic cognitive, emotional, and volitional dispositions are initiated when we are young. The demands made by our then role partners are converted into beliefs, emotions, and decision-making propensities that became part of who we are. Once in place, these patterns continue to influence us even after the persons responsible for implanting them are no longer present. But this does not mean that we suddenly become isolated. To the contrary, we remain in interaction with others. More than this, these persons continue to make demands to which we respond. In other words, our behaviors persist in being shaped by the individuals with whom we remain in contact. These pressures, in effect, serve as social scripts and supplement the internal ones. Because of this, it matters a great deal with whom we interact. Their influence can be decisive in what we choose.

Unfortunately, many people decide to remain in contact with troublesome role partners. They fail to follow their parents' advice and become entangled with a rough crowd. Having grown up around certain types of people, they wind up associating with individuals who mirror those of their youth. This is not a problem if their earlier associates were helpful. It can be disastrous if these others were abusers. Amazing as it seems, children who were physically abused tend to be attracted to adult abusers. For reasons they do not understand, they develop romances with men who beat them and/or are employed by bosses who berate them. They do not realize that their internalized beliefs, emotions, and decision-making strategies predispose them to gravitate to the sorts of persons they once knew. Sigmund Freud described this as the repetition compulsion. Many consider it a form of neurosis, but it constitutes no more than doing what feels natural. Most people hope to correct childhood mistakes, but they instead recapitulate them with partners who keep them trapped in woeful ways of life. These patterns are so deeply embedded that they are unconsciously replicated.

It may be harsh to say, but this applies to political ways of life too. People who grow up conservative tend to surround themselves with conservatives when they become adults. So too do liberals, albeit with liberals. In other words, the internalized political scripts to which people are committed tend to be reinforced by the role partners with whom they consort. Instead of being exposed to new ways of life, they hear the same shopworn beliefs, experience the same old emotions, and are prompted to follow familiar norms and values. So deeply entrenched are the messages they receive, that they never consider alternatives. Even when these are in error, they persist in reanimating them. They then go along with the crowd to which they have always belonged, partly because its demands are as potent as ever and partly because they are echoed from within.

Intergenerational Change

Because personal scripts can be persistent, change is difficult. Cultural lag is not merely a social phenomenon, but a personal one. Individuals remain committed to their accustomed perspectives precisely because they are customary. From where they sit, these seem valid. What is more, they seem normal to those with whom they maintain contact. Theirs is in essence an insular world that they carry around with them. Outside influences leave them unaffected; hence they never experience a need for change. If it happens that they are fixated on a fantasy, they do not perceive it as unreal because their internal and external scripts validate it. All too often, they go to the grave without realizing that they have been committed to an illusion.

If I may be personal for a moment, I have reached an age where I see many of my contemporaries attached to the same beliefs they had when we were young. For a large number, the Vietnam War and the Civil Rights Movement remain as vivid as ever. The values and ideals they formed back then are as salient as when they were created. These have not been revised; they have merely been rationalized. Despite the intervening years, no effort has been made to rethink conclusions reached long gone. If anything, these are simply updated as if they were perpetually valid. Thus, as a college professor, I witness colleagues teaching lessons from their youth as if these were scientific truths. They do not revise their syllabi because they still consider them relevant.

This tendency implies that large-scale social changes must frequently be intergenerational. Individuals caught in an ideological time warp do not save themselves. To the contrary, they depend on the next generation to extract the community from their errors. Of course, sometimes the young are so thoroughly indoctrinated in the shibboleths of the old that they repeat them unaltered. One sees this on the college level where the good students replicate the positions of their teachers. They bask in having their work praised and being awarded the best grades. As to the older generation, it tends to coalesce into an established elite that propounds an academic orthodoxy. As gatekeepers for university employment and academic publications, its members ensure that only ideologically pure ideas filter through.

Happily, the practice of self-replication is not foolproof. There is a tendency for well-established attitudes to perpetuate themselves, but there is also a mechanism that subverts them. While many career-minded individuals attempt to ingratiate the reigning powers, others strike out in new directions. Instead of going along to get along, they search for unexplored territories in which to stake novel claims. By being different, they hope to fashion an independent reputation for expertise. Hence rather than be followers, they elect to be leaders. Their advantage is that they never fully commit to the old verities. Because their personal scripts do not include all of the beliefs, emotions, and volitional dispositions of their teachers, they are more flexible. They therefore perceive factors their elders do not. The upshot is that for the sake of being winners, they slough off the old in favor of something to call their own. As a result, they make changes rather than be subservient to the older generation.

This is the probable fate of liberalism. Many of today's committed liberals will never extricate themselves from their positions. They will never save themselves from being dead-ended in an ideology that is destined to implode. Older liberals, in particular, will remain as dedicated to their ideals as when they were college sophomores. But there is a younger generation coming. Some of its members will be content to conform to the threadbare lessons of their instructors, but others will not. They will be open to unfamiliar perspectives and prepared to make unexpected discoveries. It is consequently they who will lead the way out of an ancient morass. This is one of the ways in which societies have always advanced. Progress—genuine progress—results from an intergenerational dance. Older and younger generations play off each other and the conditions in which they respectively live so as to produce innovations no one has foreseen. In an effort to be independent, the young sort through options their elders never considered so as to discover improvements they can implement.

A sort of social selection, more Lamarckian than Darwinian in nature, produces evolutionary surprises. Unprecedented social characteristics are generated in response to social pressures, which are then bequeathed to the next generation. If the new patterns are effective, they are perpetuated. In sociology, we say that they become institutionalized. In other words, these new versions of reality develop into the conventional wisdom. If they do not, then some members of the next generation seek untried solutions. These are then tested and if they work, are adopted. If not, the game continues with other unencumbered minds striking out in yet to be considered directions. Eventually innovative cultural and structural formats emerge. New roles evolve in concert with other roles, fresh beliefs rise to the surface, and altered norms and values gain a wider following. In the end, what once seemed natural comes to be viewed as old-fashioned. So it was with the absolute monarchies of medieval Europe. So it will be with contemporary liberalism.

Intragenerational Change

On an individual level moving from one ideological commitment to another is a more formidable challenge. My father used to say that "you can't teach an old dog new tricks." Even as a relatively young man, he prided himself on constancy. The truth was that he was afraid to change. He was terrified of digging into a past that had been a nightmare. He did not want to examine his personal scripts lest they demonstrate that he was crazy. Intergenerational change, in contrast, occurs when one cohort moves beyond another. It does not have to investigate why the older generation was wrong so much as replace it. Intragenerational change is different. It requires people to confront their previous mistakes. This can be alarming; hence it makes individual change more demanding. As a result, it is unlikely that many nonprofessionalized adults will professionalize or that committed liberals will abandon their liberalism.

Nevertheless, personal change is possible. People can save themselves from their own mistakes. There is a mechanism for doing so. It is called resocialization. Most people do not avail themselves of this process because it is lengthy and painful. Even so, they need to be aware that it exists. Like cultural lag, individual tendencies toward conservatism are reactions to loss. When people fail to get what they need, they repeat old errors in the hope of correcting them. They assume that if they do what they formerly did, they can do it better the second time around. In this, they do not recognize that what was lost is frequently beyond reclamation; that the only way to make things better is to let go of what is gone and replace it with something else.

Resocialization essentially allows individuals who are trapped in unfortunate childhoods to grow up. It permits them to become strong adults who can win victories in competition with others. Now able to operate as self-motivated experts, they are able to achieve hierarchical, personal relationship, and social roles successes. In order to arrive at this point, however, they must first reexperience their past losses, protest against them, mourn them, and finally renegotiate improvements. This can take years, but it is doable. They can, if they desire, acquire the courage to disengage from comforting fantasies so as to participate in more satisfying realities.

I have discussed the nature of resocialization in greater detail elsewhere;[1] hence I only allude to it here. The point is that we are not condemned to dreams of salvation. We can achieve them. We can do this socially and individually. To repeat, life is frightening and social living is challenging, but we do not have to live with lies. Liberalism is a form of communal prevarication. It is an ancient fairytale that prevents us from achieving as much as we can. The time has thus come to let go. We should do this intergenerationally and, if we can, intragenerationally. Let liberalism die. History is not on its side. Nor is it the only alternative. Most of us can grow up, if we so decide. Indeed, we will be better off when we see liberalism in the rearview mirror.

The Star Spangled Banner proclaims that America is "the land of the free and the home of the brave." If this is true, then many Americans will eventually find the courage to relinquish their liberal fantasies. They will face their fears and liberate themselves for timeworn fairy tales. Instead of passively dreaming of salvation, they will embrace professionalization. And when they do, they will not only become experts in their economic and political vocations, but in the art of living. Should they choose to do so, the rewards will be ample. Not only will they fulfill the promise with which their nation was born, but they will fulfill the promise that lies within themselves.

Note

1.   Fein, M. 2011. *On Loss and Losing: Beyond the Medical Model of Personal Distress.* New Brunswick, NJ: Transaction Publishers.

Bibliography

Abrams, R.M. 2006. *America Transformed: Sixty Years of Revolutionary Change, 1941–2001.* New York: Cambridge University Press.

Acton, Lord. 1887. *Letter to Bishop Mandell Creighton.*

Adams, J.C. 2011. *Injustice: Exposing the Racial Agenda of the Obama Justice Department.* Washington, DC: Regnery Publishing.

Alterman, E. 2003. *What Liberal Media?: The Truth about Bias and the News.* New York: Basic Books.

Anderson, M. 1992. *Imposters in the Temple: American Intellectuals Are Destroying Our Universities and Cheating Our Students of Their Future.* New York: Simon & Schuster.

Armstrong, K. 1993. *A History of God: The 4000-Year Quest of Judaism, Christianity and Islam.* New York: Ballantine Books.

Asch, S.E. 1952. *Social Psychology.* New York: Prentice-Hall.

Ashton, T.S. 1965. *The Industrial Revolution 1760–1830.* New York: Oxford University Press.

Auchincloss, L. 1989. *The Vanderbilt Era: Portraits of a Gilded Age.* New York: Scribner.

Bailey, B.J. 1998. *The Luddite Rebellion.* New York: New York University Press.

Bailyn, B. 1992. *The Ideological Origins of the American Revolution.* Cambridge, MA: The Belknap Press.

Baker, P. 2000. *The Breach: Inside the Impeachment and Trail of William Jefferson Clinton.* New York: Scribner.

Ball, T. and Dagger, R. 1999. *Political Ideologies and the Democratic Ideal.* New York: Longman.

Banfield, E.C. 1961. *Political Influence: A New Theory of Urban Politics.* New York: The Free Press.

Bannister, R.C. 1979. *Social Darwinism: Science and Myth in Anglo-American Social Thought.* Philadelphia: Temple University Press.

Barlett, D.L. and Steele, J.B. 1996. *America: Who Stole the Dream?* Kansas City: Andrews and McMeel.

Baron-Cohen, S. 2003. *The Essential Difference: The Truth about the Male and Female Brain.* New York: Basic Books.

Barone, M. 2001. *The New Americans: How the Melting Pot Can Work Again.* Washington, DC: Regnery Publishing.

Barone, M. 2004. *Hard America Soft America*. New York: Crown Forum.

Barzun, J. 2000. *From Dawn to Decadence: 500 Years of Western Cultural Life*. New York: HarperCollins Publishers.

Bell, D. 1978. *The Cultural Contradictions of Capitalism*. New York: Basic Books.

Bellah, R.N., Madsen, R., Sullivan, W.M., Swindler, A., and Tipton, S.M. 1985. *Habits of the Heart: Individualism and Commitment in American Life*. Berkeley: University of California Press.

Bergmann, B.R. 1996. *In Defense of Affirmative Action*. New York: Basic Books.

Bernstein, C. and Woodward, B. 1974. *All the President's Men*. New York: Simon & Schuster.

Bernstein, R. 1994. *Dictatorship of Virtue: Multiculturalism and the Battle for America's Future*. New York: Alfred A. Knopf.

Bernstein, W.J. 2008. *A Splendid Exchange: How Trade Shaped the World*. New York: Grove Press.

Best, J. 2001. *Damned Lies and Statistics: Untangling Numbers from the Media, Politicians, and Activists*. Berkeley: University of California Press.

Betzig, L.L. 1986. *Despotism and Differential Reproduction: A Darwinian View of History*. New York: Aldine.

Biazine, E. 1992. *Liberty, Retrenchment, and Reform: Popular Liberalism in the Age of Gladstone 1860–1880*. New York: Cambridge University Press.

Blankenhorn, D. 1995. *Fatherless America: Confronting Our Most Urgent Social Problem*. New York: Basic Books.

Blass, T. 2004. *The Man Who Shocked the World: The Life and Legacy of Stanley Milgram*. New York: Basic Books.

Bloom. A. 1987. *The Closing of the American Mind*. New York: Simon & Schuster.

Blumin, S.M. 1989. *The Emergence of the Middle Class: Social Experience in the American City 1760–1900*. New York: Cambridge University Press.

Blyth, M. 2004. *Spin Sisters: How the Women of the Media Sell Unhappiness and Liberalism to the Women of America*. New York: St. Martin's Press.

Boehm, C. 1999. *Hierarchy in the Forest: The Evolution of Egalitarian Behavior*. Cambridge, MA: Harvard University Press.

Boone, J.L. 2000. "Status Signaling: Social Power, and Lineage Survival." In: Diehl, M.W. (Ed.), *Hierarchies in Action: Cui Bono?* Carbondale, IL: Center for Archaeological Investigations.

Boorstin, D.J. 1987. *Hidden History: Exploring Our Secret Past*. New York: Harper & Row.

Boot, M. 1998. *Out of Order: Arrogance, Corruption, and Incompetence on the Bench*. New York: Basic Books.

Bork, R. 1996. *Slouching Toward Gomorrah: Modern Liberalism and American Decline*. New York: Regan Books.

Bourdieu, P. 1990. *The Logic of Practice*. Stanford, CA: Stanford University Press.

Bowlby, J. 1969. *Attachment*. New York: Basic Books.

Bowlby, J. 1973. *Separation: Anxiety and Anger*. New York: Basic Books.

Bowlby, J. 1980. *Loss: Sadness and Depression*. New York: Basic Books.

Bowlby, J. 1990. *Charles Darwin: A New Life*. New York: W.W. Norton.

Bowles, S. and Gintis, H. 1976. *Schooling in Capitalist America: Educational Reform and the Contradictions of Capitalist Life*. New York: Basic Books.

Bozell, L.B. 2004. *Weapons of Mass Distortion: The Coming Meltdown of the Liberal Media*. New York: Crown Forum.

Brands, H.W. 2001. *The Strange Death of American Liberalism*. New Haven: Yale University Press.

Braudel, F. 1979a. *The Structures of Everyday Life: Civilization & Capitalism 15th–18th Century*, Vol. 1. New York: Harper & Row.

Braudel, F. 1979b. *The Wheels of Commerce: Civilization & Capitalism 15th–18th Century*, Vol. 2. New York: Harper & Row.

Braudel, F. 1979c. *The Perspective of the World: Civilization & Capitalism 15th–18th Century*, Vol. 3. New York: Harper & Row.

Brimelow, P. 2003. *The Worm in the Apple: How the Teacher Unions Are Destroying American Education*. New York: HarperCollins Publishers.

Brooks, D. 2000. *Bobos in Paradise: The New Upper Class and How They Got There*. New York: Simon & Schuster.

Brooks, D. 2004. *On Paradise Drive*. New York: Simon & Schuster.

Brown, D.E. 1988. *Hierarchy, History, and Human Nature: The Social Origins of Historical Consciousness*. Tucson: The University of Arizona Press.

Brownmiller, S. 1975. *Against Our Will: Men, Women and Rape*. New York: Bantam.

Brownstein, H.H. 2000. *The Social Reality of Violence and Violent Crime*. Needham Heights, MA: Allyn & Bacon.

Bruce, T. 2001. *The New Thought Police: Inside the Left's Assault on Free Speech and Free Minds*. Roseville, CA: Prima Publishing.

Bruegman, R. 2005. *Sprawl: A Compact History*. Chicago: University of Chicago Press.

Bruhn, J. 2001. *Trust and the Health of Organizations*. New York: Kluwer/Plenum.

Bugliosi, V. 1975. *Helter Skelter: The True Story of the Manson Murders*. New York: Bantam Books.

Burns, E. 2004. *The Spirits of America: A Social History of Alcohol*. Philadelphia, PA: Temple University Press.

Campos, P.F. 1998. *Jurismania: The Madness of American Law*. New York: Oxford University Press.

Cannadine, D. 1999. *The Rise and Fall of Class in Britain.* New York: Columbia University Press.

Cannadine, D. 2006. *Mellon: An American Life.* New York: Random House.

Cantor, N.F. 1997. *Imagining the Law: Common Law and the Foundations of the American Legal System.* New York: HarperCollins Publishers.

Caplow, T., Hicks, L., and Wattenberg, B.J. 2001. *The First Measured Century: An Illustrated Guide to Trends in America, 1900–2000.* Washington, DC: The AEI Press.

Carter, S.L. 1991. *Reflections of an Affirmative Action Baby.* New York: Basic Books.

Carter, S.L. 1998. *Civility: Manners, Morals and the Etiquette of Democracy.* New York: Basic Books.

Cashman, S.D. 1981. *Prohibition: The Lie of the Land.* New York: Free Press.

Charen, M. 2003. *Useful Idiots: How Liberals Got It Wrong in the Cold War and Still Blame America First.* Washington, DC: Regnery Publishing.

Charen, M. 2004. *Do-Gooders: How Liberals Hurt Those They Claim to Help.* New York: Sentinel.

Chatfield, C. 1992. *The American Peace Movement: Ideals and Activism.* New York: Twayne Publishers.

Cheney, D. 2011. *In My Time: A Personal and Political Memoir.* New York: Simon & Schuster.

Cheney, L. 1995. *Telling the Truth.* New York: Simon & Schuster.

Cherlin, A.J. 1992. *Marriage, Divorce, and Remarriage.* Cambridge, MA: Harvard University Press.

Chernow, R. 1990. *The House of Morgan: An American Banking Dynasty and the Rise of Modern Finance.* New York: Grove Press.

Chernow, R. 1998. *Titan: The Life of John D. Rockefeller.* New York: Random House.

Chirot, D. 1986. *Social Change in the Modern Era.* New York: Harcourt, Brace, Jovanovich.

Chirot, D. 1994a. *How Societies Change.* Thousand Oaks, CA: Pine Forge Press.

Chirot, D. 1994b. *Modern Tyrants.* Princeton, NJ: Princeton University Press.

Clements, K.A. 1987. *Woodrow Wilson: World Statesman.* Boston: Twayne.

Clinton, H. 1996. *It Takes a Village: And Other Lessons Children Teach Us.* New York: Simon & Schuster.

Codevilla, A.M. 2009. *The Character of Nations: How Politics Makes and Breaks Prosperity, Family, and Civility.* New York: Basic Books.

Coleman, J.S., Campbell, E.Q., Hobson, C.J., McPartland, J., Mood, A.M., Weinfeld, F.D., and York, R.L. 1966. *Equality of*

Educational Opportunity. Washington, DC: U.S. Government Printing Office.

Collier, P. and Horowitz, D. 1976. *The Rockefellers: An American Dynasty*. New York: Holt, Rinehart and Winston.

Collier, P. and Horowitz, D. 1989. *Destructive Generation: Second Thoughts about the '60s*. New York: The Free Press.

Coltrane, S. 1996. *Family Man: Fatherhood, Housework, and Gender Equity*. New York: Oxford University Press.

Colville, J. 1985. *The Fringes of Power: 10 Downing Street Diaries 1939–1955*. New York: W.W. Norton.

Connerly, W. 2000. *Creating Equal: My Fight against Race Prejudices*. San Francisco: Encounter Books.

Cook, A.E., Jelen, T.G., and Wilcox, C. 1992. *Between Two Absolutes: Public Opinion and the Politics of Abortion*. Boulder: Westview Press.

Coontz, S. 1992. *The Way We Never Were: American Families and the Nostalgia Trap*. New York: Basic Books.

Corey, L. 1935. *The Crisis of the Middle Class*. New York: Columbia University Press.

Coulter, A. 2002. *Slander: Liberal Lies about the American Right*. New York: Crown Publishers.

Coulter, A. 2003. *Treason: Liberal Treachery from the Cold War to the War on Terrorism*. New York: Crown Forum.

Courtois, S., Werth, N., Panne, J.L., Paczkowski, A., Bartosek, K., and Margolin, J.L. 1999. *The Black Book of Communism: Crimes, Terror, Repression*. Cambridge, MA. Harvard University Press.

Cranston, M. 1982. *Jean-Jacques*. New York: W.W. Norton.

Crawford, J. 1989. *Bilingual Education: History, Politics, Theory, and Practice*. Trenton, NJ: Crane Publishing.

Cronk, L., Chanon, N., and Irons, W. (Eds.) 2000. *Adaptation and Human Behavior: An Anthropological Perspective*. New York: Aldine de Gruyter.

Crossman, R.H. (Ed.) 1963. *The God that Failed*. New York: Harper & Row.

Crozier, M. 1964. *The Bureaucratic Phenomenon*. Chicago: University of Chicago Press.

Cumston, C.C. 1987. *The History of Medicine: From the Time of the Pharaohs to the End of the XVIII Century*. New York: Dorset Press.

Dahl, R. 1967. *Pluralist Democracy in the United States*. Chicago: Rand McNally.

Dahrendorf, R. 1959. *Class and Class Conflict in Industrial Society*. Stanford, CA: Stanford University Press.

Dalrymple, T. 2001. *Life at the Bottom: The Worldview that Makes the Underclass*. Chicago: Ivan R. Dee.

Darwin, C. 1979. *The Origin of Species*. New York: Avnel Books.

Davies, T. 1997. *Humanism*. New York: Routledge.

Dawes, R.M. 2000. *Everyday Irrationality: How Pseudo-Scientists, Lunatics, and the Rest of Us Systematically Fail to Think Rationally.* Boulder, CO: Westview Press.

De Beauvoir, S. 1978. *The Second Sex.* New York: Alfred A. Knopf.

Demott, B. 1990. *The Imperial Middle: Why American Can't Think Straight about Class.* New Haven: Yale University Press.

Deveaux, M. 2000. *Cultural Pluralism and Dilemmas of Justice.* Ithaca, NY: Cornell University Press.

Diamond, J. 1997. *Guns, Germs, and Steel: The Fates of Human Societies.* New York: W.W. Norton.

Diamond, J. 2005. *Collapse: How Societies Choose to Fail or Succeed.* New York: Penguin Books.

Diehl, M.W. (Ed.) 2000. *Hierarchies in Action: Cui Bono?* Carbondale, IL: Center for Archeological Investigations.

Doty, C.S. (Ed.) 1969. *The Industrial Revolution.* New York: Holt, Rinehart and Winston.

Douthat. R. 2005. *Privilege: Harvard and the Education of the Ruling Class.* New York: Hyperion.

D'Souza, D. 1991. *Illiberal Education: The Politics of Race and Sex on Campus.* New York: The Free Press.

D'Souza, D. 2000. *The Virtue of Prosperity: Finding Values in an Age of Techno-Affluence.* New York: The Free Press.

D'Souza, D. 2010. *The Roots of Obama's Rage.* Washington, DC: Regnery Publishing.

Dunbar, R., Knight, C., and Power, C. (Eds.) 1999. *The Evolution of Culture.* New Brunswick, NJ: Rutgers University Press.

Duncan, O.D. 1965. "The Trend of Occupational Mobility in the United States." *American Sociological Review,* 30: 491–98.

Durant, A. and Durant. W. 1967. *Rousseau and the Revolution.* New York: MJF Books.

Durkheim, E. 1915. *The Elementary Forms of Religious Life.* New York: The Free Press.

Durkheim, E. 1933. *The Division of Labor in Society.* New York: The Free Press.

Durkheim, E. 1961. *Moral Education.* New York: The Free Press.

Dye, T.R. 1975. *Power and Society: An Introduction to the Social Sciences.* Belmont, CA: Wadsworth Publishing.

Easton, D. 1964. *The Political System: An Inquiry into the State of Political Science.* New York: Alfred. A. Knopf.

Ebenstein, A. 2001. *Friedrich Hayek: A Biography.* New York: Palgrave.

Eberhard, W. 1977. *A History of China.* London: Routledge & Kegan Paul.

Eberstadt, M. 2004. *Home-Alone America: The Hidden Toll of Day Care, Behavioral Drugs, and Other Parent Substitutes.* New York: Sentinel.

Eckstein, H. and Gurr, T.R. 1975. *Patterns of Authority: A Structural Basis for Political Inquiry.* New York: John Wiley & Sons.

Edin, K. and Kefalas, M. 2005. *Promises I Can Keep: Why Poor Women Put Motherhood before Marriage*. Berkeley: University of California Press.

Edman, I. (Ed.) 1928. *The Works of Plato*. New York: The Modern Library.

Edmonds, D. and Eidinow, J. 2006. *Rousseau's Dog: Two Great Thinkers at War in the Age of Enlightenment*. New York: HarperCollins Publishers.

Eisenstadt, S.N. 1971. *Social Differentiation and Stratification*. Glencoe, IL: Scott, Foresman.

Elias, N. 1982. *Power and Civility*. New York: Pantheon Books.

Elias, N. 1983. *The Court Society*. New York: Pantheon Books.

Ellis, J.J. 1993. *Passionate Sage: The Character and Legacy of John Adams*. New York: W.W. Norton.

Ellis, J.J. 1996. *American Sphinx: The Character of Thomas Jefferson*. New York: Alfred A. Knopf.

Ellis, J.J. 2000. *Founding Brothers: The Revolutionary Generation*. New York: Alfred A. Knopf.

Ellis, J.M. 1997. *Literature Lost: Social Agendas and the Corruption of the Humanities*. New Haven: Yale University Press.

Ellis, R.J. 1998. *The Dark Side of the Left: Illiberal Egalitarianism in America*. Lawrence: University of Kansas Press.

Elshtain, J.B. 1995. *Democracy on Trial*. New York: Basic Books.

Engels, F. 1972. *The Origin of the Family, Private Property, and the State*. New York: International Publishers.

Entine, J. 2000. *Taboo: Why Black Athletes Dominate Sports and Why We're Afraid to Talk About It*. New York: Public Affairs.

Entwisle, D.R., Alexander, K.L., and Olson, L.S. 1997. *Children, Schools & Inequality*. Boulder, CO: Westview Press.

Epstein, C.F. 1970. *Woman's Place: Options and Limits in Professional Careers*. Berkeley: University of California Press.

Epstein, J. 2002. *Snobbery: The American Version*. Boston: Houghton Mifflin.

Erikson, E. 1968. *Identity: Youth and Crisis*. New York: W.W. Norton.

Erikson, E. 1969. *Gandhi's Truth: On the Origins of Militant Non violence*. W.W. Norton.

Etzioni, A. 1993. *The Spirit of Community: Reinvention of American Society*. New York: Simon & Schuster.

Faludi, S. 1991. *Backlash: The Undeclared War against American Women*. New York: Crown Publishers.

Farber, D.A. and Sherry, S. 1997. *Beyond All Reason: The Radical Assault on Truth in American Law*. New York: Oxford University Press.

Farley, R. 1996. *The New American Reality: Who We Are, How We Got Here, Where We Are Going*. New York: Russell Sage Foundation.

Farrell, W. 2005. *Why Men Earn More*. New York: Amacom.

Feagin, J.R. and Sikes, M.P. 1994. *Living with Racism: The Black Middle-Class Experience*. Boston: Beacon Press.

Fein, M. 1993. *I.A.M.: A Common Sense Guide to Coping with Anger*. Westport, CT: Praeger.

Fein, M. 1997. *Hardball without an Umpire: The Sociology of Morality*. Westport, CT: Praeger.

Fein, M. 1999. *The Limits of Idealism: When Good Intentions Go Bad*. New York: Kluwer/Plenum.

Fein, M. 2005. *The Great Middle Class Revolution: Our Long March toward a Professionalized Society*. Kennesaw, GA: Kennesaw State University Press.

Fein, M. 2010. *A Professionalized Society: Our Real Future*. Kindle.

Fein, M. 2011. *On Loss and Losing: Beyond the Medical Model of Personal Distress*. New Brunswick, NJ: Transaction Publishers.

Fein, M. 2012. *Human Hierarchies: A General Theory*. New Brunswick, NJ: Transaction Publishers.

Ferguson, N. 2001. *The Cash Nexus: Money and Power in the Modern World, 1700–2000*. New York: Basic Books.

Festinger, L. 1957. *A Theory of Cognitive Dissonance*. Evanston, IL: Row, Peterson.

Festinger, L., Riecken, H.W., and Schachter, S. 1956. *When Prophesy Fails: A Social and Psychological Study of a Modern Group that Predicted the Destruction of the World*. New York: Harper & Row.

Fischer, D.H. 1989. *Albion's Seed: Four British Folkways in America*. New York: Oxford University Press.

Fischer, L. 1964. *The Life of Lenin*. New York: Harper & Row.

Fisher, H.E. 1982. *The Sex Contract: The Evolution of Human Behavior*. New York: William Morrow.

Fisher, H.E. 1992. *Anatomy of Love: The Natural History of Monogamy, Adultery and Divorce*. New York: W.W. Norton.

Fishman, R. 1987. *Bourgeois Utopias: The Rise and Fall of Suburbia*. New York: Basic Books.

Flynn, D.J. 2004a. *Intellectual Morons: How Ideology Makes Smart People Fall for Stupid Ideas*. New York: Crown Forum.

Flynn, D.J. 2004b. *Why the Left Hates America: Exposing the Lies that Have Obscured Our Nation's Greatness*. New York: Three Rivers Press.

Folsom, B. 2008. *New Deal or Raw Deal?: How FDR's Economic Legacy Has Damaged America*. New York: Simon & Schuster.

Forbes, J.D. 1981. *J.P. Morgan Jr.* Charlottesville, VA: University of Virginia Press.

Ford, G.R. 1979. *A Time to Heal: The Autobiography of Gerald R. Ford*. New York: Harper & Row.

Fornara, C. 1991. *Athens from Cleisthenes to Pericles*. Berkeley: University of California Press.

Fox-Genovese, E. 1996. *Feminism is Not the Story of My Life: How Today's Feminist Elite Has Lost Touch with the Real Concerns of Women*. New York: Doubleday.

Frank, S.A. 1998. *Foundations of Social Evolution*. Princeton, NJ: University of Princeton Press.

Frankel, N. and Dye, N.S. (Eds.) 1991. *Gender, Class, Race and Reform in the Progressive Era*. Lexington, KY: University of Kentucky Press.

Franklin, D.L. 1997. *Ensuring Inequality: The Structural Transformation of the African-American Family*. New York: Oxford University Press.

Freeman, D. 1983. *Margaret Mead and Samoa: The Making and Unmaking of an Anthropological Myth*. Cambridge, MA: Harvard University Press.

Freidel, F.B. 1973. *Franklin Roosevelt: Launching the New Deal*. Boston: Little, Brown.

French, M. 1992. *The War against Women*. New York: Summit Books.

Freud, A. 1966. *The Ego and the Mechanisms of Defense*. New York: International Universities Press.

Freud, S. 1953–1974. *The Standard Edition of the Complete Psychological Works of Sigmund Freud*. Edited by J. Strachey. London: Hogarth Press and Institute for Psychoanalysis.

Freud, S. 1961. *Civilization and Its Discontents*. New York: W.W. Norton.

Friedan, B. 1963. *The Feminine Mystique*. New York: W.W. Norton.

Friedman, M. 1962. *Capitalism and Freedom*. Chicago: University of Chicago Press.

Fromm, E. 1941. *Escape from Freedom*. New York: Holt, Rinehart and Winston.

Fukuyama, F. 1995. *Trust: The Social Virtues and the Creation of Prosperity*. New York: Free Press.

Fukuyama, F. 1999. *The Great Disruption: Human Nature and the Reconstitution of Social Order*. New York: Free Press.

Fussell, P. 1983. *Class: A Guide through the American Status System*. New York: Simon & Schuster.

Galbraith, J.K. 1958. *The Affluent Society*. Boston: Houghton Mifflin.

Galileo. 1997. *Galileo on the World Systems*. Berkeley: University of California Press.

Gambino, R. 1975. *Blood of My Blood: The Dilemma of the Italian Americans*. Garden City, NY: Doubleday.

Gans, H.J. 1962. *The Urban Villagers: Group and Class in the Life of Italian-Americans*. New York: The Free Press,

Gans, H.J. 1967. *The Levittowners: Way of Life and Politics in a New Suburban Community*. New York: Alfred A. Knopf.

Gans, H.J. 1988. *Middle American Individualism: Political Participation and Liberal Democracy.* New York: Oxford University Press.

Garbarino, J., Schellenbach, C.J., and Sebes, J. 1986. *Troubled Youth, Troubled Families.* New York: Aldine De Gruyter.

Garder, R.D. 1978. *Horatio Alger: Or the American Hero Era.* New York: Arco Publishers.

Garreau, J. 1991. *Edge City: Life on the New Frontier.* New York: Random House.

Gelles, R.J. 1997. *Intimate Violence in Families* (3rd ed.). Beverly Hills: Sage Publications.

Gelles, R.J. and Straus, M.A. 1989. *Intimate Violence: The Causes and Consequences of Abuse in the American Family.* New York: Touchstone Books.

Gerson, M. (Ed.) 1996. *The Essential Neo-Conservative Reader.* Reading, MA: Addison-Wesley Publishing.

Gerth, H. and Mills, C.W. (Eds.) 1946. *From Max Weber: Essays in Sociology.* New York: Oxford University Press.

Gibbon, E. 1963. *The Decline and Fall of the Roman Empire.* New York: Dell Publishing.

Gibbs, J. 1989. *Control: Sociology's Central Notion.* Chicago: University of Illinois Press.

Giddens, A. 1973. *The Class Structure of the Advanced Societies.* New York: Harper & Row.

Gilligan, C. 1982. *In a Different Voice.* Cambridge, MA: Harvard University Press.

Giuliani, R.W. 2002. *Leadership.* New York: Miramax Books.

Gladwell, M. 2000. *The Tipping Point: How Little Things Can Make a Big Difference.* Boston: Little, Brown.

Glass, I.B. (Ed.) 1991. *The International Handbook of Addiction.* New York: Tavistock/Routledge.

Glazer, N. 1997. *We Are All Multiculturalists Now.* Cambridge, MA: Harvard University Press.

Glendon, M.A. 1991. *Rights Talk: The Impoverishment of Political Discourse.* New York: Free Press.

Glendon, M.A. 2011. *The Forum and the Tower: How Scholars and Politicians Have Imagined the World, from Plato to Eleanor Roosevelt.* New York: Oxford University Press.

Glendon, M.A. and Blankenhorn, D. (Eds.) 1995. *Seedbeds of Virtue: Sources of Competence, Character, and Citizenship in American Society.* Lanham, MD: Madison Books.

Glenn, N. 1997. *Closed Hearts, Closed Minds: The Textbook Story of Marriage.* New York: Institute for American Values.

Goffman, E. 1959. *The Presentation of Self in Everyday Life.* Garden City: Doubleday.

Goffman, E. 1969. *Strategic Interaction.* New York: Ballantine Books.

Goffman, E. 1974. *Frame Analysis.* New York: Harper & Row.

Goldberg, B. 2002. *Bias: A CBS Insider Exposes How the Media Distort the News*. Washington, DC: Regnery Publishing.

Goldberg, B. 2009. *A Slobbering Love Affair: The True (and Pathetic) Story of the Torrid Romance between Barack Obama and the Mainstream Media*. Washington, DC: Regnery Publishing.

Goldberg, J. 2007. *Liberal Fascism: The Secret History of the American Left from Mussolini to the Politics of Meaning*. New York: Doubleday.

Goldberg, S. 1973. *The Inevitability of Patriarchy*. New York: William Morrow.

Goldsworthy, A. 2006. *Caesar: Life of a Colossus*. New Haven: Yale University Press.

Goldwater, B.M. 1964. *Conscience of a Conservative*. New York: MacFadden-Bartell.

Goleman, D. 1995. *Emotional Intelligence: Why It Can Matter More Than IQ*. New York: Bantam Books.

Goleman, D. 2006. *Social Intelligence: The New Science of Human Relationships*. New York: Bantam Books.

Good, T.L. and Braden, J.S. 2000. *The Great School Debate: Choice, Vouchers, and Charters*. Mahwah, NJ. Lawrence Erlbaum Associates.

Goodall, J. 1990. *Through a Window: My Thirty Years with the Chimpanzees of Gombe*. Boston: Houghton Mifflin.

Goodwin, D.K. 1995. *No Ordinary Time: Franklin and Eleanor Roosevelt*. New York: Simon & Schuster.

Gordon, M.M. 1964. *Assimilation in American Life: The Role of Race, Religion, and National Origins*. New York: Oxford University Press.

Gottfredson, M.R. and Hirschi, T. 1999. *A General Theory of Crime*. Stanford, CA: Stanford University Press.

Gould, S.J. 1973. *Ever Since Darwin: Reflections on Natural History*. New York: W.W. Norton.

Gould, S.J. 1981. *The Mismeasure of Man*. New York: W.W. Norton.

Gouldner, A.J. 1954. *Patterns of Industrial Bureaucracy*. New York: The Free Press.

Graglia, F.C. 1998. *Domestic Tranquility: A Brief against Feminism*. Dallas, TX: Spence Publishing.

Graham, T. 1996. *Patterns of Deception: The Media's Role in the Clinton Presidency*. Alexandria, VA: Media Research Center.

Gramsci, A. 1977. *Antonio Gramsci: Selections from Political Writings*. New York: International Publications.

Granovetter, M. 1973. "The Strength of Weak Ties." *American Journal of Sociology*, 78: 1360–80.

Greer, C. and Kohl, H. 1995. *A Call to Character*. New York: HarperCollins Publishers.

Gregorovius, F. 1971. *Rome and Medieval Culture*. Chicago: University of Chicago Press.

Griswold, W. 1994. *Cultures and Societies in a Changing World.* Thousand Oaks, CA: Pine Forge Press.

Grun, B. 1979. *The Timetables of History: A Horizontal Linkage of People and Events.* New York: Simon & Schuster.

Gutmann, S. 2000. *The Kinder, Gentler Military: Can America's Gender-Neutral Fighting Force Still Win Wars?* New York: Scribner.

Halberstam, D. 1969. *The Best and the Brightest.* New York: Random House.

Halberstam, D. 1986. *The Reckoning.* New York: William Morrow.

Hall, C. 1997. *Steel Phoenix: The Fall and Rise of the U.S. Steel Industry.* New York: St. Martin's Press.

Hall, R.H. 1975. *Occupations and the Social Structure.* Englewood Cliffs, NJ: Prentice-Hall.

Hamilton, E. 1958. *The Greek Way.* New York: W.W. Norton.

Hamilton, R.F. 1996. *The Social Misconstruction of Reality: Validity and Verification in the Scholarly Community.* New Haven: Yale University Press.

Handlin, O. 1959. *The Newcomers: Negroes and Puerto Ricans in a Changing Metropolis.* New York: Doubleday.

Harris, M. 1977. *Cannibals and Kings: The Origins of Cultures.* New York: Random House.

Harrison, L.E. and Huntington, S.P. (Eds.) 2000. *Culture Matters: How Values Shape Human Progress.* New York: Basic Books.

Hayek, F.A. 1944. *The Road to Serfdom.* London: Routledge.

Hayek, F.A. 1988. *The Fatal Conceit: The Errors of Socialism.* Chicago: The University of Chicago Press.

Haynes, J.E. and Klehr, H. 2003. *In Denial: Historians, Communism and Espionage.* San Francisco: Encounter Books.

Hearn, F. 1997. *Moral Order and Social Disorder: The American Search for Civil Society.* New York: Aldine de Gruyter.

Heilbroner, R.L. 1980. *The Worldly Philosophers.* New York: Simon & Schuster.

Herrnstein, R.J. and Murray, C. 1994. *The Bell Curve: The Reshaping of American Life by Differences in Intelligence.* New York: Basic Books.

Hewitt, J.P. 1998. *The Myth of Self-Esteem: Finding Happiness and Solving Problems in America.* New York: St. Martins.

Himmelfarb, G. 1995. *The De-Moralization of Society: From Victorian Virtues to Modern Values.* New York: Alfred A. Knopf.

Himmelfarb, G. 1999. *One Nation, Two Cultures.* New York: Alfred A. Knopf.

Hobbes, T. 1956. *Leviathan: Part I.* Chicago: Henry Regnery.

Hochschild, A.R. 1983. *The Managed Heart: Commercialization of Human Feeling.* Berkeley: University of California Press.

Hochschild, J. 1995. *Facing Up to the American Dream.* Princeton, NJ: Princeton University Press.

Hoffer, E. 1951. *The True Believer: Thoughts on the Nature of Mass Movements*. New York: Harper & Row.

Hoffer, P.C. 2004. *Past Imperfect: Facts, Fictions, Fraud—American History from Bancroft and Parkman to Ambrose, Bellesiles, Ellis and Goodwin*. New York: Public Affairs.

Hoffman, A. 2001. *The Autobiography of Abbie Hoffman*. New York: Four Walls Eight Windows.

Hollander, P. 1992. *Anti-Americanism: Critiques at Home and Abroad 1965–1990*. New York: Oxford University Press.

Hoogenboom, A.A. 1968. *Outlawing the Spoils: A History of the Civil Service Reform Movement 1865–1883*. Urbana: University of Illinois Press.

Horowitz, D. 1997. *Radical Son: A Generational Odyssey*. New York: The Free Press.

Horowitz, D. 1998. *Betty Friedan and the Making of the Feminine Mystique*. Amherst, NY: University of Massachusetts Press.

Horowitz, D. 2003. *Left Illusions: An Intellectual Odyssey*. Dallas, TX: Spence Publishing.

Horowitz, I.L. 1983. *C. Wright Mills: An American Utopian*. New York: The Free Press.

Horowitz, I.L. 1994. *The Decomposition of Sociology*. New York: The Oxford University Press.

Howard, P.K. 1995. *The Death of Common Sense: How Law Is Suffocating America*. New York: Random House.

Howard, P.K. 2001. *The Lost Art of Drawing the Line: How Fairness Went Too Far*. New York: Random House.

Howe, I. 1976. *The World of Our Fathers*. New York: Harcourt, Brace, Jovanovich.

Howell, J.T. 1973. *Hard Living on Clay Street: Portraits of Blue Collar Families*. Prospect Heights, IL: Waveland Press.

Hughes, R. 1993. *Culture of Complaint: The Fraying of America*. New York: Oxford University Press.

Humphrey, H.H. 1964. *War on Poverty*. New York: McGraw-Hill.

Hunt, A. 1999. *Governing Morals: A Social History of Moral Regulation*. New York: Cambridge University Press.

Hunter, F. 1953. *Community Power Structure: A Study of Decision Makers*. Chapel Hill: University of North Carolina Press.

Hunter, J.D. 1991. *Culture Wars: The Struggle to Define America*. New York: Basic Books.

Hunter, J.D. 2000. *The Death of Character: Moral Education in an Age without Good and Evil*. New York: Basic Books.

Huntington, S.P. 1996. *The Clash of Civilizations and the Remaking of World Order*. New York: Simon & Schuster.

Huntington, S.P. 2004. *Who Are We?: The Challenges to America's National Identity*. New York: Simon & Schuster.

Ignatiev, N. 1995. *How the Irish Became White*. New York: Routledge.

Isaacson, W. 2003. *Benjamin Franklin: An American Life*. New York: Simon & Schuster.

Jackson, K.T. 1985. *Crabgrass Frontier: The Suburbanization of the United States*. New York: Oxford University Press.

Jacobs, R. 1997. *The Way the Wind Blew: A History of the Weather Underground*. New York: Verso.

Jagger, A.M. 1988. *Feminist Politics and Human Nature*. Totowa, NJ: Rowman & Littlefield.

Jakle, J.A. and Sculle, K.A. 1999. *Fast Food: Roadside Restaurants in the Automobile Age*. Baltimore: Johns Hopkins University Press.

Jardine, L. 1999. *Ingenious Pursuits: Building the Scientific Revolution*. New York: Doubleday.

Jencks, C. 1972. *Inequality: A Reassessment of the Effect of Family and Schooling in America*. New York: Basic Books.

Jencks, C. 1992. *Rethinking Social Policy: Race, Poverty and the Underclass*. Cambridge, MA: Harvard University Press.

Jencks, C. 1994. *The Homeless: Rethinking Social Policy*. Cambridge, MA: Harvard University Press.

Johnson, V.E. 2002. *Grade Inflation: A Crisis in College Education*. New York: Springer.

Kagan, D. 2003. *The Peloponnesian War*. New York: Penguin Books.

Katz, L.D. (Ed.) 2000. *Evolutionary Origins of Morality: Cross-Disciplinary Perspectives*. Bowling Green, OH: Imprint Academic.

Keats, J. 1820. "Ode to a Grecian Urn." In: Quiller-Couch, A. (Ed.) (1919), *The Oxford Book of English Verse*. Oxford: Clarendon.

Kendall, P.M. 1971. *Louis XI: The Universal Spider*. New York: W.W. Norton.

Kennedy, P. 1987. *The Rise and Fall of the Great Powers: Economic Change and Military Conflict from 1500 to 2000*. New York: Random House.

Kennedy, R. 2003. *Nigger: The Strange Career of a Troublesome Word*. New York: Vintage Books.

Kimball, R. 1990. *Tenured Radicals: How Politics Has Corrupted Our Higher Education*. Chicago: Ivan R. Dee.

Kinder, R.R. and Sanders, L.M. 1996. *Divided by Color: Racial Politics and Democratic Ideals*. Chicago: University of Chicago Press.

Kirk, R. 1993. *The Politics of Prudence*. Wilmington, DE: ISI Books.

Kirk, R. 1997. *Edmund Burke: A Genius Reconsidered*. Wilmington, DE: Intercollegiate Studies Institute.

Klein, M. 2003. *The Change Makers: From Carnegie to Gates*. New York: Times Books.

Klein, R.G. and Elgar, B. 2002. *The Dawn of Human Culture: A Bold New Theory on What Sparked the "Big Bang" of Human Consciousness*. New York: John Wiley & Sons.

Kloppenberg, J.T. 2011. *Reading Obama: Dreams, Hope, and the American Tradition*. Princeton, NJ: Princeton University Press.

Knight, R.H. 1998. *The Age of Consent: The Rise of Relativism and the Corruption of Popular Culture*. Dallas, TX: Spence Publishing.

Kohn, B. 2003. *Journalistic Fraud: How the New York Times Distorts the News and Why It Can No Longer Be Trusted*. Nashville: WND Books.

Kohn, M.L. 1969. *Class and Conformity: A Study in Values*. Homewood, IL: The Dorsey Press.

Kohn, M.L. and Schooler, C. 1983. *Work and Personality: An Inquiry into the Impact of Social Stratification*. Norwood, NJ: Ablex Publishing.

Kors, A.C. and Silverglate, H.A. 1998. *The Shadow University: The Betrayal of Liberty on America's Campuses*. New York: The Free Press.

Kramer, H. and Kimball, R. 1999. *The Betrayal of Liberalism: How the Disciples of Freedom and Equality Helped Foster the Illiberal Politics of Coercion and Control*. Chicago: Ivan R. Dee.

Kramer, R. 1991. *Ed School Follies: The Miseducation of America's Teachers*. New York: The Free Press.

Krimmerman, L.I. (Ed.) 1969. *The Nature and Scope of Social Science: A Critical Anthology*. New York: Appleton-Century-Crofts.

Kubler-Ross, E. 1969. *On Death and Dying*. New York: Macmillan.

Kurtz, P. 2000. *Humanist Manifesto 2000: A Call for a New Planetary Humanism*. Amherst, NY: Prometheus Books.

Lacey, R. 1986. *Ford: The Man and the Machine*. Boston: Little, Brown.

Ladd, E.C. 1999. *The Ladd Report*. New York: The Free Press.

Lamont, M. 1992. *Money, Morals, and Manners: The Culture of the French and the American Upper-Middle Class*. Chicago: University of Chicago Press.

Landry, B. 1987. *The New Black Middle Class*. Berkeley: University of California Press.

Lantham, R. (Ed.) 1983. *The Illustrated Pepys: Extracts from the Diary*. Berkeley: University of California Press.

Lareau, A. 2003. *Unequal Childhoods: Class, Race, and Family Life*. Berkeley: University of California Press.

Lareau, A. and Conley, D. (Eds.) 2008. *Social Class: How Does It Work?* New York: Russell Sage Foundation.

Larson, M.S. 1977. *The Rise of Professionalism: A Sociological Analysis*. Berkeley: University of California Press.

Lasch, C. 1979. *The Culture of Narcissism: American Life in an Age of Diminishing Expectations*. New York: Warner Books.

Leaky, R. 1981. *The Making of Mankind*. London: Michael Joseph.

Lenski, G. 1966. *Power and Privilege: A Theory of Social Stratification*. New York: McGraw-Hill.

Leo, J. 2001. *Incorrect Thought: Notes on Our Wayward Culture*. New Brunswick, NJ: Transaction Publishers.

Lewis, M. and Saarni, C. (Eds.) 1985. *The Socialization of Emotions.* New York: Plenum Press.

Lichter, S.R., Lichter, L.S., and Rothman, S. 1994. *Prime Time: How TV Portrays American Culture.* Washington, DC: Regnery Publishing.

Lindsey, B.B. and Evans, W. 1927. *Companionate Marriage.* New York: Boni & Liveright.

Lindzey, G. and Aronson, E. (Eds.) 1985. *Handbook of Social Psychology* (3rd ed.). New York: Random House.

Link, A.S. 1954. *Woodrow Wilson and the Progressive Era 1910–1917.* New York: Harper.

Lipset, S.M. 1996. *American Exceptionalism: A Double-Edged Sword.* New York: W.W. Norton.

Loewen, J.W. 1995. *Lies My Teacher Told Me: Everything Your American History Textbook Got Wrong.* New York: The New Press.

Lofland, L.H. 1973. *A World of Strangers.* New York: Basic Books.

Lomborg, B. 2001. *The Skeptical Environmentalist: Measuring the Real State of the World.* New York: Cambridge University Press.

Lorber, J. 1994. *Paradoxes of Gender.* New Haven: Yale University Press.

Lortie, D.C. 1975. *Schoolteacher: A Sociological Study.* Chicago: University of Chicago Press.

Loseke, D.R. 1999. *Thinking about Social Problems: An Introduction to Constructivist Perspectives.* New York: Aldine de Gruyter.

Lott, J.R. 1998. *More Guns, Less Crime: Understanding Crime and Gun Control Laws.* Chicago: University of Chicago Press.

Lowery, R. 2003. *Legacy: Paying the Price for the Clinton Years.* Washington, DC: Regnery Publishing.

Lynch, F.R. 1997. *The Diversity Machine.* New York: The Free Press.

Lyons, M. 1994. *Napoleon Bonaparte and the Legacy of the French Revolution.* New York: St. Martin's Press.

MacDonald, H. 2000. *The Burden of Bad Ideas: How Modern Intellectuals Misshape Our Society.* Chicago: Ivan R. Dee.

MacDonald, H. 2003. *Are Cops Racist?: How the War Against the Police Harms Black Americans.* Chicago: Ivan R. Dee.

MacKinnon, C.A. 1987. *Feminism Unmodified: Discourses on Life and Law.* Cambridge, MA: Harvard University Press.

MacMillan, M. 2001. *Paris 1919: Six Months that Changed the World.* New York: Random House.

McBride, J. 1996. *The Color of Water: A Black Man's Tribute to His White Mother.* New York: Riverhead Books.

McCullough, D. 1992. *Truman.* New York: Simon & Schuster.

McCullough, D. 2001. *John Adams.* New York: Simon & Schuster.

McElvaine, R.S. 1984. *The Great Depression: America 1929–1941.* New York: Times Books.

McFeely, W.S. 1981. *Grant: A Biography.* New York: W.W. Norton.

McFeely, W.S. 1991. *Fredrick Douglass.* New York: W.W. Norton.

McGowan, W. 2001. *Coloring the News: How Crusading for Diversity Has Corrupted American Journalism.* San Francisco: Encounter Books.

McNeill, W.H. 1963. *The Rise of the West: A History of the Human Community.* Chicago: University of Chicago Press.

McNeill, W.H. 1977. *Plagues and Peoples.* New York: Doubleday.

McShane, C. 1994. *Down the Asphalt Path: The Automobile and the American City.* New York: Columbia University Press.

McWhorter, J. 2001. *The Power of Babel: A Natural History of Language.* New York: HarperCollins Publishers.

McWhorter, J. 2003. *Authentically Black: Essays for the Black Silent Majority.* New York: Gotham Books.

Madison, J, Hamilton, A., and Jay, J. 2000. *The Federalist Papers.* London: Phoenix Press.

Madsen, A. 2001. *John Jacob Astor: America's First Multimillionaire.* New York: John Wiley & Sons.

Magnet, M. 1993. *The Dream and the Nightmare: The Sixties Legacy to the Underclass.* New York: William Morrow.

Malkin, M. 2009. *Culture of Corruption: Obama and His Team of Tax Cheats, Crooks, and Cronies.* Washington, DC: Regnery Publishing.

Mannheim, K. 1936. *Ideology and Utopia.* New York: Harcourt, Brace, & World.

Mapp, A.J. 1987. *Thomas Jefferson: A Strange Case of Mistaken Identity.* Lanham, MD: Madison Books.

Maraniss, D. 1995. *First in His Class: The Biography of Bill Clinton.* New York: Simon & Schuster.

Marcuse, H. 1972. *Counterrevolution and Revolt.* Boston: Beacon Press.

Markmann, C.L. 1965. *The Noblest Cry: A History of the American Civil Liberties Union.* New York: St. Martin's Press.

Marshall, P.D. 1977. *Celebrity and Power: Fame in Contemporary Culture.* Minneapolis, MN: The University of Minnesota Press.

Marx, K. 1967. *Das Capital.* Edited by F. Engels. Translated by Samuel Moore and Edward Aveling. New York: International Publishing.

Marx, K. and Engels, F. [1848] 1935. *The Communist Manifesto* (In: *Selected Works*) London: Lawrence and Wishart.

Massey, D.S. 2007. *Categorically Unequal: The American Stratification System.* New York: Russell Sage Foundation.

Mathiesen, M.M. 2000. *Global Warming in a Politically Correct Climate.* San Jose: Writers Club Press.

Matthews, K.D. 1964. *The Early Romans: Farmers to Empire Builders.* New York: McGraw-Hill.

Merton, R. 1949. *Social Theory and Social Structure.* New York: Free Press.

Meyer, E.P. 1974. *"Not Charity, But Justice," The Story of Jacob A. Riis.* New York: Vanguard Press.

Michael, R.T., Gagnon, J.H., Laumann, E.O., and Kolata, G. 1994. *Sex in America: A Definitive Study.* New York: Warner Books.

Mill, J.S. 1857. *Utilitarianism.* Indianapolis: Bobbs-Merrill.

Mill, J.S. 1863. *On Liberty.* London: Longman, Roberts and Green.

Miller, Z. 2003. *A National Party No More: The Conscience of a Conservative Democrat.* Atlanta: Stroud & Hall Publishing.

Mills, C.W. 1951. *White Collar: The American Middle Classes.* New York: Oxford University Press.

Mills, C.W. 1956. *The Power Elite.* London: Oxford University Press.

Moir, A. and Jessel, D. 1989. *Brain Sex: The Real Difference between Men and Women.* New York: Delta.

Money, J. and Ehrhardt, A. 1972. *Man and Woman: Boy and Girl.* Baltimore: Johns Hopkins Press.

Montefiore, S.S. 2004. *Stalin: The Court of the Red Tsar.* New York: Alfred A. Knopf.

Moore, G.E. 1960. *Principia Ethica.* Cambridge: Cambridge University Press.

Moore, M. 2001. *Stupid White Men . . . and Other Sorry Excuses for the State of the Nation.* New York: ReganBooks.

Moore, S. and Simon, J.L. 2000. *It's Getting Better All the Time: 100 Greatest Trends of the Last 100 Years.* Washington, DC: Cato Institute.

Morgan, H.W. 1981. *Drugs in America 1800–1980.* Syracuse: University of Syracuse Press.

Morin, R. 1969. *Dwight D. Eisenhower: A Gauge of Greatness.* New York: Simon & Schuster.

Morris, E. 1999. *Dutch: A Memoir of Ronald Reagan.* New York: Random House.

Morris, E. 2001. *Theodore Rex.* New York: Random House.

Morris, H. (Ed.) 1961. *Freedom and Responsibility.* Stanford, CA: Sanford University Press.

Morris, K.E. 1991. *Jimmy Carter, American Moralist.* Athens: University of Georgia Press.

Morris, R.B. 1985. *Witnesses at the Creation: Hamilton, Madison, Jay, and the Constitution.* New York: New American Library.

Mortimer, E. 1982. *Faith and Power: The Politics of Islam.* New York: Random House.

Moynihan, D.P. 1965. *The Negro Family: The Case for National Action.* Washington, DC: U.S. Govt.

Moynihan, D.P. 1993. "Defining Deviancy Down." *American Scholar,* Winter, 17–30.

Murray, C. 1986. *Losing Ground: American Social Policy.* New York: Basic Books.

Murray, C. 2012. *Coming Apart: The State of White America 1960–2010.* New York: Crown Forum.

Murray, D., Schwartz, J., and Lichter, S.R. 2001. *It Ain't Necessarily So: How Media Make and Unmake the Scientific Picture of Reality.* Lanham, MD: Rowman & Littlefield.

Myrdal, G. 1944. *An American Dilemma: The Negro Problem and American Democracy.* New York: Harper & Row.

Nasaw, D. 2000. *The Chief: The Life of William Randolph Hearst.* Boston: Houghton Mifflin.

National Center for Educational Statistics. 2001. *Digest of Educational Statistics, 2001.* Washington, DC: Government Printing Office.

Nauert, C.G. 1995. *Humanism and the Culture of Renaissance Europe.* New York: Cambridge University Press.

Neill, A.S. 1960. *Summerhill: A Radical Approach to Child Rearing.* New York: Hart Publishing.

New York Times Correspondents. 2005. *Class Matters.* New York: Henry Holt and Company.

Norris, C. 1997. *Against Relativism: Philosophy of Science, Deconstruction and Critical Theory.* Oxford, UK: Blackwell Publishers.

Obama, B.H. 1995. *Dreams from My Father.* New York: Three Rivers Press.

Obama, B.H. 2006. *The Audacity of Hope.* New York: Crown.

Oberschell, A. 1995. *Social Movements: Ideologies, Interests, and Identities.* New Brunswick, NJ: Transaction Press.

Ogbu, J.U. 1974. *The Next Generation: An Ethnography of Education in an Urban School.* New York: Academic Press.

Ogburn, W. [1922] 1966. *Social Change with Respect to Culture and Original Nature.* New York: Heubsch.

Olasky, M. 1992. *The Tragedy of American Compassion.* Washington, DC: Regnery Publishing.

Oliver, M.L. and Shapiro, T.M. 1997. *Black Wealth/White Wealth: A New Perspective on Racial Inequality.* New York: Routledge.

Olson, R.E. 1999. *The Story of Christian Theology: Twenty Centuries of Tradition and Reform.* Dowers Grove, IL: Intervarsity Press.

Olson, S. 2000. *Mapping Human History: Discovering the Past through Our Genes.* Boston: Houghton Mifflin.

Olson, W.K. 1992. *The Litigation Explosion.* New York: Truman Talley Books.

Olson, W.K. 1997. *The Excuse Factory: How Employment Law is Paralyzing the American Workplace.* New York: The Free Press.

O'Neill, J.E. and Corsi, J.R. 2004. *Unfit for Command: Swift Boat Veterans Speak Out about John Kerry.* Washington, DC: Regnery Publishing.

O'Neill, N.O. and O'Neill, G.O. 1972. *Open Marriage: A New Life Style for Couples.* New York: M. Evans.

O'Reilly, B. 2007. *Culture Warrior.* New York: Broadway Books.

O'Reilly, B. 2003. *The No Spin Zone: Confrontations with the Powerful and Famous in America.* New York: Broadway Books.

Orwin, C. and Tarcov, N. (Eds.) 1997. *The Legacy of Rousseau*. Chicago: University of Chicago Press.

Packard, V. 1959. *The Status Seekers*. New York: D. McKay.

Paine, T. 1953. *Common Sense and Other Political Writings*. Edited by Nelson F. Adkins. New York: Liberal Arts Press.

Pareto, V. 1991. *The Rise and Fall of Elites: An Application of Theoretical Sociology*. New Brunswick, NJ: Transaction Publishers.

Park, R. 1950. *Race and Culture*. Glencoe, IL: Free Press.

Parsons, T. 1951. *The Social System*. New York: The Free Press.

Partridge, W.L. 1973. *The Hippie Ghetto: The Natural History of a Subculture*. New York: Holt, Rinehart and Winston.

Patterson, O. 1982. *Slavery and Social Death: A Comparative Study*. Cambridge, MA: Harvard University Press.

Payne, R. 1965. *The Rise and Fall of Stalin*. New York: Avon Books.

Perrow, C. 1970. *Organizational Analysis: A Sociological View*. Belmont, CA: Cole/Brooks.

Peter, L.J. and Hull, R. 1969. *The Peter Principle*. New York: William Morrow.

Pew Research Center. 2010. *The Decline of Marriage and the Rise of New Families*. Washington, DC: Pew Research Center.

Pfeiffer, J.E. 1977. *The Emergence of Society: A Prehistory of the Establishment*. New York: McGraw-Hill.

Piven, F.F. and Cloward, R.A. 1977. *Poor People's Movement's: Why They Succeed, How They Fail*. New York: Vintage.

Plato. 1928. *The Works of Plato* (Jowett translation). New York: The Modern Library.

Plumb, J.H. 1961. *The Italian Renaissance*. New York: American Heritage.

Plutarch. 1959a. *Lives of Noble Greeks*. Edited by Edmund Fuller. New York: Nelson Doubleday.

Plutarch. 1959b. *Lives of Noble Romans*. Edited by Edmund Fuller. New York: Nelson Doubleday.

Pollock, W. 1999. *Real Boys: Rescuing Our Sons from the Myths of Boyhood*. New York: Henry Holt.

Popenoe, D. 1996. *Life Without Father: Compelling New Evidence that Fatherhood and Marriage Are Indispensable for the Good of Children and Society*. New York: The Free Press.

Popper, K.R. 1959. *The Logic of Scientific Discovery*. London: Hutchinson.

Popper, K.R. [1945] 1971. *The Open Society and Its Enemies* (5th ed.). Princeton, NJ: Princeton University Press.

Posner, G.L. 1993. *Case Closed: Lee Harvey Oswald and the Assassination of JFK*. New York: Random House.

Powell, C. and Persico, J.E. 1995. *My American Journey*. New York: Random House.

Powell, J. 2003. *FDR's Folly: How Roosevelt and His New Deal Prolonged the Great Depression*. New York: Crown Forum.

Putnam, R.D. 1993. *Making Democracy Work: Civic Traditions in Modern Italy*. Princeton, NJ: Princeton University Press.

Putnam, R.D. 2000. *Bowling Alone: The Collapse and Revival of American Community*. New York: Simon & Schuster.

Pyatt, S.E. 1986. *Martin Luther King, Jr.: An Annotated Bibliography*. New York: Greenwood Press.

Radosh, R. and Radosh, A. 2005. *Red Star Over Hollywood: The Film Colony's Long Romance with the Left*. San Francisco: Encounter Books.

Raskin, J. 2004. *American Scream: Allen Ginsberg's Howl and the Making of the Beat Generation*. Berkeley: University of California Press.

Ravitch, D. 2000. *Left Back: A Century of Failed School Reforms*. New York: Simon & Schuster.

Ravitch, D. 2003. *The Language Police: How Pressure Groups Restrict What Students Learn*. New York: Alfred A. Knopf.

Rawls, J. 1971. *A Theory of Justice*. Cambridge, MA: The Belknap Press.

Regnery, A.S. 2008. *Upstream: The Ascendance of American Conservatism*. New York: Simon & Schuster.

Reisman, D. 1950. *The Lonely Crowd*. New Haven: Yale University Press.

Reynolds, A. 2006. *Income and Wealth*. Westport, CT: Greenwood Press.

Rice, E. 1997. *The O.J. Simpson Trial*. San Diego, CA: Lucent Books.

Rice, L. and Greenberg, L. (Eds.) 1984. *Patterns of Change*. New York: Guilford Press.

Richardson, J. 1977. *Victoria and Albert*. New York: The New York Times Book.

Ridely, J. 1982. *Statesman and Saint: Cardinal Wolsey, Sir Thomas More and the Politics of Henry VIII*. New York: The Viking Press.

Riech, C.A. 1971. *The Greening of America*. New York: Bantam.

Ritzer, G. 2000. *The McDonaldization of Society*. Thousand Oaks, CA: Pine Forge Press.

Robinson, R. 2000. *The Debt: What America Owes to Blacks*. New York: Dutton.

Rochester, J.M. 2002. *Class Warfare: Besieged Schools, Bewildered Parents, Betrayed Kids and the Attack on Excellence*. San Francisco: Encounter Books.

Rochon, T.R. 1998. *Culture Moves: Idea, Activism, and Changing Values*. Princeton, NJ: Princeton University Press.

Roiphe, K. 1993. *The Morning After: Sex, Fear, and Feminism on Campus*. Boston: Little, Brown.

Rose, P.I. 1997. *Tempest-Tost: Race, Immigration, and the Dilemmas of Diversity*. New York: Oxford University Press.

Rossi, A.S. (Ed.) 1973. *The Feminist Papers: From Adams to de Beauvoir*. New York: Bantam Books.

Rothwax, H.J. 1995. *Guilty: The Collapse of Criminal Justice*. New York: Random House.

Rousseau, J.J. [1762] 1968. *The Social Contract*. Translated by Maurice Cranston. New York: Penguin Books.

Rousseau, Jean-Jacques [1762] 1979. *Emile*. Translated by A. Bloom. New York: Basic Books.

Rousseau, J.J. 1992. *The Discourse on the Origins of Inequality*. Edited by Roger D. Masters and Christopher Kelly. Hanover, NH: University Press of New England.

Rove, K. 2010. *Courage and Consequence: My Life as a Conservative in the Fight*. New York: Simon & Schuster.

Rubin, L.B. 1972. *Busing & Backlash: White against White in an Urban School District*. Berkeley: University of California Press.

Rudolph, F. 1990. *The American College and University: A History*. Athens: University of Georgia Press.

Russell, B. 1929. *Marriage and Morals*. New York: H. Liveright.

Sale, K. 1973. *SDS*. New York: Random House.

Salvatore, N. 1982. *Eugene V. Debs: Citizen and Socialist*. Urbana: University of Illinois Press.

Samuelson, R. 1996. *The Good Life and Its Discontents: The American Dream in the Age of Entitlement 1945–1995*. New York: Times Books.

Samuelson, R. 2008. *The Great Inflation and Its Aftermath: The Past and Future of American Affluence*. New York: Random House.

Sandeen, E.R. 1970. *The Roots of Fundamentalism: British and American Millinarianism 1800–1930*. Chicago: University of Chicago Press.

Sanderson, S.K. 1995. *Social Transformations: A General Theory of Historical Development*. Oxford, UK: Blackwell.

Sanderson, S.K. 2010. *Revolutions: A Worldwide Introduction to Social and Political Contention* (2nd ed.). Boulder: Paradigm Publishers.

Sanderson, S.K. and Alderson, A.S. 2005. *World Societies: The Evolution of Human Social Life*. Boston: Pearson/Allyn & Bacon.

Santayana, G. 1905. *The Life of Reason*. New York: Scribners.

Sarton, G. 1962. *The History of Science and the New Humanism*. Bloomington: Indiana University Press.

Satel, S. 2000. *PC, M.D.: How Political Correctness is Corrupting Medicine*. New York: Basic Books.

Schama, S. 1989. *Citizens: A Chronicle of the French Revolution*. New York: A. Knopf.

Schippers, D.P. 2000. *Sell Out: The inside Story of President Clinton's Impeachment*. Washington, DC: Regnery Publishing.

Schlesinger, A.M. 1992. *The Disuniting of America*. New York: W.W. Norton.

Schumpeter, J.A. 1942. *Capitalism, Socialism and Democracy*. New York: Harper & Brothers.

Scott, J. 2011. *A Singular Woman: The Untold Story of Barack Obama's Mother*. New York: Riverhead Books.

Sears, D.O. and McConahay, J.B. 1973. *The Politics of Violence: The New Urban Black and the Watts Riot*. Boston: Houghton Mifflin.

Seigel, J.E. 1999. *Bohemian Paris: Culture, Politics, and the Boundaries of Bourgeois Life, 1830–1930*. Baltimore: Johns Hopkins Press.

Seligman, A.B. 1992. *The Idea of Civil Society*. Princeton, NJ: Princeton University Press.

Sennett, R. and Cobb, J. 1966. *The Hidden Injuries of Class*. New York: The Free Press.

Seward, K. 1978. *The American Family: A Demographic History*. Beverly Hills: Sage Publications.

Shapiro, B. 2004. *Brainwashed: How Universities Indoctrinate America's Youth*. Nashville, TN: WND Books.

Sheed, W. 1975. *Muhammad Ali: A Portrait in Words and Photographs*. New York: Crowell.

Sheehy, G. 1999. *Hillary's Choice*. New York: Random House.

Sherif, M. 1936. *The Psychology of Social Norms*. New York: Harper & Brothers.

Shilts, R. 1988. *And the Band Played On: Politics, People and the AIDS Epidemic*. New York: Penguin Books.

Shirer, W.L. 1960. *The Rise and Fall of the Third Reich*. New York: Simon & Schuster.

Shogan, R. 2001. *Bad News: Where the Press Goes Wrong in the Making of the President*. Chicago: Ivan R. Dee.

Sidanius, J. and Pratto, F. 1999. *Social Dominance: An Intergroup Theory of Social Hierarchy and Oppression*. Cambridge: Cambridge University Press.

Silberman, C.E. (Ed.) 1973. *The Open Classroom Reader*. New York: Random House.

Simon, H.A. 1947. *Administrative Behavior*. New York: Macmillan.

Sinclair, U. 1988. *The Jungle*. Urbana: University of Illinois Press.

Skocpol, T. 2000. *The Missing Middle: Working Families and the Future of American Social Policy*. New York: W.W. Norton.

Skrentny, J.L. 1996. *The Ironies of Affirmative Action: Politics, Culture, and Justice in America*. Chicago: University of Chicago Press.

Sleeper, J. 1997. *Liberal Racism*. New York: Viking.

Smaje, C. 2000. *Natural Hierarchies: The Historical Sociology of Race and Caste*. Oxford: Blackwell Publishers.

Smigel, E.O. (Ed.) 1963. *Work and Leisure*. New Haven: College & University Press.

Smith, A. 1776. *An Inquiry into the Nature and Causes of the Wealth of Nations*. London: W. Strahan & T. Cadell.

Smith, H. 1988. *The Power Game: How Washington Works*. New York: Random House.

Sommers, C.H. 1994. *Who Stole Feminism: How Women Have Betrayed Women*. New York: Simon & Schuster.

Sommers, C.H. 2000. *The War against Boys: How Misguided Feminism is Harming Our Young Men*. New York: Simon & Schuster.

Sommers, P.M. (Ed.) 1982. *Welfare Reform in America: Perspectives and Prospects*. Boston: Kluwer and Nijhoff.

Sowell, T. 1981. *Ethnic America*. New York: Basic Books.

Sowell, T. 1999. *The Quest for Cosmic Justice*. New York: The Free Press.

Sowell, T. 2004. *Affirmative Action around the World: An Empirical Study*. New Haven: Yale University Press.

Sowell, T. 2007. *A Conflict of Visions: Ideological Origins of Political Struggles*. New York: Basic Books.

Sowell, T. 2009. *Intellectuals and Society*. New York: Basic Books.

Spencer, H. [1899] 1969. *The Principles of Sociology* (3 Vols.) Edited by S. Andreski. New York: Macmillan.

Spencer, R.W. 2008. *Climate Confusion: How Global Warming Hysteria Leads to Bad Science, Pandering Politicians and Misguided Policies that Hurt the Poor*. New York: Encounter Books.

Stampp, K.M. 1956. *The Peculiar Institution: Slavery in the Ante-Bellum South*. New York: Knopf.

Stampp, K.M. 1965. *The Era of Reconstruction: 1865–1877*. New York: Vintage Books.

Stanford, C.B. 1999. *The Hunting Apes: Meat Eating and the Origins of Human Behavior*. Princeton, NJ: Princeton University Press.

Starr, P. 1982. *The Social Transformation of American Medicine*. New York: Basic Books.

Starr, P. 2004. *The Creation of the Media: Political Origins of Modern Communications*. New York: Basic Books.

Steele, S. 1990. *The Content of Our Character: A New Vision of Race in America*. New York: St. Martin's Press.

Steele, S. 1998. *A Dream Deferred: The Second Betrayal of Black Freedom in America*. New York: HarperCollins Publishers.

Steffens, L. 1957. *The Shame of the Cities*. New York: Hill and Ward.

Stein, H. 2000. *How I Accidentally Joined the Vast Right-Wing Conspiracy (and Found Inner Peace)*. New York: Delacorte Press.

Stein, H. and Foss, M. 1999. *The Illustrated Guide to the American Economy* (3rd ed.). Washington, DC: AEI Press.

Steinbeck, J. 1986. *The Grapes of Wrath*. New York: Penguin Books.

Steinem, G. 1992. *Revolution from Within: A Book of Self-Esteem*. Boston: Little, Brown.

Stengel, R. 2000. *You're Too Kind: A Brief History of Flattery*. New York: Simon & Schuster.

Stossel, J. 2004. *Give Me a Break: How I Exposed Hucksters, Cheats, and Scam Artists and Became the Scourge of the Liberal Media*. New York: HarperCollins Publishers.

Straus, B.R. 1987. *The Catholic Church*. London: David & Charles.

Sumner, W.G. 1960. *Folkways*. New York: New American Library.

Suskind, R. 2011. *Confidence Men: Wall Street, Washington, and the Education of a President*. New York: HarperCollins Publishers.

Suttles, G.D. 1972. *The Social Construction of Communities*. Chicago: University of Chicago Press.

Swanberg. W.A. 1972. *Luce and His Empire*. New York: Scribner.

Swartz, D. 1997. *Culture and Power: The Sociology of Pierre Bourdieu*. Chicago: University of Chicago Press.

Tallentyre, S.G. 1969. *The Life of Voltaire*. New York: Kraus Reprint.

Talmon, J.L. 1985. *Political Messianism: The Romantic Phase*. Boulder: Westview Press.

Tanenhaus, S. 1997. *Whittaker Chambers: A Biography*. New York: Random House.

Tannen, D. 1990. *You Just Don't Understand: Women and Men in Conversation*. New York: William Morrow.

Tarbell, I. 1904. *The History of the Standard Oil Co.* New York: McClure, Phillips.

Taylor, F.W. 1911. *The Principles of Scientific Management*. New York: Harper & Brothers.

Thernstrom, S. and Thernstrom, A. 1997. *America in Black and White: One Nation, Indivisible*. New York: Simon & Schuster.

Thernstrom, S. and Thernstrom, A. 2003. *No Excuses: Closing the Racial Gap in Learning*. New York: Simon & Schuster.

Thomas, A. 2001. *Clarence Thomas: A Biography*. San Francisco: Encounter Books.

Thomas, H. 1997. *The Slave Trade: The Story of the Atlantic Slave Trade: 1440–1870*. New York: Simon & Schuster.

Thomas, R.M. 1997. *Moral Development Theories—Secular and Religious*. Westport, CT: Greenwood Press.

Thomas, W.I. and Thomas, D.S. 1928. *The Child in America: Behavior, Problems and Progress*. New York: Knopf.

Thomas, W.I. and Znaniecki, F. 1918/1958. *The Polish Peasant in Europe and America*. New York: Dover Publications.

Thucydides. 1998. *The Peloponnesian War*. Translated by Walter Blanco. New York: W.W. Norton.

Tilly, C. 1998. *Durable Inequality*. Berkeley: University of California Press.

Tilly, C. 2004. *Social Movements: 1768–2004*. Boulder: Paradigm Publishers.

Tipton, S.M. 1982. *Getting Saved from the Sixties*. Berkeley: The University of California Press.

de Tocqueville, A. 1966. *Democracy in America*. Translated by George Lawrence. New York: Harper & Row.

Toennies, F. [1887] 1966. *Community and Society*. New York: Harper Row.

Toland, J. 1980. *No Man's Land: 1918, The Last Year of the Great War*. New York: Ballantine Books.

Troyat, H. 1984. *Ivan the Terrible*. New York: E.P. Dutton.

Tuchman, B.W. 1966. *The Proud Tower: A Portrait of the World Before The War: 1890–1914*. New York: Macmillan.

Tumminia, D.G. 2005. *When Prophesy Never Fails: Myth and Reality in a Flying Saucer Group*. New York: Oxford University Press.

Turner, R.H. 1962. "Role Taking: Process vs. Conformity?" In: Rose, A.M. (Ed.), *Human Behavior and Social Processes*. Boston: Houghton Mifflin.

Twain, M. 1915. *The Gilded Age*. New York: Harper.

U.S. Census Bureau. 1997. *American Housing Survey for the United States: 1997*. Washington, DC: Government Printing Office.

U.S. Department of Labor. 1991. "Research Summaries." *Monthly Labor Review*, December. Washington, DC: Government Printing Office.

U.S. Department of Labor, Bureau of Labor Statistics. 1980. *Occupational Outlook Handbook* (1980–81 ed.). Washington, DC: Government Printing Office.

U.S. Department of Labor, Bureau of Labor Statistics. 2000. *Dictionary of Occupational Titles*. Washington, DC: Government Printing Office.

U.S. Department of Labor, Bureau of Labor Statistics. 2001. *2001 National Occupational Employment and Wage Estimates*. Washington, DC: Government Printing Office.

Valenstein, E.S. 1986. *Great and Desperate Cures: The Rise and Decline of Psychosurgery and Other Radical Treatments for Mental Illness*. New York: Basic Books.

Valentine, C.A. 1968. *Culture and Poverty: Critique and Counter Proposals*. Chicago: University of Chicago Press.

Van Hoffman, N. 1968. *We Are the People Our Parents Warned Us Against*. Chicago: Quadrangle Books.

Van Tine, W. 1977. *John L. Lewis: A Biography*. New York: Quadrangle/New York Times.

Veblen, T. [1899] 1967. *The Theory of the Leisure Class*. New York: Viking Penguin.

Vidich, A. and Bensman, J. 1958. *Small Town in Mass Society: Class, Power, and Religion in a Rural Community*. Princeton, NJ: Princeton University Press.

Vollmer, H. and Mills, D. (Eds.) 1968. *Professionalization*. Englewood Cliffs, NJ: Prentice-Hall.

de Waal, F. 1982. *Chimpanzee Politics*. New York: Harper & Row.

de Waal, F. 1989. *Peacekeeping among Primates*. Cambridge, MA: Harvard University Press.

de Waal, F. 1996. *Good Natured: The Origins of Right and Wrong in Humans and Other Animals*. Cambridge, MA: Harvard University Press.

de Waal, F. (Ed.) 2001. *Tree of Origin: What Primate Behavior Can Tell Us about Human Social Evolution*. Cambridge, MA: Harvard University Press.

Waite, C.J. and Gallagher, M. 2000. *The Case for Marriage: Why Married People are Happier, Healthier, and Better off Financially*. New York: Doubleday.

Wallace, J. 1993. *Hard Drive: Bill Gates and the Making of the Microsoft Empire*. New York: HarperBusiness.

Wallenstein, J.S., Lewis, J.M., and Blakesee, S. 2000. *The Unexpected Legacy of Divorce: A 25 Year Landmark Study*. New York: Hyperion.

Waller, W. 1967. *The Sociology of Teaching*. New York: John Wiley & Sons.

Watson, J.B. 1928. *Psychological Care of Infant and Child*. New York: W.W. Norton.

Wead, D. 2003. *All the Presidents' Children: Triumph and Tragedy in the Lives of America's First Families*. New York: Atria Books.

Weber, M. 1947. *The Theory of Social and Economic Organization*. New York: Free Press.

Weber, M. 1958. *The Protestant Ethic and the Spirit of Capitalism*. New York: Charles Scribner's Sons.

Weiss, R.S. 1975. *Marital Separation: Coping with the End of Marriage*. New York: Basic Books.

Weiss, R.S. 1990. *Staying the Course: The Emotional and Social Lives of Men Who Do Well at Work*. New York: Free Press.

Wells, S. 2002. *The Journey of Man: A Genetic Odyssey*. Princeton, NJ: Princeton University Press.

West, D. 2007. *The Death of the Grown-Up: How America's Arrested Development Is Bringing Down Western Civilization*. New York: St. Martin's Press.

Westermarck, E. 1960. *Ethical Relativity*. Paterson, NJ: Littlefield, Adams.

Whitehead, B.D. 1998. *The Divorce Culture: Rethinking Our Commitments to Marriage and the Family*. New York: Random House.

Whiting, J. and Child, I. 1953. *Child Training and Personality*. New Haven: Yale University Press.

Whittier, N. 1995. *Feminist Generations: The Persistence of the Radical Women's Movement*. Philadelphia: Temple University Press.

Whyte, W.F. 1943. *Street Corner Society*. Chicago: University of Chicago Press.

Whyte, W.H. 1956. *The Organization Man*. New York: Simon & Schuster.

Wicker, T. 1991. *One of Us: Richard Nixon and the American Dream*. New York: Random House.

Wiener, D. and Berley, M. 1999. *The Diversity Hoax: Law Students Report from Berkeley*. New York: FAST.

Williams, J. 1998. *Thurgood Marshall: American Revolutionary*. New York: Times Books.

Williams, T.I. 1984. *A Short History of Twentieth Century Technology*. New York: Oxford University Press.

Wilson, J.Q. 1975. *Thinking about Crime.* New York: Basic Books.

Wilson, J.Q. 1993. *The Moral Sense.* New York: The Free Press.

Wilson, J.Q. 1997. *Moral Judgment.* New York: The Free Press.

Wilson, J.Q. 2002. *The Marriage Problem: How Culture Has Weakened Families.* New York: HarperCollins Publishers.

Wittfogel, K.A. 1957. *Oriental Despotism: A Comparative Study of Total Power.* New Haven: Yale University Press.

Wolfe, A. 1989. *Whose Keeper?* Berkeley: University of California Press.

Wolfe, A. 1996. *Marginalized in the Middle.* Chicago: University of Chicago Press.

Wolfe, A. 1998. *One Nation, After All: What Middle-Class Americans Really Think.* New York: Viking.

Wolfe, A. 2001. *Moral Freedom: The Search for Virtue in a World of Choice.* New York: W.W. Norton.

Wolfe, A. 2003. *The Transformation of American Religion: How We Actually Live Our Faith.* New York: The Free Press.

Wood, G. 1991. *The Radicalization of the American Revolution.* New York: Random House.

Wood, P. 2003. *Diversity: The Invention of a Concept.* San Francisco: Encounter Books.

Woodward, B. 2002. *Bush at War.* New York: Simon & Schuster.

Wrangham, M. 2009. *Catching Fire: How Cooking Made Us Human.* New York: Basic Books.

Wright, R. 2000. *Nonzero: The Logic of Human Destiny.* New York: Vintage Books.

Wuthnow, R. 1987. *Meaning and Moral Order: Explorations in Cultural Analysis.* Berkeley: University of California Press.

Wuthnow, R. 1996. *Poor Richard's Principle: Recovering the American Dream through the Moral Dimension of Work, Business, & Money.* Princeton, NJ: University of Princeton Press.

Zarefsky, D. 1986. *President Johnson's War on Poverty.* University, AL: University of Alabama Press.

Zigler, E. and Valentines, J. (Eds.) 1979. *Head Start: A Legacy of the War on Poverty.* New York: Free Press.

Zinsser. H. 1935. *Rats, Lice and History.* Boston: Little, Brown.

Index

Bohemians, 49
Bolsheviks, 70, 261
Bonaparte, Napoleon, *see* Napoleon
  Bonaparte
bourgeoisie, 46; *see also* capitalists
Bowlby, John, 147, 171, 261-262; *see
  also* attachment, mothering
brain trust, the, 15, 60, 64, 113
Brands, H.W., 1-2
Brazil Nut Tree, 227-228
Broken Window Theory, 25, 95, 115
Brook Farm, 45
Brooks, David, 66-67
brotherhood, 15
Browning Robert, 27
Bryant, William Jennings, 54
Buddhism, 35
Buffet, Warren, 125
bureaucracy, 38, 54, 140-141, 223,
  229-235, 236-243; *see also* Weber, Max
Burke, Edmund, 134
Bush Derangement Syndrome, 130
Bush, George H.W., 76, 126
Bush, George, W., 76, 123-124, 126,
  128, 130, 131-132, 214, 268, 270, 280,
  314
business, cycle, 109-110, 263, 289

C

Calvinism, 106
Cambodia, 72
Cantor, Eric, 271
Carnegie, Andrew, 50-51
Carter, Jimmy, 18, 76, 123, 126, 266
capital gains, 267; *see also* taxes
capitalism, 16, 20, 44, 60, 70, 82-83, 124,
  167, 214
capitalists, 47, 78, 236
Catholics, Roman, 53, 280; *see also*
  Christianity
CIA, 130
central planners, 152, 242
centered, 304
centralization, 152, 241-242, 248, 263,
  265, 281; *see also* decentralization
Chamberlin, Neville, 92, 94
Chamberlin, Wilt, 95
change, 13, 111-112; intragenerational,
  318-319; intergenerational, 316-318;
  social, 181-183, 272
charity, 267

cheating, 126, 136, 314; *see also* lies
Chicago, 277
childrearing, 250-251, 256-258, 276,
children, 82
chimpanzees, 148, 165, 176, 178-179
China, 48, 70, 72, 77, 93, 105, 204, 272
Christianity, 5, 10, 15, 35-39, 69, 185,
  198, 207, 212; *see also* religion
Church, the, 53; *see also* Christianity
Churchill, Winston, 14
civil rights, 2, 25, 65, 78; movement, 316
Civil War, American, 32, 56, 76
class warfare, 263; *see also* lower class,
  middle class, working class
Clinton, Bill, 2, 76, 89, 99, 126-129, 131,
  190, 314
Clinton, Hillary, 127, 212
Code Pink, 93
cognitive dissonance, 6
cognitive order, 158, 281-282; constraints, 163-164; *see also* Social
  Domain Theory
cohabitation, 250
Cold War, 2, 64, 77, 91-92
Coleman, James, 100-101, 265
collectivism, 4, 27, 70
colleges, 53-54, 66-67
commerce, 39-43, 201-203; *see also*
  exchange, social
commitments, 316-318
commodification, 83
Common Sense, 246
communication, 31
communicators, effective, 303
communism, 47-48, 72, 134, 261
communist man, *see* new communist
  man
communists, 34, 45
community effects, 53, 106
comparable worth, 80
compassion, 20, 120-124; *see also*
  sympathy
competition, 234-235
complexities, 13
con games, 133
concentration camp, 61
conflict theorists, 181; *see also*
  Marxists
conflicts, social, 286
congress, 3, 55
consensual validation, 163-164, 282

E

F

G

Inequality, 78-79; *see also* equality
Innovation, 242-243; technological, 260;
  see also technology
Inquisition, Spanish, 287
Intelligence, 13, 120, 243; superior,
  113-120
Intellectuals, 27, 119, 155-156; *see also*
  best and the brightest
Intelligentsia, 113
Intimate relations, 98; *see also* relation-
  ships, personal
Inverse force rule, 159, 185-192, 215,
  274
Investments, 118, 217, 269
Iraq, 261, 270
Iraq War, 13, 92, 123, 130-131
Iron cage, 54, 238
Iron rice bowl, 72
Irrationality, 259, 281, 283-285
Islam, 119, 133, 198
Israel, 124, 133

J

Japan, 61, 92, 170
Jazz band, 224-226
jealousy, 45, 288
Jefferson Thomas, 22, 27-28, 190
Jencks, Christopher, 117
Jews, 9, 61, 124, 134, 142
Job description, 238
Jobs, 238, 269; professional, 238
Johnson, Lyndon B., 18, 65, 76
journalists, 248; *see also* media
Judaism, 35
Jungle, the, 52
Justice,81, 97, 263; cosmic, 23-26;
  environmental, 20, 25; economic, 18;
  moral, 21, 26; social, 1, 18, 24

K

Keats, John, 167, 220
Kennedy, John F., 62-63, 77
Kennedy, Robert, 300-301
Kennedy, Ted, 3
keepers, social, 5
Kennesaw State University, 141-142,
  192
Kerry, John, 76, 131
Keynesian economics, *see* economics,
  Keynesian
kinship, 193; *see also* family

Klein, Benjamin, 134-135
Kiev, 35
knowledge, 31, 189, 213, 282-283, 290,
  302-303, 306; interpersonal, 246;
  political, 253
Kodak, 118
Korean War, 77
Kulaks, 261

L

lag, cultural, 181-182, 259-263, 318
language 164-165; police, 119
Lasch, Christopher, 202
Laughead, Charles, 6-7; Lillian, 6-7
laws, 152-153; interpretation of, 153
lawyers, 31, 67, 231-232, 237-238
learners, life-long, 304
Leary, Timothy, 63
Lenski, Gerhard, 109, 168-169
Lewinsky, Monica, 89, 126-127, 314
Lewis, Oscar, 98
liberalism, death of, 1, 3; *see also* death
  throes
libertarianism, 34, 107, 219-220
liberte, egalite, fraternite, 42-43
liberty, 16; *see also* freedom
lies, 126, 130-133, 215-217, 270-271,
  287, 313-314
limitations, 281-289; social, 149-155
limits with latitude, 258; *see also*
  childrearing
Lincoln, Abraham, 50
Lindsey, John, 136
Lobbyists, 258
losers, 69
loss, 262, 311, 318-319; *see also*
  attachment
Louis XIV, 40, 146, 243-244
love, 87, 95, 163, 250-251, 254, 288,
  295-296, 299, 310-311; free, 18, 57,
  212, 249; universal, 15, 26, 47, 210,
  263
lower class, 284; *see also* poverty
Luddites, 44

M

McCain, John, 14-15, 129, 268
McCarthy, Joseph, 123
McClellan, George, B., 76, 302
male-bashing, 97-98
Marat, Jean-Paul, 244

material constraints, 168-170
material order, 158; *see also* Social
   Domain Theory
Mao Tse-tung, 72
Martin, Dorothy, 6-7
marriage, 19, 86-87, 116, 251-252, 255,
   276; collaborative, 252-253, 256;
   companionate, 252; trial, 86
Marx, Karl, 10, 45-49, 51, 54, 57, 69-70,
   77, 105, 108, 151, 155-156, 169, 185,
   200, 201, 236
Marxism, 16, 60, 64, 69, 72-73, 138, 178,
   181
Matthews, Christopher, 131
maturity, 299
mean-spirited, 7, 11, 154, 162, 209
mechanical energy, 201
media, 127, 131-132, 213
Medicaid, 82, 100, 110, 117, 266, 271
Medicare, 27, 82, 100, 110, 117, 266, 271
Medieval Europe, 201
mediocrity, 23, 28
mentally ill, 20, 139
methadone, 137
Middle Ages, 37, 39, 279
middle class, 257-258; society, 29, 31,
   62, 70
migrations, 148
Milgram, Stanley, 284
military, 239-240
Millay, Edna St. Vincent, 57
mistakes, 8, 288-289, 291
mobility, social, 182
modernists, 273
money, 21, 176, 198-199, 201
Montesquieu, 243
moral indignation, 189; rules, 189
morality, 17, 21, 26, 126-127, 155,
   160-162, 215, 286-287; *see also* moral
   order, moral rules, relativism, moral
Moore, Michael, 131
More, St. Thomas, 5
Morgan, J.P., 50-52
Mormons, 10, 122
mothering, 171
movements, social, *see* social movements
Moveon.org, 11
Mr. Mom, 97
Murray, Charles, 142
Mussolini, Benito, 58
multi-cultural, 79
myths, 8

N

N-word, 79, 123
naiveté, 12
Napoleon Bonaparte, 244, 285
Nast, Thomas, 9
nation states, 201
nationalism, new, 5
Nazism, 12, 58, 61, 203, 260
Negotiation skills; *see* skills, negotiation
negotiations, dual concern, 254;
   marital, 252, 254-255, 288; moral,
   287; polarized, 162; role, 177-178,
   232-234, 242, 244, 281, 291; social,
   226, 228, 245, 275-276, 287, 303-304
neo-conservatives. 151-152, 154, 209;
   see also conservatives
nepotism, 238
Netherlands, the, 243
neurosis, 314
new communist man, 48, 155
New Deal, 59-60, 62, 110, 125, 263-264
New Harmony, 45
New Lanark, 45
New York City, 277
Newport, R.I., 50
Newspapers, 52, 137-138; *see also*
   journalists, media
Newspeak, 217
niceness, 17, 28, 42, 47, 65-66, 73-74,
   121, 215
Nietzsche, Friedrich, 295
ninety-nine percent, the, 4
Nixon, Richard, 64, 129, 131
No child left behind, 24, 100, 265
noble savages, 146, 155
normative constraint, 160-162
normative order, 158
norms, 312-313; moral, 312; *see also*
   rules
nurses, 232-233

O

OVR, 140-141
O'Reilly, Bill, 10, 35
Obama, Barack, 2, 4, 9, 13-14, 76-77,
   101, 120, 125, 128-129, 132, 138, 162,
   167, 214-216, 259, 264-271, 295, 314
ObamaCare, 11, 100, 132, 217, 266; *see
   also* health care
obedience, 284
Occupy Wall Street, 9